A Guide to the Louvre

A Guide to the Louvre

Texts by

Anne Sefrioui
From palace to museum
Arts of Islam
Paintings
Objets d'art
Graphic Arts

Bérénice Geoffroy-Schneiter
Oriental antiquities
Egyptian antiquities
Greek, Etruscan and Roman antiquities
Arts of Africa, Asia, Oceania and the Americas

Manuel Jover
Sculptures

Translation from the French
David Wharry

We would like to thank the following for their invaluable comments and suggestions: D. Alcouffe, G. Bresc-Bautier, A. Caubet, J.-R. Gaborit, A. Pasquier, V. Pomarède, F. Richard, F. Viatte, C. Ziegler and their teams, particularly S. Allard, B. André-Salvini, A. Benoit, M. Bormand, S. Cluzan, F. Demange, S. Descamps, E. Fontan, J. Foucart, E. Foucart-Walter, F. Gaultier, C. Giroire, S. Guillot de Suduiraut, J. Habert, C. Jail, V. Jeammet, S. Laveissière, I. Lemaistre, S. Loire, S. Makariou, J.-L. Martinez, O. Meslay, D. Roger, C. Scailliérez, G. Scherf, A. Sérullaz and D. Thiébaut. Our thanks also go to G. Viatte of the Musée du Quai Branly.

Contents

Foreword

First-time visitors to the Louvre can hardly fail to be overwhelmed by the sheer size and wealth of its collections. The Louvre Museum is an extraordinary time machine. As one passes from one room to another, one travels through centuries, entire civilisations, faced always with the same dilemma: how to choose among so many treasures?

This guide, like the visitor, is necessarily selective. Its aim is not to show everything, but to cover everything. Through a choice of some six hundred masterpieces from Antiquity to the mid-nineteenth century, the reader is given as comprehensive as possible an idea of all the departments today comprising the Louvre, including the recently created Islamic Arts department and the collection of African, Asian, Oceanic and American arts now on view.

Accompanying the commentaries on the Louvre's foremost masterpieces, presentations of the various periods and collections situate each in its artistic context and throw light on the personalities of its most famous artists. Visitors can consult this book as a prelude to their visit and return to it afterwards to learn more about their discoveries. And because it cannot encompass the Louvre in its entirety, this guide proposes the ideal visit.

Henri Loyrette
President-Director of the Louvre

From palace to museum

From palace to museum

The art treasures of the Louvre Museum are today housed in an impressive group of buildings which has earned the museum the reputation of being the 'largest in the world'. But besides being a great museum the Louvre is also an exceptional work of architecture, a monument fashioned by eight centuries of often turbulent, sometimes tragic history, that of France and her monarchs.

The medieval fortress

The Louvre's architectural history began in the late 12th century when, at the southwest corner of what is today the Cour Carrée, Philippe Auguste (1165–1223) built a formidable circular keep surrounded by outer walls with towers and living quarters. Intended to protect Paris from attack by the English, the fortress was erected on a site known as 'Lupara', the origin of the word Louvre (the French for wolf being *loup*) and the source of countless etymological hypotheses, the most fanciful being that there was once a wolf kennel on the site.

The military edifice, whose remains were excavated in 1984–85 and are now on view in the museum's basement, gradually lost its defensive raison d'être. It was used as a prison, as an arsenal, and under Philip the Fair as royal treasury. The living quarters, however, were seldom used by the kingdom's successive monarchs, who led an itinerant existence moving from château to château until Charles V (1338–80), having built a new, larger wall around Paris, decided to take up residence there. Raymond du Temple, charged with refurbishing the Louvre and in so doing exalting royal power, transformed the fortress into a comfortable and luxurious abode. He raised the ancient living quarters, and the two new main buildings, reached by a magnificent spiral staircase, the '*grande vis*', were given stained glass windows and their interiors decorated with frescoes and wood panelling. In this beautiful Gothic residence, the king installed his famous library of rare manuscripts, his jewels and precious objects.

But the Louvre's new vocation as royal residence was to be short-lived. France was about to traverse many a troubled decade – the madness of Charles VI, civil unrest, the Hundred Years War – during which the kings of France abandoned Paris for the Loire Valley and Île-de-France.

The Louvre's Renaissance

France had to wait until a great builder, Francis I (1494–1547), came to the throne before the abandoned fortress could become a palace worthy of the kingdom's capital. In 1528 the original keep, La Grosse Tour, was demolished and replaced by a courtyard, and in 1540 the buildings were transformed into a residence befitting of Charles V. Then in 1546, the decisive transformations began. On the foundations of the old ramparts parallel to the Seine the architect Pierre Lescot erected a new residence, commissioning Jean Goujon to decorate the facades. We also owe this remarkable artist the magnificent sculptures in the Caryatids Room, originally the royal residence's ceremonial hall and today housing part of the antique sculpture collection. The building's three-tiered inner facade, with large windows, protruding bays, cornices and engaged columns is a masterpiece of French Renaissance architecture. It determined the Louvre's ensuing architectural development, serving as both inspiration and model for the palace's subsequent enlargements.

Lescot's work, the bulk of which was carried out during Henry II's reign (1547–59), continued with the construction of a wing a right angles, linked to the previous one by the King's Pavilion. While work continued under Charles IX (1560–74) with a small gallery in the Italian style on the Seine side, Catherine de Médicis, Henry II's widow, had a palace built outside the city limits, 500 metres west of the Louvre, on land known as the Tuileries because of the tile kilns previously on the site. The architect Philibert Delorme designed an enormous quadrilateral composed of several buildings but the building project, continued by his successor Jean Bullant, was only carried out in part. Only the Italian garden was completed, with a picturesque little grotto decorated with glazed terracottas by Bernard Palissy.

The 'Grand Design'

Although short, Henry IV's reign (1589–1610) proved to be a watershed in the palace's history. Intent on imposing Paris as France's political and intellectual epicentre, he decided to link the Louvre to the Tuileries. The plan was to complete the Petite Galerie perpendicular to the Seine and above all add a very long building along the riverfront, the Grande Galerie or 'Galerie du bord de l'eau'. The 460-metre-long edifice was finished in 1608 by Louis Métezeau and Jacques II Androuet du Cerceau, and an ambitious ensemble of buildings and courtyards was planned to complete the King's cherished project of a royal palace complex and residence for artists.

Henry IV, murdered in 1610, never saw his 'Grand Design' completed, but his son Louis XIII (1610–43) took charge of the ongoing project. He entrusted the painter Nicolas Poussin with the Grande Galerie's interior decoration and Jacques Le Mercier with completing the Cour Carrée and removing the last vestiges of the medieval Louvre. The architect lengthened Lescot's wing and built the Pavillon de l'Horloge, the Louvre palace's 'linchpin'. Additional enlargements were carried out under Louis XIV (1643–1715) by Louis Le Vau, who closed off the quadrilateral with a west wing. A competition was held for the exterior facade, for which Bernini produced a design, but his project was considered too 'Italian' and Claude Perrault's austere colonnade was chosen instead.
The building work forced the court to withdraw to the Tuileries palace, modified in 1666 and now looking out over formal gardens designed by Le Nôtre. But Louis XIV's heart lay at Versailles and, deciding to take up permanent residence there, he left Paris in 1678. By the late 18th century, the unfinished Louvre palace, long forsaken by France's kings, parts of it with no roof, had become a complex of workshops and lodgings for a population of artists and other inhabitants.

The resumption of the 'Grand Design'

The ensuing decades of political unrest were hardly favourable for ambitious architectural projects. Despite Napoleon I's professed desire to resume work, his architects Percier and Fontaine only had time to erect the triumphal arch of the Carrousel at the entrance to the Tuileries and begin work joining up the Louvre's palaces on the north side along the Rue de Rivoli, created in 1802. Not until a half-century later would Henry IV's 'Grand Design' again be the order of the day.

Further sections of the north wing were built under the Restoration, but it was Napoleon III (1808–73), who had taken up residence in the Tuileries on his accession to the throne, who resumed the full-scale building programme that produced the imposing ensemble we know today. Louis Visconti and Hector Lefuel, the successive directors of this gargantuan building project, demolished the quarter that had existed for centuries between the two palaces, completed the existing palace buildings, built new pavilions on either side of the present-day Cour Napoleon and unified the facades, destroying ancient work in places to do so. Part of the palace extension was given over to the administration and Napoleon III moved into a suite in the north wing. The 'New Louvre' was inaugurated by the emperor on August 14th 1857.

No sooner had the 'imperial city' been completed than war broke out between France and Germany in 1870. In 1871, in the wake of France's defeat, the Tuileries Palace was destroyed by fire during the civil insurrection known as the Paris Commune. The huge trapezium formed by the Louvre had been breached. The restoration of the Tuileries was envisaged for a while but the palace was finally demolished in 1883. Only its extremities, the Marsan and Flore pavilions, were left standing.

The twentieth century

The Louvre was constantly added to and also considerably modified inside, the purpose of these ongoing refurbishments no longer being to glorify the monarchy but to do justice to the ever-increasing number of artworks the palace now housed. The culmination of this long-term programme was the 'Grand Louvre' project launched by President François Mitterand in 1981. Its most spectacular visual feature, the glass pyramid in the Cour Napoleon, designed by the Chinese-American architect Ieoh Ming Pei, was the crowning achievement of a mammoth undertaking: the extension of the museum into wings previously occupied by government offices, and the conversion of the palace's basements into technical facilities and to ensure optimum management of the flow of visitors. This enhancement of the collections, still in progress, is part of the Louvre's now bicentennial history as a museum.

From palace to museum

The 'Muséum Central des Arts' was officially opened amid the tumult of the French Revolution, on 10th August 1793. Yet the idea of a museum open to the general public had originated under the Ancien Régime and been pursued by successive directors of the King's Buildings. In 1768, the Marquis de Marigny, supported by the writers and philosophers of the Enlightenment, submitted to Louis XV the first project for a public exhibition of the royal collections in the Grande Galerie. Turned down at the time, the project was taken up again and developed by Count d'Angiviller who, with a view to creating a 'muséum', made an inventory of the royal collections stored in the Louvre, bought works and restored pictures. The painter Hubert Robert, who was in charge of the paintings, took part in the museum project and drew up plans for overhead natural lighting.

Financial difficulties and the political unrest which culminated in the Revolution prevented completion of the ambitious project begun under the Ancien Régime, but in 1791 a commission of artists began preparing the opening of the Muséum. Pictures were to be exhibited in the Grande Galerie and antiquities on the ground floor of the Petite Galerie. The royal collection, now the property of the nation, was enriched by works seized from religious buildings and émigrés' houses during the Revolution, and subsequently by requisitioning in the Netherlands, Italy and Germany during the Napoleonic wars. Renamed the 'Musée Napoléon' in 1803, the Louvre, under Vivant Denon's directorship, boasted an exceptional number of masterpieces in rooms specially refurbished for their exhibition.

The growth of the collections

At the end of the Empire in 1815, the museum, 'royal' anew, had to return all requisitioned works except around 100 which had been negotiated or exchanged – among them Veronese's *The Wedding Feast at Cana.* But new collections were very quickly developed, notably with the transfer to the Louvre of the sculptures in the short-lived Musée des Monuments Français, closed in 1816, and above all thanks to archaeological discoveries; these broadened the public's knowledge of other civilisations and filled the museum with treasures such as the *Venus de Milo*, which entered the Louvre in 1821. The influx of Greek, Roman, Egyptian and Near Eastern antiquities led to the museum's reorganisation into specialised museums, especially in the buildings around the Cour Carrée: the Musée Égyptien, of which Champollion was appointed director in 1826, and the Musée Assyrien, created in 1847, reigned over by the winged bulls of Khorsabad.

Gifts and acquisitions enriched the museum over the ensuing decades, to the extent that it had to be reorganised into separate departments. The Louvre's eight departments today have some thirty thousand works on exhibit, with the Department of Graphic Arts showing works on a rotary basis in temporary exhibitions. Each of these departments, like the rooms housing the Arts of Africa, Asia, Oceania and the Americas, has its own rich history, which is outlined in each chapter of this guide to the Louvre collections.

Oriental antiquities

THE HISTORY OF THE LOUVRE'S DEPARTMENT OF ORIENTAL ANTIQUITIES is inseparable from that of French archaeological discoveries in the Near and Middle East. The first explorations were undertaken by diplomats posted in what was then the vast and powerful Ottoman Empire. One of their dreams was to discover the traces of the peoples mentioned in the Bible. Paul-Emile Botta, French Consul at Mosul (present-day northern Iraq) set out with the idea of finding ancient Nineveh. His search took him to the site at Khorsabad where, instead of discovering the long-lost city there, he unearthed the remains of the palace of Sargon II, king of Assyria in the 8th century BC. Some of the works dug up, catalogued and drawn by the talented painter Eugène Flandrin, were sent back to the Louvre, which in 1847 opened the first Assyrian museum. This fieldwork also led to the deciphering of cuneiform writing.
EXPEDITIONS THEN TURNED TO THE LANDS OF THE LEVANT. Learned travellers such as F. de Saulcy and E. Guillaume Rey were the first to bring back antiquities from Cyprus and the Holy Land. Ernest Renan's expedition to the Lebanon revealed the Phoenician civilisation. Ernest de Sarzec, a diplomat posted to Basra (in present-day southeast Iraq), explored southern Mesopotamia. At Telloh, he unearthed an impres-

sive series of stone effigies of Gudea, prince of the Sumerian city state of Lagash, who reigned around 2130 BC. It was due to the many inscriptions discovered there that the very name of the Sumerians first came to light. We owe this people one of mankind's fundamental inventions: writing. Iran was to find its major explorer in the French engineer Marcel Dieulafoy. Aided by his intrepid wife, he undertook for the Louvre the excavation of the town of Susa, where the ruins of the palace of Darius were still visible. His most outstanding discovery there, the famous 'Archers of Darius' frieze, is one of the gems of the department. Following in Dieulafoy's footsteps, Jacques de Morgan unearthed the most ancient layers of Susa, capital of the kingdom of Elam before being that of the Persians.

After the First World War and the collapse of the Ottoman Empire, teams of French archaeologists continued the fieldwork. From 1929 onwards, Claude Schaeffer excavated Ras Shamra, ancient Ugarit, while in 1933 André Parrot discovered ancient Mari. The department's curators are pursuing their work today, in collaboration with local authorities, and their discoveries now remain in their country of origin.

'Land between the rivers'

It was the Greek historian Polybius who, in the 2nd century BC baptised the alluvial valley of the Tigris and the Euphrates 'Mesopotamia', 'land between the rivers'. This region covering present-day Iraq and part of Syria owed its wealth to the fertile plains irrigated by these two long rivers. The Bible records the efforts to transform them into cultivable fields: the Garden of Eden, the earthly paradise in the book of Genesis, is located 'to the east'.

The 'Neolithic revolution' (as the archaeologist Gordon Childe termed it) took place over a vast area encompassing Mesopotamia and the regions close to the Levant. Gradually, over several millennia, man became 'possessor and master' of nature. From 7000 BC, the Iraqi Al-Jazirah (plain between the two rivers) became covered with village communities living from cattle-rearing and agriculture. There soon appeared the first hand-fashioned terracotta recipients, whose varied forms and colours have enabled archaeologists to compare and classify these 'prehistoric' cultures. The so-called 'Hassuna' civilisation, for instance, which developed in the Middle Tigris region in the early 6th millennium, produced distinctive, still unrefined ceramic ware with incised and painted decoration. The Samarra and Halaf cultures, which emerged in the areas stretching from the Zagros mountains to the Middle Euphrates, in turn created vases heightened with geometric motifs, sometimes even with animal and floral decorations.

The second 'revolution', the transition from village to town and the emergence of the city-state, did not take place until the middle of the 4th millennium. In this intensely hierarchical society there emerged a dominant figure whom archaeologists have baptised the 'priest-king', while the first written archives appeared around 3300 BC. The sculptors, for their part, developed art forms destined for a brilliant future: relief and sculpture in the round.

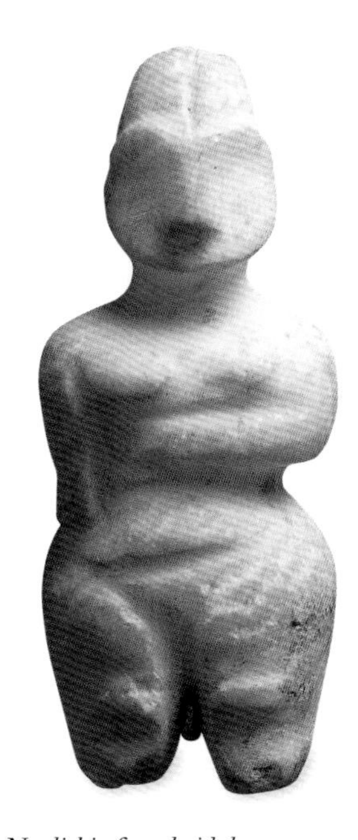

1 *Neolithic female idol*

Tell es-Sawwan (Middle Tigris)
Early 6th millennium BC
Alabaster. H. 5.4 cm
Loaned by the Baghdad Museum, 1981
DAO 33

The tombs of this region of the Middle Tigris, dug beneath houses built to a regular ground plan, have yielded very refined stone tableware and alabaster statues. These are the first composite female figurines, combining several materials, and bear witness to the existence in Mesopotamia of cults venerating fecundity and motherhood.

2 *Priest-king*

Southern Mesopotamia
Uruk period, *c.*3300 BC
Limestone. H. 25 cm
Early acquisition. AO 5718

3 *Prince Ginak*

Mesopotamia
Early Archaic Period, *c.*2700 BC
Gypsum. 26 x 10.8 cm
Gift of the Société des Amis du Louvre, 1951
AO 20146

For most of the 3rd millennium, Mesopotamia was divided into numerous city-states. Princes and high-ranking dignitaries had themselves represented in prayer, with their hands joined in a timeless gesture of devotion. The statuette of this prince from northern Mesopotamia is no exception. A hieratic figure, with a schematised body, prominent nose, long hair and stylised beard, he is wearing the characteristic garment of his rank: the *kaunakes*, a kind of loincloth trimmed with woollen braids. The inscription on the back of the statuette tells us that he is 'Ginak, prince of Edin-E', an unknown town.

4 *The 'Vulture Stele'*

Telloh (ancient Girsu)
c.2450 BC
Limestone. 1.80 x 1.30 m
E. de Sarzec excavations
AO 50. 2346, 2347, 2348, 16109

5 *Vase of Entemena, King of Lagash*

Telloh (ancient Girsu)
c.2400 BC
Silver and copper. 35 x 18 cm
E. de Sarzec excavations.
Gift of Sultan Abd-ul-Hamid, 1896
AO 2674

Like his first-dynasty predecessors, Entemena in turn showed his profound devotion to the great god of his kingdom, Ningirsu. This exceptionally fine vase, made from a single sheet of beaten silver, is dedicated to him. The superbly engraved decoration around the body shows Ningirsu's animal attribute, the lion-headed eagle Anzu, successively gripping stags or goats in his lion's claws. The seven squatting heifers around the vase's shoulder, symbols of fertility, also evoke the wealth of the divine herd. The inscription around the collar states that this particularly precious recipient belonged to 'the god's table service' and that at that time 'Dudu was priest of Ningirsu'.

6 *Relief of Ur-Nanshe, king of Lagash*

Telloh (ancient Girsu)
*c.*2500 BC
Limestone. 40 x 47 cm
E. de Sarzec excavations, 1888
AO 2344

Ur-Nanshe founded the first dynasty of Lagash in around 2500 BC. If we are to believe the many inscriptions he left us, he was a tireless builder of sanctuaries, digger of canals and erector of sculptures in honour of the gods. In this large perforated relief, the Sumerian sovereign had himself portrayed laying the foundations of a temple, with a basket of bricks balanced on his head. In the bottom register, Ur-Nanshe, sitting enthroned amidst members of his family and dignitaries, goblet in hand, is celebrating the edifice's completion. The inscriptions tell us that the temple was built in honour of the two principal divinities in the pantheon of the state of Lagash, Ningirsu and Nanshe, and that precious wood was imported from Dilmun (present-day Bahrain) for its construction.

7 *The Mari 'Standard'*

Mari (Middle Euphrates), temple of Ishtar
*c.*2400 BC
Shell and mosaic
A. Parrot excavations, 1934–1936
AO 19820

8 *Temple guardian lion*

Mari, temple of Dagan
19th century BC
Copper with inlay. 38 x 70 cm
A. Parrot excavations, 1936–1937
AO 19824

The flourishing kingdom of Mari

The kingdom of Mari, founded on the Euphrates on the borders of Syria and Mesopotamia in the 3rd millennium BC, bore witness to the spread of Sumerian culture into regions to the north. The excavations André Parrot carried out from 1933 revealed the existence of a capital which played a major role in Mesopotamian history from the mid-3rd millennium until its destruction by Hammurabi of Babylon around 1750 BC. The city had a luxurious palace decorated with frescoes and numerous temples, from which were unearthed over 20,000 texts written in cuneiform script. These archives paint a moving picture of daily life in an oriental city four thousand years ago. But it is above all in the burgeoning art of sculpture that we most vividly experience the fervour of the people of Mari. Many were the faithful who placed ex-voto of themselves in the temple of Ishtar, goddess of love and war. These magnificent idealised 'portraits' – king, miller, head of the cadastre, cupbearer, singer, priestess, all gazing at us with their eyes inlaid with colour – have survived in exceptionally good condition. Recognisable among the female statuettes are portrayals of priestesses. Impassively sitting enthroned, with their high *polos* headdress, in their left hand they hold a reed, symbol of their intervention in the fertility of nature. The statue of Superintendant Ebih-il [9], the masterpiece of the period, achieves a miraculous balance between realism and religious convention, and is rendered even more priceless by the eyes in lapis lazuli, imported from Afghanistan.

In the wealthy city of Mari, the sumptuary arts also flourished, as illustrated by the numerous chlorite vases imported from eastern Iran, and the *Mari 'Standard'* [7], a genuine precursor of the comic strip, with its tiny figures cut out of mother-of-pearl. The Mari excavations, directed by Jean-Claude Margueron since 1978, are constantly adding to our knowledge of the extent of this city's refinement.

9 *Ebih-il, Superintendent of Mari*

Mari (Middle Euphrates), temple of Ishtar
*c.*2400 BC
Alabaster. H. 52 cm
A. Parrot excavations, 1934
AO 17551

'Statue of Ebih-il, the superintendent. To Ishtar the Virile, has he dedicated it,' reads the inscription on the back of this striking alabaster statuette. Ebih-il, his head shaven as was the custom, sports an impeccably groomed beard, its undulating locks ending in graceful twirls. His eyebrows have lost their inlay but his eyes, set in bitumen, still sparkle with the brilliance afforded by the combined use of shell and lapis lazuli. It is the naturalistic rendition of the *kaunakes* which is the most surprising, however: it is as if every last tuft of sheep's fleece has been painstakingly represented. Yet behind its superficial realism, this statue retains all its sacred detachment, a magnificent testament to fervour and devotion.

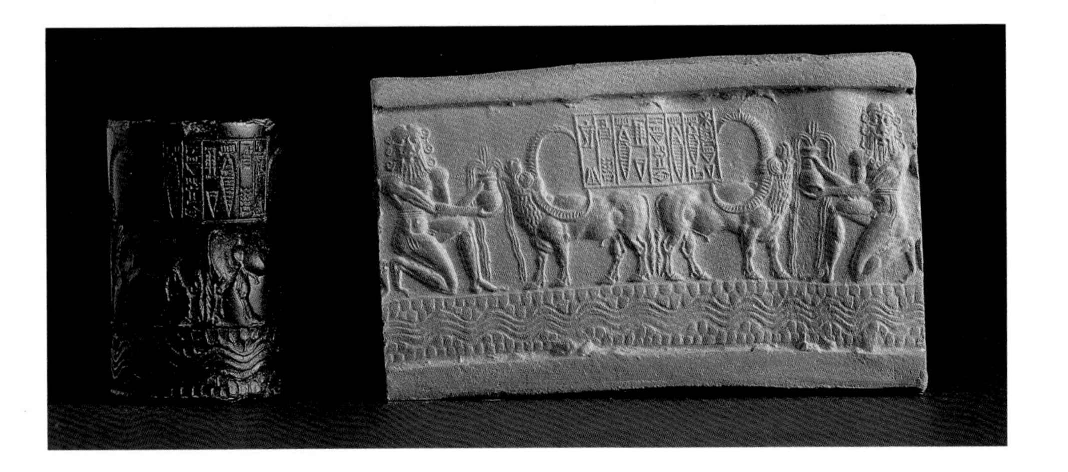

The Akkad empire (*c.*2340–2200 BC), or art in the service of power

It was Sargon ('just king' or 'true king' in Akkadian) who put an end to Mesopotamia's political division. Legend has it that he was born in a small town on the banks of the Euphrates, to a priestess who did not have the right to raise children, was adopted by a gardener and, owing to the favour of the goddess Ishtar, became a cupbearer at the king's court and then a prince himself. But one can assume that this young adventurer gathered around him a band of the affluent Semites of the Syrian desert, men who hired themselves out in the rich oases of Mesopotamia as day labourers or soldiers. Soon after founding the town of Akkad around 2300 BC, Sargon overthrew the king of Uruk, Lugalzagesi, subjugated Lower Mesopotamia and went on to push back Mesopotamia's frontiers as none of his predecessors had succeeded in doing. His unified, centralised empire now encompassed the countries of Sumer and Akkad, northern Mesopotamia, and the Diyala and Elam regions. His son, Manishtusu, and grandson, Naram-Sin, carried on his work. The reigns of the sovereigns of Akkad were marked by grandiose achievements. Art was used essentially to glorify the royal person and express the coherence and stability of a highly centralised military empire. The genius of the artists of Akkad is best expressed in the historiated reliefs and statuary. Clarity, elegance and severity are the hallmarks of this aesthetic.

Around 2200 BC, mountain peoples from the east wrought anarchy in Mesopotamia for nearly a century. In the Sumerian south, the state of Lagash regained its autonomy under the authority of a pacific and pious monarch, Prince Gudea.

10 *Cylinder seal of the scribe of Sharkalisharri, King of Akkad*

*c.*2340-2200 BC
Chlorite. 3.9 x 2.6 cm
Gift of H. de Boisgelin, 1967
Formerly in the De Clercq Collection
AO 22303

11 *Victory stele of King Naram-Sin*

Susa
Akkadian period, *c.*2230 BC
Pink sandstone. 2 x 1.05 m
J. de Morgan excavations, 1898
Sb 4

The incontestable masterpiece of Akkadian art, this stele commemorates the triumph of the fourth king of the Akkad dynasty over the Lullubi, a rebellious mountain people from Zagros. With a consummate sense of drama, the sculptor has managed to convey his sovereign's ascent towards victory. The tall, central, isolated figure of the king, dominates the entire composition, symbolically ascending the mountain armed with a short spear. The horns on his helmet confer divine status on him. The astral signs at the top of the stele also signify the protection of the gods. An official propaganda monument, it was taken away as war booty in the 12th century BC by Elamite conquerors. It was discovered by French archaeologists among the remains of the town of Susa.

12 *Lady with a Scarf*

Telloh (ancient Girsu)
Neo-Sumerian Period, *c.*2150 BC
Chlorite. 17 x 9 cm
E. de Sarzec excavations, 1881
AO 295

Statuettes of princesses, far more modest in size and material than effigies of the sovereign himself, sometimes attain great artistic heights. The famous *Lady with a Scarf* is one example. Her hands joined in a gesture of reverence and prayer, she is wearing several necklaces, a sign that she is a member of court, and very probably of the royal family. Her chignon, held in place by a head band, is similar in sobriety to Gudea's hairstyle. Her severe expression suggests her imperviousness to earthly contingencies.

13 *Small Statue of Gudea Seated*

Telloh (ancient Girsu)
*c.*2120 BC
Diorite. 46 x 33 cm
Excavations of E. de Sarzec (head) and G. Cros (body), 1903
AO 3293/4108

14 *Bull with a Man's Head*

Telloh (ancient Girsu)
Neo-Sumerian Period, *c.*2150 BC
Steatite (soapstone). 10 x 14 cm
Acquired in 1898
AO 2752

15 *Gudea with Flowing Vase*

Telloh (ancient Girsu)
*c.*2120 BC
Dolerite. 62 x 25.6 cm
Acquired in 1967
AO 22126

The second Lagash dynasty's principal sovereign, Prince Gudea (literally 'the chosen one') was extremely anxious to ensure his posterity. He left us some twenty statues depicting him as an ideal monarch, hands joined in prayer in the kneeling pose of a worshipper or, more rarely, as here, standing holding a flowing vase, a symbol of fertility. The sovereign sports a high-rimmed cap covered with ringlets of hair. His massive face, with its prominent cheekbones and square jaw, exudes an immutable yet serene power. The statue commemorates the construction of a temple dedicated to Gudea's personal god, Ningishzidda, and his consort Geshtinanna.

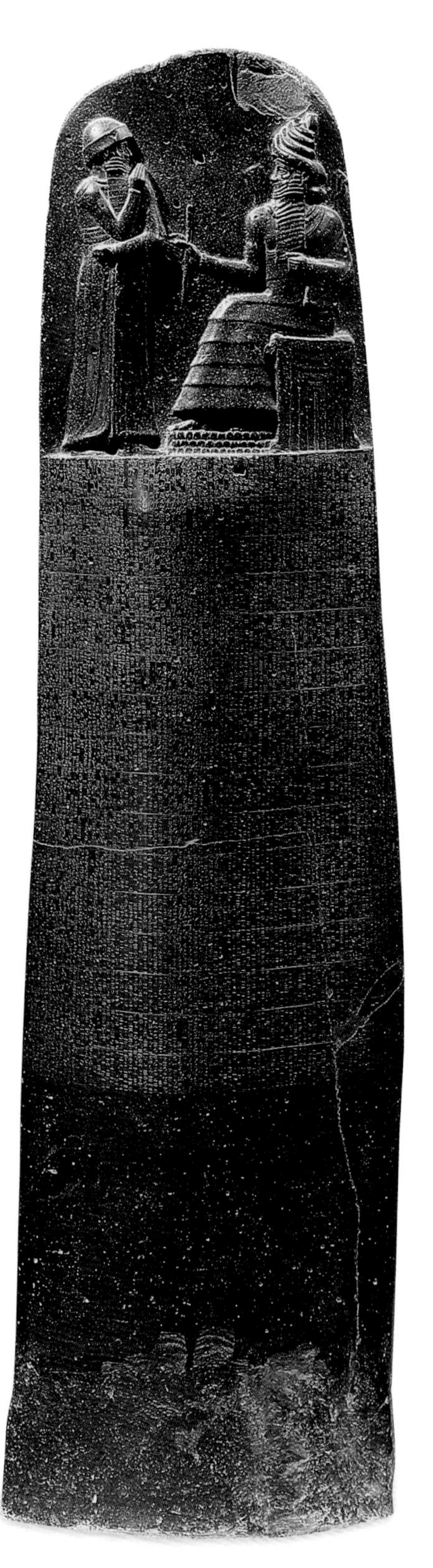

16 *The Code of Hammurabi*

Babylon, found at Susa
First half of the 18th century BC
Basalt. H. 2.25 m
J. de Morgan excavations, 1901–1902
Sb 8

Hammurabi, the sixth sovereign of the Amorite dynasty which established itself in Babylon in the early 19th century BC, transformed this small town into a brilliant capital whose power was felt throughout the Orient. But Hammurabi's name will always be remembered for the famous Code of Laws he had engraved on several steles, a complete one of which is in the Louvre. The work, carved in a fine black basalt is divided into two parts. Below the seat of divinity (the sun-god Shamash, patron-god of justice, recognisable by the flames shooting from his shoulders), runs a long text engraved in a script of great elegance. As well as being a code of law, the work became a classic of Babylonian literature and was endlessly copied. Erected in Babylon, it was taken as booty to Susa by an Elamite king in the 12th century.

17 *Royal Head*

Brought from Babylonia to Susa
First Babylonian dynasty, 19th–18th century BC
Diorite. 15.2 x 9.7 cm
J. de Morgan excavations
Sb 95

18 *The Worshipper of Larsa*

Larsa (Babylonia)
First half of the 18th century BC
Bronze and gold. 19 x 15 cm
Acquired in 1932
AO 15704

The worshipper, kneeling, his hand on his mouth in a gesture of prayer and devotion, is wearing the heavy round cap that was the royal headdress from Gudea's time onwards. It is possibly a depiction of King Hammurabi himself. This priceless statuette with its face and hands covered in gold leaf was dedicated by an inhabitant of Larsa to the god Amurru, in the hope that he would protect the life of his sovereign. The small basin at the front is for offerings.

19 *Kudurru of King Melishipak of Babylon*

Brought from Babylonia to Susa
Early 12th century BC
Grey limestone. 65 x 30 cm
J. de Morgan excavations, 1898–1899
Sb 22

This stele commemorating a donation was part of the Mesopotamian war booty found at Susa. After Hammurabi's death, the Babylonian empire broke up under the combined threats of tribes from the 'countries of the sea' and incursions of Kassite barbarians from the Zagros region. Taking advantage of the climate of instability, the Kassites took power around 1595 BC. They instated new practices such as gifts of land to prominent figures, whom they bound in their service. 'Kudurrus', massive stone steles with rounded tops officialised these donations. On one side are engraved the terms of the property transfer, and on the other, the emblems and symbols of the major deities guaranteeing the contract, Anu, god of the sky, Enlil, god of the atmosphere, Ea, god of the watery Abyss, the crescent of Sin, god of the Moon, the star of Ishtar (Venus), and the solar disc of Shamash.

20 *Stele (Kudurru) of King Marduk-Zakir-Shumi*

Uruk (southern Mesopotamia)
Mid-9th century BC
Limestone. 32 x 15 cm
Acquired in 1914
AO 6684

In the late 2nd millennium BC, Babylonia sank again into chaos and turmoil before recovering its brilliance under the neo-Babylonian dynasty in the late 7th century. Despite political unrest, the region preserved its religious and intellectual aura, as illustrated by this small stele carved in light-coloured limestone. At the top, the familiar figure of a priest, the donation's addressee, depicted standing before the sovereign. The principal gods, represented by their attributes, act as the contract's guarantors.

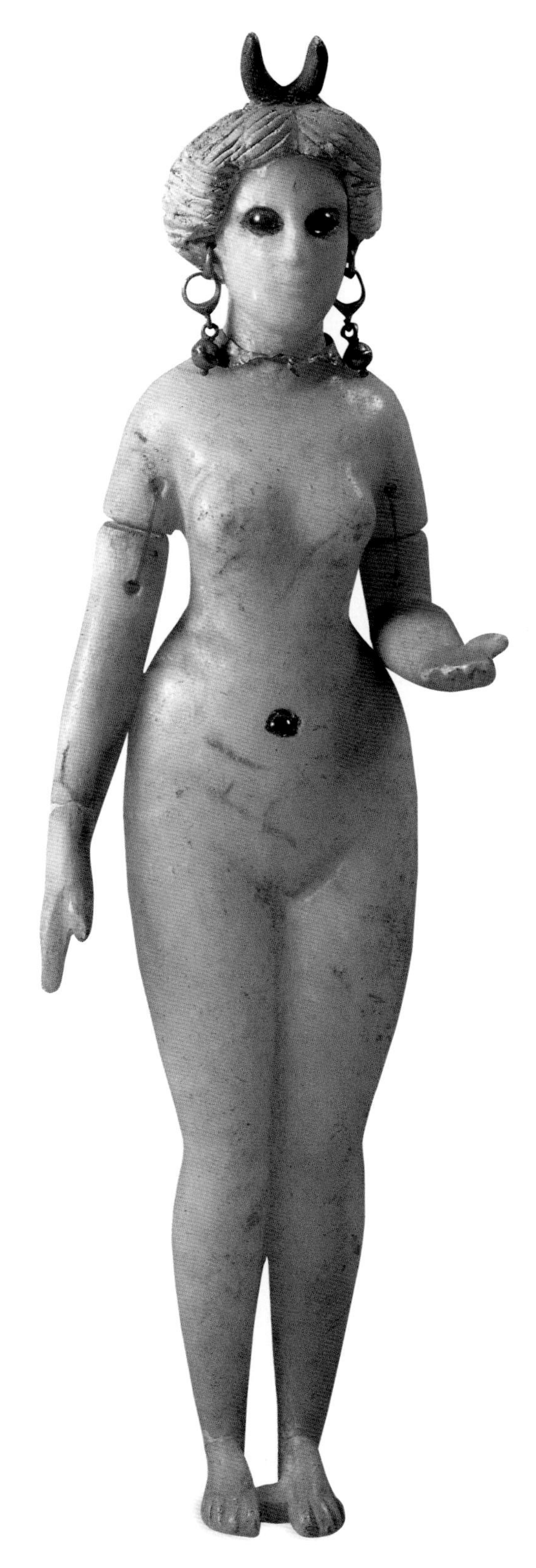

21 *Statuette of the goddess Ishtar*

Babylon
*c.*250 BC
Alabaster, gold, bronze and rubies. H. 25 cm
Pacifique Delaporte Donation, 1866
AO 20127

Babylon was the intellectual capital of Mesopotamia. The elite of priests, scribes and soothsayers employed beyond the kingdom's frontiers, as far afield as Syria and the Hittite court, was recruited from the clergy of the god Marduk. Instead of dying out with the arrival of Alexander the Great in the 4th century BC, Babylonian culture continued to flourish, and with it part of the Babylonians' science and religion. An example of this is this delicate statuette of the goddess Ishtar, recognisable by her crescent moon, and whose forms are borrowed from the sensual anatomy of the Greek Aphrodite. The Mesopotamian tradition of composite sculpture combining different materials is continued here. The opening towards India favoured by Alexander's expedition into the East is manifest here in the use of rubies from the Far East, inlaid in the eyes and navel.

22 *Assurbanipal in a chariot*

Nineveh, Palace of Assurbanipal
668–630 BC
Relief, gypsum. 1.62 x 0.77 m
Gift of Rawlinson to the Place Expedition
Entered the Louvre in 1856
AO 19904

23 *Exorcism plaque*

Assyria
Late 8th–7th century BC
Bronze. 13.5 x 8.5 cm
Gift of H. de Boisgelin, 1967
AO 22205

24 *Median tribute bearers*

Khorsabad (Assyria), Palace of Sargon II
721–705 BC
Relief, gypsum. 1.62 x 3.66 m
P.-E. Botta excavations, 1843–1844
AO 19887

25 *Door guarded by winged Assyrian bulls*

Khorsabad, Palace of Sargon II of Assyria
721–705 BC
Gypsum. 4.20 x 4.36 m
P.-E. Botta excavations, 1843–1844
AO 19857

When Sargon II decided on the location of his new capital, some 15 kilometres north of Nineveh, he envisaged not merely a palace but a city of gigantic size. The building of the city from scratch on the site of present-day Khorsabad required a massive work force. The doors of the palace, symbols of this immoderation, were guarded by winged creatures with bull's bodies, benevolent monsters whose role was to ward off hostile forces whilst guaranteeing the edifice's stability. These *lamassu* with gentle human faces, their proportions governed by mathematically calculated proportions, exude calm, serenity and harmony.

26 *Hittite god*

Yozgat, Bogazkoy region
Ancient Hittite Empire, 1600–1400 BC
Gold. H. 3.8 cm
Chantre Collection
AO 9647

Around 1650 BC, a Hittite prince united the many small kingdoms of central Anatolia under his authority and set up his capital at Hattusha (now Bogazkoy). The town, protected by a rampart, had several sanctuaries where devotional practices are manifested by small figurines in bronze or precious metals very close to Syrian statuettes of the time. This gold pendant depicts a divinity wearing a high conical tiara, the traditional short loincloth and boots with turned-up toes, characteristics to be found on Hittite rock reliefs.

27 *Double idol*

Cappadocia
Early Bronze Age, *c.*2000 BC
Alabaster. H. 12 cm
AO 8794

The site at Kultepe (Kanesh) has yielded a remarkable series of 'idols' carved in marble or gypsum, whose stylised anatomy has affinities with the figurines of the Cyclades. These images are related to beliefs linked to fertility.

Anatolia

Anatolia played an appreciable role as 'bridge' between Europe and the world of the high plateaux of Iran. Attracting many peoples with its varied resources, compartmented by its mountain ranges and subjected to diverse influences, this region would not experience true political and cultural unity until the period of the Hittite empire (17th–13th century BC).

The first traces of Neolithic communities date from the 8th millennium. On the high plain of Konya, the settlement of unbaked brick houses at Catal Huyuk covered twelve hectares. At the dawn of the early Bronze Age (3500–2300 BC), the land's geographic divisions favoured the emergence of numerous small cultures, each developing its own artistic language. To the west, the necropolis at Yortan has yielded a series of stone figurines reminiscent of the idols of the Aegean world and the Cyclades, while Cappadocia produced double-headed figurines during the 3rd millennium. In the early 2nd millennium, Mesopotamian merchants founded colonies in Cappadocia to control the transport of tin. Then, during the 17th century BC, the Hittites succeeded in unifying the land and developing a monumental art.

28 *Goblet from Susa I*

Susa, archaic necropolis
4th millenium BC
Terracotta. 28.5 x 16 cm
J. de Morgan excavations, 1907–1909
Sb 3174

Painted ceramics are incontestably the most refined aspect of the art of Susa in the 5th millennium. Made from a very smooth paste, they fall into two main categories: bowls and goblets. Most of these recipients come from the tombs excavated by J. de Morgan, but it is probable that this luxury ware was not solely funerary. These vases are striking in their formal perfection and decoration, in which man is rarely depicted. It is the animal who triumphs, represented by geometrical forms.

Iran

To the west of Mesopotamia, high mountains and a high plateau stretch to the Indus plain and beyond to the steppes of Central Asia. The harshness of the climate and the mountainous terrain profoundly influenced its cultures. To the southeast, Elam, or the 'high country', dominated a small plain, an extension of the Mesopotamian plain, whose capital was Susa. Its culture was open to Mesopotamian influences and to the traditions of the mountain peoples, the dual factors which forged Susa's identity. Susa, located by the Englishman K. Loftus and excavated by Marcel Dieulafoy, who explored the Persian Achaemenid palace, has yielded remains dating back to the 4th millennium BC, which the French geologist and prehistorian Jacques de Morgan was the first to attempt to identify in 1897. Unfortunately, the excavation methods he used to unearth remains in unbaked brick left much to be desired. Among the discoveries in the religious and administrative acropolis are a number of Elamite pieces and works brought from Babylonia as war spoils, notably the Code of Hammurabi and the Stele of Naram-Sin, king of Akkad.

29 *Female worshipper*

Susa
Uruk period, *c.*3200 BC
Alabaster. 6.3 x 3.8 cm
J. de Morgan and R. de Mecquenem excavations, 1909
Sb 70

'One of the most striking representations of prayer' was how Pierre Amiet described this wonder of geometrical refinement. In the late 4th millennium, Susa, then under the influence of Mesopotamian culture, in turn developed the art of sculpture in stone in a spirit all its own, full of humour. These statuettes of male and female worshippers were discovered in two 'archaic stores'. They are both expressions of popular piety and universal masterpieces of sculpture.

30 *Openwork pinhead with amorous scene*

Southeast Iran
*c.*2000 BC
Copper. Pin: 24.8; head: 5.85 x 5.1 cm
Gift of M. Foroughi, 1975
AO 26068

31 *Ovoid vase*

Decorated with intertwined snakes surrounding
a motif representing two identical vases from which female
heads are emerging
Bactria
Mid-3rd millenium BC
Chlorite and mother-of-pearl and white stone inlay
H. 24.5 cm
Gif of the Société des Amis du Louvre, 2002
AO 31883

Bactria: an aristocratic society

In the late 3rd and early 2nd millennium, this region of northern Afghanistan irrigated by the ancient Oxus (modern Amu Darya) river and its tributaries developed a brilliant culture which Pierre Amiet described as 'exterior Iran'. It was here that the Greeks who settled in the wake of Alexander the Great's conquest built their capital, Bactra, after which the country was named. The merchant aristocracy, closely associated with Elamite territories, lived in their château-like fortresses in great style judging by the precious objects and furniture found in their tombs: alabaster vases, stone cosmetic or perfume jars, round mirrors with anthropomorphic handles, lapis-lazuli, gold and kaolin pearls, silver pendants in the form of dogs, etc. The mythological repertoire of the compartmented arsenic-copper seals is both Iranian and Central Asian: a winged spirit with a bird of prey's head perching on mountains, a goddess seated on a one-horned snake-dragon spitting flames. The more conventional precious vases have episodes in the life of the local aristocracy engraved on their sides: banquets, hunting scenes, ploughing, chariot races – the same repertoire as that of the Median and Persian nobles at Persepolis during Darius's reign.

Bactrian sculpture bears witness to traditions borrowed from the cultures of the Iranian plateau and Mesopotamia. Certain tombs have yielded composite statuettes in white limestone and chlorite depicting women wearing full 'crinoline' skirts [33] next to a spirit with a scarred face and body covered with snake's scales [32]. They were probably two dominant mythological figures.

The community of Bactrian merchant-lords appears to have been refined, cosmopolitan and at the crossroads of several cultures, yet it collapsed in the late 17th century BC, at the same time as the Harappan civilisation in the Indus Valley.

32 *Mythological spirit* known as *'Scarface'*

Bactria
Limestone, chlorite, iron
H. 11.7 cm
Acquired in 1961
AO 21104

Although the regions of the Oxus in Bactria and Margiana have yielded a great many feminine effigies known as 'Princesses', only four statuettes of this enigmatic figure, called 'Scarface' by archaeologists, have so far been unearthed. His body, draped in a short loin-cloth, is covered with snake's scales emphasising the ophidian nature of the dragon he is embodies. He is bearded and bears a long scar perhaps symbolising some ritual destruction. The 'Princesses' are probably representations of the Great Goddess, and 'Scarface' both a celestial and chtonian, benign and malevolent figure.

33 *Composite statuette*

Bactria
Early 2nd millenium BC
Chlorite and limestone. H. 18.3 cm
Acquired in 1969
AO 22918

These Ladies of Bactria are dressed in an ample dress with woollen braids recalling the Sumerian *kaunakes*. The head and arms are always in limestone, the garment and headdress – hair, hat or turban – in steatite or chlorite. Some, such as the Louvre statue, are shown standing. They are generally recognisable as a divinity or priestess.

34 *Elamite god*

Susa
Early 2nd millennium
Bronze and gold. 17.5 x 5.5 cm
Sb 2823

35 *Ibex cup*

Susa
20th–19th century BC
Bitumen. H. 9 cm; Ø 22 cm
R. de Mecquenem excavations, 1924
Sb 2740

The 'Susa V' period encompasses, at Susa, a culture similar to that of the neo-Sumerians. The kings of the country called Simashki, contemporaries of the kings of Ur around 2000 BC, were followed by the Sukkalmah dynasty. Although there a few traces of the architecture of this period, the sarcophagus tombs have yielded rich furnishings attesting to the existence of a prosperous aristocracy. The favourite material of this luxurious art seems to have been bitumen putty, from a natural deposit near Susa, out of which they fashioned bowls and vases decorated with animal protomes. The masterpiece of this series is a tripod dish with feet in the form of kneeling ibex. Here, it is the animal's entire body which forms the recipient itself.

36 *Funerary head of an Elamite*

Susa
15th–14th century BC
Painted unbaked clay. 24 x 15 cm
R. de Mecquenem excavations, 1926
Sb 2836

37 *Elamite worshipper*

Susa
12th century BC
Statuette, gold and bronze. 7.5 x 2.4 cm
J. de Morgan excavations, 1904
Sb 2758

This gold statuette was discovered by the French archaeologist R. de Mecquenem in 1904, during the excavations on the acropolis at Susa. It was found with an identical figurine cast in silver. These statuettes are clearly effigies of ordinary worshippers bringing a goat as an offering to the god, or perhaps of the sovereign himself leading the sacrificial animal to the altar.

38 *Model of an Elamite place of worship*

Susa
c. 1150 BC
Cuprous alloy. 80 x 40 cm
J. de Morgan excavations, 1904–1905
Sb 2743

This model is the only known representation of an act of worship carried out in the open air. In the middle of a rectangular area, two nude, squatting figures with shaven heads (probably priests) seem to be ritually washing themselves in the early morning before the day's offerings and sacrifices. They are surrounded by the accoutrements of worship: altars (sometimes thought to be ziggurats), offering tables, basins, and steles and bushes evoking the 'temples of the wood' mentioned in the inscriptions. The name of the object and the person who commissioned it are engraved on the right side of the base: 'I, Shilhak-Inshushinak, son of Shutruk-Nahhunte, beloved servant of Inshushinak, king of Anzan and Susa, enlarger of the empire, protector of Elam, sovereign of the land of Elam, have fashioned a sunrise (*Sit-shamsi*) in copper.'

39 *Vase in the form of a humpbacked bull*

Marlik
Red lustred ceramic. H. 24 cm
Gift of M. Foroughi, 1962
AO 21112

The Marlik civilisation, which established itself in the rich province of Gilan to the south of the Caspian Sea, is known solely through its necropolises. The craftsmen of this flourishing nomadic culture were clearly inspired clay sculptors and excellent metal-workers. Among their most beautiful creations are their anthropomorphic or zoomorphic vases with vigorous shapes, such as this bull. The liquid was poured from a spout in the muzzle.

40 *Horse bit in the form of a human-headed winged bull trampling an animal*

8th–7th century BC
Bronze
Acquired in 1958, J. Coiffard Collection
AO 20530

41 *Vase with winged monsters*

Marlik region (northern Iran)
14th–13th century BC
Electrum. H. 11 cm; Ø 11.2 cm
Acquired in 1956
AO 20281

The precious metalworkers of Marlik borrowed their decorative repertoire from the glyptics of their powerful Elamite neighbours, as this magnificent goblet illustrates. A majestic winged monster with two heads and entwined scaled legs is clutching gazelles or goats. This prestigious recipient recalls the very beautiful goblet with winged bulls in the Iran Bastan Museum. It has the same virtuosity in the treatment of volumes and details but also that 'savage energy' that is the hallmark of the art of the peoples of the steppes. A few centuries later, the Scythian nomads would rekindle this tradition.

43 *Achaemenid vase handle*

5th–4th century BC
Silver and gold. 27 x 15 cm
Formerly in the Tyszkiewicz Collection
Acquired in 1898
AO 2748

42 *The Archers of Darius*

Susa
*c.*500 BC
Relief, glazed terracotta bricks. H. 2 m
M. Dieulafoy excavations, 1884–1886
AOD 488

It was a Persian prince of the Achaemenid family, Darius I (522–486 BC), who would unite Iran and create a Persian Empire stretching from the Indus to the Aegean Sea and Egypt. He undertook the construction of his immense palace on the northwest hill of Susa. The 'Archers Frieze' is the most famous and sumptuous decoration from the residential part of the palace. In the Babylonian tradition, it consisted of large courtyards surrounded by rooms whose walls were covered with coloured bricks. The hieratic, severe figures of this frieze, wearing the Persian pleated robe and with their heads garlanded, walk bearing bow, quiver and spear. This elite corps, whom the Greek historian Herodotus called the 'Immortals', symbolises the Persian people in arms, completely devoted to its monarchy and king.

45 *Sassanid pitcher*

Dailaman province, northern Iran
5th–7th century BC
Silver gilt. H. 18.1, Ø 10.6 cm
Acquired in 1966
MAO 426

44 *Capital from the Apadana, Palace of Darius I*

Susa, Palace of Darius I
Achaemenid period
Reign of Darius I, *c.*510 BC
Limestone. H. 7.60 m
Dieulafoy Mission, 1885–1886
AOD 1

Darius's palace was composed of two distinct ensembles: a Babylonian-style palace decorated with coloured bricks, and a vast audience chamber called the 'Apadana' in the Iranian tradition, with six rows of six columns. Outside, a double row of six columns supported each of the porticos of the three north, east and west facades. The capitals, carved in grey limestones form the Zagros mountains, are decorated with bull and griffin protomes. Their vigorous profiles echo a Mesopotamian pictorial repertoire dating from the 3rd millennium and also used by the Assyrians.

46 *Male statuette*

Safadi, Negev
Chalcolithic Period, 3500–3000 BC
Hippopotamus ivory. H. 24 cm
J. Perrot excavations, 1958
AO 21406

The Levant, crossroads of the Near East

The Levant, at the hub of the Aegean world, Anatolia, Mesopotamia and Egypt, comprised the modern countries of Syria, Lebanon and Israel and the island of Cyprus. From the 7th millennium BC, all the prerequisite conditions were in place for the emergence of numerous villages connected by commercial exchanges. Neolithic towns such as Hacilar, Jericho and Byblos owed their prosperity to the trade in obsidian from Anatolia, then copper from the Sinai. The urbanisation of the Levant took place in the 3rd millennium, when contacts were intensifying with the land of the Pharaohs as well as the Aegean world and the Syro-Mesopotamian interior. At Byblos, which controlled the trade in cedarwood from Mount Lebanon, the Egyptian sovereigns offered sumptuous gifts in exchange for wood. Luxury objects and works of art, when not directly imported from the banks of the Nile, were Egyptian in style. Even the 'Lady of Byblos', the city's tutelary goddess, is depicted with the features of the Egyptian divinity Hathor.
The 2nd millennium was just as fertile in commercial, diplomatic and artistic exchanges. Every merchant in the Mediterranena and Asia seems to have passed through the Levantine crossroad where, despite these many influences, there burgeoned an original and sumptuous culture. There emerged a tradition of luxury craftwork of exceptional quality, which developed themes, motifs and techniques shared by all the cultures around the Levant. And the success of these pieces was the measure of their virtuosity. From Knossos to Ugarit, from Mycenae to Enkomi and from Cyprus to Megiddo, the furnishings of the palaces, residences and the tombs of the elite are outstanding in their beauty. Polychrome earthenware caskets, cosmetic boxes, ivory toilet effects, gold paterae, cornelian jewellery and ceremonial objects in alabaster bear witness to an artistic community which would in turn be imported into the Greek world during its 'Orientalist' phase.

47 *Fertility Idol*

Cyprus
Chalcolithic Period, late 3rd millennium BC
Painted and incised terracotta. H. 12.9 cm
Couchoud Mission
AM 1176

48 *Seated sphinx*

Syria
Middle Bronze Age, *c.* 1600 BC
Ivory. H. 8.4 cm
Acquired in 1993
AO 30256

Ivory carving was one of the principal means of artistic expression in the Levant. Hippopotamus ivory was the most commonly used material, with elephant ivory usually being reserved for palaces and temples. This plaque probably decorated a piece of furniture. The sphinx, Egyptian in inspiration, has the Asian features of the enemies of the land of the Pharaohs.

49 *'Eyed idol'*

Northern Syria
c. 3300–3000 BC
Terracotta. H. 27 cm
Gift of the Société des Amis du Louvre, 1991
AO 30002

In northern Syria, urbanisation in the 4th millennium was accompanied with profound spiritual mutations. Forsaking the generous forms of the Neolithic 'mother goddesses', clay sculptors fashioned stylised figures verging on the sign or abstraction, such as this extraordinary, exceptionall carved 'eyed idol', which belongs to a type widespread from the Euphrates (Tell Brak excavations) to Mesopotamia (Susa).

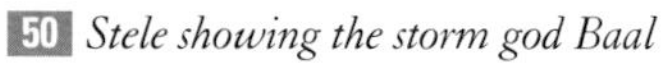

50 *Stele showing the storm god Baal*

Ras Shamra (ancient Ugarit)
14th–13th century BC
Limestone. H. 1.42 m
C. Schaeffer excavations, 1930
AO 15775

Ugarit, present-day Ras Shamra on the Syrian coast, was the capital of a flourishing kingdom in the 2nd millennium. Two large temples in the form of towers dominated its acropolis, one dedicated to Dagan, a god of the infernal forces, the other to the storm god Baal. It is the latter divinity who is depicted on the Louvre stele, brandishing a mace and striking a spear into the ground. The spear shaft transformed into a leafy reed indicates the effectiveness of his action which, by unleashing rain, has regenerated the vegetation. Under his arm the king of Ugarit is depicted praying under the protection of his god.

51 *Idol of the storm god Baal*

Minet el-Beida (port of ancient Ugarit)
14th–12th century BC
Bronze and gold. H. 17.9 cm
C. Schaeffer and G. Chenet excavations, 1929
AO 11598

As at Byblos, the deities of Ugarit were honoured in the form of statuettes that were installed in places of worship throughout the city. This figure of the god Baal, wearing an Egyptian-style high crown, is strikingly slender and dynamic in pose.

52 *The 'Mistress of the Animals'*

Minet el-Beida (port of ancient Ugarit), tomb III
14th–13th century BC
Cosmetic box cover, elephant ivory
H. 13.7 cm
C. Schaeffer excavations, 1929
AO 11601

The use of elephant tusks gave rise to the emergence in the 14th and 13th centuries of new models such as these cylindrical pyxes, cosmetic or unguent boxes, carved from the hollow base of the tusk. This box lid is particularly remarkable for its technical virtuosity and iconography. It shows a 'Mistress of the Animals' feeding corn cobs to wild goats standing up on their hind legs. Her long tiered skirt, her pose and sensuous nature recall the traditions of Crete and Mycenae.

53 *Dish with hunting scene*

Ras Shamra (ancient Ugarit)
14th–12th century BC
Gold. Ø 18.8 cm
C. Schaeffer and G. Chenet excavations, 1933
AO 17208

54 *Stele of Si Gabbor, Priest of the Moon God*

Neirab, near Aleppo, northern Syria
6th century BC
Basalt. H. 95 cm
Acquired in 1897
AO 3027

55 *Model of a sanctuary decorated with nude goddesses*

Meskene (ancient Emar, on the Euphrates)
12th century BC
Terracotta. H. 44 cm
J.-C. Margueron excavations, 1975
Gift of the Syrian Arab Republic
AO 27905

56 *Grimacing mask*

Carthage, Dermech necropolis
Late 7th–early 6th cenury BC
Terracotta. H. 19.5 cm
Delattre excavations. Gift of P. Gauckler
AO 3242

Organised into city-states along the coastal strip of present-day Lebanon, the Phoenicians, intrepid mariners, were constantly opening up new trade routes in the eastern Mediterranean and establishing trading posts along them. The town of Carthage in North Africa is traditionally said to have been founded in 814 by the king of Tyre's sister, Dido. A mere colony at the outset, this prosperous town grew into a metropolis and became the hub of a civilisation that flourished in the 9th and 8th centuries before being swallowed up by the Romans in 146 BC. This grimacing terracotta mask was intended to ward off evil spirits.

57 *Statuette of an ibex*

Southern Arabia (Yemen)
1st century BC–1st century AD
Bronze. H. 19 cm
Acquired in 2001
AO 31571

58 *Divine triad*

Palmyra region
1st half of the 1st century AD
Limestone. 60 x 72 cm
Acquired in 1945
AO 19801

The ancient Arab world, from the last centuries BC until the advent of Islam, saw the emergence of a series of cultures, of which Palmyra, in modern Syria, was one of the most dazzling. Dominating trade throughout the Orient, the rich families of merchants established in this oasis embellished their city with colonnaded monuments, reliefs and Roman-style statues. They also developed a funerary art of great beauty, with monumental tombs in which funerary portraits preserved the image of the deceased. Large temples were built for the worship of astral deities. In this relief, the three major Palmyrene deities are depicted as Roman soldiers, yet their frontal and hieratic pose is Oriental.

Egyptian antiquities

THOSE WHO HAVE NEVER HAD THE CHANCE to visit the banks of the Nile can easily console themselves in the treasure-filled Egyptian rooms in the Louvre. The Egyptian Department, with its wealth of over 50,000 works, recently entirely redesigned its exhibition spaces (the work was finished in December 1997), which now combine thematic and chronological presentations to take the visitor on a journey through 4,000 years of Egyptian civilisation. All the themes vital for an understanding of Egyptian thought and the Egyptian world (writing, the tomb, the temple, the gods, and so forth) are explored alongside the major masterpieces that have contributed to the Louvre's fame.

THE DEPARTMENT'S HISTORY is still inseparable from its first curator, Jean-François Champollion. An order signed by Charles X on 15 May 1826 created an Egyptian monuments section in the Musée Royal du Louvre, under the directorship of the decipherer of Egyptian writing. Although Champollion failed to acquire the splendid Drovetti Collection in Turin, he managed to obtain some 4,000 pieces amassed by Salt, the British Consul in Cairo. This exceptional purchase included the Great Sphinx from Tanis [65] and the enormous pink granite sarcophagus of Ramses III.

CHAMPOLLION WAS CHARGED NOT ONLY WITH ENRICHING THE MUSEUM but also its design and arrangement. From the outset, the Egyptologist sought to reconcile aesthetic pleasure and the didactic dimension. Despite sometimes clashing with the architect Fontaine (to whom we owe the imitation marble, the Egyptian-style grisailles, the ceiling decorations painted by the greatest painters of the time, and the cupboards decorated with gilt bronze), Champollion retained control of the museum's design: there was a room devoted to the gods, a secular room and two funerary rooms. The second Drovetti collection, bought in 1827, comprised over 500 pieces including the famous Djehuty cup [93] and the colossal effigies of Ramses II.

In the second half of the 19th century, European museums began to be enriched in a new way: objects unearthed during excavations in Egypt were now shared with the Egyptian government. Some 6,000 objects discovered by Mariette at the Serapeum at Memphis entered the Louvre in this way, including the famous *Seated Scribe* [86]. But it was above all the creation of the Institut Français d'Archéologie Orientale in Cairo (1880) which brought the richest 'harvests': the excavation of the pyramid of Djedefre at Abu Ruwaysh in 1901 [82], the excavation of the Coptic monastery at Bawit in 1901–1902 [120], the excavations at Assiut which yielded the funerary ensemble of Chancellor Nakhti [87] and the excavation of the workers' village at Deir el-Medineh [72].

Besides acquisitions, exceptional donations continue to enrich the museum's collections, such as the colossal statue of Amenophis IV, offered as a gesture of thanks for the French effort in saving the treasures in Nubia [101], and the Louise, Atherton and Ingeborg Curtis Bequest of some 1,500 pieces.

The land and its inhabitants

The annual cycle of the Nile

Like Herodotus, many Egyptologists have maintained that the Egypt of the pharaohs was a 'gift of the Nile'. Behind this conventional idea there lies a geographical and cultural reality, which the objects and paintings discovered in the tombs brilliantly illustrate. Whatever their social status, men and women lived their lives according to the rhythm of the annual flooding of a capricious river over 6,670 kilometres long, which they worshipped as the god Hapy, a paunchy, androgynous spirit with its arms full of plants symbolising fertility.

The prosperity of the entire kingdom closely depended on the lush green oasis bordering the banks of the Nile. Beyond this narrow strip fertilised by the silt deposited by the river stretched an arid desert into which the Egyptians ventured only to hunt, or to travel to the western oases and the quarries in the mountains to the east. Egypt's only other geographical division was a political one. Lower Egypt and Upper Egypt became separate political entities very early on. Menes, the first pharaoh, saw the economic advantage of unifying the two territories, from the first cataract to the sea. And history would prove him right. As soon as a sovereign's grip loosened, local particularisms spawned ephemeral princedoms which created divisions in the valley and attracted foreign invasions.

The High Dam at Aswan was built in the 1960s to regulate the water supply throughout Egypt. But it sounded the knell of a host of secular practices, such as the offerings of figurines which villagers threw into the river in July to joyfully welcome the arrival of the life-saving annual inundation.

59 *Paintings from the tomb of Ounsou*

c.1450 BC (18th dynasty)
Left bank at Thebes, now Luxor
Painting on silt. 94 x 68 cm
N 1431

Egypt's entire wealth depended on its unlimited labour force, comprised mainly of peasants. They worked hard on large farms for private landowners, in sanctuaries, or on land belonging to the Pharaoh. Rather like photographers, the painters of the tomb of Ounsou, the very official and powerful scribe of the grain stores of the god Amon, painstakingly recorded daily labour, the harvest, its transport, the loading of stocks of grain and its storage in the temple warehouse. Occasionally a scene introduces a touch of humour into these rural chronicles, such as this woman bringing a snack to the harvesters.

60 *Mastaba of Akhethotep*

c.2400 BC (5th dynasty)
Saqqâra
Bas-relief, painted limestone
E 10958 A

Scenes sculpted in shallow bas-relief and heightened with colour (alternating brown skinned men and light skinned women) immortalise the lifestyle and duties of the tomb's owner, a wealthy landowner of the Old Kingdom. We also see young servant women advancing in single file, each personifying one of Akhethotep's farms. In the Middle Kingdom, these offering bearers, destined to ensure the deceased's physical survival in afterlife, became veritable three-dimensional models of rural life, sculpted in the round in wood.

61 *Offering bearers*

c. 1950 BC (12th dynasty)
Excavations at Assiut and Antinoe
Painted wood. H. max. 63 cm; max. depth 33 cm
E 11990, E 11991, E 11992, E 20575, E12001

Writing and the scribes

A civilisation of the sign

Hieroglyphs were everywhere, carved on temple pylons or on obelisks, or carpeting the walls of tombs like papyri. Writing appeared in Egypt shortly before 3,000 BC, after the region's political unification. The administration, now powerful and organised, immediately saw it as a tool for transcribing and recording the Pharaoh's orders throughout the Nile Valley. The key figure in this system, the scribe, had a privileged status in Egyptian society, 95 per cent of whom were illiterate peasants. The scribe knew how to read, write and draw and these noble activities dispensed him from all unpleasant tasks. 'You are under nobody's orders, you have no one above you. Because out of all those who work, the scribe is chief', one reads in the *Satire of the Trades*. But there was of course a gulf of rank and wealth between the modest bureaucrat and the royal scribe, the intimate confidant of the sovereign. Writing was always considered a precious knowledge inherited from the gods. Many sculptures show the scribe with the head of Thoth, the baboon, patron god of the scribes. Although women were largely excluded from this profession, some had themselves depicted in the tomb with writing equipment under their chair. The mastery of the written word was one of the prerequisite conditions for communication with the gods and the beings in the beyond. By virtue of their power to create and recreate worldly possessions at will, hieroglyphs possessed virtually all the magical power that Egyptian civilisation conferred on the image, which could be benevolent or malevolent but never harmless or gratuitous.

62 *Scribe's palette*

*c.*1300 BC (18th dynasty)
Thebes region
Wood, reed, remains of blocks of colour
33.3 x 5.5 x 1.4 cm
Salt Collection. N 3023

Many palettes discovered in tombs are replicas and were therefore never used. Although this one is covered with the classic funerary formulae, it is extraordinarily like the real thing. Narrow and elongated, it has a cavity for brushes (usually reed stems with crushed ends) and four receptacles for blocks of colour, which were mixed with water. The most frequently used colours were black and red. Black was obtained from soot and used for writing most text. Red was made with ochre and natural iron oxide.

63 *Mastaba of Akhethotep: scribes*

c. 2400 BC (5th dynasty)
Saqqâra
Bas-relief, painted limestone
E 10958

The temple

64 *The goddess Sekhmet*

Probably from the Temple of Mut at Karnak, where it was transported from its place of origin on the east bank at Thebes
Reign of Amenophis III,
c. 1391–1353 BC (18th dynasty)
Statue, diorite
1.78 (without restored sun disk) x 0.55 x 0.95 m
A 8

These majestic statues of the lion-headed goddess Sekhmet, sculpted during the reign of the great builder pharaoh Amenophis III, were supposed to welcome and impress worshippers arriving at the temple and channel through their negative energy all the forces of evil at work in Egypt. Here and there in this row of different-sized sculptures one notices a more ornate wig or a more harmonious polish, the barely perceptible marks of an individual sculptor transcending the dictates of an official commission.

A closed world

Unlike the sanctuaries of classical Antiquity or churches, the Egyptian temple was not a public place of worship. On the contrary, it was a closed world reserved for the priesthood. Laymen could only enter restricted areas outside: the forecourt and the outer enclosures. With its high walls and small doors, it was a like a fortress built to rigorous specifications in stone, unlike the homes of the living and even royal palaces. It was a stable environment in which ritual could be carried out in the secure conditions indispensable for the manipulation of the divine.

Although its ground plan varied according to liturgies and local theologies, the Egyptian temple usually had a quay on the Nile, an avenue lined with sphinxes and a door in a massive mud-brick outer wall. Inside this door, a courtyard (which worshippers were allowed to enter) preceded a room with columns or hypostyle hall which gave on to the sanctuary proper. The sanctuary comprised a modest-sized room housing the altar, where offerings were placed, and the *naos*, a kind of stone tabernacle containing the statue of the deity. But the god's 'domain' extended much further. Priests' quarters, storerooms and workshops, and the House of Life, where scribes copied religious texts, were all essential components of the temple complex, which could be a genuine town within the town. The material life of the temple was ensured by its surrounding properties, fields, herds and even mines and quarries. During the 18th dynasty, the fortune of the Temple of Amon was greater than that of the pharaohs, who were only too aware of it.

65 *The Great Sphinx*

Tanis
Pink granite. 1.83 x 4.80m
Salt Collection. Acquired in 1826. A 23

66 *Naos*

Reign of Amasis, 570–526 BC (26th dynasty)
Pink granite. 2.55 x 1.61 x 1.50 m
Drovetti Donation. D. 29

The *naos*, a small edifice carved in stone with a wooden door, was the Egyptian 'Holy of Holies'. It housed the statue of the god, which each day was the object of meticulous attention. Every morning, priests opened the temple and prepared the deity's food. The highest-ranking priest opened the *naos* while offerings were placed on an altar. The statue was washed, clothed and perfumed. At midday, the god received libations, fumigations of incense and aspersions. The morning rituals were performed again in the evening, after which the statue was put back in the *naos*, which was locked and sealed until the following morning.

Death

67 *Funerary servant of Ramses IV*

*c.*1153–1147 BC (20th dynasty)
Statuette, painted wood. H. 32.5 cm
N 438

A perilous journey

Preparing one's passage into afterlife seems to have been the major preoccupation of the Egyptians, who built their tombs during their lifetime. Those at the bottom of the social ladder contented themselves with a simple ditch, or even matting placed on the ground. But the great majority spent their time, fortune and energy building stone houses for themselves for eternity. The form of the tomb evolved down the centuries. In the most ancient times it was a simple round hole, which became oval then rectangular. It usually had two distinct parts: one accessible to the living, where priests came to officiate and place offerings, the other sealed for ever, containing the funerary pit in which the coffin with its elaborate furniture (crockery, linen, toilet articles, jewellery, funerary statuettes, food, and so on) was placed.
However, the deceased could only survive in the underworld if his or her children or a member of the staff of a temple regularly brought the necessary provisions. As an extra precaution, the deceased was often depicted on the chapel wall in front of an offerings table piled high with food. If a passer-by, or the deceased himself, recited the ritual words, these images were magically transformed into real food.
But ensuring the perpetual conservation of the body by mummification and equipping the tomb and the deceased for afterlife was only one aspect of funerary ritual. The deceased also had to be defended against the many perils awaiting him in the underworld and which could cause him to die a second death. This ultimate protection was ensured by the 'funerary texts', a kind of armour of signs and a passport for resurrection and eternal life.

68 *Model of a boat*
c.1900 BC (12th dynasty)
Painted wood. L. 81 cm; H hull 38.5 cm
Assiut burial ground excavations,
tomb of Chancellor Nakhti. E 12027

It is no coincidence that graceful models of boats have been discovered in great numbers in tombs. Death was likened to the crossing of a river. In Egyptian, the word 'travel' was written with a hieroglyph in the form of a boat. Having this supreme form of transport in the eternal darkness of the tomb reflects the Egyptians' wish to continue their 'journey' in afterlife.

70 *Statuette of a hippopotamus*

c.2033–1710 BC (early Middle Empire)
Siliceous faience. 12 x 20 x 8 cm
Acquired in 1883. E 7709

69 *Burial scene*

From the 'Book of the Dead of Nebqued'
c.1400 BC (18th dynasty)
Painted papyrus. H. approx. 30 cm
N 3068

71 *Sarcophagi of Lady Tamutneferet*

Third Intermediate Period (21st dynasty)
Wood. H. max. 1.92 m
N 2631 - 2571 - 2620 - 2623 - 2598

72 *Sarcophagus of Madja*

c. 1490–1470 BC (18th dynasty)
Painted wood. 0.62 x 1.84 m
Deir el-Medineh excavations. E 14543

As was customary in the New Kingdom, the sarcophagus of Lady Madja is shaped like her body, thereby guaranteeing that she will remain unchanged for eternity. There are no funerary inscriptions on this type of coffin except the name of the deceased. The texts enabling the deceased to enter the kingdom of Osiris were now written on a papyrus known as the *Book of the Dead*. Bound in its wrappings, the mummy of Lady Madja can now set out on its long journey.

73 *Sarcophagus of Imeneminet* (back)

Third Intermediary Period
Agglomerated canvas, stuccoed and painted
1.87 x 0.48 m
Rousset Bey Collection. E 5534

The first sarcophagi, veritable protective boxes for the mummy, appeared in the late 12th dynasty, when they were considered a kind of 'substitute' for the body of the deceased. During the New Kingdom their use became widespread, with the deceased portrayed as the god Osiris. Their form and decoration varied, depending on the social status of their owner but also on the period and evolving religious concepts. During the Third Intermediate Period, sarcophagi were decorated with grand scenes depicting the deceased's rebirth and his integration into the Osirian and solar cycles. An 'armour' of hieroglyphs completed his eternal protection.

74 *Mummy of a man*

3rd or 2nd century BC
L. 1.67 m.
N 2627

Religion

75 *The god Horus*

Third Intermediate Period (*c.* 1069–664 BC)
Statue, bronze. H. 95 cm
E 7703

The name Horus originally designated several gods. At the outset it was a celestial divinity represented as a falcon 'with multicoloured feathers', whose eyes were the Sun and the Moon. Lord of Hierakonpolis, he very quickly became a dynastic god and was subsequently included in the Osirian cycle, in which he was identified with Osiris's son, 'Horus the Child', whom the Greeks assimilated to Harpocrates, a very popular god during the Late Period.
This magnificent bronze portrays the god as young and robust, his arms reaching out in a regal gesture of ritual purification. The statue has unfortunately lost it original coating, probably gold, and the wig was probably inlaid with multicoloured ceramic.

Gods and sacred animals

There were hundreds of gods in ancient Egypt. Each nome, district and city had its own god, each with its own attributes and appearance: man, woman, lion, hippopotamus, falcon, vulture, ram, bull, sycamore tree, lotus, arrows, and so forth. Despite their animal or vegetable origin, these divinities usually took on a human appearance. Artists subtly adapted the head of the lioness, cow or dog to a male or female human body. These hybrid beings belonged to a complex pantheon and were linked by dynastic or family bonds. The best known example is the Theban triad of Amon, the great father, Mut, the great mother, and the youthful god Khonsu. The legend of Osiris also played a fundamental role in the development of religious thought. Isis's quest to find the scattered pieces of her brother's bodies and husband's and the resurrection she brings about with her magical powers are a metaphor for the cycle of life, death and rebirth, symbolised by the annual life-giving Nile flood.
Far from being a mere by-product of religious belief, magic appears to have been a special means of communication between men and gods. The Egyptians believed names had great power. To know the name of a god or enemy was to have a form of power over him. During the New Kingdom innumerable books of magic formulae and spells were produced and talismans on folded paper were worn around the neck.

76 *'Healing' statue of Padimahes*

4th century BC
Grauwacke. H. 67.7 cm
Tyszkiewicz Collection. E 10777

Scribes collected texts recounting the misfortunes of the gods, victims of scorpion and snake bites, or stricken by terrible headaches, which only the intervention of a supreme deity could relieve. It was believed that these accounts could save humans suffering from the same afflictions. Another popular 'recipe' was the use of healing statues. All one had to do to heal was drink water which had flowed over a stele covered with magic formulae, a ritual usually carried out on temple forecourts.

77 *Seated cat*

*c.*700–600 BC
Statuette, bronze; eyes surrounded with blue glass
33 x 25 cm
N 4538

78 *The god Apis*

Nectanebo II?
Limestone. 1.26 x 1.76 m
Serapeum. Mariette excavations
N 390

Prehistory and the first two dynasties (Thinite Period, *c.*3100–2700 BC)

79 *The Gebel el-Arak dagger*

Predynastic Period, *c.*3500 BC
Flint blade, ivory handle
H. 25 cm; H. handle 9.8 cm
Probably from Gebel el-Arak, south of Abydos
E 11517

The flint blade with its undulating surface contrasts curiously with the ivory handle carved on both sides with historiated scenes of great formal power. It depicts a battle between two distinct groups of warriors, one with shaven heads, the other with long braided hair. One side, divided into four registers, shows a sea battle at the bottom and hand-to-hand combat on land at the top. Even more enigmatic, though, is the bearded figure on the other side, flanked by two wild cats, a motif also found in Mesopotamian art. Whatever this fascinating knife was used for, it is a brilliant demonstration of the consummate art of the first Egyptian sculptors.

The birth of Egyptian art

The silhouette of the Sphinx rising out of the desert, the three great pyramids crowning the Giza plateau, the breathtaking mask of Tutankhamen… no matter how spectacular these testaments to the splendour of Ancient Egypt are, they are only a minute portion of the art produced on the banks of the Nile. Before these perfect forms were achieved, there was a long artistic prehistory, which archaeologists are constantly redefining with each new discovery. After the Neolithic Period (10,000–4,000 BC) and the transition to sedentary life, with its natural consequence, the beginnings of craftwork, the Naqadah civilisation saw the emergence of new artistic forms and techniques whose sophistication continues to surprise us. Ivory and bone combs and spoons were decorated with incised motifs and elegant basalt, porphyry, serpentine and diorite vases were carved in the form of frogs, lizards, birds and hippopotamuses. One of this civilisation's most beautiful stylistic achievements are the makeup palettes found in tombs, whose purified forms were carved with extremely stylised bas-reliefs [80]. The *Gebel el-Arak dagger* [79], whose ivory handle is masterfully carved with war and hunting scenes, is one of the masterpieces of the period.

But it was around 3000 BC that Egyptian history began in earnest with the establishment of a monarchy, the beginnings of hieroglyphic writing and the appearance of a monumental architecture dedicated to asserting temporal and religious power. All these achievements would survive on the banks of the Nile for millennia to come. The art of the bas-relief attained summits of mastery, as illustrated by the *Stele of the Snake-King* [81], a masterpiece of balance and sobriety.

80 *Palette framed with quadripeds, hyenas or wolves*

*c.*3200 BC (late Naqadah II period)
Grauwacke. 32 x 17.7 cm
E 11052

81 *Stele of the Snake-King*

*c.*3000 BC (1st dynasty)
Limestone. 1.43 x 0.55 m
Abydos excavations, tomb of the Snake-King
Amélineau Collection. E 11007

This extraordinary stele, found broken into three pieces in the royal necropolis at Abydos, is perhaps 'the most beautiful piece of writing in Egyptian art' (J.-L. de Cénival). Carved in shallow bas-relief, a powerful falcon is regally perching above a snake within the confines of a palace. But there is nothing decorative about this image. It is intended to be read rather than looked at. The falcon is the personification of the god Horus, of whom the king is the embodiment on earth. The snake is the hieroglyph for the sound 'dj', the sign used to write the word 'cobra'. Read together, they make a royal name: the Snake-King.

The Old Kingdom (*c*.2700–2200 BC)

82 *Head of King Djedefre*

c.2560 BC (4th dynasty)
Red sandstone. 26 x 33.5 x 28 cm
Abu Ruwaysh excavations. E 12626

This admirable portrait of Cheops' successor was unearthed on a temple site next to the pyramid at Abu Ruwaysh. The form of the break at the neck suggests it may have been the head of a sphinx. The pharaoh Djedefre, wearing the royal insignia of the cobra and *nemes* headress, is portrayed as a demigod.

In the shadows of the pyramids

The apparatus of the state, already developed during the first centuries of the 3rd millennium, developed into absolute monarchy during the Old Kingdom. This temporal power soon began to use all forms of artistic expression – architecture, painting, sculpture – to represent its unitary and unifying point of view. The model proposed by the pharaonic monarchy was the sole and only valid one. Stone, difficult to carve but almost indestructible, became the ideal material in which to transcribe a vision of the world in which everything had to be represented in its perfection and immutability. The work of art, not at all realist even though often based on direct observation of nature, had a life of its own since it perpetuated the object or figure represented in the reproduction. Most sculptures which have survived were not intended for public view, and in their static and repetitive nature challenge the notions of immediacy and spontaneity. Whether prototypes, copies or models, they were meant to endure for Eternity.
During this sovereign period, architecture emerged as the queen of artistic disciplines. The use of stone, until then used merely to line the walls of a few royal tombs, became widespread and soon produced true masterpieces. During the 3rd dynasty, King Djoser's brilliant architect Imhotep built his first step pyramid on the Saqqâra plateau. During the 4th dynasty, his successors developed this type of monument to its supreme perfection, first with the pyramid of Cheops, whose perfect proportions the Greeks so admired they rated it one of the Seven Wonders of the World, then those of Chephren and Mycerinos. Erected on the Giza plateau not far from Cairo, these three pyramids have come to symbolise the refinement and science attained by pharaonic civilisation.

83 *Raherka and Merseankh*

c.2350 BC (4th or 5th dynasty)
Painted limestone. 52,8 x 21,3 cm
Gift of L., I. and A. Curtis. E 15592

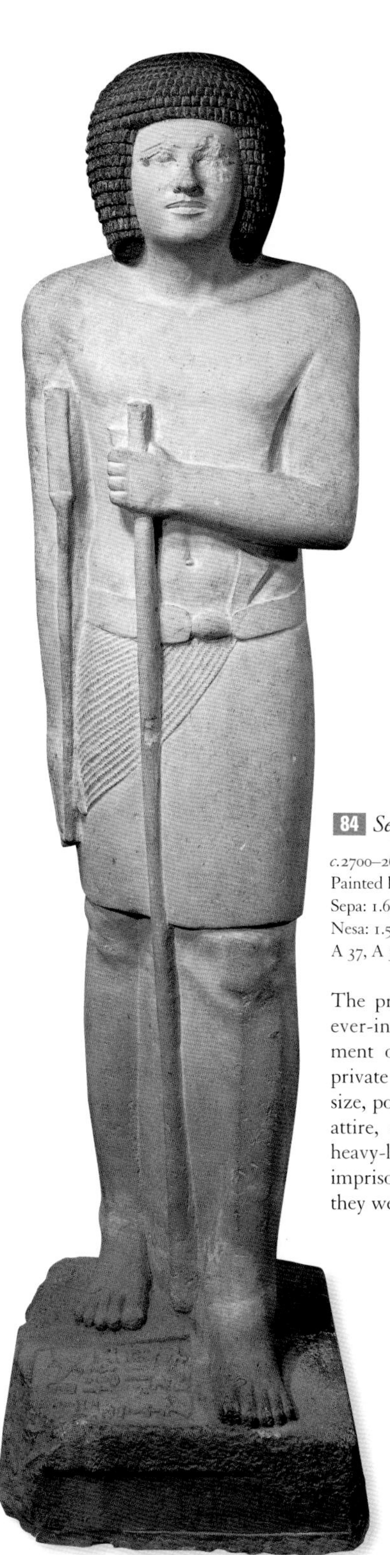

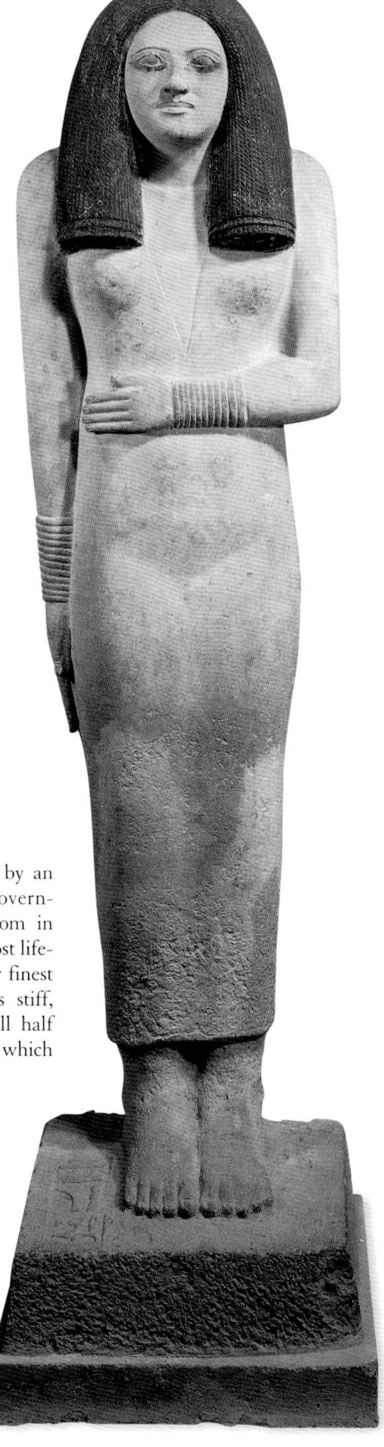

84 *Sepa and Nesa*

*c.*2700–2620 BC (3rd dynasty)
Painted limestone.
Sepa: 1.65 x 0.40 x 0.55 m
Nesa: 1.54 x 0.41 x 0.39 m
A 37, A 38

The practice of funerary rites by an ever-increasing number of government officials prompted a boom in private statue production. Almost life-size, posing for eternity in their finest attire, makeup and wigs, this stiff, heavy-limbed couple seems still half imprisoned in the stone from which they were carved.

85 *Stele of Nefertiabet*

*c.*2590 BC (4th dynasty)
Painted limestone. 37.5 x 52.5 cm
From Giza. Gift of L., I. and A. Curtis. E 15591

The polychromy of this stele discovered in a tomb at Giza, not far from the pyramid of Cheops, is still extraordinarily fresh. A young woman wearing a panther skin and jewellery, sitting on a stool with bull's legs, is reaching towards a table laden with provisions: loaves cut in two, an ox's foot, a trussed goose, and so on. Above her, a hieroglyphic list of the offerings she will receive in the next world, including incense, green and black makeup, wine and cakes. The beautiful Nefertiabet, daughter or sister of King Cheops, can begin her long journey with her mind at ease.

86 *The Seated Scribe*

*c.*2600–2350 BC (4th or 5th dynasty)
Statue, painted limestone, eyes in rock crystal set in copper
53.7 x 44 x 35 cm
Saqqâra excavations. E 3023

Sitting cross-legged and leaning slightly forward, a papyrus unrolled across his white loincloth, his missing brush poised ready to write, this scribe could be about to note down the orders of some high-ranking official. The face is just as realistically depicted as the body: a rather aquiline nose, thin lips and above all the eyes, inlaid with quartz set in metal. His slight stoutness reflects his comfortable social status, within a complex and centralised administration. The freshness of the colours (ranging from ebony black to his red ochre flesh tint) enhances the charm and vivacity of this fascinating portrait.

The Middle Kingdom (2033–1710 BC)

Realism and idealisation: the advent of a new language

After two centuries of turmoil, Egypt was reunified by the pharaoh Mentuhotep III, a native of Thebes. Little remains of the temples and altars built during this period. The state then used low-cost materials or simply lighter materials such as limestone and unbaked bricks, and many New Kingdom pharaohs systematically demolished their successors' edifices to build their own monuments on their ruins. Yet the Middle Kingdom was a period of exceptional artistic activity, particularly in sculpture. One of the most famous inventions of the period was the 'cube statue', a cubic form individualised by a head, arms and legs.
The absence of instructions from a central power combined with the relative freedom enjoyed by provincial artisans favoured the emergence of a less exclusive and more direct artistic language. Even if most works of art were still forms of official propaganda, they began to be perceived by the spectator as 'messages'. Royal power was beginning to gradually relinquish its super-human status, as illustrated by the magnificent portraits of Sesostris III. The pharaoh is first depicted as a graceful, full-cheeked youth, then with the etched features of maturity. Some interpret these portraits as the king's participation in the cycle of the sun and his victory over time.
In parallel, the new strongmen of the regime, the nomarchs (governors of a nome) had themselves buried in great pomp in their native region. Their wooden effigies, sculpted at Assiut in Middle Egypt, brilliantly illustrate their social status. The statue of Chancellor Nakhti is a fine example.

87 *Statue of Chancellor Naḳhti*

c.2033–1710 BC (early Middle Kingdom)
Acacia. 1.79 x 1.07 m
Assiut burial ground excavations. E 11937

88 *Offering bearer*

*c.*1950 BC (early 12th dynasty)
Painted ficus. H. 1.08 m; depth base 0.32 m
Acquired in 1879. E 10781

This elegant young woman, a three-dimensional version of the figures hitherto depicted on the walls of tomb chapels, is carrying an ox's leg on a dish on her head. The symbolism here is of course funerary. The presence of statues like this in the tomb ensured the perpetual nourishment of the deceased. This graceful and elongated figure is one of the masterpieces of this fertile period of Egyptian art.

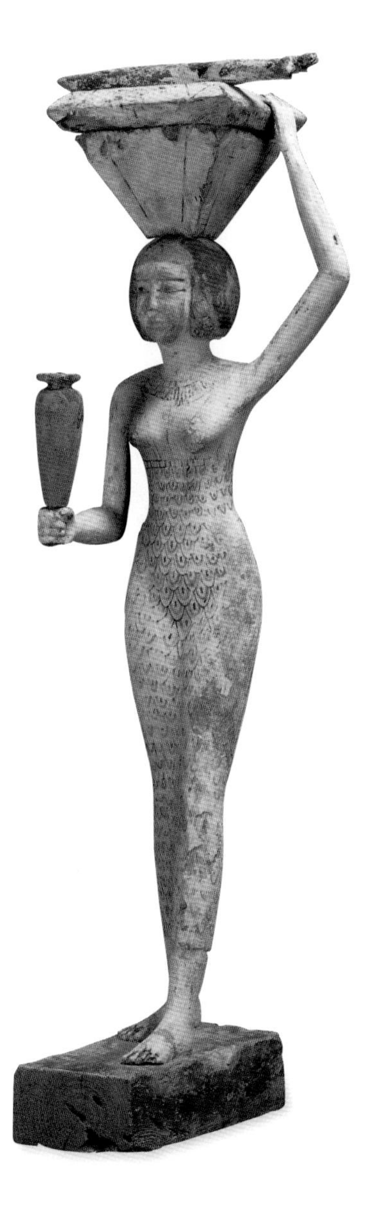

89 *Amenemhat III*

1843–1798 BC (12th dynasty)
Grauwacke. 21.4 x 10 cm
N 464

At the end of the 12th dynasty, a certain brutality seems to have gained the upper hand, at least if the austere effigies of Pharaoh Amenemhat III are anything to go by. Like Sesostris III, he reigned for a long time and led numerous campaigns in Nubia. He also developed the Fayyum and reorganised the kingdom's administration. According to the conventions of the time, his youthful body contrasts with his realistically depicted head and exaggeratedly large ears.

The New Kingdom (*c.*1550–1069 BC)

90 *Head of a king (Amenophis II?)*

*c.*1427–1401 BC (18th dynasty)
Quartzite. H. 21 cm
E 10896

The triumph of elegance

The New Kingdom marked the beginning of one of the most fertile and most brilliant periods of Egyptian civilisation. The pharaohs restored the unity of the kingdom by expelling invaders (the Hyksos from the Middle East) and embarked on a series of campaigns which won them new possessions in Asia, Nubia and to a lesser extent, Syria. These considerable enrichments and the new contacts with foreign peoples they brought favoured the emergence of a luxurious and refined art which at times even bordered on the flashy.

In this glorious and prosperous context, architecture again became majestic and colossal. Sanctuaries for the gods were built on the east bank of the Nile at Thebes, while the west bank was reserved for the houses of the dead. To the east, the sanctuary at Luxor built by Amenophis III brilliantly symbolised the supremacy of the god Amon. A few kilometres further north stretched the vast area of the 'world' of Karnak, with its host of pylons, chapels and temples, a veritable city within the city, with processional ways, courtyards with kiosks, altars, repositories of the arts of sacred boats and obelisks. In parallel, the arts of relief, statuary and painting attained unequalled refinement. Slender anatomy, the idealisation of features and sobriety of colour were the hallmarks of a supreme sense of taste, as illustrated by the portraits of the young Amenophis III and the magnificent bas-reliefs in the tombs of Ramose, governor of Thebes. But this perfect balance and harmony rapidly disintegrated during the reign of the heretic pharaoh Akhenaton. The veritable ideological and aesthetic revolution which took place during the Armana period (Akhenaton built a new capital at Armana) engendered a violent and expressive language bordering on caricature. It was not until the Ramessid period that a more 'sensible' and elegant style would be re-established, although sometimes with a certain cold aloofness.

91 *Amenophis III*

*c.*1391–1353 BC (18th dynasty)
Diorite. H. 32.5 cm
A 25

This portrayal of Amenophis III, with his full, sensual lips, almond eyes, small but full chin, smooth cheeks and rebellious nose, is typical of the elegant idealisation with discreet notes of realism which characterised the royal portraits of the early 18th dynasty. The pharaoh's crown still bears traces of stippling, which suggests it may originally have been painted blue.

92 *Senynefer and Hatshepsut*

c. 1400 BC (18th dynasty)
Painted sandstone. 62 x 8.2 cm
E 27161

This slightly smaller than life-size couple would have originally been placed in a tomb chapel to receive funerary offerings. Everything here is delicateness and refinement: the beauty of the two faces gazing serenely towards eternity, the treatment of the wigs and jewellery heightened with colour, the delicate modelling of their bodies sheathed in their severe white tunics. It is a dazzling example of the mastery attained in private statuary at the dawn of the New Kingdom.

93 *Cup bearing the name of General Djehuty*

Reign of Thutmosis III, *c.* 1479–1425 (18th dynasty)
Gold. Ø. 17.9 cm; H. 2.2 cm
N 713

94 *Chair*

c.1500–1200 BC (18th–19th dynasty)
Wood inlaid with ivory (or bone), modern leather upholstery
91 x 47.5 x 59 cm
N 2950

The decorative arts attained heights of elegance and virtuosity during the New Kingdom. Although we do not know the exact provenance of this chair in inlaid exotic woods, it has stylistic similarities with the furniture in the tomb of Tutankhamen (the same lion-paw legs and technique used for the chair back), even if it is far more luxurious in design. The style of these chairs has had a considerable influence on modern European furniture.

95 *Spoon with a swimmer*

c.1400–1350 BC (18th dynasty)
Wood and ivory (or bone). 29 x 5 cm
E 218

Much has been written about the extremely fragile and refined cosmetic spoons produced during the reign of Amenophis III. Far from being simple toiletry or beauty articles, these 'object-sculptures', in the form of a nude young woman holding a water fowl were in fact ritual offering spoons. Their iconography is puzzling, though: could this nubile swimmer in fact be the wife of Geb, god of the earth, that is, Nut, goddess of the sky?

96 *Touy*

c.1400–1350 BC (18th dynasty)
Statuette, African grenadilla wood
33 x 7 x 17 cm
E 10655

Lady Touy, with voluptuous curves exalted by her diaphanous clinging garment, is one of the most ambitious creations of the New Kingdom. There has been much speculation as to the identity of this elegant woman with a heavy plaited wig. The *menat* necklace she is holding in her left hand suggests she may have belonged to the priesthood of Akhmim, the birthplace of Amenophis III's parents-in-law, to whom she might have been related. It has even been suggested she may be Tuyu, the pharoah's mother-in-law.

97 *Flask*

c. 1400–1300 BC (18th dynasty)
Glass. 10 x 7 cm
AF 2032

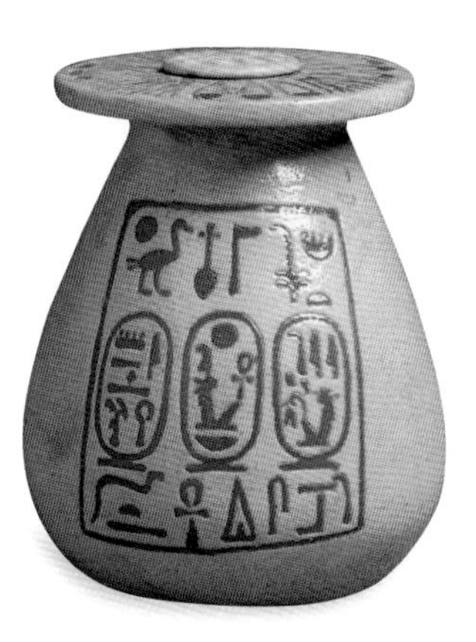

98 *Jar*

c. 1400–1300 BC (18th dynasty)
Siliceous ceramic. 8.4 x 6.6 cm
E 4877

99 *Head of a princess*

Reign of Amenophis IV-Akhenaton,
*c.*1353–1337 BC (18th dynasty)
Painted limestone. 15.4 x 10 cm
E 14715

This beautiful young face is typical of a gentler phase in Amarnian art. The extremely sophisticated hairstyle falling on one side of the head is a sign of the princely rank of this young woman, who was probably one of Akhenaton's daughters.

100 *Body of Nefertiti?*

Reign of Amenophis IV-Akhenaton,
*c.*1353–1337 BC (18th dynasty)
Statuette, red quartzite. H. 29 cm
E 25409

Egyptian art rarely permitted itself such sensuality and fullness of form. The voluptuously beautiful body beneath the clinging, diaphanous dress was for a long time thought to be that of Amenophis IV's beautiful wife, Nefertiti. The striking contrast between the soberly modelled breasts and the over-developed thighs is typical of the expressionist style of the heretic pharaoh's reign.

101 *Statue of Amenophis IV*

East Karnak
Sandstone. H. 1.37 m
E 27112

During his 14-year reign, Amenophis IV upturned thousands of years of religious and political immobilism. He not only moved his capital from Thebes to an unoccupied site at Armana but changed his name to Akhenaton, 'he who is beneficial to Aton'. This dissidence was accompanied by an unprecedented aesthetic revolution. This extraordinary, almost caricatured statue is an example. The pharaoh is shown with a prognathous jaw, distended stomach, skeletal chest and effeminate hips – distinctive features that the monarch established as the official 'canon'.

102 *Imenmes and Depet, parents of General Imeneminet*

New Kingdom, 18th dynasty
Bas-relief, limestone. 56 x 66 cm
B6

103 *Amon and Tutankhamen*

Reign of Tutankhamen, *c.* 1336–1327 BC
(18th dynasty)
Diorite. 2.14 x 0.44 x 0.785 m
E 11609

The task of re-establishing the order disrupted by Akhenaton and his short-lived Armarnian revolution fell to a young boy. His name, Tutankhamen, became world-famous overnight when his tomb was accidentally discovered by Howard Carter in 1922. In this imposing diorite statue, the pharaoh is depicted under the protection of his tutelary god, Amon, who, much taller than him, seems to be protecting him with his powerful arms. The proportions of the heavy, thickset bodies and features are typical of the post-Armarnian aesthetic. General Horemheb, Tutankhamen's successor, removed all effigies of the young pharaoh after his premature death.

104 *Piay, Gatekeeper of the Royal Palace*

c. 1300 BC (late 18th or early 19th dynasty)
Shea wood and acacia base
H. 54.4 cm; base 10.9 x 31 cm
E 124

During the post-Amarnian period, private statues acquired an aura of grace and refinement. The sculptor of this delicately carved effigy had not forgotten the stylistic innovations of Akhenaton's reign, though. A plump chest and stomach are perceivable beneath the folds of his garment, and the face, framed by his heavy wig is surprisingly gentle, almost effeminate. The offering formula engraved on the dorsal pillar is Memphite in origin.

105 *Mourning women*

Reign of Tutankhamen. *c.* 1330 BC (18th dynasty)
Bas-relief, limestone. 75 x 30 cm
From a tomb at Saqqâra
B 57

This magnificent relief, from an as yet unidentified Memphite tomb, depicts a scene of lamentation with rare dramatic power. No expression of pain seems to have been omitted: the arms of the mourning women waving in all directions, some even pulling out their hair, the men, their heads shaven, beating their foreheads as a sign of powerlessness. The sophisticated staggering of foreground and background is characteristic of the Armarnian style.

107 *Pendant in the form of a ram-headed bird of prey*

c. 1254 BC (19th dynasty)
Gold, turquoise, carnelian, lapis lazuli
Wingspan 13 cm; length 7 cm
From the Serapeum at Saqqâra. E 80

106 *A king (probably Seti I) presenting the goddess Maat*

c. 1294–1279 BC (19th dynasty)
Statuette, gold plated silver. H. 19,5 cm
Ganay Donation. E 27431

Seti I can be considered the true founder of the 19th dynasty. His son Ramses II, who reigned for almost 67 years, continued his work by driving back the Hittites at the battle of Kadesh, which was depicted on all the principal temples in Egypt. A warlike ideology seems to have tinged artistic production, which attained unprecedented technical perfection. This statuette, moulded in silver, a rarely used material in Egypt, and partially gilded, shows the king (probably Seti I) ritually offering Maat, goddess of truth and justice and present at the judgement of the dead. The pharaoh's exaggeratedly raised arms indicate that he originally stood on a processional boat.

108 *The goddess Hathor and Seti I*

c. 1294–1279 BC (19th dynasty)
Bas-relief, painted limestone. 2.26 x 1.05 m
From the tomb of Seti I in the Valley of the Kings,
Brought from Egypt by Champollion. B 7

The goddess Hathor, crowned with horns, the solar disk and the cobra, is welcoming Seti I into the beyond. Here, however she is not the goddess of love, joy and dance, but the Lady of the West (and therefore of the dead), goddess of the Theban necropolis. The pharaoh, an erect cobra on his forehead, is taking the *menat* necklace which the goddess is handing him for protection. Although this relief has been much restored, its technical perfection is dazzling. Sculptors and painters combined their talents to capture the figures' fine silhouettes, sumptuous clothes and delicate wigs.

The Third Intermediate Period, the Saite Period, and the last native dynasties (*c.*1069–332 BC)

109 *Stele of Taperet*

*c.*900–700 BC
Painted wood. 31 x 29 cm
Batissier Donation. E 52

In these difficult and troubled times, the great tradition of mural painting died out, replaced by smaller and more modest formats and materials (wooden steles, mummies' sheaths). The *Stele of Taperet*, like a little picture, was part of this trend. On both sides, the deceased is shown adoring the sun. On side A, the sun, in its morning Re-Horakhty form, bathing Taperet with its lily-shaped rays; on side B, the setting sun, personified by the god Aton. Arched around the top of the stele, the star-studded body of the goddess Nut, who swallows the sun in the evening and returns it to the world in the morning. This form of visual theology, previously confined to royal tombs, would now become widespread in private funerary art.

Successive invasions

During the Late Period, an era of internal strife and numerous changes of dynasty, Egypt fell prey to a series of invasions, notably by the Assyrians and the Persians, before the arrival of the Greeks then the Romans. During the Third Intermediary Period, a distinct geographic division of power established itself between the North, where the pharaoh had his capital, and the South, under the supreme authority the High Priest of Amon and later the 'divine consort' or 'adorer' of the god. The unity of the country was only briefly re-established during the 25th dynasty, of Nubian origin.
Despite this political instability and impoverishment, art did not experience the decadence one might have expected. However, a certain nostalgia for archaism became dominant. New techniques such as the use of damascened bronze, electrum and silver were experimented with, as illustrated by the extraordinarily graceful statue of *Karomama, Divine Consort of Amon* [110], a masterpiece of these troubled times.
Taking advantage of quarrels over succession, the princes from the town of Sais, in the Delta, seized power and opened a brilliant period of the 26th dynasty. Their sculptors, strongly influenced by archaism, produced some true masterpieces. But in 525 BC, Egypt fell under Persian domination before bowing to the authority of the Greek Ptolemaic sovereigns, of whom Cleopatra was the seventh and last.

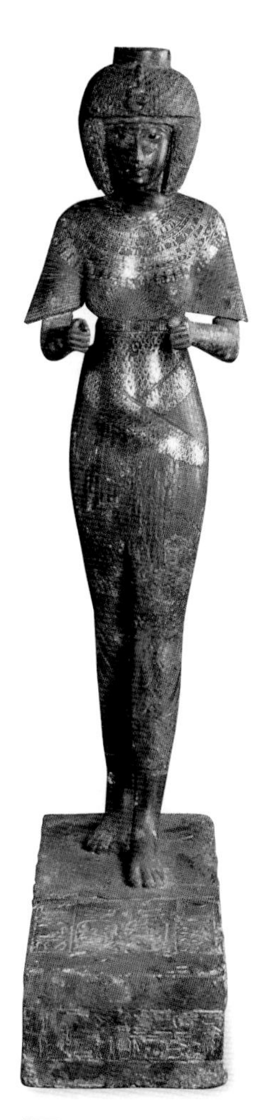

110 *Karomama, 'divine consort of Amon'*

*c.*850 BC (22nd dynasty)
Statuette, bronze inlaid with gold, silver and electrum
59.5 x 12.5 x 35 cm
Acquired in Egypt by Champollion. N 500

This hieratically elegant and majestic priestess seems to be slowly advancing towards the viewer with tranquil assurance. Her layered hairstyle frames her rather narrow smiling face, and her pleated dress hugs her slender and harmonious body. Champollion acquired this exceptional bronze during his visit to Egypt in 1829. The extraordinary virtuosity of the cast inlaid with precious metals makes this statue a masterpiece of Egyptian art of any era. Karomama probably originally held sistra in each hand.

111 *The Triad of Osorkon*

Reign of Osorkon II, *c.*874–850 BC (22nd dynasty)
Gold, lapis lazuli, glass. 9 x 6 cm
E 6204

The same consummate mastery is to be found in the jewellery of the period. *The Triad of Osorkon*, which was probably originally a pectoral, is a masterful combination of gold and lapis lazuli. The god Osiris, squatting on a pedestal, is flanked and protected by his sister and wife Isis and his son Horus. But this priceless piece of jewellery had an even greater talismanic value: according to the text engraved on the pedestal, it guaranteed king Osorkon, who reigned from 889 to 886 BC, triumph, victory and a reign as long as the god Re's. Despite their minute size, these figures of divinities exude great power.

112 *Bust of an old man*

Saite period. *c.*525 BC (26th dynasty)
Peridotite. 25.2 x 18.5 cm
N 2454

The Saite period, a veritable 'Renaissance' in Egyptian civilisation, attempted to recapture the grandeur of former eras. Vast building programmes were undertaken in all the temples in the land, and statuary benefited from a new dynamism. This strikingly sober portrait was clearly inspired by the purified and Archaic forms of the Old Kingdom. The high cheekbones, faint smile, and above all the smooth hard stone give the subject a grandeur and majesty that is a far cry from the excesses of Amarna and the refined elegance of the Ramessid era.

113 *Body of Isis or a queen*

Greek period, 3rd to 2nd century BC
Statuette, diorite. H. 63 cm
Hoffmann Donation. E 11197

Many Greeks who settled in Egypt were gradually took to Egyptian religion, funerary customs and gods. In his depiction of the goddess Isis, the talented sculptor of this statuette subtly combined two artistic languages. He has associated the stiff, hieratic frontality of the pharaonic tradition with a sensual female body revealed by folds in the Greek style. The temples built by the Ptolemaic sovereigns on the banks of the Nile more or less successfully combined both artistic styles, while the portraits of Cleopatra are both 'Egyptian' and 'Greek'.

114 *Head of a man with a shaven head*

Last Egyptian dynasties, 4th century BC
Grauwacke. H. 12.9 cm
Lami Donation. E 25577

Roman Egypt
(30 BC–4th century AD)

The long Ptolemaic dynasty came to an end in 30 BC when the great Cleopatra, the seventh queen of the same name, committed suicide and Egypt became a province of the Roman Empire. The gods and rituals of the newly subjugated land of the pharaohs would fascinate its new masters. For many a century, the emperors Nero, Vespasian, Trajan and Septimus Severus had themselves immortalised on the walls of their temples in the frozen and hieratic poses of the Egyptian monarchs.

But if there is one aspect of pharaonic civilisation which immediately appealed to the Greeks then the Romans it was its funerary practices. In the 5th century BC, the historian Herodotus was the first to describe the complex process of mummification that transformed a simple mortal into Osiris for eternity. Formerly a practice reserved solely for the elite, it became accessible to other classes during the Roman period and this led to a certain decline in ancestral techniques. Yet the magnificent coffin of Chenptah demonstrates that in the late 1st century AD all the elements indispensable for survival in afterlife – the ambalming ritual ensuring the deceased's divinisation, the use of gold to prevent corruption and identify him with the gods, the preservation of his name transcribed into hieroglyphs, and the use of linen canvas – were still present.

But apart from the stucco mortuary masks, whose gaze was sometimes enlivened with a thin film of transparent glass, the principal innovation in funerary practice was the 'mummy portraits'. Incorrectly called 'Fayyum portraits' (they have been found well beyond that region, as far away as Upper Egypt), these fascinating 'icons' are dazzling testimonies to the meeting of Greco-Roman pictorial genius and pharaonic Egpyt.

115 *Mortuary mask of a woman*

Early 3rd century AD
Painted plaster. 34 x 62 x 26 cm
Antinoe excavations. E 21360

116 *Funerary portrait of a man*

2nd century AD
Encaustic on wood. 38 x 24 cm
AF 6883

117 *Portrait of a woman*

AD 120–130
Cedarwood wood painted with encaustic and gilt
42 x 24 cm
MND 2047 (P 217)

Painted in encaustic (wax emulsion) or tempera (using a binder soluble in water) on a wooden board (lime, pine, cedar, oak) or on the canvas of the shroud, these funerary portraits from Roman Egypt captivate us by their presence and painterly virtuosity. A far cry from the impersonal gilded masks of the pharaohs, these pictures give us glimpses of an entire society in afterlife: an ambiguously graceful young ephebe haloed by a crown of gold leaves, an elegant, sensual woman bubbling with life, a mature man whose hieratic face heralds the art of the icons.

118 *Funerary hanging*

Late 1st century AD
Encaustic and tempera on linen canvas
1.75 x 1.25 m
Saqqâra. N 3076

This funerary hanging is a fine example of the hybrid art of the period. It combines the model of the Egyptian funerary stele, with the deceased standing between the gods Osiris and Anubis, and Greek stylistic innovations such as highly individualised facial features. But this symbiosis is not solely aesthetic. The deceased is represented barefoot on a pedestal because, according to Greek belief, he is a hero, that is, half-human and half-divine. He is holding the crown of the 'justified before Osiris', folded into a knot, the symbol of eternal life. Anubis, god of death and regeneration, will enable him to at last attain eternal life. He is now Osiris Hydreios, the Hellenised form of Osiris.

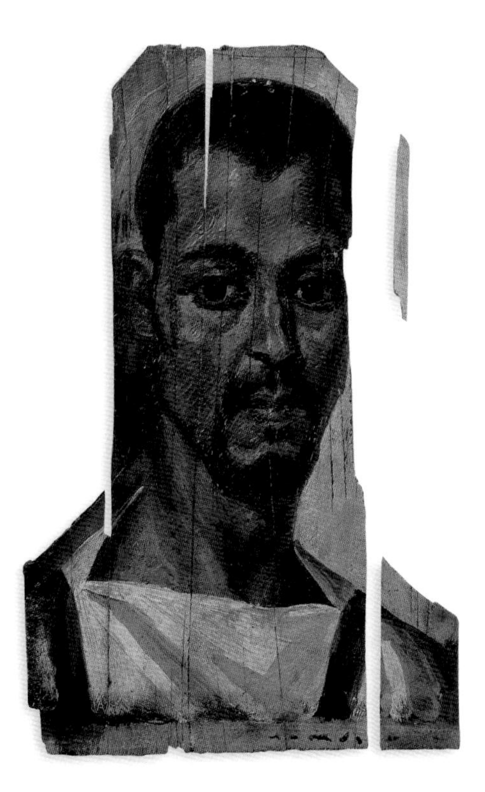

Coptic Egypt

119 *Censer with eagle*

9th century
Openwork bronze. 28 x 20 cm
Acquired in 1925. E 11708

A meeting of two worlds

The Louvre's exceptional Coptic section complements the collections of the Coptic Museum in Cairo. The reason for this is simple. The excavations carried out at the end of the 19th century by Albert-Jean Gayet on the site at Antinoe, followed by those undertaken at the turn of the 20th century by Jean Clédat and Jean Maspero in the monastery at Bawit, graced the museum with major pieces not only in the domains of architecture, sculpture and painting, but also in weaving and glassware. For a long time relegated to the status of simple, even mediocre, craftwork, since 1997 they have been displayed in a redesigned exhibition space that does full justice to their aesthetic ambitions and delightful artistic language. They brilliantly illustrate the singular culture of these Egyptian Christians whose language lives on in modern liturgy.

Unlike pharaonic or Byzantine art, Coptic art was never an art of major commissions. Its vein was more local, even popular. Showing dazzling technical mastery, artists and artisans drew their inspiration from the Greco-Roman repertoire, which they very soon adapted to the context of the Nile region but also and above all to the new Christian religion. The 4th century seems to have been a crossroads between the first tentative forms of a paleo-Christian art, and satyrs, bacchantes, Aphrodites and cupids. The Copts neglected the mosaic and in-the-round sculpture, but channelled their talents into reliefs, which were usually heightened with colours. But their verve, and sometimes even humour, was primarily expressed in their shimmering textiles, discovered by the thousand in their tombs, such as the sumptuous *Tapestry with Fish from Antinoe* (shared by the Louvre and the Musée des Tissus in Lyons), or the department's masterpiece, *Sabine's Shawl* [123], in fact a fragment of a shroud decorated with pastoral and mythological scenes. Could one imagine a more beautiful garment in which to embrace eternity?

120 *Church at Bawit*

6th–7th century
Facade of the South Church

When the archaeologist Jean Clédat unearthed the South Church of the monastery at Bawit in Middle Egypt in 1900, the monument had been buried in the sands for around eight centuries. Later excavations revealed mural paintings and magnificent capitals. The fruit of these discoveries was shared between the Louvre and the Coptic Museum in Cairo. France was lucky to keep the 6th-century paleo-Christian Church, whose sculpted decor was still intact. Visitors can now admire its intricate lacework in stone and wood thanks to a presentation recreating the monument's original volumes.

121 *Virgin Annunciate*

Late 5th century
Bas-relief, fig wood. 28 x 14 x 2 cm
Acquired in 1945. E 17118

The Virgin Mary, her huge eyes wide open in surprise, spindle suspended in mid-air, has suddenly stopped her work. The Archangel Gabriel (of whom there remains only a leg, at the side) has just announced the coming of the Infant Jesus. Taken from the Apocrypha, this scene showing Mary weaving a veil for the Temple of Jerusalem at the moment of the Annunciation would play a major role in Christian iconography. As Christ's mother, she is the primary intercessor between the faithful and her son. Her image would decorate the niches of oratories and, as was probably the case here, an item of furniture such as a chest, choir screen or door.

122 *Christ and Abbot Mena*

8th century
Tempera. 57 x 57 cm
IFAO excavations, monastery at Bawit, 1901–1902
E 11565

Found during the excavation of the monastery at Bawit (although it is not certain that it comes from the South Church), this beautiful painting on wood is the only Coptic icon in the Louvre. Christ is easily recognisable by his name inscribed on the side ('the Saviour' in Copt) and his halo stamped with the cross. Dressed in a long brown tunic, the Son of God is holding the New Testament and has his other hand on the shoulder of Abbot Mena, the monastery's superior. Only the difference in the size of the faces indicates the hierarchy between the two figures. With their hieratic appearance and large eyes with dark rings under them, these two figures recall the hypnotic magic of Roman Egyptian funerary portraits.

123 *Sabine's Shawl*

4th–5th century
Woollen tapestry. 1.10 x 1.40 m
Antinoe, A. Gayet excavations, 1902–1903. E 29302

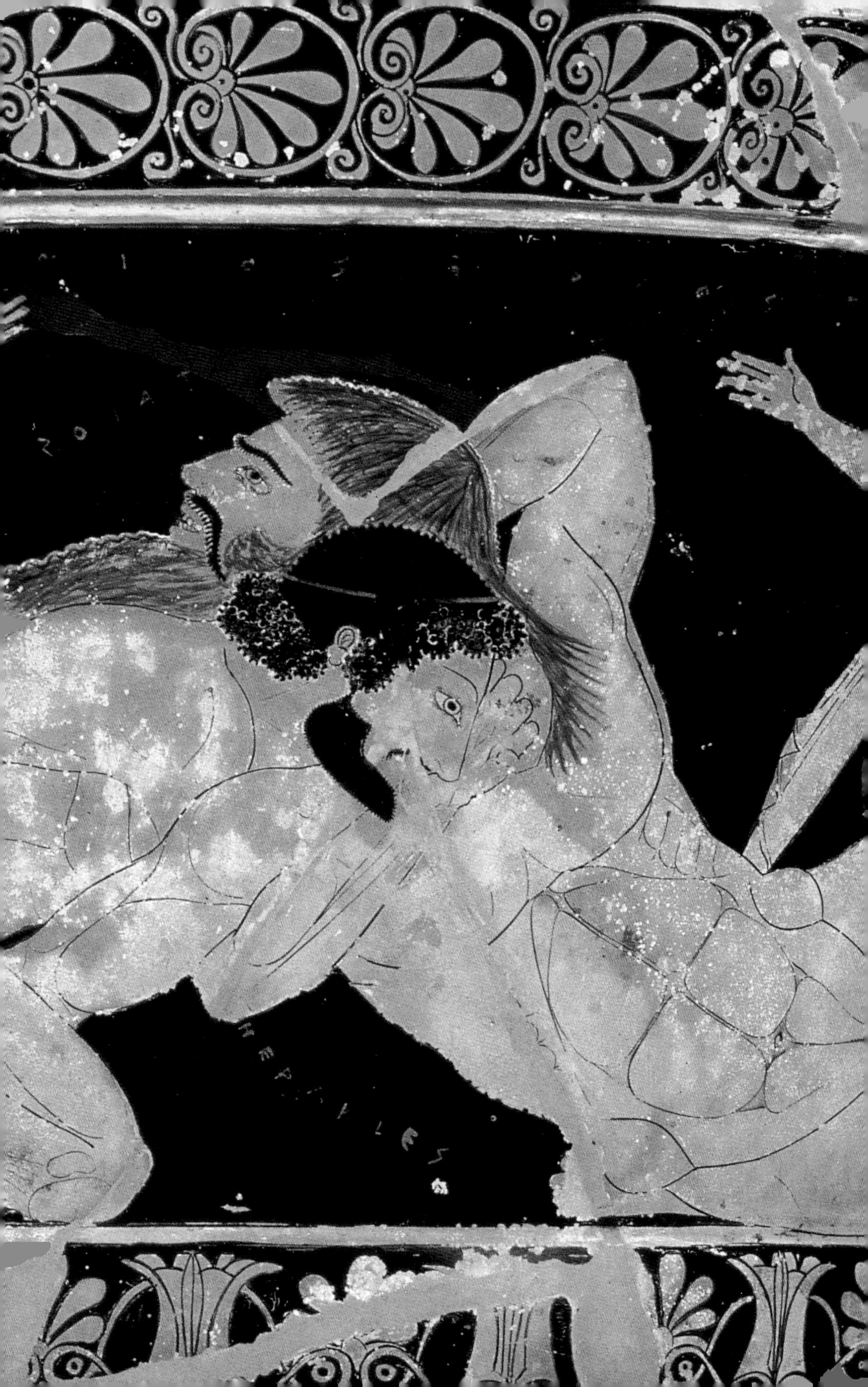

Greek, Etruscan and Roman antiquities

THE DEPARTMENT OF GREEK, ETRUSCAN AND ROMAN ANTIQUITIES is one of the Louvre's oldest departments. Planned when the Muséum Central des Arts was created in 1793 and then called the 'Musée des Antiques', it did not open until 1800 and was inaugurated by the First Consul. The core of Greek and Roman works in the former royal collection was considerably enlarged by antiquities seized during the Revolution and booty from the Napoleonic campaign in Italy. In 1807, Napoleon's purchase of the Borghese Collection (including over 500 marbles) immediately transformed the Louvre into one of the world's foremost museums of antiquities.
THE KINGS WHO SUCCEEDED THE EMPEROR were also intent on enlarging the collections. One of the most momentous events was the entry of the *Venus de Milo*, donated by Louis XVIII, who had himself received it from the Marquis of Rivière, French Ambassor to the Sublime Porte. During Charles X's reign, fragments of metopes from the Temple of Zeus at Olympia were presented to France by the newly-founded Greek republic. In parallel, prestigious purchases complemented the collections. In 1818, the arrival of the Tochon Collection of 574 vases marked the true beginning of the Greek ceramics section. Napolean III's reign also brought major additions: apart from extensive restoration work, major marbles joined the collections including the

Winged Victory of Samothrace, sent by the French Consul at Adrianople. 3,500 vases entered the Louvre with the acquisition of the vast Campana Collection in 1861.

The late 19th century was no less fruitful, with a series of excavations, purchases and donations. The kouroi from Actium arrived in 1874, and the *Hera* from Samos in 1881. The excavations carried out by Salomon Reinach at Myrinia in Asia Minor swelled the ranks of the small objects with 1,700 terracotta figurines. Certain patrons showed great generosity, notably Gustave and Edmond de Rothschild, who acquired most of the Roman silver from the Boscoreale Treasure for the Louvre.

The 20th century saw prestigious acquisitions (the *Head of Athena* from Egina in 1917 and the Campanian krater illustrated with the *Massacre of the Pretenders* in 1985) and a vast redeployment of the collections. As part of the 'Grand Louvre' project, the Preclassical Greek Gallery was recently refurbished, the presentation of the metopes from Olympia was entirely modified, the Campana Room and the Bronzes Gallery were reorganised, and all the terracotta statuettes and reliefs were moved to the rooms in the Galerie Charles X.

The pre-Hellenic age

124 *'Sauceboat'*

Heraia of Arcadia (Peloponnese)?
*c.*2200 BC
Gold. 17 x 10 x 14.4 cm
Acquired in 1887
MNC 906 (Bj 1885)

125 *Female Statuette (Syros group)*

Island of Paros
Early Cycladic II
(2700–2300 BC)
Spedos type
Marble. H. 39.3 cm
Hinstin Donation, 1876
Ma 2707

The Cycladic civilisation

During the Bronze Age, in the Aegean archipelago, the natural link between the Greek mainland and Asia Minor, there emerged a brilliant civilization of seafarers called the Cycladic culture. These small islands forming a circle around the island of Delos (the future sanctuary of Apollo) in turn became the theatre of an aesthetic and spiritual revolution. Although these islanders were hunters, fishermen and farmers, they also knew how to work metal and clay and extract and exploit obsidian and silver-bearing lead.
But it was in their brilliant, crystalline white marble that the inhabitants of the Cyclades would express their genius to the full in a remarkable production of 'idols', raging from roughly hewn pebbles to the most sophisticated and harmonious sculptures. Pure line, sober form and extreme abstraction – even if a certain naturalism expressed itself here and there – are the hallmarks of their fascinatingly modern statuary. Yet the eye discerns an infinite variety of form, subtlety of composition and even the mark of individual sculptors and regional styles. Almost a hundred statuettes, whole or fragmented, have been attributed to an artist known as the 'Master of Goulandris', reproductions of which have been found on Syros, Keros and Amorgos.
But apart from these stylistic attributions, many a mystery remains as to the true purpose of these stone figurines. Were they fertility idols, concubines of the deceased, or depictions of the Great Mother Goddess? Whatever the answer, these both skilful and 'primitive' statuettes are testaments to the first encounter of the Greek genius with white marble.

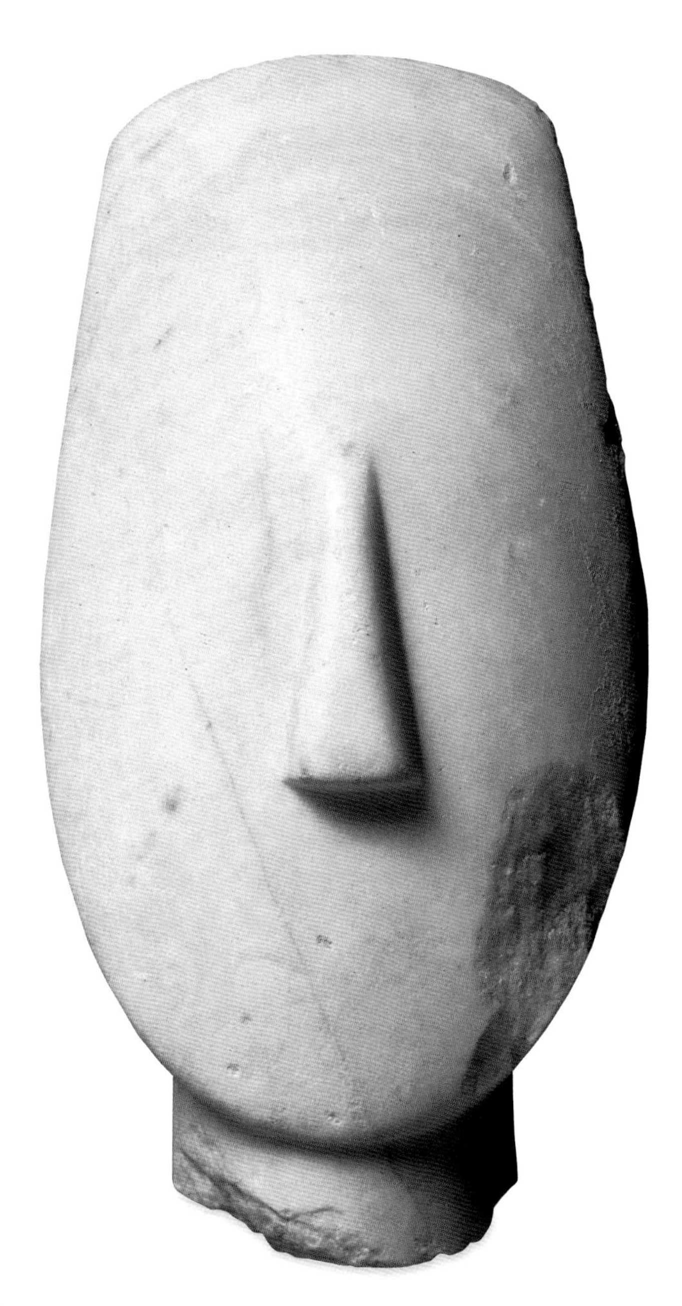

126 *Female head*

Keros
c. 2700–2400 BC
Marble. 27 x 14.5 x 9.5 cm
Rayet Donation, 1873
MNB 509 (Ma 2709)

In all probability, this marble head, exceptional in size and treatment, originally had a body. The formal harmony of the truncated oval face, vigorously sculpted nose and delicately drawn ears presupposes considerable knowledge of geometry. The 20th century, with its passion for abstraction, rediscovered the refined forms of these enigmatic 'idols', so similar to the works of Modigliani and Brancusi. One should however bear in mind that this sovereign face was originally decorated with red or blue motifs, possibly ritual make-up.

Archaic Greek art

127 *Attican Geometric lidded vase*

Athens, *c.*740 BC
Terracotta
H. 22.3 cm; Ø 34 cm
A 567

These lidded vases are circular, slightly flattened served as jewellery or unguent receptacles. In this very beautiful example, the harmony between the structure of the vase and its decoration attain perfection. Four horses crown the lid and the sides are elegantly decorated with swastikas (an ancient motif of Indo-European origin), four-petalled rosettes, checkerboards patterns and diamonds. Made in a workshop in Athens, this sumptuous vessel probably had a funerary use and was destined to accompany the deceased in afterlife.

From the Geometric to the Orientalising Style

It is now certain that the peoples who developed the brilliant Mycenaean Civilisation during the 2nd millennium were already fully-fledged Greeks. Their initially unpolished art soon forged a language of rigour and abstraction, as the famous gold masks discovered by Heinrich Schliemann in the late 19th century BC so brilliantly illustrate. But however powerful and prosperous they were, the Mycenaean kingdoms collapsed in the 12th century BC, falling prey to invasions by Northern peoples and the turmoil reigning throughout the Mediterranean. It was at this point that the Dorians entered the Hellenic peninsula and the history of the Greek people.

After the period known as the 'Dark Ages', art re-emerged in the constraining and severe forms of the Geometric style. There is not the slightest fantasy in these vases or clay figurines whose decoration and composition obey a strict repertoire of circles, triangles, wavy lines, diamonds, chevrons and zigzags, and so on. Ceramics had their first period of glory. Vases, stored in huge quantities, were sometimes imposingly large and perfectly executed. Some were placed in graves with the deceased or contained the body or ashes, others were placed on the tomb to receive the offerings destined to appease the deceased in the next world.

In the late 8th century BC, Greek boats criss-crossing the Mediterranean discovered new lands where towns soon sprang up. A new aesthetic emerged which gradually forsook geometric rigour for an ornate and sometimes exuberant style. On the Greek mainland, city states vied with one another in their artistic prowess and 'orientalised' their style, each in their own way. Corinth emerged as winner of this commercial and artistic contest and began flooding the entire Mediterranean market with its small, gracefully decorated aryballoi (jars for perfumed oil).

128 *Orientalising-style oinochoe* known as *the 'Lévy oinochoe'*

Miletus?
*c.*650 BC
Terracotta. H. 39.5 cm
Acquired in 1891
E 658

This exceptionally large oinochoe or spouted wine vase was clearly based on a metallic model. Its refined floral decoration is in the Orientalising Style. A procession of fantastic and real and fantastic animals (ibexes, goats, stags, dogs, sphinxes and griffins) stands out against a white slip applied to brown clay, with a profusion of small vegetable motifs invading the field. The 'Wild Goat Style', for a long time attributed to the workshops on the island of Rhodes, developed in several cities in Ionia, particularly at Miletus.

129 *Boeotian bell-idol*

*c.*700 BC
Terracotta
H. 39.5 cm
CA 573

130 *Amphora-loutrophoros*

Attributed to the 'Painter of Analatos'
Attica, *c.*680 BC
Terracotta. H. 81 cm
Acquired in 1935
CA 2985

This elegant amphora contained water for ritual ablutions during marriages or funerals and illustrates the transition between the late Geometric Period and the Orientalising Style. One of the most brilliant representatives of this 'aesthetic revolution' was the Painter of Analatos, who painted another decoration found on the same site. Stylised vegetable decoration (braids, rosettes, spirals, and so on) mingles with imaginary creatures and humans (sphinxes with long wavy hair, dancing couples, chariot processions). Another innovation, the use of incisions for details, heralds the emergence of the black-figure vase technique in Athens less than a century later.

131 *Aryballos*

Corinth
*c.*640 BC
Terracotta. H. 6.3 cm
Acquired in 1898
CA 931

Greece did not borrow solely new materials from the Orient. Certain forms, the small aryballos or perfume jar, for instance, came from Cyprus and further afield. The aryballos owed its success largely to the development of sport and rubbing of perfumed oil into the skin. The neck of this beautiful, particularly carefully executed aryballos is in the shape of a woman whose layered hairstyle is reminiscent of the 'Lady of Auxerre'. The belly is decorated with extraordinarily lively hunting and battle scenes.

132 *Pendant*

Rhodes (Camiros)
*c.*630 BC
Electrum. H. 8.5 cm
Salzmann Collection. Loaned by the Department of Oriental Antiquities, 1949
S 1208 (Bj 2169-10)

During the Orientalising Period there was an unprecedented fashion for the minor arts. In the growing cities there emerged a new middle-class clientele who bought precious vases and objects and, concerned with their elegance, commissioned jewellery (very little of which has survived). This small pendant in electrum illustrates the virtuosity of Greek metalworkers, who had assimilated oriental techniques such as granulation and filigreeing. The two female faces in the middle of this Egyptian-inspired bestiary are the hallmark of the so-called 'Dedalic' style.

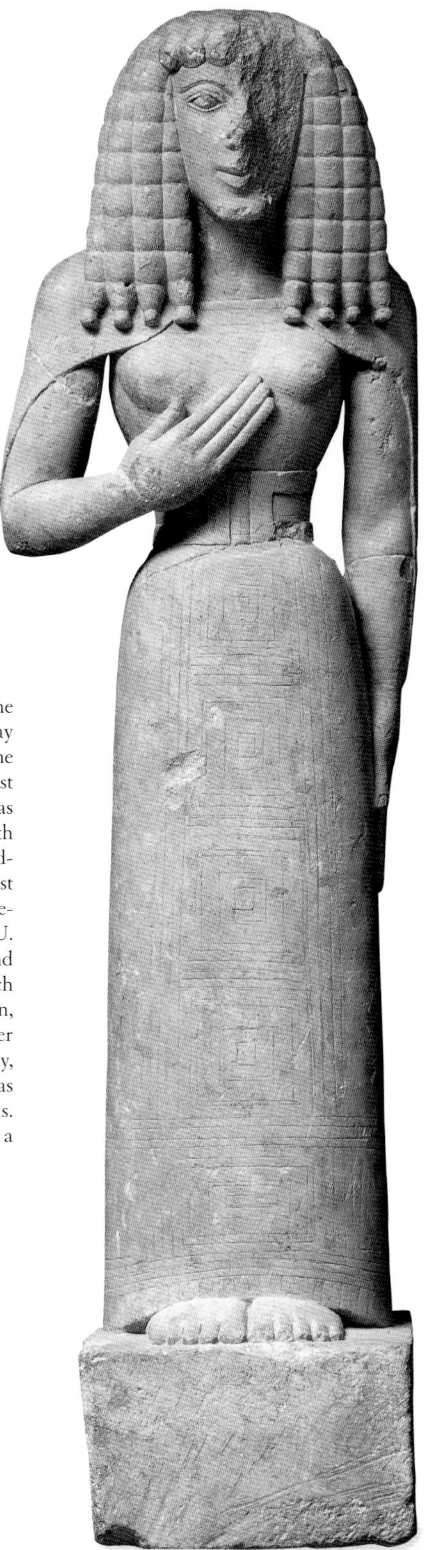

133 *Female statue*
known as *the 'Lady of Auxerre'*
Crete?
*c.*630 BC
Limestone. H. 75 cm including base
Exchanged with the Musée d'Auxerre, 1909.
MND 847 (Ma 3098)

This small statue, discovered in 1907 in the storerooms of the Musée d'Auxerre, is today considered the absolute masterpiece of the Dedalic style, named after Dedalus, an artist said to have worked for King Minos. It was on Crete that these limestone figures with tight-fitting garments and delicately modelled breasts were produced in the greatest number. The face, framed by a thick trapezoidal hairstyle is shaped like a splayed U. The forehead is low, the eyelids fringed and the lips are thick. But it is her gesture which focuses our attention. Is it one of adoration, or that of a fertility goddess designating her breasts, sources of life. Whether a deity, priestess or worshipper, this sculpture was originally enlivened with painted details. The incised decoration probably served as a 'canvas' on which to apply colours.

134 *Head of a Sphinx*

Thebes
Corinthian Style, *c.*530 BC
Terracotta. H. 18 cm
Acquired in 1895
Ca 637

135 *Kore from the Cheramyes group*

Island of Samos
*c.*560 BC
Marble. H. 1.92 m
Ma 686

After the prelude of the 'Dedalic' style, during the next century a school of great marble sculpture emerged. The two types of Archaic statuary appeared simultaneously: the kouros, a young standing nude male with his arms by his sides, and the kore, a draped young woman. This very sensual 'statue-column' with its curved stomach and delicately suggested breasts belongs to the second type. The inscription 'Cheramyes dedicated me to Hera as an offering' is carved in Greek down the veil's hem. We now know, due to the recent discovery of a twin statue in the sanctuary on the island of Samos, that this sculpture was part of a funerary monument created around 560 BC.

136 *Head of a horseman*

Athens
*c.*550 BC
H. 27 cm
Georges Rampin Bequest, 1896
MNC 2128 (Ma 3104)

This graceful effigy of a horseman, missing its torso and part of its mount (in the Acropolis Museum, Athens), shows the East Grecian influence. With his smiling lips, slightly bulging slanting eyes and braided hairstyle surmounted by a crown, this young man cuts a fine figure. In ancient Greece, the horse was the privilege of the aristocratic elite. It has been suggested that this figure may be an Athenian nobleman commemorating a sporting victory.

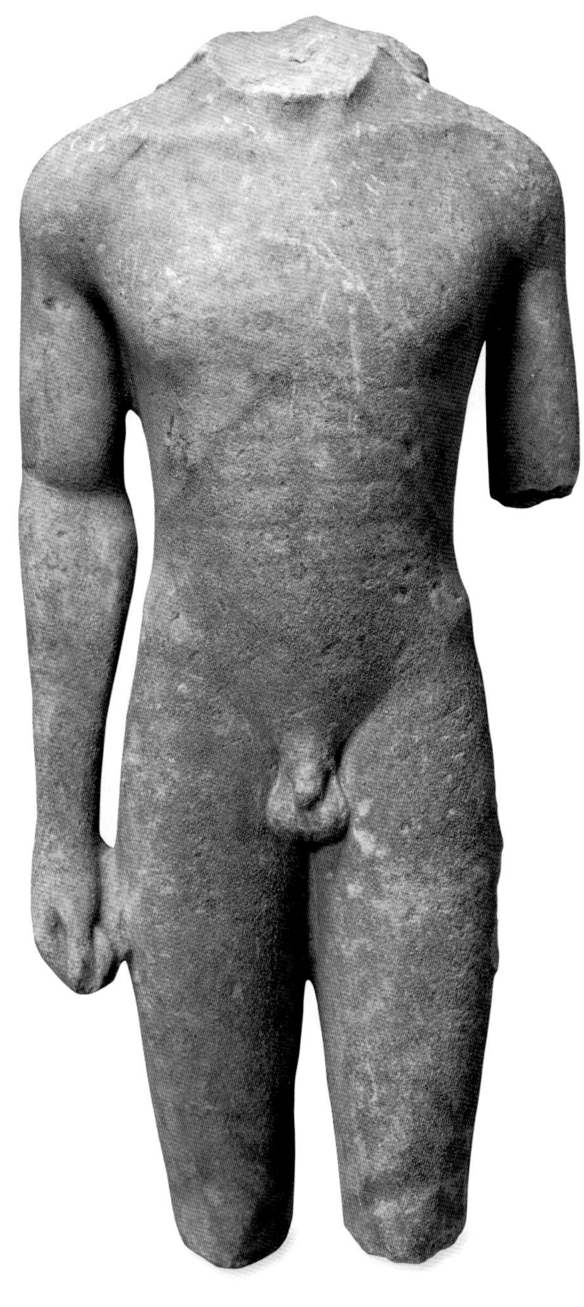

137 *Kouros*

Found at Actium
Naxian style, *c.*560 BC
Marble. H. 1 m
Acquired in 1874. MNB 788 (Ma 687)

138 *Black-figure amphora*

Signed by Exekias, potter
Attica
*c.*540 BC
Terracotta. H. 50 cm with lid
Acquired in 1883
F 53

139 *Red-figure amphora*

Signed by Andokides, potter
Attica, *c.*530 BC
Terracotta. H. 58 cm
Acquired in 1843
G 1

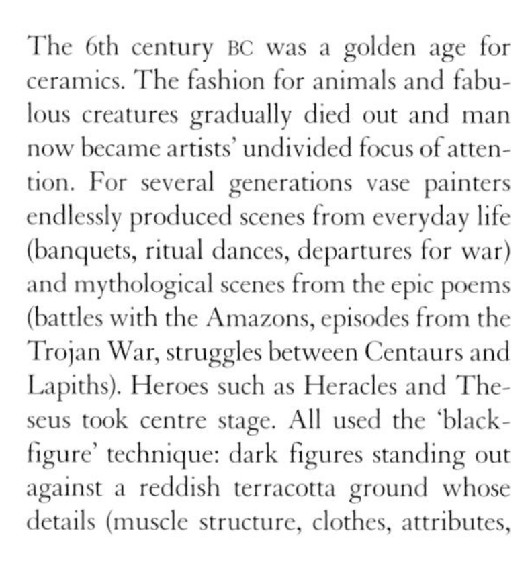

The 6th century BC was a golden age for ceramics. The fashion for animals and fabulous creatures gradually died out and man now became artists' undivided focus of attention. For several generations vase painters endlessly produced scenes from everyday life (banquets, ritual dances, departures for war) and mythological scenes from the epic poems (battles with the Amazons, episodes from the Trojan War, struggles between Centaurs and Lapiths). Heroes such as Heracles and Theseus took centre stage. All used the 'black-figure' technique: dark figures standing out against a reddish terracotta ground whose details (muscle structure, clothes, attributes, and so on) are incised. The most famous painters, such as Exekias, signed their works out of pride, but also to spread the name of the firm for which they worked.

A major innovation transformed the world of pottery around 530 BC, the invention by Athenian painters of the 'red-figure' technique. Light-coloured figures now stood out against a dark ground, with their internal details modulated with brushwork. In less than a generation masterpieces were created, such as the krater signed by Euphronius – on which we see Heracles defeating the giant Antaeus, his face contorted with suffering.

140 *Red-figure krater*

Signed by Euphronios, painter
Attica
*c.*510 BC
Terracotta. H. 46 cm
Campana Collection. Acquired in 1863
G. 103

141 *Chalice-shaped krater*

Southern Italy
*c.*330 BC
Terracotta. H. 57; Ø 81 cm
Acquired in 1825
N 3157

142 *Mirror stand*

First quarter of the 5th century BC
Bronze. H. 41 cm
Acquired in 1888
MNC 992 (Br 1688)

Classical Greek art

143 *Athlete making a libation*

Parian style?
c.470 BC
Statuette, bronze. H. 28.4 cm
David-Weill Donation, 1937
MND 1891 (Br 4236)

144 *Dionysus?*

Olympia?
c. 460 BC
Bronze. H. 23.5 cm
Acquired in 1894
Br 154

The golden age of statuary

The preceding periods had established local particularities, even styles, but no major personality had yet imposed his aesthetic on his contemporaries. For almost twenty years, Phidias the Athenian, a close friend of Pericles, supervised the work on the Parthenon. Other sculptors emerged, of course, such as Myron, whose *Discus Thrower*, leaning forward, arm stretched behind him, is on the verge of disequilibrium. But Phidias and his disciples took another direction. The 5th century BC was a virile, glorious, heroic and anthropocentric century, or at least this is the image it projects of itself in its marbles and bronzes. It was a century of artistic effervescence and social change during which statues of heroes were erected in Athens' central square, the Agora (the *Tyrannoktonoi* group by Kritios and Nesiotese celebrating the downfall of tyranny and the advent of the new regime) and Attica became an enormous construction project to which craftsmen flocked from all over Greece.
The sculptor Polycletes was another great figure of the Classical Period. His *Doryphoros*, whose perfect proportions (the head contained sevenfold within the body) obey the strictest 'canons', can be considered its manifesto. Based on a subtle balance between the limbs, many sculptures endlessly applied this arithmetic system based on measure and balance.

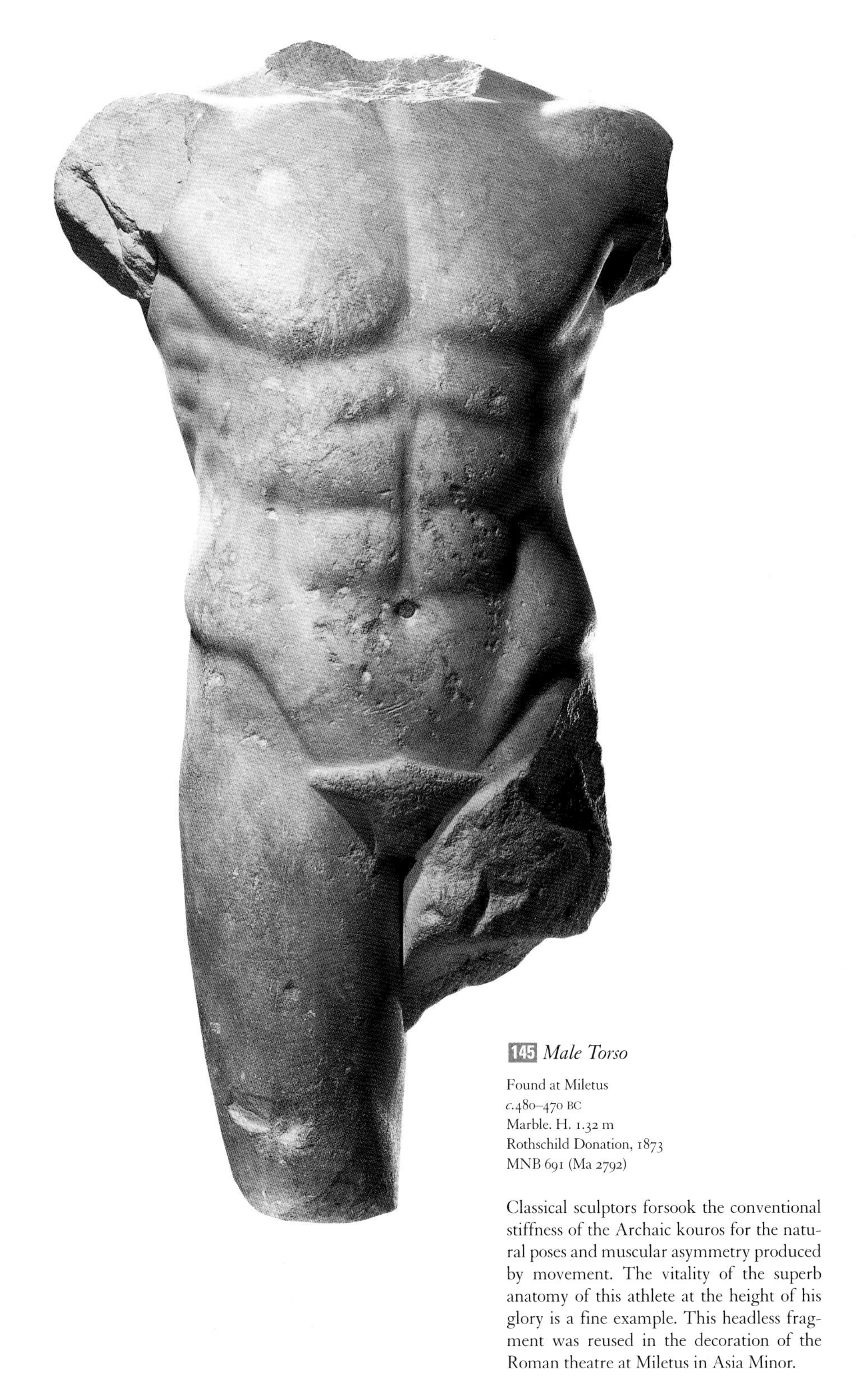

145 *Male Torso*

Found at Miletus
*c.*480–470 BC
Marble. H. 1.32 m
Rothschild Donation, 1873
MNB 691 (Ma 2792)

Classical sculptors forsook the conventional stiffness of the Archaic kouros for the natural poses and muscular asymmetry produced by movement. The vitality of the superb anatomy of this athlete at the height of his glory is a fine example. This headless fragment was reused in the decoration of the Roman theatre at Miletus in Asia Minor.

146 *Apollo and the Nymphs*

Thasos, Passageway of the Theoroi
*c.*480 BC
Relief, marble. 0.92 x 2.09 m
Acquired in 1864
Ma 696

This imposing relief discovered on Thasos in 1864 originally decorated a road called the 'Passageway of the Theoroi' after the magistrates whose annual council of three members governed worship. A procession of Nymphs and Charites passes, their hieratic profiles barely freed from the stone. In their midst is Apollo, a cithara under his left arm and looking at the woman crowning him. Is she a muse or a goddess? Despite his long tunic with vertical folds, the god's lively pose echoes that of Hermes 'the orator' on the other relief. These reliefs prefigure the stylistic innovations that would be developed during the decades to come.

147 *Funerary stele*

Pharsalus
*c.*460 BC
Marble. H. 80 cm
Acquired in 1882
Ma 701

148 *Red-figure krater*

Attributed to the 'Painter of the Niobids'
Attican style
*c.*460 BC
Terracotta. H. 54 cm
Acquired in 1883
G 341

Breaking with previous traditions, this krater depicts the massacre of Niobe's children by Artemis and Apollo in a rocky landscape. The experimentation with perspective, staggering of foreground and background and expressive facial expressions all show the combined influence of sculpture and painting.

149 *Helmeted female head*

Aeginetan style
*c.*460 BC
Marble. H. 28 cm
Vogüé Donation, 1917
MND 1053 (Ma 3109)

150 *Metope fragment: Heracles and the Cretan Bull*

c.460 BC
Paros marble. 1.14 x 1.52 m
Gift of the Greek Senate, 1830
Ma 716

151 *Plaque from the frieze of the Parthenon*

The Acropolis, Athens
c.440 BC
Bas-relief, marble. 0.96 x 2.07 m
Choiseul-Gouffier Collection.
Seized during the Revolution
MR 825 (Ma 738)

The 'Ergastines' (Greek: 'workers') is the name by which these delightful young women carved in marble are known to posterity. Their vitally important job was to weave the sacred *peplos* (mantle) which the Athenians offered to their protectress

The incomparable beauty of the original

Marbles copies of bronze originals, most of which have disappeared, half-antique half-modern statues, fragments whose meaning is not always clear, the tattered remains of great paintings, many are the 'filters' which have clouded our perception of 'classical' works which we are unable to designate for certain as Greek or Roman, authentic or extensively restored, profane or sacred. We have no way of identifying sculptures from architectural decorations since no 'filter' guides the eye. This is true of the fragments from the Temple of Zeus at Olympia, presented to the French Government by the Greek Senate in thanks for France's aid during the Greek War of Independence. This temple decoration, probably sculpted around 460 BC, is one of the masterpieces of the Severe Style, whose bywords seems to have been 'measure', 'rigour' and 'clarity', as illustrated by this west metope depicting Heracles' struggle with the Cretan Bull. Under Phidias's supervision, the decoration of the Parthenon attained heights of excellence and virtuosity. The building work attracted the finest sculptors in the Greek world. The Louvre has five fragments from this prestigious monument which, although never properly speaking a temple, contained the treasure of the city and Phidias' priceless gold and ivory statue of Athena.

152 *Metope from the south Doric frieze of the Parthénon*
Centaur and Lapith Woman

Acropolis, Athens
447–440 BC
High-relief, marble. 1.35 x 1.41 m
Acquired in 1818. Collection Choiseul-Gouffier
Ma 736

Phidias' eminently political decoration of the Parthenon includes every mythological and religious episode relating to the history of Athens. The pediments depict the Athena's miraculous birth and her quarrel with Poseidon for the possession of Attica. The Doric frieze depicts the battle between the gods and the giants, the Greeks' victory over the 'barbarian' Amazons, the birth of Erichthonios, the city's founder, the taking of Troy and centaur fighting. This metope depicts a centaur attempting to abduct a Lapith woman, but their ruthless struggle could almost be some graceful dance.

Athena on the Parthenon. The Louvre fragment of the continuous sculpted frieze which ran round the temple's colonnade shows six young women in a musical procession. The fluidity of their progress is interrupted by two priests, one carrying a basket apparently containing the sacrificial knife.

114
Greek, Etruscan and Roman antiquities

153 *Aphrodite,* known as the *Venus of Arles*

Roman copy of an original attributed to Praxiteles
Late 1st century BC
Marble. H. 1.94 m
Found at Arles, gift of the town of Arles to Louis XIV, 1683
MR 365 (Ma 439)

Sparta's victory over Athens in 404 BC marked the end of the certainties of Pericles' time. The hour was now one of doubt and questioning. Shaken by successive crises, Greek artists turned to the countries of Asia, the only ones now rich enough to provide them with major commissions. Three sculptors emerged during this period known as the 'Second Classicism', Scopas, Lysippus and Praxiteles. The latter, in the commissions he executed at Cnidus, retained above all a taste for sensuality. Heightened by the brush of his colleague Nicias, his sculptures gradually unveiled the nudity of Aphrodite, the most beautiful and desirable of all the goddesses, while he transformed Apollo into an Adonis-like young man in a languid pose.

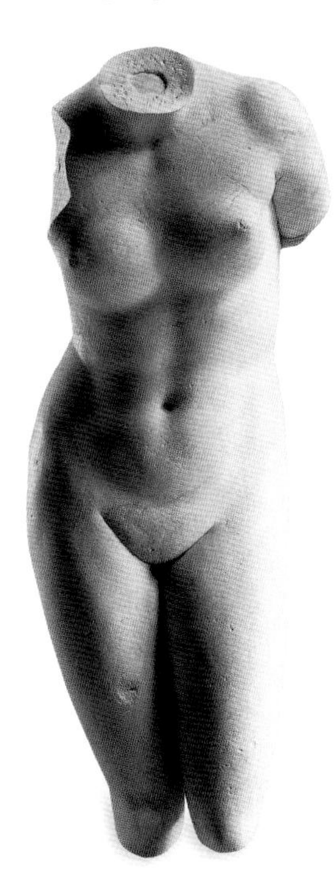

154 *Aphrodite*

Roman copy of an original attributed to Praxiteles
*c.*350 BC
Marble. H. 1.22 m
Ma 2184

155 *Apollo Sauroctonos*

Roman copy of the original attributed to Praxiteles
*c.*350 BC
Marble. H. 1.49 m
Ma 441

The Hellenistic world

156 *Statuette of Victory*

Myrina
Early 2nd century BC
Terracotta. H. 27 cm
Loaned by Lyon University, 1983
LY 1651

157 *Tanagraean,* known as *'the Sophoclean'*

Tanagra (Beotia), attributed to the 'Workshop of the Lady in Blue'
*c.*330–300 BC
Terracotta. H. 25 cm
Acquired in 1874
MNB 585

Between archaism and invention

It would be artificial to clearly demarcate the Hellenistic Period from the preceding one. Many of the creations of Second Classicism carried the seed of later stylistic developments. An artist such as Lysippus had already abundantly explored the arts of portraiture and the setting of figures in space. This sculptor from Sikyon was summoned by Alexander the Great to execute all his sculpted effigies. Lysippus' influence can be discerned in many creations from the 3rd century BC, such as the sensual *Crouching Aphrodite* [159], whose pyramidal volumes can be viewed from all angles.

The era which followed the death of the great Macedonian conqueror (323 BC) explored different paths of experimentation. The female body, unveiled by Praxiteles in the 4th century BC, continued to fascinate sculptors, with a hitherto restrained sensuality. Similarly, infancy and its opposite, old age, inspired creations of rare presence and a far cry from the impassiveness of the triumphant athletes of the 5th century. In parallel, a taste for the bizarre and the exotic began to manifest itself.

It was no longer to Athens but to the cities of Egypt and the Orient such as Alexandria, Rhodes and Antioch that people turned for inspiration. Small terracotta figurines became increasingly in demand and popularised themes such as the winged Victory or Nike. Painting was for a long time believed to have disappeared, the copies found in Pompeian villas a few centuries later thought to be the only remaining traces. But recent discoveries in northern Greece (ancient Macedonia), notably the sepulchral frescoes at Vergina have thrown this into question.

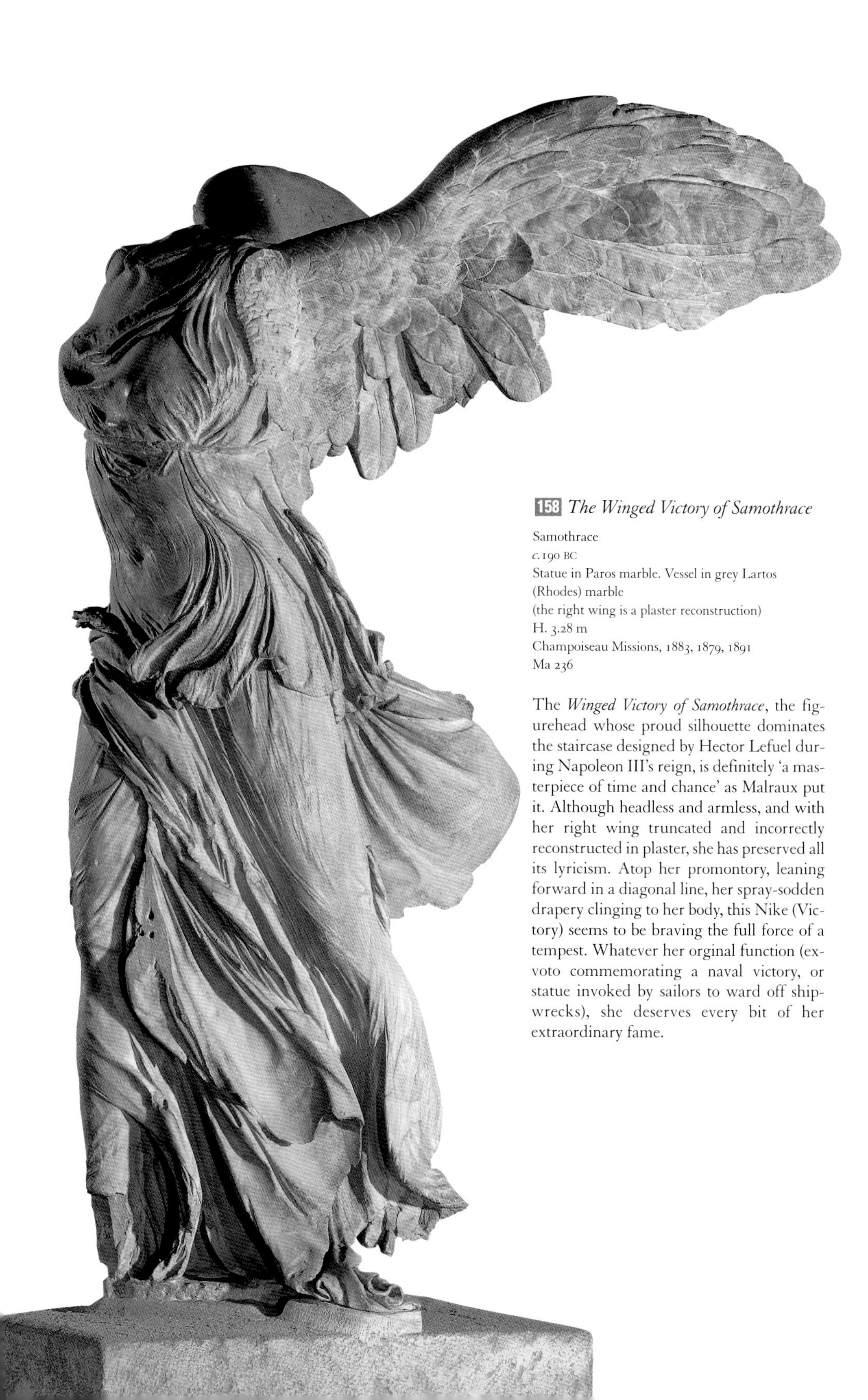

158 *The Winged Victory of Samothrace*

Samothrace
c. 190 BC
Statue in Paros marble. Vessel in grey Lartos (Rhodes) marble
(the right wing is a plaster reconstruction)
H. 3.28 m
Champoiseau Missions, 1883, 1879, 1891
Ma 236

The *Winged Victory of Samothrace*, the figurehead whose proud silhouette dominates the staircase designed by Hector Lefuel during Napoleon III's reign, is definitely 'a masterpiece of time and chance' as Malraux put it. Although headless and armless, and with her right wing truncated and incorrectly reconstructed in plaster, she has preserved all its lyricism. Atop her promontory, leaning forward in a diagonal line, her spray-sodden drapery clinging to her body, this Nike (Victory) seems to be braving the full force of a tempest. Whatever her orginal function (ex-voto commemorating a naval victory, or statue invoked by sailors to ward off shipwrecks), she deserves every bit of her extraordinary fame.

159 *Crouching Aphrodite*

Roman work from the Imperial Period
1st–2nd century AD
Sainte-Colombe (Isère)
Marble. H. 96 cm
Formerly in the Gerantet Collection
Acquired in 1878
MNB 1292 (Ma 2240)

160 *Aphrodite*,
known as the *'Venus de Milo'*

Mílos
c. 130–100 BC
Statue, marble. H. 2.02 m
Acquired in 1821
LL 299 (Ma 399)

'Our Lady of Beauty', as Henri Heine called her, is one of the jewels of the Louvre's Greek collections. Half-nude and continuing a stylistic effect pioneered by Praxiteles, this goddess (Aphrodite or possibly Amphitrite, a marine deity particularly venerated on the island of Mílos) is sensual yet restrained, innovatory yet harking back to the classic themes of the past. In her severe and slightly heavy-featured face, some have seen reminiscences of the great Phidias.

161 *Aphrodite*,
known as the *'Kaufmann Head'*

After the original by Praxiteles
2nd century BC
Marble. H. 35 cm
Acquired in 1951
MND 2027 (Ma 3518)

A Hellenistic recreation of a Praxitelian subject (the head of the Cnidus Aphrodite is known only from Roman copies), this face exudes a sensual fragility which the great Athenian sculptor would never have dared to portray two centuries earlier. We are a far cry from the *thambos*, the formidable cosmic force that the goddess of love was to inspire in the spectator. The moist gaze and slightly open lips of this Aphrodite could almost be human.

162 *Hermaphrodite Sleeping*

Roman copy of an original dating from the 2nd century AD
(the mattress was added by Bernini)
Marble. 1.69 x 0.89 m
Found in Rome in the 16th century
Acquired in 1808. Borghese Collection
Ma 231

The voluptuous anatomy of this beautiful, languid young creature, the fruit of the loves of Hermes and Aphrodite, is both masculine and feminine. This strange and ambiguous theme was bound to fascinate the sculptors of the pre-Hellenistic period, who were masters of surprise and theatrical effects. This creature 'of flesh and marble' is reclining on a mattress added in the 17th century by the sculptor Bernini, which gives the work an anecdotal dimension light years away from the Greek artist's original intentions.

163 *Homer*

Rome. 2nd century AD
Bust. Marble. H. 55 cm
Acquired in 1797
MR 530 (Ma 440)

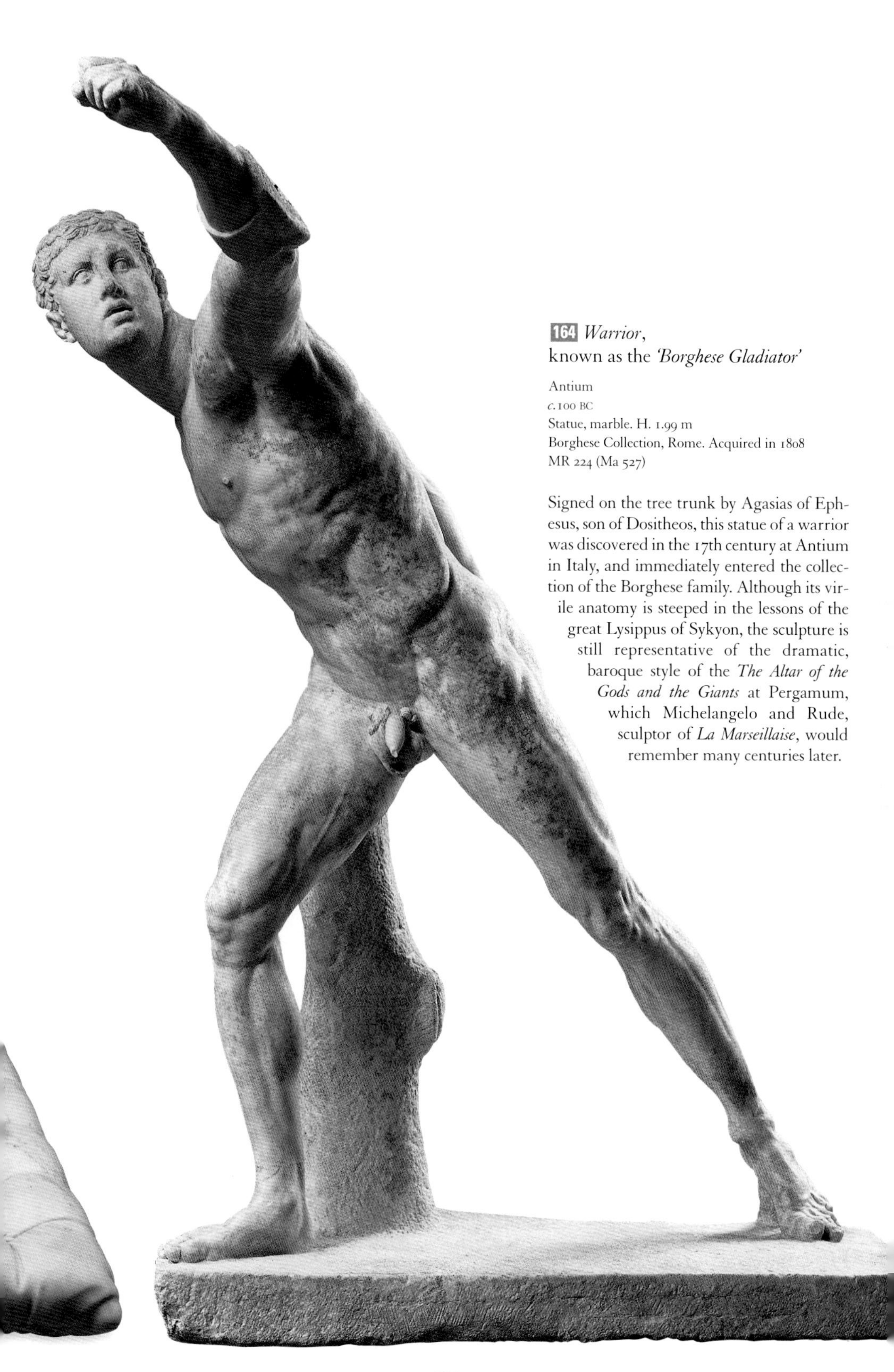

164 *Warrior*,
known as the *'Borghese Gladiator'*

Antium
c. 100 BC
Statue, marble. H. 1.99 m
Borghese Collection, Rome. Acquired in 1808
MR 224 (Ma 527)

Signed on the tree trunk by Agasias of Ephesus, son of Dositheos, this statue of a warrior was discovered in the 17th century at Antium in Italy, and immediately entered the collection of the Borghese family. Although its virile anatomy is steeped in the lessons of the great Lysippus of Sykyon, the sculpture is still representative of the dramatic, baroque style of the *The Altar of the Gods and the Giants* at Pergamum, which Michelangelo and Rude, sculptor of *La Marseillaise*, would remember many centuries later.

The Etruscans

Between Greece and Rome, an art of influences

A great deal has been written about the obscure origins of this mysterious people. Although their language is still little understood, the place of the Etruscans in the ancient Italian and Mediterranean world is being constantly re-evaluated. At the dawn of the 10th century BC saw yhe blossoming of a civilisation which archaeologists called the Villanovan culture after the village of Villanova near Bologna, where a large quantity of roughly fashioned biconical clay urns were found containing ashes of the dead. This culture had clear links with certain Hallstattian cultures in Central Europe. The Greeks, however, attracted by the plains of southern Italy and the rich mineral deposits in Etruria, would considerably modify the region's cultural landscape. Objects imported from mainland Greece and the ever-changing repertoire of forms and techniques brought by immigrant or itinerant artists gradually fashioned the particular flavour of Etruscan art, an art nurtured by influences, admittedly, but a generous and inventive one that endlessly adapted, reinterpreted and recreated the imagery of its neighbours. A style of small bronzes with organic outlines developed and a thinner type of ceramic, turned on a wheel, reproduced Eubean models in the Geometric style. But soon the repertoire of the Greek Orientalising style with its cortege of fabulous creatures seduced the local aristocracy eager for luxury and refinement. Etruscan artists demonstrated their skill in parallel, however, as attested by the magnificent jewellery discovered in the great princely tombs at Cerveteri and Prenestino. A second phase of Hellenisation, whose intensity waned in the late 6th century, enriched Etruscan art. The Ionian influence in terracottas and bronzes was so strong that on an artistic level Etruria became a genuine province of Greece. But with the expansion of Rome, Etruscan art would again change face, swapping its former models for those of its august conqueror.

165 *Terracotta plaque*

Caere
Second half of the 6th century BC
Painted terracotta. 1.23 x 0.58 m
Campana Collection. Acquired in 1883
Cp 6627

In Etruria, terracotta reigned supreme and adorned the temples. The theme depicted on this plaque, discovered with five other pieces (also in the Louvre) in a tomb at Cerveteri, is difficult to interpret. Is the winged figure a depiction of a spirit taking the soul of the deceased away into the beyond? Whatever the answer, this plaque shows the influence of Asian Greece, the absolute model for the Etruscan artists of the 6th century BC.

166 *Sarcophagus of a married couple*

Caere
Late 6th century BC
Terracotta. 1.14 x 1.90 m
Campana Collection. Acquired in 1863. Cp 5194

The Etruscan genius perhaps achieved its most beautiful expression in funerary art. This imposing, vividly polychromed sarcophagus, in fact a large clay cinerary urn, has immortalised a deceased couple tenderly embracing for eternity. The radiant grace of their smiling faces is the hallmark of Ionia, and their gesture of offering perfume originated in Asia Minor. But the vivifying role of wine has not been neglected: the two cushions are wineskins. The presence of the deceased woman, half-reclining with her husband, shows that in Etruria, unlike Greece, women and men were equals.

167 *Achelous*

*c.*480 BC
Gold. H. 4 cm
Campana Collection. Acquired in 1863
Bj 498

168 *Portrait of a Man*

Fiesole area
*c.*300 BC
Head, bronze. H. 21 cm
Acquired in 1864
Br 19

This painstakingly executed bronze effigy (the hair is depicted lock by lock) stands out from the average production of the time. Derived from both Italic expressionism and Greek naturalism, this determined looking young man's face in many ways prefigures the psychological acuity of Roman portraiture. Yet it is still a far cry from the verism that developed in Rome in the next centuries.

169 *Cinerary urn: 'Chariot Journey'*

Volterra
Late 2nd–early 1st century BC
Alabaster. 84 x 60 cm
Ma 2357

Echoing the decline of Etruscan civilisation, the art of the Hellenistic Period seems to have sunk into dull repetition. This cinerary urn is an exception. The lid depicts the deceased in the ritual banqueting pose but the urn itself is decorated with a scene of a freshness and vivacity unknown in Greek art. The deceased is journeying towards the next world on a modest chariot drawn by mules, a scene close to everyday life heralding the great achievements of Gallo-Roman art.

The Roman world

170 *'Marcellus'*

Rome, 23 BC
Signed 'Cleomenes the Athenian'
Statue, marble. H. 1.80 m
Collection of Louis XIV
Ma 1207

With its classical Greek reminiscences, this idealised portrait of Augustus' nephew and first son-in-law is a striking juxtaposition of an athletic physique in the purest Polykleitan tradition and a face whose features are highly reminiscent of the Emperor himself. Portrayed in the pose of Hermes the orator, the young man has let the drapery slip down onto a tortoise, emblem of Venus, from whom the entire Julio-Claudian line dynasty claimed to be descended.

An ambiguous art

Is there really such a thing as Roman art? Hellenic canons would continue to prevail in portraits, sarcophagi, paintings and bronze for many a century. But Roman genius succeeded in finding its own inspiration, in which every element served a moral and political ideology. The artist effaced himself in the service of his client (often the Emperor himself) and the task in hand (the glorification of Roman values such as Justice, Peace and Order). The preeminent art was architecture. The building of temples of the gods and places of political assembly, and later, during the Imperial period, public buildings (baths, theatres) was the means by which the regime ensured the adhesion of the masses. But sculpture's role was just as pragmatic. Under the Republic, it served above all to immortalise men of state in bronze or marble.
Sometimes there was a strong temptation to break free of the straightjacket of official art and create works full of poetry, reverie and abandon. The rich landowners around Rome and Pompeii adorned their villas with mural frescoes of gardens peopled with birds and flowers, vividly coloured fantastic worlds pushing back the frontiers of the real.

171 *Relief 'of Domitius Ahenobarbus': scenes of a census*

Rome, *c.* 100 BC
Relief, marble. L. 2.05 m
Acquired in 1824
Ma 975

In Roman art in the 1st century BC, eclecticism was the norm. This long relief from a monument originally erected on the Campus Martius by a consul called Domitius Ahenobarbus, now shared by Paris and Munich, combines two aesthetics. One, narrative and Roman, shows a census scene consecrated by a sacrifice, the other, in the Hellenistic tradition, depicts a procession of marine deities.

172 *Ara Pacis: imperial procession*

Rome, 13–9 BC
Relief, marble. 1.20 x 1.47 m
Campana Collection. Acquired in 1863
Ma 1088

Looking at this marble relief, it is hard not to think of the absolute model in this field, the frieze of the Panathenaic Procession on the Parthenon, a fragment of which is in the Louvre. But whereas Greece honoured its sculptor, Phidias, we know nothing of the artist (Greek or Roman?) who sculpted this work. He seems to have been more concerned with glorifying his emperor than preserving his name for posterity.

173 *Portrait of a Man*

Rome, *c.* 110 BC
Head, marble. H. 37.5 cm
Acquired in 1888
Ma 919

174 *Juba I*

Cherchel, Algeria
Late 1st century BC
Head, marble. H. 45 cm
Acquired in 1895
Ma 1885 - MNC 1920

175 *Livia*

c. 30 BC
Head, basanite. H. 34 cm
Acquired in 1860
Ma 1233

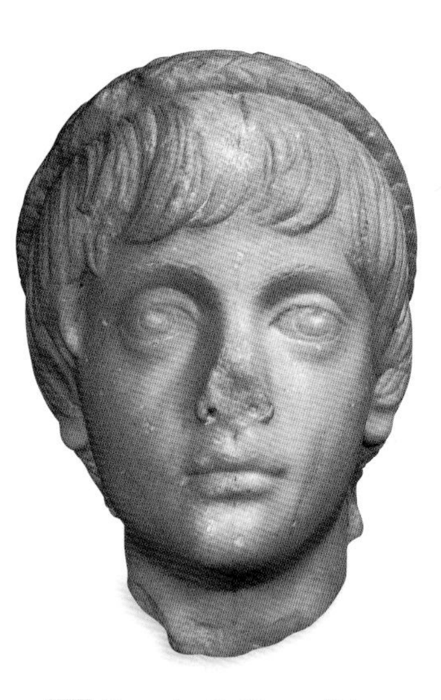

176 *Portrait of a Young Prince*

Annaba, Algeria?
c. 170
Head, marble. H. 21 cm
Acquired in 1955
Ma 3539

177 *Hadrian*

*c.*140
Head, bronze. H. 43 cm
Acquired in 1984
Br 4547

Portraiture in Rome, split between classical tendencies and realism, attained a high level of perfection. Bronze or marble effigies were very often intended to convey the subject's social status and moral virtues, but effects varied depending on the period and emperor. They could be conventional and cold like the basalt head of the empress Livia, or bubbling with life and inspired like this portrait of a man dated 110 BC. Others harmoniously combined aesthetic qualities and political propaganda. The effigies of Hadrian convey the philhellenic emperor's lofty humanist ideals, symbolised by his beard, which identifies him with the poets and philosophers. The unusual severity of this bronze, however, sculpted posthumously during the reign of Hadrian's successor, Antoninus Pius, indicates the intention to ensure the dynasty's continuity.

178 *Sarcophagus: 'Dionysos discovering Ariadne'*

Rome
*c.*235
Marble. 0.98 x 2.08 x 0.62 m
Found at Saint-Médard-d'Eyrans
Acquired in 1845
Ma 1346

The decoration of Roman sarcophagi, reflecting anxieties and questions about life after death, lend new moral virtues to Greek mythology. A lion hunt, the aristocratic activity par excellence, becomes a pretext for a demonstration of the supreme Roman ethical value, courage; a marriage between gods becomes an allusion to that other cardinal virtue, the *concordia* required of spouses. But

alongside these messages, funerary art indulges in all manner of aesthetic experimentation, such as the play of light and shadow, accentuated down the centuries by the use of the trepan. The first Christian sarcophagi, more austere in treatment, would soon forsake these ostentatious effects for clarity and symmetry.

179 *Sarcophagus: 'lion hunt'*

Rome, *c.*235–240
Marble. 0.88 x 2.20 m
Borghese Collection. Acquired in 1808
Ma 346

180 *Sarcophagus: 'marine procession'*

Rome
*c.*140–150
Marble. 0.95 x 2.37 x 0.60 m
Church of San Francesco a Ripa, Rome
Entered the Louvre in 1796
Ma 342

181 *Wrestler*

1st century?
Statuette, bronze. H. 27 cm
Autun. Acquired in 1870
Br 1067

The sheer energy of this small bronze is a gauge of how much Roman artists owed the great masters of the Hellenistic period. Vivacity and mastery of volume and space are some of this work's exceptional qualities, and the theme, a wrestler in the heat of action, must have captivated clients fascinated by such lively little slices of life.

182 *Old Woman Crouching*

2nd century
Vase, bronze. H. 9.2 cm
Vichy. Acquired in 1895
Br 2936

This pathetic huddled figure of an old woman, her wrinkled face tense with suffering, is a direct descendent of the style developed at Alexandria, where there emerged a taste for the strange, deformed, grotesque and bizarre – a vein which Roman sculptors must have had in mind when they in turn began producing statuettes with the same exaggerated dramatic effects.

183 *Bacchus and Pan*

Second half of the 2nd century
Figure group, bronze inlaid with silver. H. 18.7 cm
Augst (Switzerland). Acquired in 1865
Br 1061

184 *Aphrodite as Universal Divinity*

Roman period
Statuette, bronze. H. 20 cm
From Amrit (Syria). Acquired in 1868
Br 4425

185 *Cup with skeletons*

Boscoreale, near Pompeii
1st century
Silver-gilt. H. 10.4 cm
Boscoreale Treasure. Rothschild Donation, 1895
Bj 1923

186 *Cup*

Boscoreale
Late 1st century BC
Partially gilded silver. Ø 22.5 cm
Boscoreale Treasure. Rothschild Donation, 1895
Bj 1969

The Pompeian villas

The villas of Pompeii have left us a vivid testimony to the luxury in which rich Romans lived in the 1st century BC. The small cities of Pompeii, Boscoreale, Herculaneum and Stabiae, buried when Vesuvius erupted in AD 79, bear witness to their particularly refined lifestyle. The frescoes unearthed at Pompeii are all the more valuable in that virtually none of the great painting of classical Greece has survived. Art historians are constantly re-evaluating their freshness and stylistic variety with each new discovery. Admittedly, most compositions reuse formulas invented several centuries earlier by Greek artists. The genius of the Pompeian painters is to be seen more in their delicate little pictures of flowers, fruits and animals. Other artists produced imaginary landscapes that have all the grace of Chinese wash drawings or Japanese prints. The 'fourth' style, as it has been classified by archaeologists, takes the viewer into imaginary architectures peopled with fantastic beings. But the Pompeian villas were not adorned solely with mosaics and frescoes. They have also yielded thousands of pieces of furniture and tableware of extraordinary beauty. The Boscoreale Treasure revealed an epicurean vein, as illustrated by this cup decorated with skeletons.

187 *Calliope*

Pompeii, villa of Julia Felix
Between 62 and 79
Fresco. 46 x 36 cm
Gift of Ferdinand IV, King of Naples, 1802
P. 4

This magnificent panel perfectly illustrates the philhellenic manner so popular with the Pompeian elite. Calliope, Muse of epic poetry, is recognisable by the scroll in her hands and the inscription mentioning her name on the edge of the small pedestal.

188 *The Judgement of Paris*

Antioch (Turkey), 'House of the Atrium'
Shortly after 115
Mosaic, marble, limestone and glass paste.
1.86 x 1.86 m
Acquired in 1936
Ma 3443

190 *Preparations for a Banquet*

Carthage (Tunisia)
*c.*180
Mosaic, marble and glass paste. 2.25 x 2.40 m
Acquired in 1891
Ma 1796

191 *Phoenix on a ground of Roses*

Daphne (Turkey)
Late 5th century
Mosaic, marble and limestone. 6 x 4.25 m
Acquired in 1936
Ma 3442

From Augustus' time, the most luxurious residences had decorative floors playing on the contrast of black motifs on a white ground. It was during the reigns of Trajan and Hadrian that often very large mosaics of men and animals began to be incorporated into their design. Provincial schools emerged, as illustrated by these polychrome floors from the Orient and North Africa harmoniously combining mythological and exotic scenes.

189 *Hunting Scenes*

Daphne (Turkey), 'Constantinian Villa'
*c.*325
Mosaic, marble, limestone and glass paste.
8.07 x 8.04 m
Acquired in 1939
Ma 3444

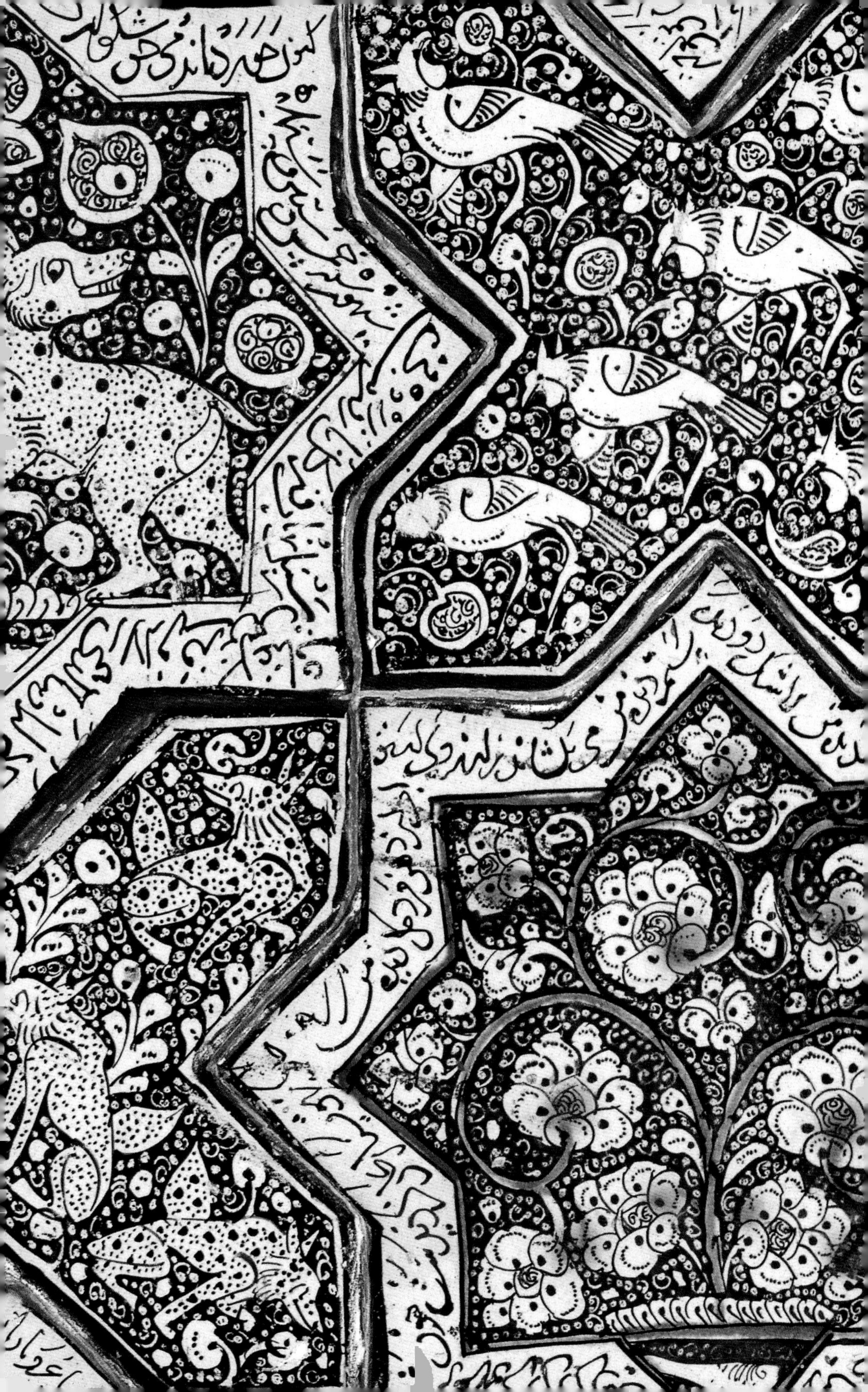

Arts of Islam

The creation in 2003 of the department of Islamic Arts – the Louvre's eighth department – marked the culmination of a long story that had begun in the second half of the 19th century, at a time when museums were first showing an interest in the art of the Muslim world. The museum's first Islamic section was established in 1890, at the instigation of two curators of the Department of Objets d'Art, Emile Molinier and Gaston Ligeon, whose decision was prompted notably by the major donation by Charles Sauvageot in 1856. The next stage came fifteen years later, in 1905, with the inauguration of the first room of 'Muslim Art'. The Baronness Alphonse Delort de Gléon Bequest enabled the opening of a second series of rooms after the First World War, in 1922. The baronness added to this gift of the large collection ammassed by her husband in Egypt and the Near East a large sum of money. In 1945, following the creation of the Objets d'Art and Asian Arts sections, the Islamic arts were incorporated into the Oriental Antiquities department until 2003.

The enrichment of the Louvre's collections over the ensuing decades with exceptional acquisitions and above all by generous donations created a pressing need for more exhibition space. In 1993, this need was partially satisfied by the opening in the Richelieu Wing of rooms for the presentation of a larger array of works. However, of the ten thousand pieces in the Louvre's Islamic Arts collection, only around three hundred were on public exhibit. The aim of the new Department of Islamic Arts, enriched with objects from other national collections, notably from the substantial Musée des Arts Décoratifs collections and the loan from the Musée du Quai de Branly, was to redeploy these collections and cover the particularly vast cultural realm of Islamic civilisation, whilst providing a measure of its chronological scope.

THE WORKS SHOWN IN THE FOLLOWING PAGES give an overview of the Islamic treasures in the Louvre. For instance, from the fine collection of metalwork pieces from Khurasan, Egypt and elsewhere, the *Baptistère de Saint Louis* [200], part of the treasury of the Sainte-Chapelle du Château de Vincennes. The wealth of ceramics from the most diverse regions and from virtually all periods – the most ancient come from excavations at Susa – is illustrated by an Abbasid *Bowl* [193] and the *Peacock Plate* [202], a magnificent example of the production at Iznik. Glassware, textiles and sculpted ivory and wood are also illustrated, as are the bibliographic arts, whose central role in Islamic tradition is widely known. This selection of works provides a varied geographical and historical panorama of the flourishing civilisations which have fired Western imagination for many a century.

The beginnings of Islamic art: 7th–10th century

The death of the prophet Mohammed in 632 marked the beginning of the lightning conquest of territories previously occupied by Byzantium and the Sassanids. Ten years later the Arabs reigned over Syria, Egypt, Iran and Mesopotamia, and by the beginning of the 8th century, Islam's uninterrupted territorial expansion had extended to western North Africa and into Spain and, to the east, into Central Asia and India. It was therefore a truly vast empire that the first Muslim dynasty, the Umayyads (661–750), had to master and administrate.

Coming from a region with no real artistic tradition, these first Arab conquerors initially contented themselves with borrowing those of the countries they invaded and using their techniques and decorative vocabulary. But they soon laid the foundations of a specific art forbidding the representation of God – an attitude akin to that of the Byzantine iconoclasts and the Judaic tradition – and, in the religious context in general, any representation of man and animals. Although there were notable local exceptions to the latter principle in Iran, India and Turkey, for example, the unity of Islamic art in space and time indeed manifests itself in primarily abstract ornamentation. Three essential categories illustrate this aspect: geometrical decoration, the interplay of straight lines, angles and segments; floral and vegetable decoration, drawing its motifs from nature and whose stylisation gave rise to the arabesque; and finally calligraphy, which elevated writing to the rank of a major art of Islamic civilisations.

From Islam's beginnings, works of authentic originality were produced in the Near East. Ceramics, notably, flourished under the Abbasids (8th–10th centuries), with the development of radically new techniques (*Bowl*, 193), whereas wood sculpture and marquetry developed especially in Egypt, notably under the Tulunids in the late 9th century (*Panel with stylised bird*, 192).

192 *Panel with stylised bird*

Egypt
Late 9th century
Wood (Aleppo pine), sculpted decoration
H. 73 cm
Daniel Fouquet Donation, 1892–93
OA 6023

This fragment of a sculpted panel, carved with the graceful outline of a long-necked bird surrounded by curvilinear motifs and flowerets, was probably part of a window shutter. Its matching piece is today in the Museum of Islamic Art in Cairo. The Tulunid Dynasty, Turkish in origin, which reigned over Egypt for some fifty years in the late 9th century, left a lasting mark on the art of this country. The wood pieces, notably, reveal the influence of the art of Samarra, combined with local Coptic traditions.

193 *Bowl*

Iraq
9th century
Clay ceramic, polychrome lustre decoration on opaque glaze
H. 6.3 cm, Ø 22.3 cm
Charles Vignier Collection. Acquired in 1931
OA 8179

The metal lustre process, a major innovation that appeared in the 9th century, spread throughout much of the Islamic world and into Spain. Potters had the idea of painting decoration on a pre-fired paste and glaze using metallic oxides of copper and silver. An additional firing, under complex conditions that produced a chemical reaction, enabled the thin film of tiny metallic particles to become part of the glaze. Potters were thus able to obtain decoration which shimmers when the lustre is well-preserved. Two types of decoration were used successively at the beginning of the Abbasid period, polychrome lustre, of which this bowl with its characteristic brown and yellow tones is a fine example, and monochrome lustre. Plant motifs were frequent during this period, sometimes combined with geometric designs.

The Western Muslims: 8th–15th century

The break-up of the Abbasid Empire in the 10th century had been foreshadowed in Spain as early as 756, when Abd al-Rahman I founded an independent Umayyad emirate with Cordoba as its capital. Almost two centuries later, in 929, the dynasty's greatest sovereign, Abd al-Rahman III, established the distant province of Al-Andalus as a powerful caliphate and resolute rival of Baghdad whose power extended into northern Morocco and the central Maghreb. It was during this period, considered its golden age, that the Western Muslim world developed its own particularly brilliant artistic and intellectual life.

But this era of stability was short-lived: the beginning of the 11th century ushered in a period of discord, one which would culminate in the fall of the caliphate in 1031 and the splitting up of its power among numerous small courts governed by minor Muslim rulers, the *Reinos de Taifas*. Over the centuries, the small, fragile princely courts established at Seville, Toledo and Saragossa succumbed to the advances of the Christian armies. After an energetic attempt at reunifying the Berber Almoravid and then Almohad dynasties, the last Islamic kingdom, that of the Nasrids of Grenada, finally fell in 1492 after the city was besieged by the Catholic kings, and with the fall of Grenada, celebrated for a long time with nostalgia, disappeared a culture of great refinement.

The brilliance of the Umayyad civilisation, manifest in its architecture (*Capital bearing the name of the caliph Al-Hakam II*, 195), expressed itself with equal pomp in the courtly arts practiced in the capital and the residence of the caliph. Although there are few traces of the woodworking arts and ceramics, the sculpted ivory boxes and caskets that have survived attest to the importance of the princely workshops (*Lidded box of Al-Mughira*, 194). Bronze working still flourished in the 12th and 13th centuries, as shown by the famous *Lion with an articulated tail* [196], entirely covered with delicate engraving.

194 *Lidded box of Al-Mughira*

Spain, Madinat al-Zahra, 968
Sculpted and engraved ivory
H. 15 cm
Formerly in the Riano Collection, acquired in 1898
OA 4068

The inscription around the base of the domed lid mentions the name of Al-Mughira, son of the great caliph Abd al-Rahman III, and the date 968. This is proof enough of the origin of this small box made in the court workshops that were very active during the caliphate of Cordoba. Carved from a single section of elephant tusk, it is covered with luxuriant decoration with, on the body, four medallions showing lions killing bovids, enthroned figures accompanied by a musician, the collecting of falcon's eggs, and hunters under a palm tree with leopards. This series of complex images refutes the idea that this was simply an illustration of the pleasures of the prince.

195 *Capital bearing the name of the caliph Al-Hakam II*

Spain, Cordoba
Late 10th century
Marble, sculpted decoration
H. 31; Ø base 21 cm
Acquired in 1900
OA 5022

Derived from the Corinthian order, this capital with very detailed foliated decoration is highly representative of the art which developed under the Umayyad caliphate in Spain. The thin epigraphic band crowning it bears the name of Caliph al-Hakam II, who built a major extension to the Great Mosque of Cordoba. He also commissioned the construction of several pavilions in the caliph's residence at Madinat al-Zahra, founded by his father Abd al-Rahman III. This capital, however, is from the Alcazar in Cordoba.

196 *Lion with an articulated tail*

Spain
12th–13th century
Bronze cast, engraved decoration
30 x 54 cm
Mme Louis Stern Bequest, 1926
OA 7883

The Iranian world, 9th–14th century

Conquered during the first decades of the Muslim expansion, Iran was one of the first territories to be emancipated from central power. From the 9th century onwards, several dynasties succeeded one another in Khurasan and Transoxiana, the most famous being that of the Sassanids (875–1005). Considered by Arab historians as the paragon of 'good government', their power was based on rigorous administration and ensured the region a lasting prosperity, which fostered a veritable cultural renaissance. Textiles, with a tradition inherited from the great civilisations of the past (*Saint Josse's Shroud*, Louvre), and also ceramics bear witness to the burgeoning of the courtly arts. Among the famous wares of the potters of the period are large white dishes decorated with elegant inscriptions, of which the Louvre has an example, as well as other objects whose polychrome decoration, often vegetable in inspiration, is painted using coloured slips.

Dominated by the Saljuq Turks from the mid-11th century, Iran (as well as Iraq and part of Syria) not only maintained its artistic activities but appens to have experienced an exceptional creative burgeoning. Again, ceramics illustrate this phenomenon, in the use of siliceous pastes, which potters sometimes mixed with crushed frit to obtain what later become known in the West as soft-paste porcelain. Certain types of crockery, whose delicate tints were obtained by the so-called 'low-fire' process (*Plate*, 199), have lustred decoration, sometimes borrowed from the bibliographic arts.

In the 13th century, the western Muslim world was shaken by the sudden conquest of the Mongols led by Ghengis Khan, who gave Iran to his grandson Hulagu. His Islamised descendents allowed their empire to disintegrate, to the profit of local dynasties, who nevertheless maintained the tradition of courtly arts. In the late 14th century, a new invasion, led by Timur the Lame (Tamerlane), would profoundly modify the Iranian world and give its creativity new impetus (*Candlestick*, 197).

197 *Candlestick bearing the name of Tamerlane*

Iran or central Asia
1396–97
Bronze cast, engraved decoration, inlaid with gold and silver
H. 56 cm
Georges Marteau Bequest, 1916
OA 7079, OA 7080

The gold-inlaid candle ring of this two-piece candlestick bears the name of Tamerlane. At Samarkand, his capital, but also at Bukhara and Herat, this sumptuous sovereign helped bring about the birth of the brilliant Timurid civilisation. This candlestick is one of a monumental set he commissioned for the shrine of the mystic Ahmad Yasavi, in present-day Kazakhstan. Four others are still kept in the shrine.

198 *Tiled panel*

Iran, Kachan
Second half of the 13th century
Siliceous ceramic, lustred decoration on opacified glaze, coloured highlights
78 x 49 cm
Charles Piet-Lataudrie Bequest, 1909
OA 6319

The decorative motifs of these tiles, drawn from the vegetable and animal world, are complemented with figures seated on the banks of the primordial pond, with the whole illustrating the ancient Iranian theme of the cycle of nature. There is also an extraordinary fauna of birds, hares, jackals and antelopes. One of the stars bears the astrological sign of the Lion, associated with the Sun, which would become the national emblem of Iran several centuries later. The texts, poetic or religious in inspiration, feature a date, 1267, written in figures and letters. This set of tiles comes from a mausoleum at Khurasan, where recent restoration work has revealed the rest of the panel.

199 *Plate*

Iran
Late 12th–early 13th century
Siliceous ceramic, low-fired 'Minai or 'Haft Rang' decoration and lustred decoration on opacified glaze, gold highlights.
H. 6.5, Ø 22 cm
Acquired in 1970
MAO 440

The hunt, a recurrent subject in the pictorial repertoire of the Muslim world, is evoked here by the depiction of a horseman with a falcon on his fist. The princely status of the figure is manifest in his costume and the horse's elaborate harness. The small mouth, elongated eyes, joined eyebrows and broad forehead, classical canons of the period, are partially inspired by Arab and Persian poetry. Apart from its aesthetic qualities, the singularity of this plate consists in its decoration being both metal-lustred and low-fired and heightened with gold. Iranian potters developed particularly skilled techniques such as these in the 12th century, well before Europe.

Egypt, the Near East, Anatolia: 13th–16th century

The Saljuq Turks' entry into Baghdad in 1055 marked the end of the so-called 'classic' period of the Islamic empire and coincided with the beginning of a particularly complex period of Near Eastern history. Before the weakness of the Fatimid rulers, certain governors soon claimed their independence. Salah al-Din (1138–1193) – the famous Saladin of the Crusades – founded the Ayyubid dynasty, overthrown in 1250 by the Mamluks. These former Turkish slaves efficiently subjugated Egypt, Syria and part of Arabia, until their defeat by the Ottomans in 1517. Their rule had its apogee in the 13th and 14th centuries. Great builders, they developed and embellished their capital, Cairo, and gave rise to an original and powerful art. Their ceramics are decorated with coats of arms and calligraphy with high upstrokes, as were their metalwork and glass pieces. Syria, an important centre for enamelled and gilt glass production, exported large quantities of bottles and lamps for grand buildings (*Bottle bearing the arms of Tuquztimur*, 203; *Mosque lamp*, 201). The Mamluk period was also the era in which metalworking attained its highest technical perfection (*Basin known as the 'Baptistère de Saint Louis'*, 200).

In the 16th century, the political configuration of the Near East was totally modified. Since the fall of Byzantium in 1453, a series of victories had enabled the Ottomans to exert their power over a vast territory stretching from Vienna to the banks of the Nile and from the Euphrates to the borders of Morocco. The capital, Constantinople, rivalled with the fallen Byzantium and from one end of the empire to the other, a fruitful artistic competition developed. Certain centres became famous. The ceramicists of Iznik (ancient Nicaea) achieved pinnacles of savoir-faire (*Peacock plate*, 202), Bursa was renowned for its fabrics and Ushak for its carpets. At court, silversmiths and jewellers chased precious objects, and in the workshops of painters, often Persian in origin, the main stylistic tendencies were forged. In certain miniatures depicting these workshops there are small tables in every way comparable to the one in the Louvre (*Scribe's table*, 204).

200 *Basin* known as the *'Baptistère de Saint Louis'*

Signed Muhammad ibn al-Zayn
Syria or Egypt
*c.*1320–1340
Beaten brass, engraved decoration, inlaid with chased silver and gold; black paste.
H. 23.2, Ø 50.5 cm
Formerly in the treasury of the Sainte-Chapelle du Château de Vincennes
Entered the Musée Royal in 1832
LP 16

This large basin was formerly in the collection of the French Crown – hence the presence of the arms of France on the inside – and was used as a font for the baptisms of Louis XIII and the son of Napoleon III. It could not, on the other hand, have been used for the baptism of Saint Louis – after whom it was named – since the object was not created until fifty years later. On the outside, four medallions depicting princes on horseback interrupt a cortege of figures including a falconer, a man holding a leopard on a leash, and the Master of the Royal Wardrobe. The inside is decorated with hunting and combat scenes. This masterpiece of Mamluk art was made from a single sheet of brass, inlaid with silver and gold. It is signed six times.

201 *Mosque lamp with lotus decoration*

Syria or Egypt
Mid-14th century
Blown glass with enamel and gilt decoration
H. 27 cm
Baron Charles Davillier Bequest, 1885
OA 3110 bis

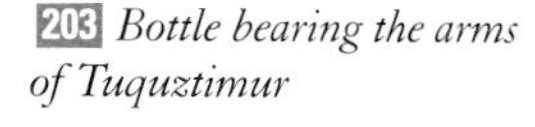

203 *Bottle bearing the arms of Tuquztimur*

Syria or Egypt
First half of the 14th century
Enamelled and gilt glass
H. 50.5 cm
Spitzer Collection. Acquired in 1893
OA 3365

The inscription on the bottle's belly was written with the tall upstrokes typical of the Mamluk period. It is interrupted by a medallion bearing the arms of Tuquztimur, cupbearer of Sultan Nasir al-Din Mohammed, who later became viceroy of Syria, a white eagle over a cup. A phoenix with spread wings surrounds the base of the bottle's neck, with delicate floral motifs completing the decoration. Enamelled and gilt decoration, often dominantly blue, was particularly fashionable under the Mamluks.

202 *Peacock plate*

Turkey, Iznik
2nd quarter of the 16th century
Siliceous ceramic, decoration painted over slip and transparent underglaze
H. 8; Ø 37.5 cm
Raymond Koechlin Bequest, 1932
K 3449

The activity of the potters of Iznik began as soon as the Ottoman empire was founded in the 13th century and flourished during the reign of Suleyman the Magnificent (1520–1566). The principal colour used was cobalt blue, enriched during the second half of the 16th century by grey mauve and lime green. This was the colour used for this plate's central motif, a large stylised flower with scaly petals, beneath which is a peacock. Around it are large dentated leaves and blooming flowers, with Chinese-inspired clouds around the rim. The decoration is typical of the *saz* style developed in the 1520s and 1530s in the imperial workshops of Istanbul, in which one can see central Asian influences that had reached the banks of the Bosporus via Iran.

204 *Scribe's table*

Turkey, late 16th–early 17th century
Inlaid wood, mother-of-pearl, tortoiseshell on gilt paper, rosewood, ebony, tin
32 x 66 x 37 cm
Acquired in 1992
MAO 871

205 *Kilim with historiated scenes*

Iran, Kashan
Late 16th–early 17th century
Silk and silver thread, tapestry
2.49 x 1.39 m
Félix Doisteau Donation, 1904
OA 5946

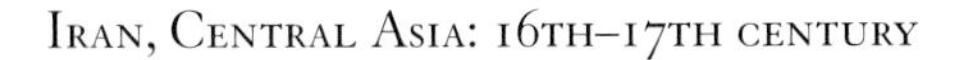

Iran, Central Asia: 16th–17th century

The devastation perpetrated by the Mongols in the 13th century long time eclipsed the brilliant achievements of their reign. By founding his empire and dynasty in the heart of Iran, Hulagu drew the frontiers for a territory which would develop its own original civilisation over the ensuing centuries. After the Timurids, descendents of Tamerlane, it was the Safavids who seized power in 1501. They established Shiism as the official religion and maintained a political stability which led them to be considered the founders of modern Iran.

The most outstanding figure of this dynasty was Shah Abbas I (1587–1629), who succeeded in repulsing the Ottomans and forging a long period of prosperity that facilitated trade relations with Europe. A great builder, he embellished his royal town of Ispahan, while the arts of the miniature, textiles, ceramics and precious metalworking underwent a brilliant period of development. Flower-scattered gardens peopled with elegant figures and animals are among the favourite themes and were depicted in all kinds of materials: they embellished mural tiles (*Scene in a Garden*, Louvre) and decorated fine carpets framed with vegetable arabesques, echoing the quatrains sung with consummate refinement by the poets (*Kilim with historiated scenes*, 205).

Thanks to princely patronage, the bibliographic arts flourished, notably in manuscript painting (*Page from an album*, 206). The depiction of epic stories enabled artists to express their sensibility and quest for dramatic intensity. In the 17th century, the vogue shifted to war scenes and portraits (*Portrait of Shah Abbas I*, 207). The influence of Chinese art, and to an even greater degree of relations with the West, explains the evolution of painting, in which modelling and chiaroscuro effects appeared, while the demand for realism grew.

206 *Page from an album*

Nasta'liq calligraphy, signed Mir Ali
Iran, 16th century (calligraphy)
India, c.1650 (margins)
Ink, gouache and gold on paper
Received from Georges Demotte
Georges Marteau Bequest, 1916
OA 7157

207 *Portrait of Shah Abbas I and his page*

Signed Muhammad Qasim
Iran, former Ispahan
12 March 1627
Ink, colour and gold leaf on paper
27.5 x 16.8 cm
Acquired in 1975
MAO 494

Under the Safavids, depictions of sovereigns became more realistic, notably their faces and details of their dress. The ruler depicted in this miniature with floral decoration is Shah Abbas I. He has a drooping moustache and on his shaven head he wears the wide-brimmed conical hat which he had made fashionable. The page at his side is handing him a cup of wine poured from the bottle in his other hand. On the right, beneath the foliage of the tree, the artist has inscribed his name, the portrait's date and a short poem: 'May life bring you all you desire from the three lips, those of your lover, the river and the cup.' The river flowing in the foreground was originally silvered.

Mogul India: 16th–18th century

After reaching northern India in the 8th century, the Arabs were unable to maintain their power over this territory due to lack of forces, and over the ensuing decades the region broke up into numerous autonomous states. For the next three centuries, successive dynasties reigned in the Muslim sultanate of Delhi until the advent of Prince Babur in 1526. A descendant of Genghis Khan and Timur and heir to the kingdom of Samarkand, Babur dreamed of reconstituting the ephemeral Mogul empire and extended his domination to Afghanistan and the Punjab. Although he never achieved this, he did found the Mogul empire, stamping it with his rich personality and leaving us an autobiography revealing both his conquering spirit and thirst for knowledge. During the reign of Akbar, a grandson worthy of his succession, Islam developed alongside other religions. A remarkable administrator, integrated Afghans and Persians into the local elites, forging a new Mogul civilisation out of this conjunction of cultures. During his reign and those of his successors Jahangir and Shah Jahan (1582–1666), towns were enriched with elegant edifices (Shah Jahan built the Taj Mahal at Agra), while the court arts blossomed, supported by the imperial manufactories, which were run by Iranians. At its apogee, Mogul art distinguished itself by its harmonious synthesis of Indian and Iranian influences and by a marked taste for realist figuration. The pieces from Mogul India in the Louvre – a carpet, metal objects, weapons and miniatures – also reflect the omnipresence of more or less stylised floral motifs. The blown glass *Hookah* [209] is decorated with graceful poppies, while the handle of the *Horse-head dagger* [208] is inlaid with a flower of admirable finesse.

208 *Horse-head dagger*

India, 17th century
Blade: steel, decoration inlaid with gold
Handle: jade, sculpted decoration inlaid with gold and semiprecious stones
L. 50.5 cm
Salomon de Rothschild Collection. Acquired in 1927
R. 890 (ex OA 7891)

This elegantly curved dagger has a damascened steel blade and a jade handle delicately inlaid with precious stones. But the beauty of this ceremonial weapon lies above all in the extraordinary expressive power of the horse's head: mouth half open, nostrils flared, it seems to be rearing. Jade, a costly material greatly appreciated at the Mogul court, was also used for jewellery and caskets.

209 *Hookah*

India, 18th century
Blown glass, enamel and gilt decoration
H. 16 cm
Acquired in 1985
MAO 739

India, the word *hookah* designates the water pipes that are elsewhere called narghileh. Much used in the Islamic world and made from a variety of materials, they take different forms depending on the country. In India, they have a single orifice, like this one in enamelled and gilt glass. Again the favourite motif of the Mogul artists, flowers, is well in evidence, in this case poppies, depicted with extraordinary realism.

Paintings

The most universally known painting in the Louvre, the *Mona Lisa* or *La Gioconda* was purchased by Francis I during Leonardo da Vinci's lifetime or shortly after the artist's death at Amboise in 1519. This treasure was one of the ensemble of masterpieces bought by this enlightened monarch in the early 16th century which formed the original core of the royal collection. Enriched by subsequent kings, during the Revolution it became the property of the nation, eventually constituting the Louvre's Department of Paintings. Constantly added to over the last two centuries, the department now has over 6,000 works dating from the late 13th century to the early 19th century.

Francis I's acquisitions were mainly Italian but his successors had more eclectic tastes. Henry IV, Marie de Médicis and Louis XIII commissioned pictures from artists of European renown such as Rubens, Vouet and Poussin, to whom they entrusted the decoration of their palaces and whose masterpieces are today in the Louvre. But the most spectacular enrichment of the royal collections took place under Louis XIV, during whose reign some 1,500 paintings were acquired, many by the greatest French painters of the time, Poussin, Le Brun and Claude Lorraine. In the 18th century, acquisitions grew scarcer until Louis XVI appointed the Count d'Angiviller as his Superintendent of Buildings. With his mind set on creating a 'muséum', and pursuing a curator's policy in the fullest modern sense of the term, he commissioned pictures and sought others to fill gaps in the collections.

The Fall of the Ancien Régime ushered in a prosperous period for the Louvre collection. The Muséum Central des Arts', as it was now called, housed pictures confiscated from churches, monasteries and the homes of the émigrés. Under the Empire these were joined by the spoils of the Napoleonic conquests, prestigious works confiscated all over Europe, a hundred of which remain in the Louvre. The enrichment of the national collection continued, although in a less spectacular manner, with judicious acquisitions and donations (the major La Case Bequest in 1869), and thanks to the exemplary efforts of the Société des Amis du Louvre, founded in 1897. More recently, the law authorising payment of inheritance tax with works of art has enabled further contributions.

Around two thirds of the pictures in the Louvre are French, followed by the Italian and Flemish schools respectively, a proportionality naturally reflecting France's art history and geographical proximity. From the outset, however, the Louvre asserted its encyclopaedic vocation, and its Hispanic, Germanic and Scandinavian collections have also been regularly enriched. Organised into national schools in 1794, the Department of Paintings today reflects every facet of European artistic culture.

France

The French Primitives – 14th–15th century

The first masters of French painting were discovered only relatively recently because until the second half of the 19th century art historians had taken little interest in their works, hitherto often neglected or attributed to foreign schools. This belated recognition was partially due to the rarity of pre-16th-century French pictures, above all the result of the iconoclastic manifestations of the Wars of Religion and compounded two centuries later by the ravages of the French Revolution. The Louvre is the museum with the finest and most coherent ensemble of paintings from this period.
With the exception of Jean Clouet's *Portrait of Francis I* [222], the entry of the French Primitives into the national collections began during the reign of Louis-Philippe (1830–48). Jean Fouquet's *Portrait of Guillaume Jouvenel des Ursins* [214] was bought in 1835 and his *Portrait of Charles VII* [215] three years later. The second picture was then considered a 'Greek work', such was the misappreciation of its value. Louis-Philippe acquired it solely on documentary grounds, for the history gallery he was compiling at Versailles.
Several decades later, however, the enrichment of the museum's collection of medieval paintings became, on the contrary, a major preoccupation. The Louvre's curators sought to acquire works either by purchase or through gifts, the most noteworthy being Henri Bellechose's *Saint-Denis Altarpiece* [212], donated by one of them, Frédéric Reiset, in 1863. The major acquisitions begun in 1864 with Jean Malouel's *Large Round Pietà* [211], were complemented after the exhibition devoted to the French Primitives in 1904 by the *Boulbon Altarpiece* and Jean Hey's *Portrait Presumed to be of Madeleine of Burgundy* [218], and the *Crucifixion for the Parlement de Paris* [213] was returned to the Louvre by the Court of Appeal. The efforts of the Société des Amis du Louvre enabled the acquisition of an absolute masterpiece, *The Villeneuve-lès-Avignon Pietà* by Enguerrand Quarton [216]. More recently, gaps in the collection were filled by pictures by painters such as Nicolas Dipre and Jean de Baumetz, hitherto absent or represented only by minor works. Josse Lieferinxe's *Calvary* [217] was acquired in 1962.

210 School of Paris
Mid-14th century
Portrait of John the Good
*c.*1350
Wood. 60 x 44.5 cm
On loan from the Bibliothèque Nationale de France, 1925. RF 2490

This anonymous work is the oldest surviving French easel painting and also the earliest known individual portrait in Europe. Despite portraying his subject in profile, the painter has succeeded in giving his subject a profoundly human trueness to life. As proclaimed by the inscription above his head, the man portrayed is John the Good (1319–1404), second king of the house of Valois. His reign during the Hundred Years War was fraught with difficulties. Defeated and taken prisoner by the English at the battle of Poitiers in 1356, he spent his captivity in London, where he signed a treaty relinquishing the French crown – a hapless fate never to be forgotten since no subsequent French king bore his name.

211 Jean Malouel

Before 1370–1415

Large Round Pietà

c.1400
Wood. Ø 64 cm
Acquired in 1864. MI 692

The term pietà generally denotes a depiction of the grieving Virgin Mary supporting the dead Christ after the descent from the Cross. The pictorial composition of this picture has sometimes been associated with the 'Throne of Grace' or 'Trinity Pietà' category, that is, a representation of the Holy Trinity in which God the Father is shown holding his Son in front of him, with the dove of the Holy Spirit in flight between them. There were many variations on this new formula, which probably originated in France. From the late 14th century, the body of Christ rests on the knees of God the Father, whose grief is thus more poignantly conveyed.

This picture is attributed to Jean Malouel, a painter of Flemish origin employed by Philip the Bold (1342–1404), Duke of Burgundy, to decorate the Carthusian monastery he founded at Champmol near Dijon in 1383. Malouel succeeded Jean de Beaumetz as court painter to the dukes of Burgundy and was himself succeeded by Henri Bellechose [212]. The subtle modelling of Christ's anatomy, the elegance of his hands and the refinement of the picture's execution are indicative of the stylistic affectation then in vogue in the European courts.

212 Henri Bellechose

Known from 1415, died *c.*1440/44

The Saint-Denis Altarpiece

1416
Wood transferred to canvas. 1.62 x 2.11 m
From the Chartreuse de Champmol.
Gift of Frédéric Reiset, 1863. MI 674

Probably like the *Large Round Pietà* [211], this altarpiece was painted for the Carthusian monastery at Champmol in the Duchy of Burgundy, a flourishing artistic centre in the late 14th and early 15th century. Henri Bellechose, a painter of Flemish origin, was appointed court painter to John the Fearless after Jean Malouel's death (1415). This work is generally attributed to him.
To the left of the Cross, Saint Denis, first Bishop of Paris and martyr, is receiving the last communion from the hand of Christ. On the right, we see the executioner about to behead him, the fate also of his two companions, the priest Eleutherius and the deacon Rusticus.

213 Master of Dreux Budé (André d'Ypres?)

Mentioned in Tournai 1428–1450

Crucifixion for the Parlement de Paris

*c.*1449
Wood. 2.26 x 2.70 m
Seized during the Revolution. RF 2065

Although at first sight its pictorial composition and three-part structure are akin to an altarpiece, this picture was not painted for a church but for a court of justice, the Great Chamber of the Parlement de Paris in the Palais de la Cité, where the work remained until the 18th century. The figures on either side of Christ are the patron saints of the French monarchy. On the left, Saint John the Baptist and Saint Louis, whose features, according to numerous commentators, are those of Charles VII; on the right, Saint Denis, the first Bishop of Paris, next to the emperor Charlemagne, patron of the kingdom of France and the Crown. Recognisable in the landscape at the top on the left are the Palais de la Cité, seat of the French Parliament, and in the foreground, further away beyond the stretch of water, the outline of the Louvre, the fortified château which Charles V had transformed into a sumptuous royal residence.
The picture is by a painter conventionally known as 'Master of Dreux Budé', who is generally identified as the Amiens-based painter André d'Ypres. After training in Tournai, where there is mention of him in 1428, he seems to have established himself in Paris in the mid-1440s.

Jean Fouquet

The 15th century saw the development throughout Europe of the art of the individual portrait, a genre brilliantly dominated in France by Jean Fouquet. We unfortunately still know very little about the life of this exceptional painter, the earliest French Renaissance artist. Born in Tours around 1420, he appears to have gone to Italy in the 1440s, where his presence is attested by an account written by the Florentine architect Filarete. Filarete reveals that Fouquet, whom he describes as a good master, 'above all in drawing from nature', painted the portrait of Pope Eugene IV, a work no longer in existence but known from engravings. Although the length and circumstances of the young painter's stay in Italy are unclear, he seems to have frequented famous artists, notably Fra Angelico, from whom he learned the mastery of three-dimensional space and geometric perspective. On the other hand, it was due to his early contact with the art of the great Flemish masters that he owes his mastery of the three-quarter portrait, whereas Italian artists would continue for a long time to represent their models in profile.

The two ceremonial paintings of *Charles VII* [215] and *Guillaume Jouvenel des Ursins* [214] give a measure of Fouquet's illustrious clientele and also, like most of his works, illustrate his remarkable talents as a portraitist. The Louvre has a priceless enamelled gold medallion on which the artist portrayed himself, the first known self-portrait by a French painter.

Fouquet was also a painter of religions subjects (the *Virgin and Child Surrounded by Angels* in Antwerp, with its strange colours, is a universally known example), and he executed a considerable number of illuminated manuscripts, sometimes aided by his studio. Despite their small format, these miniatures are true paintings in their own right, showing Fouquet's consummate mastery of perspective and masterly sense of colour.

214 Jean Fouquet
c.1415/20–1477/81
Portrait of Guillaume Jouvenel des Ursins
c.1460
Wood. 93 x 73 cm
Acquired in 1835. INV. 9619

The eminent dignitary portrayed by Fouquet is Guillaume Jouvenel des Ursins (1401–1472), who was appointed Chancellor of France by Charles VII and remained so under Louis XI. His luxurious clothes, the sumptuous moneybag hanging at his hip and the elaborate gilt architectural decor with coats of arms are clearly intended to emphasise the model's social status rather than his personality. The picture inaugurated a new type of portrait, that of the individual representing a social class, which would later gain great favour. Jouvenel des Ursins' praying pose has suggested the existence of another panel representing a devotional subject, most probably a Virgin and Child, and possibly even a third panel portraying the Chancellor's wife.

215 Jean Fouquet

*c.*1415/20–1477/81

Portrait of Charles VII

*c.*1450
Wood. 86 x 71 cm
Acquired in 1838. INV. 9106

Fouquet's model here is Charles VII (1403–1461), whose name is inscribed on the painting's original frame, which has fortunately survived. The monarch who rid France of English occupation, and beside whom Joan of Arc stood when he was crowned at Reims, is hailed as the 'très victorieux roy de France'.
The model's frontal pose, accentuated by the padded shoulders fashionable in the mid-15th century, and the framing of the subject in a confined space give this portrait extraordinary monumentality.

From Provence to the Loire – 15th century

The city of Avignon, residence of the papal court from 1316 until the end of the Great Western Schism (1417), became a centre of extraordinary creativity from the 14th century on owing to the presence of Italian artists summoned there by the popes. The Siennese painter Simone Martini arrived around 1336 followed, seven years later, by Matteo Giovanetti. The decoration of churches, the residences of the cardinals and the Palais des Papes were stimulating tasks for these artists, who were active as far afield as Aix and Marseille.

Thanks to the large clientele of churchmen, princes and rich merchants, Provence was a prosperous place for painters throughout the 15th century. The artists were of numerous different origins but many had fled the Northern countries because of political and religious conflicts. The blend of cultures and the Flemish influence combined with the Southern painter's acute sensitivity to light gave rise to a specific movement known as the 'School of Avignon', characterised by rigorous forms and compositions, and simplified volumes emphasised by bold light effects and an uncluttered atmosphere.

The Louvre has several of this Southern school's major pictures: the *Boulbon Altarpiece*, and above all the famous *Villeneuve-lès-Avignon Pietà* [216]. This undisputed masterpiece is attributed to Enguerrand Quarton, born in Laon and active in Provence from 1444 to 1466 and considered school's most representative artist. The School of Avignon's final flourish came at the end of the century with Josse Lieferinxe, another painter who came from the Northern tradition, represented here by a magnificent *Calvary* [217].

French art benefited from another flourishing centre, the court of the dukes of Burgundy, whose proved themselves to be active patrons. Philip the Bold and his successor John the Fearless employed remarkable artists, often from the North, such as Jean Malouel [211]. In the late 15th century, the courts of the dukes of Bourbon employed the painter known as the Master of Moulins, today thought to be the Dutch painter Jean Hey, whose works are characterised by their extreme refinement (*Portrait Presumed to be of Madeleine of Burgundy*, 218; *Portrait of the Dauphin Charles-Orlant*, 219).

216 Enguerrand Quarton

Known in Provence 1444–1466

The Villeneuve-lès-Avignon Pietà

*c.*1455
Wood. 1.63 x 2.18 m
Gift of the Société des Amis du Louvre, 1905. RF 1569

Enguerrand Quarton, probably from Picardy and trained in northern France, is considered the exemplary representative of the School of Avignon. This picture is attributed to the painter owing to its similarities with other works that we know for certain to be by him, notably his famous *Coronation of the Virgin* (Musée Pierre-de-Luxembourg, Villeneuve-lès-Avignon).
In this poignant, severely drawn composition, the donor is portrayed on the left, behind Saint John dressed in canon's robes. His expression is one of profound compassion at the sight of Christ's body and the stigmata of his crucifixion, as that of the Virgin and the saints, poignantly sober. The purpose of themes of devotion inspired by Christ's Passion, very frequent in the pictures of the Late Middle Ages, was to incite the faithful to meditate on their own path to salvation.

I.N.R.I.

217 Josse Lieferinxe

Active 1493–1505/08

Calvary

*c.*1500–1505
Wood. 1.70 x 1.26 m
Acquired in 1962. RF 1962-1

This *Calvary* may have been the central part of an altarpiece. In the clouds in the background, to Christ's right, the artist has depicted the scene from the Apocalypse in which Michael struggles with the fallen angels and the dragon, a combat symbolising redemption through the Cross.
We know little about Josse Lieferinxe other than that he was probably a native of the Hainaut region and that he lived in Marseilles from 1493. He seems to have worked there and in Aix until his death between 1505 and 1508.

218 Jean Hey,
known as the Master of Moulins

Active in central France 1472–c.1504

Portrait Presumed to be of Madeleine of Burgundy

*c.*1490
Wood. 56 x 40 cm
Acquired in 1904. RF 1521

219 Jean Hey,
known as the Master of Moulins

Active in central France 1472–c.1504

The Dauphin Charles-Orlant

1494
Wood. 28 x 23 cm
Carlos de Beistegui Donation. RF 1942-28

The Renaissance – 16th century

The military campaigns of French monarchs in Italy at the turn of the 16th century enabled them to discover an art and culture they would later fervently seek to import or imitate. Charles VIII brought back Italian artists to decorate his château at Amboise and Louis XII did the same, without this having any great impact on contemporary French artistic trends. Francis I in turn invited Italian painters, and great ones at that: Leonardo da Vinci and Andrea del Sarto, whose influence at the time remains little known. The decisive influence of the Italians on French art did not really begin until 1530, when the king enlisted the services of exceptional artists such as Rosso Fiorentino, Francesco Primaticcio, Serlio and Cellini to refurbish his medieval palace at Fontainebleau. The presence of these artists in France for several decades, until around 1570, was of capital importance since it was under their impetus that a new stylistic trend known as the 'School of Fontainebleau' developed through which France joined the great movement of European Mannerism.
A refined, elegant, courtly art gradually imposed itself in architecture, sculpture, decoration, engraving and easel painting. But more than a style, it was the vehicle of a new vision of the world. Religious subjects made way for mythological references and learned allegories, realism was abandoned for the imaginary, and the human body was displayed in all its elegant nudity. These were the new canons espoused by the anonymous painter of *Diana the Huntress* [220], in which a female figure is shown with bow and quiver, attributes of the goddess of hunting, and in another allegorical picture, *Eva Prima Pandora* [221] by Jean Cousin the Elder, a major exponent of the Fontainebleau style considered to be one of the most illustrious figures of the French Renaissance.

220 School of Fontainebleau
Mid-16th century
Diana the Huntress

c. 1550
Oil on canvas. 1.91 x 1.32 m
Acquired in 1840. INV. 445

Elongated anatomy and sinuous poses are two of the stylistic devices adopted by the School of Fontainebleau and that justify it being considered a Mannerist movement. Another of the school's characteristics is the primacy accorded to drawing over colour. The motif of Diana the Huntress, often interpreted as an allusion to King Henry II's liaison with Diane de Poitiers, was in fact widely depicted in the mid-16th century, particularly in sculpture and tapestries. Besides being a pretext for portraying the female nude in a natural setting, the allegory also echoed the reality of a world in which hunting played an essential part.

221 Jean Cousin the Elder

*c.*1490–*c.*1560

Eva Prima Pandora

*c.*1550
Wood. 0.97 x 1.50 m
Gift of the Société des Amis du Louvre, 1906. RF 2073

The female nude here is an allegorical portrayal of the first woman: in Biblical tradition, Eve, in Greek mythology, Pandora. Reclining with one arm resting on a skull and a snake coiled around the other, she holds an apple branch in her right hand while her left hand rests on a vase, a pictorial allusion to the box Pandora opened, inadvertently releasing all the ills that would beset mankind.

Symbols already frequently employed in medieval religious painting changed their frame of reference during the Renaissance. Their coded language now often referred to ancient texts and mythology, and to the new horizons of knowledge being opened up by the humanists, which all cultivated individuals made it their business to assimilate.

222 Attributed to Jean Clouet

1490/95–1540/41

Portrait of Francis I

c.1530
Wood. 96 x 74 cm
Collection of Francis I. INV. 3256

Jean Clouet is first mentioned as painter to Francis I in 1516. Few works have been attributed to him with certainty, but it was definitely Clouet, aided by his son François, who executed the fine series of portrait drawings of members of the great French families in 1536 and 1540 (Musée Condé, Chantilly). Jean and François Clouet are considered to be the greatest French portraitists of the 16th century. In their pictures the precise rendering of the model's features is accompanied by remarkable economy of pictorial means.

223 François Clouet

c.1505/10–1572

Portrait of Pierre Quthe

1562
Wood. 91 x 70 cm
Gift of the Société des Amis du Louvre, 1908. RF 1719

224 Antoine Caron

1521–1599

Augustus and the Tiburtine Sibyl

c.1575–1580
Canvas. 1.25 x 1.70 m
Gift of Gustave Lebel, 1938. RF 1938-101

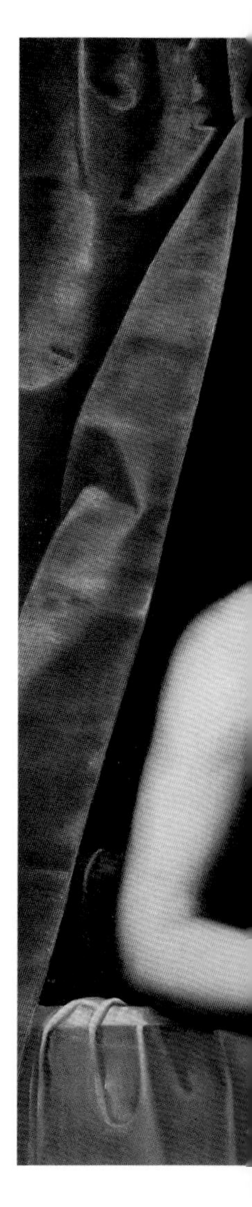

Figures in antique dress stroll through Antoine Caron's strange, fanciful architectural decor of arches, colonnades, monuments and pavilion-like edifices. The unreal, stage set-like scene the painter has created is hardly surprising, though, given his career: he worked at the court of Catherine de Médicis, notably designing decors for her fetes and entertainments. The theme here is the apparition of Virgin Mary to the Tiburtine Sibyl. Turning to the kneeling emperor Augustus, the Sibyl points skywards, weight on one leg and robes billowing in the Mannerist manner. The work encapsulates one of the Renaissance's fundamental preoccupations: reconciling the rediscovery of Antiquity and its philosophers with the fundaments of the Christian faith.

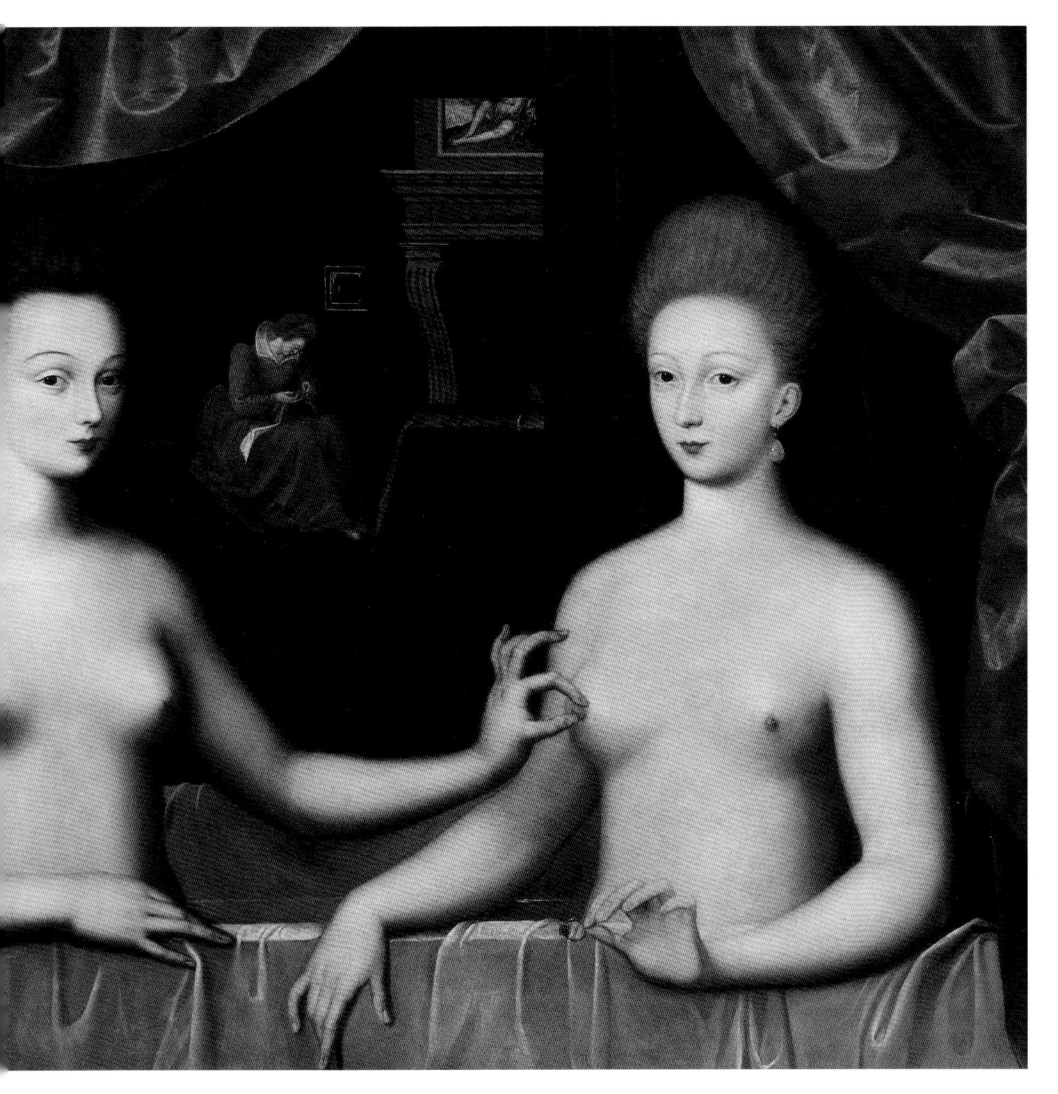

225 School of Fontainebleau

Late 16th century

Gabrielle d'Estrées and One of Her Sisters

*c.*1595 (?)
Wood. 0.96 x 1.25 m
Acquired in 1937. RF 1937-1

Definitely one of the oddest pictures in western painting, this double portrait has Lost none of its capacity to fascinate since the 16th century. Parted curtains invite us into the privacy of two pale, delicate-skinned young women sitting in a bath. Despite their reserved expressions, one is provocatively pinching the nipple of the other, who is holding a ring, a token of fidelity. The woman on the right is Gabrielle d'Estrées, Henry IV's mistress. Her companion is her sister, whose bizarre gesture is an allusion to a forthcoming pregnancy. The painting, therefore, is an announcement of the impending birth of a prince, but its symbolism was probably more complex given the taste for enigmas and word play at that time.

226 Claude Vignon
1593–1670
The Young Singer
*c.*1625
Wood. 95 x 90 cm
Gift of the Société des Amis du Louvre. RF 1966-6

17TH CENTURY – FRENCH CARAVAGGISM

The French Caravaggists, eclipsed by the major figures of the 'Grand Siècle', Poussin, Claude Lorraine and Le Brun, whose work letter suited Louis XIV's 'classical' aesthetics, were rediscovered only relatively recently, beginning with the most singular and today most universally acclaimed, Georges de La Tour [231 to 233].
Few followers of Caravaggio (died 1610) attained his dramatic power, despite the profound influence he had on certain young French painters in the first quarter of the 17th century. But they did borrow the Italian master's revolutionary use of chiaroscuro, his deceptively simple composition and dramatic staging of his subjects. They also adopted his realist vision of contemporary life: alongside traditional religious subjects, always commissions, new themes emerged, some of which, particularly tavern and music scenes, would become popular set pieces.
The Concert [227], by Valentin de Boulogne, French Caravaggism's most accomplished representative, is a fine example. Music is again the theme of *The Young Singer*, an early work by the Touraine-born painter Claude Vignon, who also spent time in Italy before returning to France, where he devoted most of his prolific output to church paintings.
The Rome of the Counter-Reformation, during the first forty years of the 17th century, was the undisputed capital of European art. It was in Rome, not Paris, that an artist could hope to makes his debut, even work for almost his entire career, as Nicolas Poussin did. Nevertheless, artists' frequentation of Italy did not prevent the emergence of a specifically French art, one which in the 17th century adopted forms as varied as they were powerful.

227 Valentin de Boulogne
1594–1632
The Concert
*c.*1628–1630 (?)
Oil on canvas. 1.75 x 2.16 m
Collection of Louis XV. INV. 8252

Born in northern France, Valentin de Boulogne spent his short career as a painter in Rome, whose cosmopolitan Bohemian circles he seems to be echoing here. Both the picture's theme and style are typical of Caravaggism, of which Valentin was an exemplary exponent: figures lit by an invisible light source, singing or playing musical instruments, standing out against a sombre background. Yet the solemn expressions, elegant poses and refined colour are his own personal interpretations of the lessons of the Italian master, whose vigour and veristic language he nevertheless succeeds in maintaining. Valentin made his name with tavern and music scenes such as this, but also painted many religious subjects, including a picture for Saint Peter's Basilica in Rome.

228 Lubin Baugin

*c.*1612–1663

The Dessert of Wafers

*c.*1630–1635
Oil on wood. 41 x 52 cm
Acquired in 1954. RF 1954-23

The bare composition and pure, cold harmony of this picture are typical of an austere trend which developed in French art under Louis XIII and which some have linked to the Protestant or Jansenist influence. This is one of the four known still lifes signed by Baugin, two of which are in the Louvre, the other being *The Five Senses (Still Life with Chessboard)*.

Lubin Baugin, a painter of religious subjects born in Pithiviers around 1612, was received into the Saint-Germain-des-Près painters' guild as a master in 1629 and spent several years in Italy, where his study of Raphael, Parmigianino, and Guido Reni led him to produce stylistically affected works still steeped in the spirit of the School of Fontainebleau.

NC DIMITTIS SERVVM

229 Simon Vouet

1590–1649

The Presentation in the Temple

1641
Oil on canvas. 3.93 x 2.50 m
Collection of the Académie Française. INV. 8492

Simon Vouet, one of the French painters who espoused Caravaggism in Italy, was far more successful than his compatriots in forging a career on his return to France. It was the fame he acquired in Italy, where he settled in 1614, which prompted Louis XIII to summon him to Paris to become first painter to the court in 1627. Retaining the king's favour, Vouet dominated the Paris art scene for the next twenty years, also executing important commissions for the nobility, the bourgeoisie and the church. *The Presentation in the Temple*, commissioned by Richelieu, is a fine example that gives us a measure of his artistic development. By 1641 he had already gravitated from the Caravaggism of his early works towards a lighter, richer, more Venetian manner, which he applied to portraiture and allegorical and history paintings.

230 Simon Vouet

1590–1649

Allegory of Wealth

c. 1640
Oil on canvas. 1.70 x 1.24 m
Collection of Louis XIII. INV. 8500

Allegory of Wealth is part a decorative series destined for Louis XIII's château at Saint-Germain-en-Laye. *Charity* and *Virtue* are also in the Louvre.

The elegance and ample-bodied generosity of this allegorical figure, and the picture's brilliant yet refined colour confirm that from 1635 to 1640 Simon Vouet infused his art with a baroque, lyrical and decorative spirit likely to seduce his elite clientele, and one which would lead him to exercise considerable influence over the French school. Painters such as Eustache Le Sueur, Charles Le Brun and Pierre Mignard rubbed shoulders in his studio, the most frequented in Paris, along with the sculptors and engravers who would widely disseminate his style.

Georges de La Tour

Famous in his time then completely forgotten, Georges de La Tour was not reinstated in his rightful, prestigious place in the history of French painting until the early 20th century. Born in Lorraine in 1593, as a young trainee painter he fully benefited from the vibrant artistic activity in his native region, whose foremost figures were the printmaker Jacques Callot and the painter Jacques Bellange, and it was there that he began his career. We have no means of ascertaining whether he travelled to Italy or not, and it is thought he may have become acquainted with Caravaggism through the Dutch painters of the Utrecht school, whose use of light effects is comparable. Having rapidly gained fame in Lorraine, he left the duchy for Paris in 1639, summoned there by Louis XIII, who appointed him 'Ordinary Painter to the King'. His fame spread and he was commanding considerable sums for his commissions by the time he died during an epidemic in 1652.

All fifty of the pictures today attributed to Georges de La Tour, only two of which are dated, are either genre scenes or religious paintings and fall into one of two categories, his so-called 'diurnal' and 'nocturnal' works. *Saint Thomas* [231] belongs in the first, *Magdalen with the Night Light* [232], showing a pensive young woman lit solely by a single candle flame, her hand resting on a skull, in the second. The latter has all the master's stylistic hallmarks: bare construction, simplified forms, a restricted palette – here ochres and browns enlivened by an area of red – and above all his consummate lighting effects conveying intense spirituality.

It was the provincial painters, notably Georges de La Tour, who kept the flame of Caravaggism burning until the mid-17th century, by which time tastes had shifted to other forms of pictorial expression.

231 Georges de La Tour
1593–1652
Saint Thomas
c. 1625–1630
Oil on canvas. 69 x 61 cm
Acquired by public subscription, 1988. RF 1988-15

The Louvre acquired this 'diurnal' La Tour in 1988 in the wake of widespread outcry and a public subscription to prevent the painting leaving France. Saint Thomas, lit by natural light, seems filled with fervour, the expression of which de La Tour became a master. Here the painter has abandoned his habitual palette of browns and reds for a subtle counterpoint of ochre and blue, whose refinement is matched by the extremely simplified treatment of the figure, cut off at the waist in typically Caravaggesque fashion.

232 Georges de La Tour
1593–1652
Magdalen with the Night Light
c. 1640–1645
Oil on canvas. 1.28 x 0.94 m
Acquired in 1949. RF 1949-11

233 Georges de La Tour

1593–1652

The Cheat with the Ace of Diamonds

c.1635
Oil on canvas. 1.07 x 1.46 m
Acquired in 1972. RF 1972-8

If this painting is one of the most famous works in the Louvre, it is because its absolute formal perfection is coupled with a highly unusual atmosphere. Who are the elegant protagonists in this scene? There can be no doubt as to the intentions of the man after whom the picture was named – on the left, cards hidden behind his back. The wealthily dressed young man on the right is too engrossed in his hand to notice the looks exchanged by the two women plying him with drink and clearly intent on divesting him of the gold on the table. The painter has frozen the scene's actors in a pregnant moment of silence, magnificently suggested, before the game takes its dramatic turn.
Georges de La Tour's psychological subtlety is at its apogee here, in the language of the players' hands and distribution of light and shade emphasising their interrelationships. The three accomplices are shown against a black ground of deceit, infinitely broader than the light ground of innocence behind their young victim.

The Le Nain Brothers

Born in Laon, then a minor but quite active artistic centre, Antoine, Louis and Matthieu Le Nain completed their training in Paris, where they subsequently worked for their entire careers. Working in close collaboration in their studio at Saint-Germain, so closely it is sometimes difficult to determine exactly who painted which of their pictures, all of which are signed simply 'Le Nain', the three brothers were admitted to the French Academy together in 1648, the year of its founding.

Success seems to have come quickly thanks to religious paintings and sporadic portraits, aspects of their output still as little-known as their 'noble paintings' of biblical and mythological subjects. Their group portraits, on the other hand, treated as genre pictures in the Dutch manner, are better known, as demonstrated by *Smokers in an Interior* [234], in which the faces of the realistically and vividly portrayed figures are lit in Caravaggesque fashion.

But if the Le Nain brothers are today ranked among the great masters of the 17th century, it is above all thanks to their depictions of peasant life. Some of these scenes are set in the open air but the most powerful are unquestionably the interiors. *The Peasant Family* [235] is a fine example: anecdote and the picturesque have been stripped away to leave only the painter's poignantly empathic observation of people in all the gravity of their human condition.

Almost forgotten by the end of the 17th century, the Le Nain brothers owe their rediscovery to the essay devoted to them in 1850 by the famous critic Champfleury, himself a native of Laon. One of their most emblematic works, *The Peasant Meal*, entered the Louvre in 1869.

234 Louis or Antoine Le Nain
c.1600/10–1648
Smokers in an Interior
1643
Oil on canvas. 1.17 x 1.37 m
Acquired in 1969. RF 1969-24

235 Louis (or Antoine) Le Nain

c.1600/10–1648

The Peasant Family

c.1640–1645
Oil on canvas. 1.13 x 1.59 m
Acquired with the arrears of the Arthur Pernolet Bequest, 1915. RF 2081

One of this picture's most striking components is its simple, masterly bas-relief construction, rendered in a sombre palette of browns and greys. But there is also its atmosphere: around the young flutist, it is as if the adults and children have momentarily suspended what they were doing to cast their calm, unsettling gazes on us. This family is portrayed in all its humble dignity and grandeur, a magnificent, universal tribute to peasant society.

236 Nicolas Poussin
1594–1665
The Rape of the Sabine Women
c.1637–1638
Oil on canvas. 1.59 x 2.08 m
Painted for Cardinal Omodei
Collection of Louis XIV. INV. 7290

Nicolas Poussin

Paradoxically, the painter whose oeuvre is considered to be the highest expression of French classicism spent most of his career in Italy. The son of a Normandy farmer, Nicolas Poussin settled in Rome in 1624 at the age of 30, and subsequently left the city only once, reluctantly, at the insistent demand of Louis XIII, who in 1640 entrusted him with the decoration of the Grande Galerie of the Louvre. The project was never finished and after a difficult two-year interlude in the French capital, Poussin left for Italy once more, never to return.

The renown of this adoptive Roman had reached his native France despite the isolated existence he led there, devoting himself exclusively to his art and producing works solely for a circle of erudite patrons and connoisseurs. Poussin considered painting to be an 'idea of incorporeal things', which he sought to convey through the expression of passion, in works intended to instil in the spectator sentiments as elevated as those of their protagonists. His emotional palette was broad, ranging from the vehement intensity of *The Rape of the Sabine Women* [236], in which the crowd is agitated by powerful forces, to the equally masterly depictions of melancholy or contemplation in the monumental religious and pagan pictures of his late period.

In the last twenty years of his life, Poussin became increasingly sensitive to the beauty of nature. Landscape took on an preponderant role in his works and the sumptuous *Four Seasons* [239 to 242], commissioned by the Duke of Richelieu and completed a year before his death, can be seen as a kind of testament. The apparent theme is nature's cyclic transformations, yet the biblical subject Poussin chose to associate with each season indicates that they also symbolised the major stages of human destiny. Or could the series be a pagan meditation on man's helplessness in the face of nature?

237 Nicolas Poussin
1594–1665
Portrait of the Artist
1650
Oil on canvas. 98 x 74 cm
Acquired in 1797. INV. 7302

During his brief two-year stay in Paris from 1640 to 1642, Nicolas Poussin became friends with one of his most fervent French admirers, Paul Fréart de Chanteloup, for whom he painted this self-portrait. He seems to have painted only one other self-portrait, today in Berlin. The artist portrays himself here at the age of 56, a serious-looking man well aware of his worth, surrounded by allegorical references to his vocation, painting. Although deemed the equal of Raphael, Poussin was not imitated by his contemporaries, who had little love for the man and disliked his violent criticisms and rigid theories.

238 Nicolas Poussin

1594–1665

The Inspiration of the Poet

*c.*1630
Oil on canvas. 1.82 x 2.13 m
Acquired in 1911. RF 1774

Apollo, god of the arts, assisted by cherubs and a muse, Euterpe or Calliope, is about to crown a poet, possibly Virgil, writing under his inspiration. Poussin painted this allegory, whose subject has yet to be fully elucidated, at a turning point in his career. The warm colours belong to his 'Venetian' period, but some commentators have seen the picture as the master's first purely 'classical' work. This is a plausible reading, given that when Poussin painted this canvas he was already in Rome, working under the patronage of the collector Cassiano dal Pozzo, who passed on his erudite knowledge of antiquity and mythology to his protégé. Later, Poussin gravitated towards an increasingly thoughtful art, conceiving each of his pictures as a philosophical or moral meditation.
The Louvre's unrivalled collection of Poussins was built up almost entirely by Louis XIV, who owned 31 of the 38 works in the museum today.

239 Nicolas Poussin

1594–1665

Spring

c. 1660–1664
Oil on canvas. 1.18 x 1.60 cm
Painted for the Duke of Richelieu
Collection of Louis XIV. INV. 7303

240 Nicolas Poussin

1594-1665

Summer, or *Ruth and Booz*

c. 1660–1664
Oil on canvas. 1.18 x 1.60 m
Painted for the Duke of Richelieu
Collection of Louis XIV. INV. 7304

241 Nicolas Poussin

1594–1665

Autumn

c.1660–1664
Oil on canvas. 1.18 x 1.60 m
Painted for the Duke of Richelieu
Collection of Louis XIV. INV. 7305

242 Nicolas Poussin

1594–1665

Winter or *The Deluge*

c.1660–1664
Oil on canvas. 1.18 x 1.60 m
Painted for the Duke of Richelieu
Collection of Louis XIV. INV. 7306

243 Eustache Le Sueur

1616–1655

Clio, Euterpe and Thalia

*c.*1652
Oil on wood. 1.30 x 1.30 m
Painted for the Hôtel Lambert, Paris
Collection of Louis XVI. INV. 8057

Eustache Le Sueur trained in Simon Vouet's studio and worked for the whole of his short career in France. This wood panel representing the muses of History, Music and Comedy is one of a set of nine panels the artist painted for a bedroom in the Lambert mansion on the Île Saint-Louis, in which he also decorated other rooms. He did not apply his classical, fluid and harmonious aesthetics exclusively to decorative commissions, however, but also to his many fine church paintings.

Landscape and interior decoration

In 17th-century Europe a new conception of nature emerged, one in which landscape ceased to be considered as a purely pictorial background convention but as a subject in its own right. The style of the Dutch landscape painters, rooted in realist observation, differed from the French conception of landscape as an idealised natural setting for the great themes of antiquity and fable. Two major artists, Nicolas Poussin and Claude Lorraine, defined the forms of the classical landscape in French painting in the 17th century. Poussin devoted himself to landscape only at the end of his career, inspired by Stoic thought, while Claude, influenced by the Northern painters he met in Rome, sought from the outset to render light and atmosphere [244].
The works of these two masters and those of the Northern naturalists disseminated by the art market, combined with the growing interest in questions of perspective, prompted a spate of landscape paintings in Paris in the second half of the century. The trend was further fuelled by a strong demand for interior decorations for the many residences built during this period of great middle-class prosperity. Among the painters who excelled at this were Eustache Le Sueur, who took part in the decoration of the Hôtel Lambert [243] on the Île Saint-Louis, 13 surviving paintings of which are in the Louvre.

244 Claude Gellée,
known as Claude Lorraine

*c.*1602–1682

The Disembarkation of Cleopatra at Tarsus

1642
Oil on canvas. 1.19 x 1.68 m
Collection of Louis XIV. INV. 4716

As was his custom, Claude Lorraine placed the scene justifying this painting's title in the foreground, in this case the Egyptian queen Cleopatra arriving at Tarsus to seduce Mark Antony and subject him to her interests. The historical episode depicted took place in the 1st century BC, and Antiquity is evoked by the totally unreal yet grandiose architecture which gives the picture its rigorous organisation and monumentality. And yet the subject is once again merely a pretext for the Lorraine-born landscape painter to create a natural world steeped in luminous atmospherics, as he did with the landscape around Rome, which he painted with his friend Nicolas Poussin. Echoes of Claude Lorraine's work, already celebrated by his contemporaries, can be seen in another great master of light and atmosphere, the 19th-century English painter J.M.W. Turner.

245 Philippe de Champaigne

1602–1674

The Ex Voto of 1662

1662
Oil on canvas. 1.65 x 2.29 m
Donated by the painter to the convent of Port-Royal, Paris.
Seized during the Revolution. INV. 1138

Philippe de Champaigne's involvement with the Jansenist convent of Port Royal in the 1640s was a major turning point in his life. The austere lifestyle of this ascetic sect had a profound effect on him. In 1662, his daughter Catherine, who had entered the convent as a nun, made a miraculous recovery from paralysis of the legs and he painted this fine mystic picture as a token of his gratitude. His association with the Jansenists led him to paint the portraits of several of the movement's leading figures, including *Robert Arnauld d'Andilly* (Louvre) and *Mother Angélique Arnauld* (Musée Condé, Chantilly), in which one sees the formal perfection and psychological truthfulness for which he became renowned during his lifetime.

246 Philippe de Champaigne

1602–1674

Cardinal Richelieu

c. 1635
Oil on canvas. 2.22 x 1.55 m
Seized during the Revolution. INV. 1136

Although born in Brussels, Philippe de Champaigne was not strictly speaking Flemish. His training and tastes, however, led him to further in France the pictorial tradition and sensual generosity of the southern Low Countries, which he later subjected to an order and discipline inspired by Poussin. He began his career in France working for Marie de Médicis in the Luxembourg Palace, and pursued it with Richelieu who, like Louis XIII, appreciated his work and commissioned him to decorate his own palace. Philippe de Champaigne was a talented portraitist and painted several portraits of the cardinal and many members of the high aristocracy and churchmen. He was a prolific painter, especially of religious pictures, commissions for which came from all over France and which he imbued with great spiritual profundity.

Charles Le Brun

Few painters have had more dazzling careers than Charles Le Brun, who dominated French art in the second half of the 17th century, during the reign of Louis XIV. A child prodigy, he entered Simot Vouet's studio at the age of 15, around 1634, and during his youth was a protégé of Chancellor Pierre Séguier, to whom he later paid tribute by painting a sumptuous ceremonial portrait [247]. This patronage enabled him to travel to Italy in 1642 with Poussin on the latter's return to Rome, where for four years he studied under the master.

It was after his return to Paris that Le Brun's career began in earnest. He soon forged a wide clientele for his religious pictures and decorative ceilings. He secured his reputation with his brilliant demonstration of his talents at Nicolas Fouquet's château at Vaux-le-Vicomte, where he painted walls and ceilings, executed cartoons for sculptures and tapestries and designed festive decorations. After the minister of finance's disgrace, he placed himself in the service of Court. Following his appointment as First Painter to the King in 1664, his overriding concern became the glorification of the monarchy. Aided by numerous assistants, he personally executed or supervised sumptuous decoration projects at the Louvre and above all at Versailles. He produced tapestry cartoons [248], reorganised the Gobelins and Savonnerie tapestry and carpet workshops into full-scale manufactories, oversaw the training craftsmen and soon succeeded in imposing the 'Louis XIV style'.

A man of inexhaustible energy, Le Brun was one of the founder members of the Académie Royale de peinture et de Sculpture in 1648 and played a preponderant role in the codification of the canons of the art of his time.

247 Charles Le Brun
1619–1690
Chancellor Séguier

c. 1655–57
Oil on cavas. 2.95 x 3.51 m
Acquired in 1942 with the aid of the Société des Amis du Louvre. RF 1942-3

248 Charles Le Brun

1619–1690

The Entry of Alexander into Babylon

1661–65
Oil on canvas. 4.50 x 7.07 m
Collection of Louis XIV. INV. 2898

In his capacity as director of the Gobelins tapestry manufactory, Charles Le Brun executed several series of huge tapestry cartoons. Four of these canvases were devoted to the history of Alexander the Great. This one, painted in 1665, shows the Greek hero entering Babylon accompanied by a sumptuous procession. The plain purpose of the picture's epic style, of which Le Brun became the paragon, was to exalt the glory and virtue of the King. The primacy Le Brun accorded to drawing rather than colour in his oeuvre led to its wide dissemination in the form of engravings in France and abroad.

249 Nicolas de Largillière

1656–1746

Family Portrait

c.1710?
Oil on canvas. 1.49 x 2 m
Dr Louis La Caze Bequest, 1869. MI 1085

Nicolas de Largillière was a brilliant and prolific portraitist – according to his contemporaries he painted over 1,500 portraits during his career – but he also left us numerous genre pictures. These two facets of his production reflect the training he received during his youth in Antwerp and England. He settled in Paris, his birthplace, in 1682, and was admitted to the Academy of Painting for his large portrait of Le Brun, now in the Louvre.

This group portrait, painted during Largillière's mature period, owes much to Van Dyck, whose fluid elegance and realism he adopted. His subjects, who appear relaxed and at ease in their surroundings, epitomise the new, more informal conception of portraiture which developed under the Regency and which would flourish a few years later under Louis XV. In this respect, Largillière's work marks a turning point between the 17th and 18th centuries.

250 Hyacinthe Rigaud

1659–1743

Portrait of Louis XIV

1701
Oil on canvas. 2.77 x 1.94 m
Collection of Louis XIV. INV. 7492

King Louis XIV was 63 years old when he posed in his coronation costume for this extraordinary ceremonial portrait. The picture, in which the Sun King is made to appear the very embodiment of absolute power, was originally destined for his grandson, King Philip V of Spain, but was so admired at court that it was decided it should stay in France. Hyacinthe Rigaud, born in Perpignan, became the darling of the European aristocracy, devoting his prolific output essentially to portraits brilliantly conveying his ample and vigorous manner.

The Regency – Watteau

At the close of the 17th century, the triumphant classicism of the first twenty years of Louis XIV's reign, over which Charles Le Brun had reigned supreme, gave way to a painting concerned more with seduction than grandeur. 'Noble painting', although brilliantly upheld by artists such as Jouvenel and Coypel, gradually sank out of favour, supplanted by the portrait (Nicolas de Largillière, *Family Portrait*, 249), the ornamental picture and the genre scene. This trend, which bloomed in the first twenty years of the 18th century, attained its highest perfection and poetry in the work of Jean-Antoine Watteau (1684–1721).

During his short, meteoric career, Watteau, born at Valenciennes in northern France, succeeded in imposing a genre of his own invention, the *fête galante*, an outdoor scene generally showing a couple or gathering of elegant figures conversing, dancing or making music in a pastoral setting. But Watteau transforms what might have been merely a scenic 'stage convention' into a musical or amorous reverie, peopled with carefree beings whose only preoccupation seems to be living life's every moment to the full. They are enveloped in a gentle, luminous atmosphere, marvellously conveyed by the gossamer touch of an artist who had assimilated the lessons of the Venetian painters.

Watteau's exceptional qualities were immediately recognised. Already destined for immense fame, he was admitted to the Académie Royale de Peinture et de Sculpture in 1717 as a 'painter of *fêtes galantes*' for his entry piece, *The Pilgrimage to Cythera* [251]. Yet he did not limit himself to this theme since he also undertook subjects drawn from mythology, and above all numerous scenes linked to the world of the theatre, in particular *commedia dell'arte* characters, then much in vogue [253].

251 Jean-Antoine Watteau

1684–1721

The Pilgrimage to Cythera

1717
Oil on canvas. 1.29 x 1.94 m
Collection of the Académie Française. INV. 8525

Strung like a garland through a vaporous *sfumato* landscape, a file of young men and women make their way down to the water two by two. They are setting out to pay homage to Venus, goddess of love, symbolised by the sculpture on the right. Watteau has created an enigmatic atmosphere in this illustration of the theme of the pilgrimage of lovers to the isle of Cythera, also found in ballets and operas of the time. We are unsure whether the lovers are arriving on the island or leaving it. And is the couple sitting on the right the same couple as the one getting up and the one already leaving for the shore, with the woman looking back over her shoulder? And could this picture, more melancholy than *gallant*, therefore be a hymn to the fleeting passage of time, to the brevity of youth?
This emblematic work is a magnificent résumé of Watteau's style. Delicateness vies with grace. The finesse of the colour, the preciosity of the costumes, the idyllic landscape, the pictorial elements as a whole combine to create a dream world rather than a real one.

252 Jean-Antoine Watteau

1684–1721

Two Cousins

*c.*1716
Oil on canvas. 30 x 36 cm
Acquired in 1990. RF 1990-8

This masterfully composed little canvas has all the ingredients of the *fête galante*: the delights of love, conversation, music, a leafy park, and another recurrent feature in Watteau's work, a woman seen from behind. With her hair worn up to reveal her slender, graceful neck, dressed in a shimmering dress, she seems lost in a dream of her own, oblivious to the banter of the couple next to her. Watteau, blessed with a prodigious gift for drawing, as the many sketches from life he left us amply illustrate, was peerless in his ability to capture a figure's elegance and every telling movement.

253 Jean-Antoine Watteau

1684–1721

Pierrot, also known as *Gilles*

*c.*1718–1719
Oil on canvas. 1.84 x 1.49 m
Dr Louis La Caze Bequest, 1869. MI 1121

Both the subject and precise purpose of this painting remain shrouded in mystery. Is this Pierrot standing stiffly with his arms dangling really the portrait of an actor posing in *commedia dell'arte* costume? Or is this, as has been suggested, a transposed self-portrait? And what should we make of the characters Watteau has placed behind him, trying to get a donkey to move on? The painting's original raison d'être is just as enigmatic. Did it perhaps serve as a sign for a theatre, or the hang in café of a retired actor? Whatever the truth may be, there is unanimous agreement on one count: that this work is one of Watteau's strangest and most personal works.

254 Jean-Baptiste-Siméon Chardin

1699–1779

Boy with a Top

Before 1738
Oil on canvas. 67 x 76 cm
Acquired in 1907 RF 1705

Chardin painted many family scenes depicting several figures, but from around 1737 to 1738, he produced a series of particularly delicate pictures whose sole subject is a child or an adolescent. Other than this *Boy with a Top,* the Louvre has *The Young Draughtsman* and *Young Man with a Violin*. Whatever the activity of his always calm and elegant young subjects – the painter's son also posed for him –, Chardin succeeds in conveying their freshness and fragility with unrivalled mastery.

The mid-18th century

The intellectual sea change brought about by the thinkers of the Enlightenment, based on a new vision of man and scepticism vis-à-vis all manner of dogmas, also swept through the arts. In his famous *Salons*, the philosopher Denis Diderot challenged the rules governing beauty and the classical ideal laid down by the Académie in the previous century, arguing that 'subjective beauty' was the only sentiment liable to determine the 'truth' of a work of art.

It was the primacy now accorded to subjectivity that lay at the root of the mid-18th century development of two categories of painting hitherto considered minor: the portrait, the ceremonialism of which was discarded in favour of psychological suggestion, and the genre scene, which became a theatre of sentiments. It was the extremely wide-ranging responses of artists to the new concepts of the Enlightenment that produced the artistic richness of the mid-century. Jean-Baptiste-Siméon Chardin's approach was sober and restrained. His genre scenes are every bit as precise as his still lifes: the same silent atmosphere and the same refined palette in the service of a 'moral' art exalting the virtues of everyday life [254–258]. Jean-Baptiste Greuze, on the other hand, pushed the expression of human sentiment to new heights of pathos in the 1770s [264]. François Boucher, famous principally for his amorous pastoral scenes, also executed genre pictures over a short period: his *Morning Coffee* [260], in which we enter the privacy of a Parisian household – that of the painter, father of two at the time – is a fresh and brilliant illustration of a new art of seeing.

255 Jean-Baptiste-Siméon Chardin

1699–1779

Saying Grace

*c.*1740
Oil on canvas 49 x 39 cm
Collection of Louis XV. INV. 3202

The Louvre has some twenty canvases by Chardin, most of which entered the museum with the Dr Louis La Caze Bequest in 1869. But it is Louis XV, who showed little inclination for art collecting, whom we must thank for the acquisition of one of the painter's most popular works. This everyday scene shows a mother gently but solemnly making sure her youngest daughter says grace properly before a meal. But although its similarity with Dutch genre pictures is manifest, Chardin's subtle rendering of material and texture, diaphanous touch and mastery of light imbue the subject with his own very personal interpretation.

256 Jean-Baptiste-Siméon Chardin

1699–1779

The Skate

Before 1728
Oil on canvas. 1.14 x 1.46 m
Collection of the Académie. INV. 3197

Chardin was admitted to the Académie de Peinture in 1728 on the strength of this painting, which he presented with another still life, *The Buffet* (Louvre). The mastery of this painter compelled the recognition of his peers, to the extent that he succeeded in transgressing the official hierarchy of painting genres. Because of his magical painterly skill and capacity to transcend the most mundane everyday objects, he is sometimes called the painter of 'silent life'. Diderot devoted admiring passages to him in his *Salons*: 'Oh, Chardin! it is not white, red and black that you mix on your palette but the very substance of things, it is air and light that you take on the tip of your brush and put on the canvas.'
The small still lifes of his late period, more rigorously composed, are masterpieces of sobriety and chromatic refinement.

257 Jean-Baptiste-Siméon Chardin

1699–1779

Still Life with Pipe and Jug

c.1737
Oil on canvas. 32 x 42 cm
Acquired in 1867. MI 721

258 Jean-Baptiste-Siméon Chardin

1699–1779

Grapes and Pomegranates

1763
Dr Louis La Caze Bequest, 1869. MI 1035

259 Jean-Honoré Fragonard

1732–1806

The Bathers

1763–1764
Oil on canvas. 64 x 80 cm
Dr Louis La Caze Bequest, 1869. MI 1055

Admitted to the Académie as a history painter, Fragonard soon gravitated from austere subjects towards more pleasurable scenes in which, without even bothering to cloak them in a mythological pretext, he exalted the beauty of naked flesh. The nude bodies of these eight rosy bathers in full bloom seem to shimmer as they gambol in this dreamlike vision of nature.
Although the picture's subject is still in the tradition of his master, Boucher, Fragonard's sensuality and highly personal touch, inspired by another master, Rubens, are all his own.

The 'painters of happiness'

Louis XV's reign, as Louis XIV's, gave rise to a style bearing the monarch's name. The lofty, ponderous classicism of Louis XV's grandfather was supplanted by a pleasant, light art, all gracefulness and curves, and the talented young painters commissioned to decorate refined and luxuriant interiors in the new '*rocaille*' spirit went by the name of Carle Van Loo, Charles-Joseph Natoire and Jean-François de Troy. But its most virtuoso and imaginative exponent was incontestably François Boucher (1703–1770), whose work has come to epitomise this period of French art history.
The brilliant career of Boucher, favourite painter of the king's mistress, Madame de Pompadour, reached its apogee in the 1750s and 1760s. Overwhelmed with French and foreign commissions for interior decorations, ceilings and overdoors, he also worked for the theatre and the opera and produced tapestry cartoons. He was appointed director of the Gobelins tapestry factory in 1755, and also designed decorations for Sèvres porcelain as well as models for engraving.
Yet despite his frenetic activity and effortless execution, he remained a painter through and through, playing with colour with great refinement and invention and transforming the most conventional subjects into celebrations of the senses: his *Diana Resting After Her Bath* [261] is a small masterpiece of sensuality and modesty.
A 'painter of happiness', as he has been described, Boucher succeeded in passing on this consummate sense of grace to one of the pupils working in his studio, Jean-Honoré Fragonard (1732–1806), who in turn celebrated love and sensual delight [259, 263].

260 François Boucher

1703–1770

Morning Coffee

1739
Oil on canvas. 8.15 x 6.55 m
Dr Achille Malécot Bequest, 1895. RF 86

261 François Boucher

1703–1770

Diana Resting After Her Bath

1742
Oil on canvas. 56 x 73 cm
Acquired in 1852. INV. 2712

Diana has laid her bow and arrows to one side to indulge in the pleasures of bathing. Boucher has used the classic theme of the goddess of the hunt resting to compose a work full of luminosity and grace. His use of colour, Venetian in its softness, is coupled with his dazzling painterly effects. The young women's delicate complexions, the silky rustle of the drapery and the still life in the bottom right-hand corner are the work of a true master.

262 Jean-Honoré Fragonard

1732–1806

Portrait of Abbé de Saint-Non

1769
Oil on canvas 80 x 65 cm
Dr Louis La Caze Bequest, 1869. MI 1061

The Abbé de Saint-Non, an erudite collector and patron of artists and himself an engraver, played a significant role in the artistic life of his time. On his repeated trips to Italy he met many of the young French painters training there, striking up friendships with some of them and supporting their careers. This was the case with Fragonard, whom Saint-Non met in Rome in 1760, and of whom he became an unconditional admirer.
This canvas belonged to a 15-picture series of 'fantastic figures', eight of which are in the Louvre (including *Diderot* and *Marie-Madeleine Guimard*). The artist wrote on the back of the picture: 'painted by Fragonard in 1769 in an hour'. And the magnificently spirited touch and powerful colour do indeed suggest the picture was feverishly dashed off in the heat of the moment. This fiery canvas heralding Romanticism is today seen as a vibrant testament to his creative energy, whereas his contemporaries dismissed it as a mere sketch.

263 Jean-Honoré Fragonard

1732–1806

The Bolt

*c.*1778
Oil on canvas. 73 x 93 cm
Acquired in 1974. RF 1974-2

Long thought to be a copy, this famous painting – of which there are several versions – was eventually recognised as a work of Fragonard himself and acquired by the Louvre in 1974. The smooth treatment and golden hues are similar to the painter's late works, when he abandoned his light palette for the chiaroscuro of the Northern painters. The theme of amorous desire, on the other hand, remained a constant throughout his career. He treats it here in a dramatically passionate vein, adding a moral dimension by placing an apple – Eve's fruit – on the table.

264 Jean-Baptiste Greuze

1725–1805

The Punished Son

1778
Oil on canvas. 1.30 x 1.63 m
Acquired in 1820. INV. 5039

This picture's pendant, *The Father's Curse* – also in the Louvre – depicts the first episode of a family drama, in which a son announces to his father that he is joining the army, only to find himself being cursed for it. In the second picture we see the son on his return, weeping by his father's deathbed, surrounded by his family. A scene of great pathos which Greuze has instilled with a kind of antique grandeur – despite the modern dress – through the gestures of its protagonists and the composition obeying the noble canons of history painting.

265 Jean-Baptiste Greuze
1725–1805
The Broken Jug
1777
Oil on canvas. 1.10 x 0.85 m oval
Seized during the Revolution. INV. 5036

The theatre of sentiments

Jean-Baptiste Greuze (1725–1805), 'a delicate, sensitive soul' according to his admirers, won considerable popular acclaim for his wholly novel conception of the genre scene. His pictures, laden with obviously moralist intent, depict dramatic situations into which the viewer is drawn, moved by the intensely psychological portrayal of their conflicting emotions. The most famous of these scenes, *The Village Betrothal* (Louvre) and *The Punished Son* [264] are full-blown domestic melodramas, whose protagonists act out their heightened sentiments in grandiose compositions worthy of history painting. In this respect, the aesthetics of his 1769 picture, *Septimus Severus Reproaching Caracalla* (Louvre), prefigures the Neoclassicism of David.

Greuze's popular success was part of a broader, literary trend towards the exaltation of sensibility, exemplified in France by Rousseau and Voltaire and in England by Richardson, an effusive vein that the painter consciously exploited, even in single-figure paintings such as *The Broken Jug* [265]. Greatly admired at the time, this picture shows a delicate young woman, hardly more than a child, carrying a jug on her right arm, whose very visible break, associated with the gesture of the hands, suggests the girl's loss of innocence.

266 Élisabeth-Louise Vigée-Le Brun

1755–1842

Self-Portrait with her Daughter Julie

1789
Oil on wood. 1.30 x 0.94 m
Seized during the Revolution. INV. 3068

Élisabeth Vigée-Le Brun, daughter of the painter Vigée, who taught her his trade, embarked very young on her brilliant career as a portraitist, whose crowning glory was her nomination as official painter to Marie Antoinette in 1779. She painted over thirty portraits of the monarch, alone or with her children, and numerous portraits of ladies at court. Fleeing the Revolution, which also dispersed her clientele, she subsequently travelled the continent painting portraits of the European, particularly Russian aristocracy. The Louvre has two of her self-portraits with her daughter Julie, born of her brief marriage with the picture dealer Jean-Baptiste Le Brun. Her portraits of men (*Hubert Robert*, Louvre) are remarkably powerful.

267 Hubert Robert

1733–1808

The Pont du Gard

1787
Oil on canvas. 2.42 x 2.42 m
Commissioned by Louis XVI. INV. 7550

Hubert Robert, a great admirer of Pannini and Piranesi, whom he discovered during his stay at the French Academy in Rome, produced a prodigious number of pictures of real or imaginary architectural subjects and ruins. This passion – which earned him the nickname 'Robert des Ruines' – had its parallel in the widespread enthusiasm in the 18th century for antique archaeology, prompted notably by the excavations of Pompeii and Herculaneum.
Intent on exalting France's archaeological heritage, the directorate of the King's Buildings commissioned Hubert Robert to paint four canvases on this theme for Louis XVI's rooms in the palace of Fontainebleau. The Pont du Gard aqueduct, built during the reign of Agrippa, in 19 BC, was one of the subjects he chose. In this picture, we see his sense of the picturesque, to which he gives free rein without compromising the extensive, balanced composition and delicate hues of the landscape, bathed in the golden glow of a Southern sunset.

Neoclassicism

Weary of the amorous mythology and frivolity of the rococo style, the artists of the second half of the 18th century reacted against the dilution of aesthetic and moral ideals in art by seeking inspiration in the canons of the classical tradition. This trend went hand in hand with a resurgence of interest in Greco-Roman art, due largely to the excavations carried out at Pompeii and Herculaneum, and the influence of the idealist theories of the German archaeologist Johann Winckelmann, who exalted the 'serene grandeur' and 'noble simplicity' of Greek art.

This pan-European movement, known as Neoclassicism, engendered forms of expression and styles so diverse it would be rash to attempt a precise definition. A number of constants do, however, prevail throughout: subject matter based on virtue and heroism, static and austere compositions, and the stylistic primacy of drawing over colour, manifest in the meticulously precise depiction of figures and their settings. These were the principles on which large history paintings inspired by Antiquity, mythology and later contemporary events were elaborated.

The major figure of the Neoclassical movement in France was unquestionably Jacques-Louis David, whose *Oath of the Horatii* [268], presented triumphantly in Paris in 1785, was regarded as a manifesto of the new painting. By exalting civic virtues in this rigorous large-format work, he was also sounding the symbolic knell of the Ancien Régime and its hedonist art. Among the pupils who studied under him in his much-frequented studio, where he taught that 'Antiquity is the greatest school for the modern painter', were artists themselves destined for fame: Gros, Gérard [272] and Girodet [273]. However, these painters sought to modulate the master's theories and elude the danger of academicism, thereby ushering in the great Romantic period that began at the dawn of the 19th century.

268 Jacques-Louis David
1748–1825
The Oath of the Horatii

1784
Oil on canvas. 3.30 x 4.25 m
Collection of Louis XVI. INV. 3682

In the account by the Roman historian Livy, the three Horatii brothers were chosen by Rome to challenge the three Curiatii, champions of the city of Alba. On the left, David shows the warriors solemnly swearing to defeat their enemies or die, as their father hands them their weapons, and on the right the desolate women of the family: their mother leaning over two grandchildren, their sister Camilla, betrothed to one of the Curiatii, and Sabine, a sister of the Curiatii betrothed to one of the Horatii. The picture's composition thus faithfully conveys the 'message' in this tragedy: the opposition of the stoicism of the men, driven solely by their patriotism, and the suffering and emotional fragility of the women, expressed by their delicate curves and colours. The picture, painted in Rome in 1784 and shown the following year in Paris, marked a major turning point in the history of painting. Its sober realism and virile inspiration became regarded as the model for the new Neoclassical school, and its triumphant reception established David as the movement's leading representative in France.

Jacques-Louis David

David's career coincided with a particularly agitated period in French history. Born during Louis XV's reign, he played an active role in the French Revolution and the Napoleonic Empire, so much so that he can be considered the archetype of the politically committed artist. Having survived these tumultuous periods, he died in exile during the reign of Charles X.
Born in Paris in 1748, David studied under Vien and attended the Académie Royale de Peinture. After several failures to win the Prix de Rome, in 1774 he finally succeeded. His five-year stay in Italy was a highly formative one. He discovered Antiquity in all its grandeur and frequented a circle of European art connoisseurs fascinated by the theories of archaeologists, particularly those of Johann Winckelmann. The concepts of the 'beautiful ideal' and art's spiritual, even moral purpose were among the concepts they impressed upon the young artist and which he sought to express in his pictures, the most exemplary in this respect being *The Oath of the Horatii* [268].
During the Revolution, David ardently threw himself into the political fray, becoming the director of festivities and, when he painted, choosing historical episodes or figures exalting revolutionary grandeur. Accused of treason after the fall of Robespierre in 1794, he was imprisoned for five months. It was during this period that David painted *The Intervention of the Sabine Women* [270]. Some time later, in 1798, he painted a study for a portrait of Napoleon Bonaparte (Louvre) and the portrait of a famous socialite, *Madame Recamier* [269]. Appointed First Painter to the Emperor in 1804, he was commissioned to paint four pictures commemorating Napoleon's coronation ceremonies, including *The Consecration of Emperor Napoleon and the Coronation of Empress Josephine* [271], which took him several years to finish.

269 Jacques-Louis David
1748–1825
Madame Récamier
1800
Oil on canvas. 1.74 x 2.44 m
Acquired in 1826. INV. 3708

270 Jacques-Louis David

1748–1825

The Intervention of the Sabine Women

1799
Oil on canvas. 3.85 x 5.22 m
Acquired in 1819. INV. 3691

In the heat of the battle between the Romans and the Sabines, the Sabine wives of the Romans attempted to stop the fighting by holding up their children amidst the fray. The woman in the middle of the picture is Hersilia, Romulus's wife, intervening between her father and her husband's readied spear. David based his magnificent staging of this historical scene on Greek bas-reliefs and, also in the manner of the Greek masters, exalted the beauty of the semi-nude, playing with drapery and according primacy to line rather than colour.

271 Jacques-Louis David

1748–1825

The Consecration of Emperor Napoleon and the Coronation of Empress Josephine in the Cathedral of Notre-Dame, Paris, 2nd December 1804

1806–1807
Oil on canvas. 6.21 x 9.79 m
Commissioned by Napoleon I. INV. 3699

David, Painter to the Emperor, painted only two of the four pictures he was commissioned to commemorate Napoleon's coronation: *The Distribution of the Eagles*, now at Versailles, and the almost ten metre-long *Consecration*. The ceremony took place in the cathedral of Notre Dame in Paris on December 2nd 1804, but instead of depicting the consecration of the Emperor himself, David chose to depict the moment when Napoleon crowns Josephine, with Pope Pius VII giving his blessing. Inspired by Rubens's *Crowning of Marie de Médicis* (Louvre), David conceived the picture as a long frieze of harmoniously arranged and subtly lit figures, the ensemble constituting a sumptuous group portrait.

272 François Gérard

1770–1837

Cupid and Psyche

1798
Oil on canvas. 1.86 x 1.32 m
Acquired in 1822. INV. 4739

Inspired by the antique canons of beauty advocated by his master, David, whose studio he frequented with passionate enthusiasm, François Gérard in turn sought an idealised purity of form. This picture, exhibited at the 1798 Salon, is a perfect illustration of the coolly graceful strain of Neoclassicism which spread throughout Europe at that time and which was echoed in the work of the Italian sculptor Canova. However, Gérard distinguished himself primarily all with his portraits (*Jean-Baptiste Isabey and his Daughter*, Louvre), painting members of the imperial family under the Empire.

273 Anne-Louis Girodet de Roussy-Trioson

1767–1824

The Burial of Atala

1808

Oil on canvas. 2.07 x 2.67 m

Acquired in 1819. INV. 4958

The heroine of Chateaubriand's novel *Atala*, published in 1801, is a young American Indian woman, a Christian, who poisons herself because a vow binding her to God prevents her from marrying the man she loves. Yet there is nothing very exotic about this funeral scene. The picture has certain Neoclassical components – the antique-inspired treatment of anatomy, purity of line and sobriety of colour – but the melancholic atmosphere created by Girodet's masterly chiaroscuro expresses a pre-Romantic sensibility already a far cry from David's precepts.

Jean-Auguste-Dominique Ingres (1780–1867)

Born in Montauban, Ingres received his first training from his father, a painter and miniaturist (who also gave him violin lessons), then attended the Académie Royale in Toulouse. On his arrival in Paris in 1797, he entered David's studio, where for several years he immersed himself in the classical and archaistic atmosphere that would have a decisive effect on his artistic development. During his stay at the French Academy in Rome from 1806 to 1810, he painted his first bathers, including *The Valpinçon Bather* [275]. *La Grande Odalisque* [274], the pinnacle of his mastery of the arabesque, was also painted during his extended stay in Rome.

Subsequently dividing his time between Paris and Italy, Ingres never ceased to study the great masters, particularly Poussin and Raphael, relentlessly drawing and researching his works. A tireless worker, he prepared his pictures with numerous drawings, ever in search of the perfect contour and flowing movement, yet recommended his pupils adopt a certain 'naivety' to better capture each model's singular qualities. His *Portrait of Louis-François Bertin* [277] is a masterly lesson in observation in this respect.

Considered revolutionary in his early career because of his opposition to David, Ingres, a master of form, in turn became the epitome of classicism for the next generation, dominated by the high priest of colour and movement, Delacroix. Yet both played their part in establishing France as the most vibrant centre of European Romanticism.

274 Jean-Auguste-Dominique Ingres
1780–1867
La Grande Odalisque

1814
Oil on canvas. 0.91 x 1.62 m
Acquired in 1899. RF 1158

Painted in Italy for Caroline Murat, Napoleon's sister, *La Grande Odalisque* was exhibited at the 1819 Paris Salon, where critics were quick to point out that the long curve of the back was anatomically incorrect, since the painter had given the odalisque three extra vertebrae. Although a meticulous observer of reality, Ingres did not hesitate to accentuate certain qualities in his models to enhance a form's expressiveness. The odalisque's Oriental accessories, intended to suggest sensual pleasure, have the opposite effect, that of emphasising the glacial perfection of her nude body.

275 Jean-Auguste-Dominique Ingres
1780–1867
The Valpinçon Bather

1808
Oil on canvas. 1.46 x 0.97 m
Acquired in 1879. RF 259

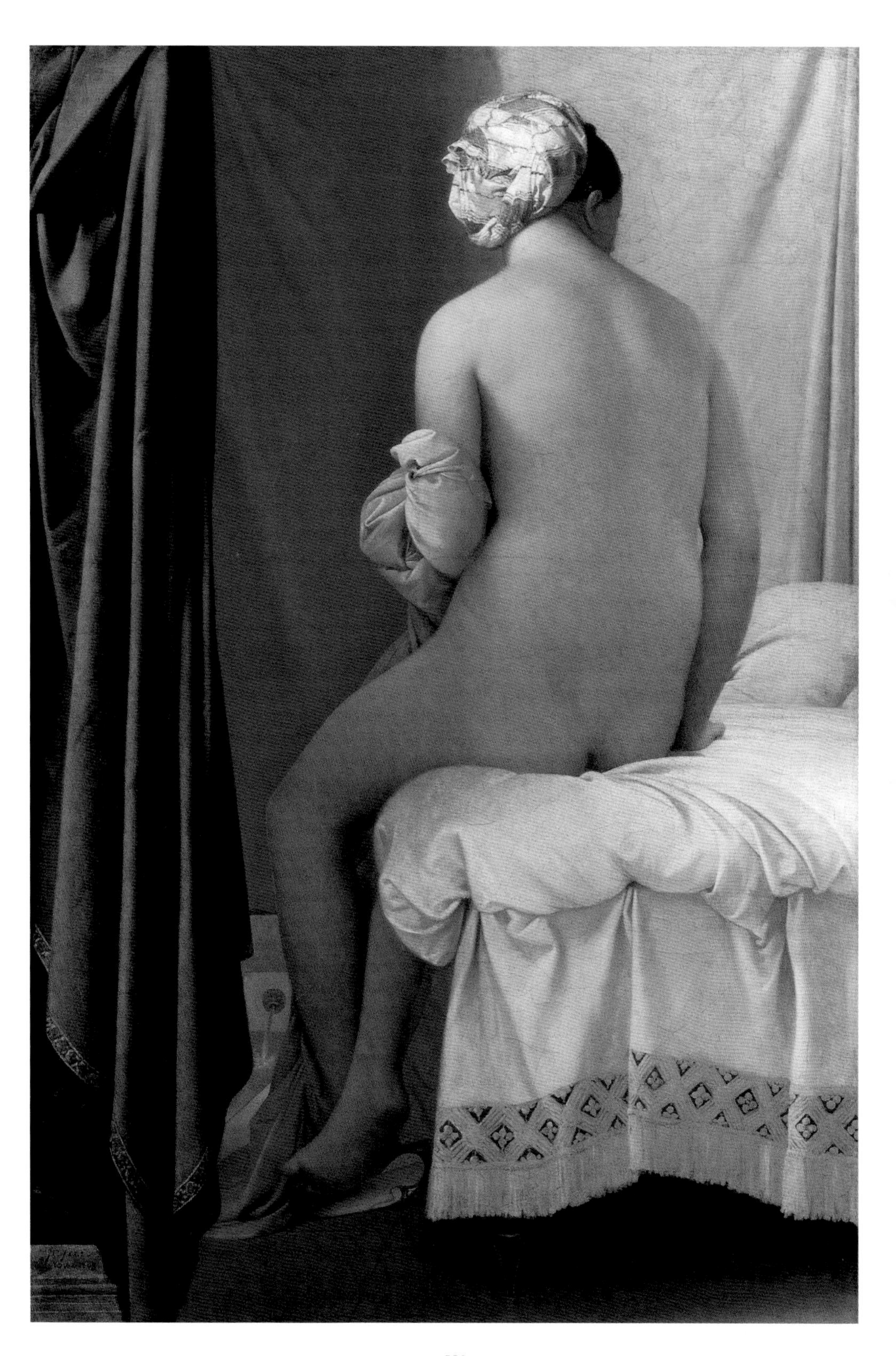

276 Jean-Baptiste-Dominique Ingres

1780–1867

Mademoiselle Caroline Rivière

Exhibited at the 1806 Salon
Oil on canvas. 1 x 0.70 m
Mme Veuve Rivière Bequest, 1870
MI 1447

Ingres painted this portrait early on in his career, in Paris, while waiting for the political situation to enable him to take up residence at the French Academy in Rome, as winner of the Grand Prix scholarship. Today this picture is considered the promising debut of his career as a portraitist, yet commentators at the 1806 Salon severely criticised his 'Gothic' style, affected precision and the harsh outlines of his faces.

277 Jean-Auguste-Dominique Ingres

1780–1867

Portrait of Louis-François Bertin

1832
Oil on canvas 1.16 x 0.95 m
Acquired in 1897. RF 1071

According to Baudelaire, Ingres was 'the only man in France who painted real portraits'. And the artist demonstrates this brilliantly in this picture, painted in less than a month, in which he combines dazzling technique and extraordinary psychological perception.
Louis-François Bertin (1766–1841), politician, businessman and owner of the influential daily newspaper, *Le Journal des débats*, epitomised the bourgeois liberal under the July Monarchy, a man sure of the validity of his values.

278 Jean-Auguste-Dominique Ingres

1780–1867

The Turkish Bath

1862
Oil on wood. 1.10 x 1.10 m
Gift of the Société des Amis du Louvre,
With the aid of Maurice Fenaille, 1911
RF 1934

Ingres was 82 years old when he finished this painting, which marked the culmination of his intensive exploration of the bathers theme. The work, originally square, was bought in 1859 by Prince Napoleon, but the painter took it back the following year and modified its format to a *tondo*. The public, had to wait until the Ingres retrospective in 1905 to see the artist's fantastical vision of a harem peopled with lascivious bodies and filled with heady perfume.

279 Théodore Chassériau

1819–1856

Esther Preparing Herself to Meet King Assuerus

1841
Oil on canvas. 45.5 x 35.5 cm
Baron Arthur Chassériau Bequest, 1934. RF 3900

Although Chassériau did not travel to the Orient until 1846, its distant and mysterious lands had fascinated him since childhood. His choice of this biblical subject gave him a pretext to paint a colourful and sensuous Oriental scene. A pupil of Ingres, Chassériau borrowed the hieratic poses of latter's figures, but the colour here is Delacroix-inspired, as would soon be his technique. 'Nature is painted like a mosaic,' he later said, definitively breaking with the precepts of his old master.

280 Hippolyte Flandrin

1809–1864

Young Man Beside the Sea

1837
Oil on canvas 0.98 x 1.24 m
Entered the Musée du Luxembourg in 1857. MI 171

Painted by Hippolyte Flandrin during his stay at the French Academy in Rome, this nude was sent back to Paris as his fourth-year piece. The perfect modelling of the body, almost fitting into a circle, is reminiscent of the virtuoso technique of Ingres, under whom he studied. Although lacking his master's genius, he nevertheless proved a staunch propagator of his theories. As well as his highly sensitive portraits (*Portrait of Madame Flandrin*, Louvre), he painted large mural compositions in the spirit of the Quattrocento painters for churches in Paris and the provinces.

281 Paul Delaroche

1797–1856

The Young Martyr

1855
Oil on canvas. 1.70 x 1.48 m
Acquired in 1895. RF 1038

Although this picture's tragic subject is typical of Romanticism, its cold, smooth treatment corresponds more closely to Neoclassical aesthetics. Throughout his career, Paul Delaroche, formerly a pupil of Gros, played on this ambiguity to the delight of bourgeois clients ever-anxious to strike the happy medium. Often drawing his subject matter from European and particularly medieval history (*The Children of Edward*, Louvre), he was an exemplary exponent of the 'troubadour' style that was so popular in the first half of the 19th century.

The birth of Romanticism

The rigour, restraint and coldness which characterised Neo-classicism at the outset gradually ceased to draw the painters of the early 19th century, who were now espousing new values. The first two decades of the century spawned the beginnings of another movement, just as complex as the one which had preceded it, and which came to be known as Romanticism.

Romanticism is complex since it cannot be reduced to a single set of aesthetics: what does the vibrant colour of Antoine Gros' *Bonaparte Visiting the Plague-Stricken in Jaffa* [282] have in common with the lunar atmosphere of Prud'hon's *Justice and Divine Vengeance Pursuing Crime* [283], or the melancholy of Girodet's *Burial of Atala* [273] with the brutal realism of Géricault's *The Raft of the Medusa* [286]? What linked these artists, therefore, was not a style but their overriding desire to express personal emotions, and even more, to exalt their excesses.

And so as Romanticism developed during the next generation it staked a new claim, the right of individuals to exist as they are, with their doubts, irrationality, hopelessness and need to escape the grim realities of everyday life. This yearning for an 'elsewhere' took diverse forms: the fascination for distant, exotic lands which manifested itself, for example, in the Orientalist works of Delacroix [289, 290] and Chassériau, and in a nostalgia for bygone eras which led painters such as Delaroche to specialise in reconstitutions of historical episodes. The urge to escape constraining social realities turned the Romantic into an isolated figure left to his own emotional devices. On the other hand, liberated from academicism, the Romantic artist assumed the right to passion, to invent a manner capable of faithfully expressing his ideals and vision of the contemporary world. The era of modern painting had begun.

282 Antoine-Jean Gros

1771–1835

Bonaparte Visiting the Plague-Stricken in Jaffa

1804

Oil on canvas. 5.23 x 7.15 m

Commissioned in 1804. INV. 5064

Political events during the Revolution and the Empire provided opportunities for artists to approach history painting in a new way. The task now was to exalt the glory of contemporary heroes, and this was what Antoine Gros set out to achieve in his depictions of several episodes of the Napoleonic saga. In this 1804 propaganda picture he shows Bonaparte, then still a young general, courageously visiting plague-stricken troops during his Syrian campaign. What really happened was a different story, but this picture is nonetheless a great piece of painting and already contains some of the components of Romanticism: warm colours, powerful naturalism, and an imaginary rather than a real Orient. Four years later, Gros painted *Napoleon on the Battlefield of Eylau* (Louvre), in which we see Napoleon visiting the wounded the day after a bloody battle with the Russian army.

283 Pierre-Paul Prud'hun

1758–1823

Justice and Divine Vengeance Pursuing Crime

1808
Oil on canvas. 2.44 x 2.94 m
Commissioned by the Paris Law Courts;
Received from the City de Paris as an exchange, 1826. INV. 7340

This allegorical picture was commissioned in 1804 by the Prefect of the Seine to decorate the Assizes Chamber of the Paris law courts. In moonlit chiaroscuro, two large flying figures, Justice and Divine Vengeance, are united in the pursuit of Crime, personified by a guilty-looking man, whose naked victim sprawled on the ground symbolises the fragility of innocence. To depict this edifying subject, Prud'hon constructed a dynamic composition with skilfully organised diagonals delimiting the celestial world of punishment and the earthly world of crime. The play of light and shade heightens the dramatic effect of the protagonists' conflicting sentiments.

284 Pierre-Paul Prud'hon

1758–1823

The Empress Josephine

1805–1809
Oil on canvas. 2.44 x 1.79 m
Collection of Napoleon I
Entered the Louvre in 1879. RF 270

Born in Martininque, Marie-Josèphe Tascher de la Pagerie was brought to France at the age of 15, where she married Viscount de Beauharnais, who was guillotined during the Reign of Terror. She married Bonaparte in 1796 and was crowned Empress in 1804. Prud'hon portrays her as thoughtful and solitary, in a forest setting in the park of her residence at Malmaison. Is her melancholy due to her inability to bear the Emperor an heir – Napoleon regretfully divorced her in 1809 – or merely a meditation on the passing of time? The picture's atmosphere, conveyed with remarkable sensitivity, is a far cry from David's spartan aesthetics. Prud'hon's treatment owes more to the masters he admired, Leonardo da Vinci and Correggio, than to Neoclassicism.

Théodore Géricault

Géricault's short career – only 12 years – helped elevate him to the status of a legend, the harbinger of the great upheavals in 18th century painting, particularly Romanticism. His eccentric temperament manifested itself during his youth in his passion for horses, and it was to master the technique of drawing them that he entered the studio of Carle Vernet, famous for his equestrian pictures. Géricault devoted a large portion of his output to this theme, and the Louvre has several examples, including *An Officer of the Imperial Horse Guards Charging* [285]. After completing his training under Pierre-Narcisse Guérin, who initiated him to the technique of David, Gericault stayed a year in Italy, where he discovered Michelangelo. The figures of his famous *Raft of the Medusa* [286] are evidence of his admiration for the Florentine master. Although nurtured on classical culture, Géricault managed to break free of it by opting for a 'modern' vision of painting, depicting contemporary subjects – horse races, portraits of madmen – with powerful realism.

285 Théodore Géricault
1791–1824
An Officer of the Imperial Horse Guards Charging
1814
Oil on canvas. 2.92 x 1.94 m
Acquired in 1851. INV. 4885

286 Théodore Géricault

1791–1824

The Raft of the Medusa

1819
Oil on canvas. 4.91 x 7.16 m
Acquired in 1824. INV. 488

The subject of this huge history painting, painted in 1819, was a harrowing news story that had fired the public imagination three years earlier: the fate of 149 passengers of the French frigate *Medusa*. When the ship foundered off the coast of Senegal, they braved the open sea on a makeshift raft, and after drifting for 12 days only 15 of them lived to tell the terrifying tale of their ordeal. Géricault prepared his realist, dramatic depiction of their plight with numerous life studies of the dying and the bodies of torture victims. This moving picture of exceptional intensity has been considered by some to be the truly seminal work of the Romantic movement. It was also the last finished work of Géricault, wounded by his lukewarm reception at the 1819 Salon.

Eugène Delacroix

The emergence of a new generation of painters during the Restoration prompted a questioning of the Neoclassical model, which some forsook for a rediscovery of the pictorial tradition of the old masters. Delacroix drew his inspiration from the Venetian painters, Michelangelo and Rubens, adopting the latter's powerful composition and sumptuous colour. Although history painting was for him an opportunity to depict subjects drawn from literature (*Dante and Virgil in Hell, The Death of Sardanapalus*, 290), he also painted, like his forebear Géricault, whom he admired, large, stormy compositions inspired by contemporary events. *The Massacre at Chios* [287] was a reference to a bloody massacre during the Greek War of Independence, a cause that had mobilised intellectuals all over Europe. His 1830 picture *Liberty Guiding the People* [288] celebrated the July uprising that had overthrown Charles X that year.
A man of his time, Delacroix in turn became fascinated by the Orient, which he discovered during a trip to Morocco in 1832, which he prolonged with a foray into Algeria. It was a revelation for the young artist – 'Rome is no longer in Rome,' he wrote – and his sketchbooks (three of which are in the Louvre) would later be a mine of inspiration for him (*Women of Algiers in Their Apartment*, 289).

287 Eugène Delacroix
1798–1863
The Massacre at Chios
1825
Oil on canvas. 4.19 x 3.54 m
Acquired in 1824. INV. 3823

288 Eugène Delacroix

1798–1863

Liberty Guiding the People

1830
Oil on canvas. 2.60 x 3.25 m
Acquired in 1831. RF 129

This very famous painting was painted shortly after the three-day uprising in July 1830 which put an end to the Restoration. 'If I did not fight for my country, at least I will paint for it,' the painter declared to his brother. After numerous preparatory sketches, it took him three months to paint this exalted tribute to Liberty, symbolised by a woman leading her comrades forward over the rubble. The work, infused with an epic spirit, perfectly sums up Delacroix's artistic precepts: the quest for a synthesis between realism and the imaginary, between a brutal subject and the depiction of a humanist ideal. The canvas, as widely acclaimed today as it was when it was exhibited at the 1831 Salon, was acquired by the French State, but because of its subversive message was not shown publicly for the next 25 years.

289 Eugène Delacroix

1798–1863

Women of Algiers in Their Apartment

1834
Oil on canvas. 1.80 x 2.29 m
Acquired at the 1834 Salon. INV. 3824

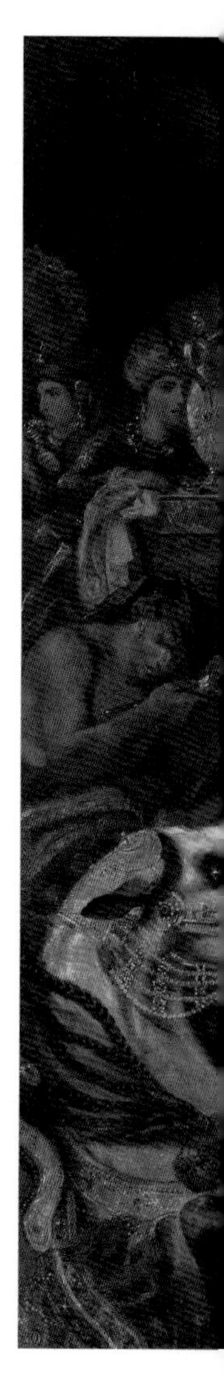

This work was the first large canvas inspired by Delacroix's trip to North Africa in 1832. It was also a remarkable demonstration of his experimentation with technique and colour. The scene is bathed in a subtle harmony of green, yellow and orange-red heightened with vibrant whites. Painted for the 1834 Salon, the picture was acquired by the State for the Musée du Luxembourg. Its success was immediate and in the next century Picasso executed a long series of variations on the work.

290 Eugène Delacroix

1798–1863

The Death of Sardanapalus

1827
Oil on canvas. 3.42 x 4.96 m
Acquired in 1921. RF 2346

This sumptuous canvas is regarded as a major manifesto of Romanticism because it combines its principal components: a lively, animated composition in the Rubens manner and a riot of warm hues vividly conveying the passionate atmosphere of the scene, set in an Oriental decor. The subject is the legendary story, drawn in part from a Byronic tragedy, of the Assyrian king Sardanapalus, who massacred his wives and family and burnt his treasures rather than abandon them to his enemies. The despot is shown on his ceremonial bed, about to die, meditating on his life's pleasures. The painter has abandoned the geometrical rigour of Neoclassical composition, entangling his figures and daring to do away with the ground and horizon. The work's sheer audacity greatly perplexed the public of the time, still entrenched in the Davidian tradition, and incurred the wrath of numerous critics.

THE METAMORPHOSIS OF LANDSCAPE

Whereas the landscape had become a genre in its own right in Holland in the 17th century, it was almost forgotten in France after Poussin and Claude Lorraine. A rediscovery of nature began in the late 18th century with the Neoclassical painters Pierre-Henri Valenciennes and Joseph Bidauld, but landscape painting, long considered a minor genre compared to 'noble painting' did not flourish until the first decades of the next century.

Of all the painters who elevated the status of landscape painting to new heights, Camille Corot is the best represented in the Louvre, with some five hundred pictures painted during his many trips to Italy (*Narni, the Augustus Bridge over the Nera*, 292) and other European countries, and of course his depictions of the French countryside such as the enigmatic *Souvenir of Mortefontaine* [293]. The peaceful forests and rivers of Île-de-France were also painted by Charles-François Daubigny and Théodore Rousseau (*Spring*, 291). In 1848, little known by the public, Rousseau moved to Barbizon near Paris, where he became a kind of model for the small colony of artists that congregated there, and paved the way for Impressionism with his innovative techniques.

291 Théodore Rousseau

1812–1867

Spring

*c.*1852

Oil on canvas. 41 x 63 cm

Thomy Thiéry Bequest, 1902. RF 1450

Unlike the solitary dreamer Corot, Théodore Rousseau was considered the leader of the 'Barbizon School', named after the hamlet on the edge of the Forest of Fontainebleau, where a group of landscape painters including Huet, Daubigny, Diaz and later Courbet congregated around him. Yet nothing had prepared Rousseau for his role as theorist. He had refused academic training, preferring instead the direct study of the old masters and taking a constant interest in his English contemporaries. His influence, however, was considerable, due to his innovative technique, a juxtaposition of coloured comma-shaped brushstrokes. The scope of this landscape reveals his profound reverence for nature, which for him had a truly metaphysical dimension.

292 Camille Corot

1796–1875

Narni, the Augustus Bridge over the Nera

Oil on paper mounted on canvas. 34 x 48 cm
Gift of Étienne Moreau-Nélaton, 1906. RF 1613

The journey to Italy had long been the painter's holy grail, since only there could one study and copy the masters and experience the power of the monuments of Antiquity at first hand. In the 19th century, this tradition continued but was accompanied by a taste for the picturesque. Corot declared that he had never been interested in the works of the ancients: it was the harmony of nature and brilliant Mediterranean light which attracted him to Italy, where he gave free rein to his sensibility, painting small canvases full of freshness and emotion, of which this is one of the most famous.

293 Camille Corot

1796–1875

Souvenir of Mortefontaine

1864
Oil on canvas. 65 x 89 cm
Acquired at the 1864 Salon. MI 692 bis

Although a keen traveller – he painted landscapes in Italy, Switzerland, the Netherlands and England – Corot remained particularly attached to the countryside around Paris. Italy had certainly taught him the power of light, but the variety of Île-de-France's ever-changing skies and colours never ceased to fascinate him. One of his favourite subjects was the Forest of Ermenonville, to the north of Paris, the setting of this famous canvas. The golden hues of his Italian landscapes have given way to a refined palette of silvery

greys, browns and light greens. The shimmering surface of the lake, seen through a faint mist, the delicate light and discreet female figures suggest a peaceful atmosphere, which Corot captures with consummate poetry. Corot's delicate touch and restrained composition are 18th-century, but his intuitive approach, modest lyricism and rejection of doctrines make him unclassifiable. Held in high esteem by his contemporaries, his oeuvre was hailed by Baudelaire as a 'miracle of the heart and mind'.

294 Camille Corot

1796–1875

Lady in Blue

1874
Oil on canvas. 80 x 50 cm
Acquired in 1912. RF 2056

Corot's prodigious output of landscapes tends to eclipse his constant interest in the human figure. He painted nudes, portraits of Italian women (*Woman with a Pearl*, Louvre) and children (*Marie-Laure Sennegon*, Louvre). Late in life, he painted numerous studies of women purely for his own pleasure, such as the melancholy *Lady in Blue*, among the works never shown during his lifetime. A woman leaning on a piece of furniture pensively clutches her fan: a magnificent piece of painting of great force and simplicity.

Italy

The Italian Primitives

There were practically no works by painters prior to Leonardo da Vinci and Raphael in the royal collections until works seized during the French revolutionary campaign in Italy entered the Louvre in 1798 (Mantegna, *Crucifixion*, 309). In 1811, the director of the new Musée Napoléon, Dominique Vivant Denon, interested in the 'primitive Italian school', personally went to Italy to requisition a number of 15th-century Florentine altarpieces, including Fra Angelico's *The Coronation of the Virgin* [301], the central panel of Filippo Lippi's *Barbadori Altarpiece* [304], Domenico Ghirlandaio's *The Visitation* [315], and even earlier works from San Francesco in Pisa such as Cimabue's *Madonna and Child Enthroned with Angels* [296]. When these pictures were officially returned in 1815, the Italian authorities allowed the Louvre to keep a number of works by the primitives, many of which were on heavy wooden panels. During the Restoration and the July Monarchy, this embryonic collection was enriched by occasional purchases, including Simone Martini's *The Carrying of the Cross* [299]. Then, under the Second Empire, came Napoleon III's momentous acquisition of works from the collection of Marquis Giampietro Campana, who had been found guilty of indiscretions as director of Rome's municipal pawnbrokers and been compelled to sell the 11,835 objects in his possession. This extraordinary purchase, which included numerous antiquities and 646 pictures, was broken up and allotted to various museums in France (the Italian primitives have fortunately since been reunited in the Musée du Petit-Palais, Avignon). The Louvre retained several masterpieces, including Paulo Uccello's *The Battle of San Romano* [306] and Cosme Tura's *Pietà* [313]. They formed the kernel of the museum's collection, which was enriched by major additions in the 20th century: Mantegna's *Saint Sebastian* [311], the five panels by Sassetta, and Piero della Francesca's *Sigismondo Pandolfo Malatesta* [303], the only picture by him in a French museum.

295 Master of San Francesco Bardi
Active in Umbria third quarter of the 13th century
Painted crucifix

1265–1270
Wood. 96 x 73 cm
Gift of the Société des Amis du Louvre, 1981.
RF 1981-48

The works known to be by the anonymous artist to whom this painted crucifix is attributed are mainly in Assisi and Perugia, indicating his probable Umbrian origin. His attempts to escape the rigid canons of the Byzantine repertoire are manifest in the expressionist treatment of Christ and the four surrounding figures.

296 Cenni di Pepi, known as Cimabue
Known from 1272 to 1302
Maestà (Madonna and Child Enthroned with Angels)

c. 1280
Tempera on wood. 4.27 x 2.80 m
San Francesco, Pisa
Entered the Louvre in 1813. INV. 254

This large altarpiece is one of the earliest testimonies to the activity of the Florentine painter Cimabue, who developed a new pictorial language in reaction to the hieratic Byzantine model. Although this *maestà* still maintains a certain formalism, the treatment of the drapery and volumes heralds new ambitions. The frame is decorated with 26 medallions representing Christ, angels, prophets and saints.

297 Pietro da Rimini

Known from 1324 to 1338

The Descent from the Cross

c.1325–1330
Wood. 43 x 35 cm
Brauer Donation, subject to usufruct, 1920
Entered the Louvre in 1932

298 Giotto di Bondone

c.1267–1337

Saint Francis of Assisi Receiving the Stigmata

c.1300
Tempera on wood. 3.13 x 1.63 m
San Francesco, Pisa.
Entered the Louvre in 1813. INV. 309

This altarpiece depicts four episodes in the life of the founder of the Franciscan order: in the main panel Saint Francis receiving the stigmata, and in the predella Pope Innocent III's vision, Innocent III approving the order's statutes and Saint Francis preaching to the birds. Already, in this early, signed work painted around the same time as the *Life of Saint Francis* frescoes in the upper basilica at Assisi, one can see the pictorial innovations – the introduction of volume and spatial depth – which revolutionised Florentine painting and prepared the way for the 'invention' of perspective in the next century.

299 Simone Martini

c.1284–1344

The Carrying of the Cross

c.1335
Tempera on wood. 30 x 20 cm
Acquired in 1834. INV. 670 bis

The pathos-charged atmosphere of this scene is conveyed by the gesture of Mary Magdalene raising her arms in pain and by the expressive faces of Christ and the Virgin Mary. The elegant drawing and refined colour are highly representative of Siennese Gothic painting, of which Simone Martini was a particularly brilliant representative. This small panel is part of a double-sided portable quadriptych whose other panels are in Antwerp and Berlin. It is thought to have been painted around 1335 in Sienna, for a member of the Orsini family.

From Trecento to Quattrocento

The pictorial renaissance brought about in Italy, notably by Giotto [298], at the end of the 13th century, in no way impaired the fascination for the Gothic style, one of whose main proponents was the Siennese painter Simone Martini. His *Carrying of the Cross* [299] already prefigured the stylistic affectedness that prevailed throughout Europe in the late 14th century and which was particularly popular among the merchant middle class. In Florence, it was a member of this rich social caste, Palla Strozzi, who commissioned Gentile da Fabriano to paint one of the most significant works of this movement in Italy, *The Adoration of the Magi*, for his family's chapel in Santa Trinita, one of whose predella panels is today in the Louvre [300].

In the first decades of the 15th century, however, Florence, influenced by the architect Filippo Brunelleschi, the sculptor Donatello and the experiments of the painter Masaccio, set out on the road to the Renaissance. Linear perspective was introduced and a new concern for realism emerged. Although he assimilated these advances, Fra Angelico remained faithful to his mystical inspiration (*The Coronation of the Virgin*, 301), Pisanello to his refined poetry (*Portrait of a Young Princess*, 302) and Sassetta to his elegant creations harking back to the previous century (*Madonna and Child Surrounded by Angels*, 305).

This new trend asserted itself in the work of Filippo Lippi, who robustly interpreted the lessons of Masaccio (*Madonna and Child Surrounded by Angels*, 304) and Piero della Francesca, a master of geometry, volume and light (*Sigismondo Pandolfo Malatesta*, 303). But none perhaps addressed the question of perspective more obsessively than the enigmatic Paolo Uccello, who in his *Battle of San Romano* [306] places his figures in space like monumental sculptures in motion.

300 Gentile da Fabriano

*c.*1370–1427

The Presentation in the Temple

1423
Tempera on wood. 26 x 66 cm
Santa Trinita, Florence
Entered the Louvre in 1812. INV. 295

The subtle colour and finesse of execution of this small panel are similar to the International Gothic style much in favour in Italy at the turn of the 14th and 15th centuries. *The Adoration of the Magi*, the main panel of the altarpiece of which *The Presentation in the Temple* was once part, today in the Uffizi Gallery, depicts a crowd of magnificently dressed figures, as requested by the painter's fabulously rich client, Palla Strozzi, whose aim was to offer his fellow Florentines the most magnificent *pala* they had ever seen.

301 Guido di Pietro, known as Fra Angelico

Known from 1417, died 1455

The Coronation of the Virgin

Before 1435
Tempera on wood. 2.09 x 2.06 m
San Domenico, Fiesole
Entered the Louvre in 1812. INV. 314

This altarpiece, the most imposing by Fra Angelico outside Italy, was one of the works chosen by Vivant Denon in 1811. It originally graced one of the three altars in the church of the Dominican monastery at Fiesole, where the painter was a monk. This work is considered to be the culmination of his artistic development from 1420 to 1430 due both to his mastery of perspective and virtuoso arrangement of figures. Fra Angelico was one of the first to understand the importance of Brunelleschi's and Masaccio's innovations and to exploit them, yet he remained committed to his personal universe and expressing his profound faith.

302 Antonio Puccio, known as Pisanello

Before 1395–1455?

Portrait of Young Princess

c. 1435
Tempera on wood. 43 x 30 cm
Acquired in 1893. RF 766

Pisanello, much in demand at Italy's most refined courts, undoubtedly painted this portrait in Ferrara, where he stayed with the Este family. The extreme purity of the profile is reminiscent of a medal, and it was in Ferrara, with its age-old tradition of engraved effigies, that the painter took up the art of the medallist, which he subsequently practiced with huge success. The picture's ground is dotted with flowers and butterflies, symbols of the youth of the model, who on her left shoulder is wearing a sprig of juniper and on her sleeve the Este family emblem, a double-handled vase.

303 Piero della Francesca

c. 1422–1492

Sigismondo Pandolfo Malatesta

c. 1450
Oil and tempera on wood. 44 x 34 cm
Acquired in 1978. RF 1978-1

This portrait is the only picture in France by the Umbrian painter Piero della Francesca. He is considered one of the most important artists of the 15th century, particularly due to his innovations in perspective geometry and treatises on painting and mathematics. The model, Sigismondo Malatesta, Lord of Rimini, was one of the most famous *condottieri* of his time. The powerful, determined figure portrayed here in profile was also a humanist, a protector of great minds and a builder. The rigorous composition, clear articulation of volumes in space and the subtle use of light are representative of the new way of seeing pioneered by Piero della Francesca, who seems to have been familiar with certain Flemish paintings present in Italy at that time.

304 Filippo Lippi

*c.*1406/07–1469

The Madonna and Child Surrounded by Angels and Saints Frediano and Augustin

(central panel of the *Barbadori Altarpiece*)
*c.*1437–1438
Wood. 2.09 x 2.06 m
San Spirito, Florence
Entered the Louvre in 1812. INV. 339

305 Stefano di Giovanni, known as Sassetta

1392?–1450

Madonna and Child Surrounded by Six Angels, Saint Anthony of Padua and Saint John the Evangelist

Between 1437 and 1444
Wood. Central panel: 2.07 x 1.18 m;
wings: 1.95 x 0.57 m
San Francesco, Borgo San Sepolcro
Acquired in 1956. RF 1956-11

These three panels painted on a gold-leaf ground were part of the double-sided polyptych Sassetta painted for the church of San Francesco at Borgo San Seplocro. The saints on either side of the Madonna and Child, Jean the Evangelist and Anthony of Padua, were originally situated together on the right, as a pendant to the Blessed Ranieri and John the Baptist. Sassetta's luxurious execution of the scene shows his fidelity to the Siennese tradition of the previous century, yet his oeuvre is widely considered to have been a decisive step towards the Renaissance.

306 Paolo di Dono, known as Uccello

1397–1475

The Battle of San Romano

c. 1435

Tempera on wood. 1.82 x 3.17 m

Campana Collection

Entered the Louvre in 1863. MI 469

Uccello depicted *The Battle of San Romano*, probably commissioned by Lionardo Bartolini Salimberi to decorate his palace in Florence, in a series of three pictures of similar format (the other two are in the Uffizi Gallery, Florence, and the National Gallery, London). They commemorate the battle between the Siennese and the Florentines in 1432, this episode showing Micheletto da Cotignola's riposte.

The huge, densely packed composition of men-at-arms and horses is given rhythm by the verticals of the legs, which are echoed above the heads by the geometric lines of the lances. Uccello, although experimenting here with the art of foreshortening with rarely-matched power, retains the ornate costumes and accessories of the Gothic style.

The dissemination of a new art

The technically sophisticated art that developed in Florence remained above all within the confines of Tuscany, Rome and Umbria until the mid-15th century, then spread astonishingly quickly throughout Italy, into court milieus very different to the mercantile republic where it had emerged. This dissemination took place as works were sent or commissioned further afield and as artists travelled to cater for widespread demand. Piero della Francesca worked at Ferrara while Filippo Lippi executed commissions in Venice and Padua, the city where Donatello had also worked at length and where the young Mantegna trained. The second generation of Florentine artists of the Quattrocento very naturally pursued the preoccupations of their forebears and further experimented with light, as illustrated by Alessio Baldovinetto (*Madonna and Child,* 307).

Meanwhile, Venice and Padua were discovering the new rules imported by great Florentines such as Uccello and Filippo Lippi, and Giovanni Bellini was learning the painter's craft from his father Jacopo. He masterfully assimilated the principles of perspective but, preoccupied also with conveying the inner landscape of the soul, painted poignantly truthful works such as *Christ Blessing* [308]. His style also owes much to his brother-in-law Andrea Mantegna, who trained in Padua and spent most of his career in the service of the dukes of Mantua (*Mars and Venus*, or *'Parnassus'*, 310).

The second half of the 15th century also saw the development of portraiture, magnificently represented in the Louvre by a work by Antonello da Messina, whose brief stay in Venice exercised considerable influence on the painters there (*Portrait of a Man*, or *'Il Condottiere'*, 312). The increasing taste for the portrayal of contemporary figures logically coincided with the rise of humanism, which made man its central focus of study, and blossomed within the broad intellectual and artistic movement known as the second Renaissance.

307 Alessio Baldovinetti

*c.*1426–1499

Madonna and Child

*c.*1460–1465
Wood. 1.06 x 0.75 m
Acquired in 1898 with the aid of the Société des Amis du Louvre
RF 1112

The attribution of this *Madonna and Child* was for a long time a matter of conjecture. Although art historians agree it dates from the mid-Quattrocento, some believe it to be an early Piero della Francesca since Baldovinetti was for a while a pupil of Domenico Veneziano, who passed on to both painters his taste for brilliant colour and sweeping landscapes. Here, the painstakingly executed landscape background, with its road, river and buildings steeped in a quite realist atmosphere, has extraordinary depth. The face of the Virgin Mary expresses gentle fervour as she gazes at the Infant Jesus placed on a balustrade. This refined and luminous work is highly representative of Florentine painting in the mid-15th century.

308 Giovanni Bellini

*c.*1430–1516

Christ Blessing

*c.*1465
Tempera on wood. 58 x 46 cm
Acquired in 1912. RF 2039

Christ resurrected, bearing the stigmata of the Passion, standing against a cloudy sky, his face still gaunt with pain, blesses humanity, on whom he is bestowing his merciful forgiveness. In his left hand he holds the Book of his word, for his disciples. Giovanni Bellini probably offered this poignant work to the monastery of Santo Stefano in Venice, his birthplace, where he was trained by his father Jacopo.

IN RI

309 Andrea Mantegna

1431–1506

Crucifixion

Late 1456 to 1460
Tempera on wood. 76 x 96 cm
San Zeno, Verona
Entred the Louvre in 1798. INV. 369

This panel is part of a triptych Mantegna painted for the church of San Zeno Maggiore in Verona. The main panels, depicting the Madonna and Child surrounded by saints, are still in place on the altar, while the central panel, *The Crucifixion*, is in the Louvre, and the *The Agony in the Garden* and *The Resurrection* in the Musée de Tours.
In this triptych, an absolute masterpiece which he painted single-handed, Mantegna demonstrates his complete mastery of perspective, stimulated by the presence in Padua, the town where he trained, of Tuscan artists such as Uccello, Lippi and Donatello. It was also there that the painter, a genuine forerunner of the Renaissance, built up a repertoire of forms inspired by classical Antiquity. His intention to create an archaeologically faithful reconstruction of the Crucifixion is manifest in the modelling of the anatomy, inspired by antique marbles, and the very precise rendering of the Roman soldiers' armour and costumes. But the scene's strangeness is due essentially to its mineral setting, with the three tall crosses placed on an area of stone paving and the hill of Golgotha depicted as a barren rock.

310 Andrea Mantegna

1431–1506

Mars and Venus, or *Parnassus*

1496–1497
Oil on canvas. 1.59 x 1.92 m
Collection of the Duke de Richelieu
Entered the Louvre in 1801. INV. 370

Presiding over this mythological allegory, the guilty lovers Mars and Venus are standing atop a rock in front of a myrtle bush or 'Venus's tree', as it was known. To the couple's left, the fruit of their union, the young Cupid, is pointing his blowpipe at the jilted husband, Vulcan. Beneath them on the left, Apollo is playing the lute, accompanying the Muses dancing in a circle, while Pegasus, about to take flight on the right, is being restrained by Mercury.

Commissioned in 1496 by Isabella d'Este, wife of Duke Francesco II of Mantua, to decorate the *studiolo* in his palace, the picture was intended to glorify the royal couple's patronage of the arts. The presence of Pegasus in particular recalls the legendary singing contest between the Pierids and the nine Muses: Mount Helicon having grown unnaturally large with pleasure, Neptune dispatched Pegasus to calm things down, and when the beast struck the mountain with its hoof, a spring flowed forth. The episode is evoked here by the stream behind the winged horse.

311 Andrea Mantegna

1431–1506

Saint Sebastian

c. 1480
Canvas. 2.55 x 1.40 m
Acquired in 1910. RF 1766

Until it was bought by the Louvre, this picture was in the Saint-Chapelle at Aigueperse, a small town in Auvergne, where it was taken after Gilbert de Bourbon-Montpensier married the daughter of Federico I Gonzaga of Mantua, Mantegna's patron, in 1481. In this very sculptural *Saint Sebastian*, with the martyr tied to an antique column and standing on Roman remains, Mantegna shows his knowledge of antiquity and demonstrates his masterfully precise draughtsmanship (he was also an exceptional engraver) and acute sense of texture in the stone and leaves on the left. As in the *Crucifixion*, he cuts off the foreground figures at chest height to accentuate spatial depth.

312 Antonello da Messina

Known in Messina 1456–1479

Portrait of a Man, or *Il Condottiere*

1475
Oil on wood. 36 x 30 cm
Acquired in 1865. MI 693

There can be no doubt as to this picture's attribution or date since Antonello da Messina took care to place a *cartellino* at the bottom, on which he wrote: *1475, Antonellus messaneus me pinxit*. The model's imperious expression and the scar on his upper lip led to the supposition in the 19th century that he was a *condottierre*, despite there being nothing to confirm this. The wonderfully simple composition and restrained palette of this portrait are highly representative of Antonello da Messina's style, all of whose models are painted in the same three-quarter pose, looking at the viewer. A Sicilian trained in Naples, a city where the new Flemish painting was well in evidence, he retained the Northern school's minutely detailed vision and masterful oil painting technique, of which he was one of the first exponents in Venice.

313 Cosme Tura

Ferrara 1430–1495

Pietà

1474 or 1480
Paint on wood transferred to canvas. 1.32 x 2.68 m
San Giorgio fuori le Mura, Ferrara.
Campana Collection
Entered the Louvre in 1863. MI 485

This *pietà* is semicircular because it was originally the top panel of a polyptych commissioned by the Roverella family in Ferrara, the central part of which is in London. The work, the most important ensemble Tura painted, is clearly influenced by Mantegna's monumental style, but the Ferrarese painter added his subtle drawing and palette and rare gift for drama. Tura executed numerous decorative projects and a few portraits. His work marked the beginning of an artistic resurgence in his city, which became one of the main centres of the Renaissance in northern Italy.

Leonardo, the universal genius

The cultural refinement in Italy at the turn of the 15th and 16th centuries is magnificently illustrated in the Louvre, notably by two frescoes by Botticelli in which we see the poetic atmosphere of his mythological works (*Venus and the Three Graces*, 314), and in pictures by another great Florentine artist, Ghirlandaio. A painter of grand architectural compositions showing his mastery of the rules of perspective, and of powerful and colourful religious scenes (*The Visitation*, 315), Ghirlandaio could also be a painter of sentiment, as proven by his very moving *Old Man and a Child* [316]. A later picture, *The Sermon of Saint Stephen at Jerusalem* [317] by the Venetian Vittore Carpaccio, also reflects the humanist culture that found its expression in a profound understanding of recent advances in pictorial art.

The most exceptional ensemble in the Louvre, however, is the museum's unique collection of paintings by Leonardo da Vinci, the most famous and priceless of which is incontestably the *Mona Lisa* [319]. It is said that the picture's royal buyer, Francis I, was so attached to his acquisition he considered it the jewel of his 'cabinet of pictures'.

Painter, sculptor, architect, engineer, musician, poet, philosopher, astronomer, anatomist, geologist and botanist, Leonardo seems to have been intent on mastering all these disciplines and was a forerunner in certain domains. He revealed himself to be a genuinely intuitive genius, and theorised on his vision of painting, which he considered a new form of philosophy and an instrument of knowledge since it enabled both intellectual speculation and visual verification through representation.

Posterity has rightfully paid tribute to this outstanding artist by transforming him into the very symbol of the Italian Renaissance. He in fact marks the turning point between an art still inspired by the Quattrocento, brilliantly represented by Botticelli, and the wholly novel art pioneered by Raphael. The Louvre provides a particularly representative panorama of his painting [318 to 321] and also has a remarkable collection of his drawings.

314 Alessandro Filipepi, known as Botticelli

c.1445–1510

Venus and the Three Graces Presenting Gifts to a Young Woman

c.1483?
Fresco. 2.11 x 2.83 m
Villa Lemmi. Acquired in 1882. RF 321

The Louvre has the rare privilege of possessing two frescoes by Botticelli, from the Villa Lemmi near Florence, which belonged to the Tornabuoni, a family allied to the Medicis. In this scene we see a young woman receiving gifts from four allegorical figures, possibly Venus and the Three Graces, while its pendant shows a young man being presented to a goddess (Venus or Minerva). They were painted after the painter returned to Rome, where he worked on frescoes in the Sistine Chapel, and after one of his most famous works, *Spring*, painted at the request of members of the Medici family. The hallmarks of Botticelli's inimitable style, the elegance of his female figures, his delicate colour and fluidly rhythmic gestures and drapery, are well in evidence.

315 Domenico di Tomaso Bigordi, known as Ghirlandaio

1449–1494

The Visitation (with Mary Jacobi and Mary Salome)

1491
Tempera on wood. 1.72 x 1.65 m
Santa Maria Maddalena dei Pazzi, Florence
Entered the Louvre in 1812. INV. 297

316 Domenico di Tomaso Bigordi, known as Ghirlandaio

1449–1494

Old Man and a Child

c. 1490
Oil on wood. 62 x 46 cm
Acquired in 1886. RF 266

The old man cuddling a little boy, probably his grandson, has not been identified, but Ghirlandaio must have had close ties with the model since he died with a drawing of him on his deathbed. The man's age-worn face is depicted with realism but also with great humanity, while his tender relationship with the child is conveyed by their intent gazes. The sobriety of the composition emphasises the intimacy of this scene, undoubtedly also a reflection on the ages of life.

A contemporary of Botticelli, with whom he occasionally worked, Domenico Ghirlandaio ran an important studio in Florence in the late 15th century. Among those who commissioned works from him were the Tornabuoni family, notably Lorenzo, for whom he painted a *pala* for the church at Cestello (now Santa Maria Maddalena dei Pazzi) in Florence [315].

317 Vittore Carpaccio

*c.*1450/54–1525/26

The Sermon of Saint Stephen at Jerusalem

*c.*1514
Oil on canvas. 1.48 x 1.94 m
Acquired by exchange from
the Pinacoteca Brera, Milan. 1812. INV. 181

In the Book of Acts, Saint Stephen, brought before the Sanhedrin for having blasphemed, having declared, 'Behold, I see the heavens opened, and the Son of Man standing on the right hand of God,' and is cast out of the city and stoned. Carpaccio tells the martyr's story in a set of six pictures executed for the Scuola dei Lanieri at San Stefano, Venice, and later dispersed when monasteries and convents were abolished in 1806. In the Louvre picture, Saint Stephen is portrayed according to the saint's iconographic tradition, as a beardless young man wearing a dalmatic. The sunny vista of Jerusalem in the background is more an exposition of the classical ideal than an attempt at realistic representation. Likewise, the figures in the foreground are more a mythical vision of the Orient than a documentary depiction of an event, despite the painter's imagination certainly having been stimulated by the many merchants of oriental origin in Venice. Here, Carpaccio again demonstrates his mastery of narrative style, following his famous cycle, *The Legend of Saint Ursula* (Venice, Galleria dell'Accademia).

318 Leonardo da Vinci

1452–1519

The Virgin of the Rocks

1483–1486
Oil on wood transferred to canvas. 1.99 x 1.22 m
Collection of Louis XII? INV. 777

The kneeling Virgin Mary has a protective hand on the infant Saint John the Baptist's shoulder while the Infant Jesus, supported by an angel, raises his chubby hand in a charming gesture of blessing. The scene's gentleness, steeped in Leonardo's characteristic *sfumato*, contrasts starkly with the strange vista of soaring rocks. In this harmonious pyramidal composition, spatial depth is created not solely by geometry but by delicate gradations of colour.
The central panel of a triptych painted for San Francesco Grande in Milan, this picture was never delivered to Leonardo's clients, for whom he painted a second version, today in the National Gallery, London.

319 Leonardo da Vinci

1452–1519

Portrait of Lisa Gherardini, known as the *Mona Lisa*

1503–1506
Oil on wood. 77 x 53 cm
Collection of Francis I? INV. 779

According to the longstanding hypothesis first formulated in the 16th century, the woman smiling the famous smile – present in many of Leonardo's pictures – is Lisa Gherardini, wife of the Florentine notable Francesco di Bartolomeo di Zanoli del Giacondo. Speculation as to her identity continues to this day, however, some commentators even believing the picture to be an androgynous self-portrait. Whoever Leonardo's model was, he defined here a feminine ideal that would exercise an enduring influence over Italian painting. The picture apparently took him five years to paint and according to Giorgio Vasari's biography, written a generation later, he never considered it finished, and this was perhaps why the painter took it with him to France, where he died in 1519.

320 Leonardo da Vinci

1452–1519

The Virgin and Child with Saint Anne

*c.*1510
Oil on wood. 1.68 x 1.30 m
Collection of Francis I? INV. 776

This picture, which Leonardo kept with him until his death, was never finished, as we can tell by the sketch still visible beneath areas of transparent paint. Taking up a rarely-used theme of medieval origin, the Virgin Mary sitting on Saint Anne's lap, the painter opted for a pyramidal yet nevertheless flowing composition, a combination of gentle curves, rounded volumes and smiling faces painted with his characteristic *sfumato* treatment. The caressing movement of the slightly pivoting Virgin Mary and the direction of the figures' gazes create an atmosphere of great tenderness between them.

321 Leonardo da Vinci

1452–1519

Saint John the Baptist

*c.*1516–1517
Oil on wood. 69 x 57 cm
Collection of Francis I? INV. 775

Executed entirely by the artist at Amboise, this is thought to be Leonardo's last picture. Saint John the Baptist, smiling, his index finger raised heavenwards, seems to have emerged from darkness to receive the Divine Light. The modelling of the face and body, obtained by a subtle gradation of light and shade and intended to create the illusion of relief, are a perfect demonstration of the *chiaroscuro* technique perfected at the turn of the 16th century, of which Leonardo was one of the pioneers.

322 Raffaello Santi, known as Raphael
1483–1520
The Virgin and Child with Saint John the Baptist or *'La Belle Jardinère'*
1507
Oil on wood. 1.22 x 0.80 m
Collection of Louis XIV. INV. 602

The hallmarks of Raphael's style during his Florentine period – clarity of composition, limpid technique, delicate colour and purity of sentiment – are well in evidence in this exquisite Madonna and Child, known as 'La Belle Jardinère' because of its rural setting. Although the form of the Virgin's face still owes much to Perugino and the pyramidal composition shows Leonardo's influence, the young painter is already asserting his own personality here, notably in the importance he accords to the representation of emotions, expressed here by the exchange of looks and the gentleness of the Virgin's maternal gestures.

The high Renaissance

Whereas the Quattrocento was characterised by its many artistic centres, dominated by the 'great workshop' of Florence, the next century saw the main hub shift to Rome and the emergence of another centre of great influence, Venice. But for the first twenty years of the Cinquecento, the artistic capital remained Florence, where Raphael had come to study Leonardo, Michelangelo and Fra Bartolommeo and master anatomy, light and the expression of feeling. One of the many Madonnas he painted during his stay there is the supremely tender *Virgin and Child with Saint John the Baptist*, known as *'La Belle Jardinère'* [322]. Summoned to Rome by Pope Julius II in 1508, Raphael was commissioned to paint frescoes for the Vatican palace, a prelude to several years of intense activity in the service of the Popes. Apart from these works, for which he employed assistants, he also executed easel paintings, notably *Saint Michael*, commissioned by Lorenzo de' Medici as a gift for Francis I and today in the Louvre along with another small *Saint Michael* and a *Saint George* [324], perhaps for the Duke of Montefeltro. Raphael also left us stunningly lifelike portraits such as the magnificent *Baldassare Castiglione* [323]. His mythical reputation, enhanced by his sudden death at the age of 37, lived on uneclipsed for the next three centuries, particularly in France.

The great Raphael was by no means the sole representative of the Renaissance movement. Others played their part in disseminating the new norms of pictorial perfection in Italy and elsewhere. Andrea del Sarto, the most outstanding representative of Florentine classicism, who succeeded in assimilating both Raphael's formal power and Leonardo's subtlety, enjoyed such renown he was summoned to France by Francis I – where he painted only one work, *Charity* [326], illustrating his ability to conceive light compositions imbued with great gentleness of feeling.

323 Raffaello Santi, known as Raphael

1483–1520

Baldassare Castiglione

*c.*1514–1515
Oil on canvas. 82 x 67 cm
Collection of Louis XIV. INV. 611

Baldassare Castiglione, the epitome of the Renaissance humanist and gentleman, was sent on ambassadorial missions to France and England and was the author of the hugely successful manual of noble conduct, *Il cortegiano* (1528), in which he defines the dialectics of the life and behaviour of the ideal courtier. He recommended in particular dressing in black, and that a costume's richness should make itself felt solely through beauty of its fabrics – a rule which, if the magnificent harmonies of black, grey and beige of this portrait are anything to go by, he seems to have obeyed himself. The only touches of colour are the model's blue eyes, whose extraordinarily piercing gaze meets the viewer's and seems to follow our every movement.

324 Raffaello Santi, known as Raphael

1483–1520

Saint George Fighting the Dragon

c. 1504
Oil on wood. 29 x 25 cm
Collection of Louis XIV. INV. 609

325 Raffaello Santi, known as Raphael

1483–1520

The Holy Family

1518
Oil on canvas. 2.07 x 1.40 m
Collection of Francis I. INV. 604

Francis I amassed an impressive collection of works by Raphael, including this *Holy Family*, which was commissioned for him, and had the painter not died prematurely, he may well have been invited to the French court. The picture's complex composition, muted tones and the elegance of the drapery show that before he died the painter was already gravitating towards a mannerist style. After a period of neglect, Raphael was rediscovered by the French in the 1650s, and until the 19th century, as the many adulatory commentaries and innumerable engravings of his works show, he was considered the greatest of all painters, the unsurpassed paragon, the very epitome of painterly genius.

326 Andrea d'Agnolo di Francesco, known as Andrea del Sarto

1486–1530

Charity

1518
Oil on cavas. 1.85 x 1.37 m
Collection of Francis I. INV. 712

A pupil of Piero di Cosimo, the Florentine Andrea del Sarto – so-named because his father was a tailor – spent his entire career in his native city except for a stay of less than a year in France, where he went at the behest of Francis I. *Charity*, an allegory of theological virtues painted while he was in France, has a pyramidal composition very similar to Leonardo da Vinci's *Saint Anne* [300]. The work is already Mannerist in tendency yet does not indulge in artificial posture, while the noble drapery of the female figure shows the artist's complete mastery of anatomy. Andrea del Sarto is considered to be most outstanding representative of Florentine classicicism.

The Venetians

Paradoxically, it was during a period of relative economic decline for Venice, in the early 16th century, that the city's intellectual and artistic life bloomed to the full. Giorgione, a product of its refined and sensitive culture, although not a prolific painter, influenced many other artists, notably Titian, with whom he worked closely. Their close ties explain why the attribution of the famous *Concert Champêtre* [327] was for a long time a bone of contention.

Gifted with an energetic and passionate temperament, Titian dominated painting in the city for almost 70 years. His pictorial language and the primacy he accorded to colour rather than drawing left a definitive mark on Venetian painting. Certain Titians in the Louvre – the remarkably psychological *Man with a Glove* [328] and the sensual *Woman with a Mirror* [330] – date from the master's early or 'classical' period, covering the first 30 years of the Cinquecento. Yet one of finest examples of his lyrical and sovereign grand manner is *The Entombment* [329], a masterly construction of formal contrasts and chiaroscuro. Among the other masterpieces in the Louvre's exceptional collection of Titians, largely acquired by Louis XIV, are *The Supper at Emmaus*, the moving *Saint Jerome* and *Christ Crowned with Thorns*, with its masterful composition of diagonals.

Some of his pupils continued his tradition in forceful style, in particular Tintoretto, who executed huge canvases for the churches of Venice and decorative cycles for public buildings: the sketch for *Paradise* [336], in the Ducal Palace, Venice, gives an idea of his ability to conceive large-scale lyrical compositions. Another of Titian's pupils, more serene in temperament, was Veronese, an exponent of brilliant colour who executed enormous, lavish compositions for the religious orders (*The Wedding Feast at Cana*, 335), and other canvases commissioned by his patrician clientele such as *The Pilgrims of Emmaus.*

327 Tiziano Vecellio, known as Titian
1488/90–1576
Concert Champêtre
c.1509
Oil on canvas. 1.10 x 1.36 m
Collection of Louis XIV. INV. 71

Although the longstanding dispute over the attribution of the *Concert Champêtre* to either Titian or Giorgione continues, there is now an emerging consensus that the picture was conceived by Giorgione and executed by Titian early in his career, a hypothesis based on the former's impasto technique and the latter's smooth brushwork. Another hypothesis is that the painting was begun by Giorgione and finished by Titian.

What appears to be a musical gathering outdoors is in fact an allegory whose meaning has been interpreted differently: is it a reflection on the relationship between music and inspiration, a reference to Virgil's Arcadia or, more broadly, a meditation on man's relationship to nature? It is today considered more likely that it is an allegory to poetry. Often copied down the centuries, *Concert Champêtre* inspired another, equally famous painting in the 19th century, Manet's *Le Déjeuner sur l'herbe* (Musée d'Orsay, Paris).

328 Tiziano Vecellio, known as Titian
1488/90–1576
Man with a Glove

c.1520
Oil on canvas. 1 x 0.89 m
Collection of Louis XIV. INV. 757

329 Tiziano Vecellio, known as Titian
1488/90–1576
The Entombment

Before 1523
Oil on canvas. 1.48 x 2.12 m
Collection of Louis XIV. INV. 749

The composition of this picture, probably painted for the Gonzagas of Mantua, was inspired by Raphael but Titian imbued it with a dramatic scale and intensity all his own. The twilight sky and masterly use of light and shade accentuate the scene's pathos-charged atmosphere, and it is with immense compassion that the painter portrayed the grief-stricken Virgin Mary by the pallid corpse of her Son.

330 Tiziano Vecellio, known as Titian

1488/90–1576

Woman with Mirrors

*c.*1515
Oil on canvas. 93 x 77 cm
Collection of Louis XIV. INV. 755

Titian's beautiful young model is attending to her hair before a mirror held up for her by a man, her back reflected in another, convex mirror behind her. The picture's serene sensuality, highly representative of the artist's style at that time, is a perfect example of the harmonious Venetian classicism which he succeeded in elevating to its most supreme expression. The exceptional ensemble of works by the painter in the Louvre also includes several male portraits, including *Man with a Glove* [328], a portrayal of a young Venetian aristocrat.

Mannerism

The style known as Mannerism began to manifest itself simultaneously in several places in Italy around 1515–20: in Sienna and Florence in the work of Pontormo and Rosso Fiorentino, and in Rome around the central figures of Michelangelo and Raphael. Finding the rigours of classicism too constraining, these artists and their followers sought to 'exceed measure with grace'. They did away with static symmetry and shunned conventional compositional formulae and faithful likeness, distorting anatomy, hypertrophying muscles and elongating limbs with the sole aim of creating harmonious forms.

Although Mannerism later became a pejorative term denoting stylistic affectation, it was at the outset, on the contrary, an art that was all lightness and imagination, as illustrated by the Florentine Pontormo's *Madonna and Child with Saint Anne and Other Saints* [333], an elegant work of rare chromatic beauty. Mannerism could also sometimes resemble a kind of painful expressionism, as in Rosso Fiorentino's *Pietà* [331], painted for Anne de Montmorency. This cultivated painter and musician, commissioned by Francis I to decorate the Château de Fontainebleau, left a lasting trace in France, but his disciples retained more his decorative talents than his dramatic power.

Another painter whose works have Mannerist tendencies was Correggio, a native of Parma, where he worked for much of his career. The undulating lines and refined atmosphere of his *Mystical Marriage of Saint Catherine* [334], a late work, are highly representative of the style's first manifestations.

331 Giovanni Battista di Jacopo, known as Rosso Fiorentino

1496–1540

Pietà

c.1530–1535
Oil on canvas. 1.27 x 1.63 m
Painted for Anne de Montmorency, Constable of France
Chapel of the Château d'Écouen
Seized during the Revolution. INV. 594

With outstretched arms, the Virgin seems to be imploring the whole of humanity to witness her grief. Embroidered on the cushions on which Christ's body is resting are the arms of the Constable of France, Anne de Montmorency, who commissioned the work for the Château d'Écouen, where it remained until it was acquired by the Louvre in the 18th century. When Rosso painted this Mannerist-inspired painting, he had just finished the Galerie Francis I at the Château de Fontainebleau. With Francesco Primaticcio and Nicolò dell'Abbate, who also worked there, he contributed to the emergence of the famous 'School of Fontainebleau' which brought France into the great pan-European movement of the Renaissance.

332 Lorenzo Lotto

*c.*1480–1556

Christ Carrying the Cross

1526
Oil on canvas. 66 x 60 cm
Acquired in 1982. RF 1982-50

Unlike the great Venetians of his generation, Lorenzo Lotto succumbed little to the charms of *sfumato*, preferring instead precise forms accentuated by saturated colour. The powerful red of Christ's robe here is a vivid illustration. Daringly framing Christ in close-up, Lotto's picture focuses on the personal tragedy of Jesus the man: in his eyes we see pain and exhaustion, while the violence to which he is being subjected is suggested by the mimicking Roman soldiers and the hand holding him by the hair. Except for a few rare mythological works and portraits, Lorenzo Lotto's entire output consists of religious works shot through with the faith that would lead him to enter a monastery as an oblate.

333 Jacopo Carucci, known as Pontormo

1494–1556

Madonna and Child with Saint Anne and Four Saints

c. 1527–1529
Oil on wood. 2.28 x 1.76 m
Couvent of Sant'Anna in Verzaia, Florence.
Entered the Louvre in 1814. INV. 232

334 Antonio Allegri, known as Correggio

1489?–1534

The Mystic Marriage of Saint Catherine

c. 1526–1527
Oil on wood. 1.05 x 1.02 m
Collection of Louis XIV. INV. 41

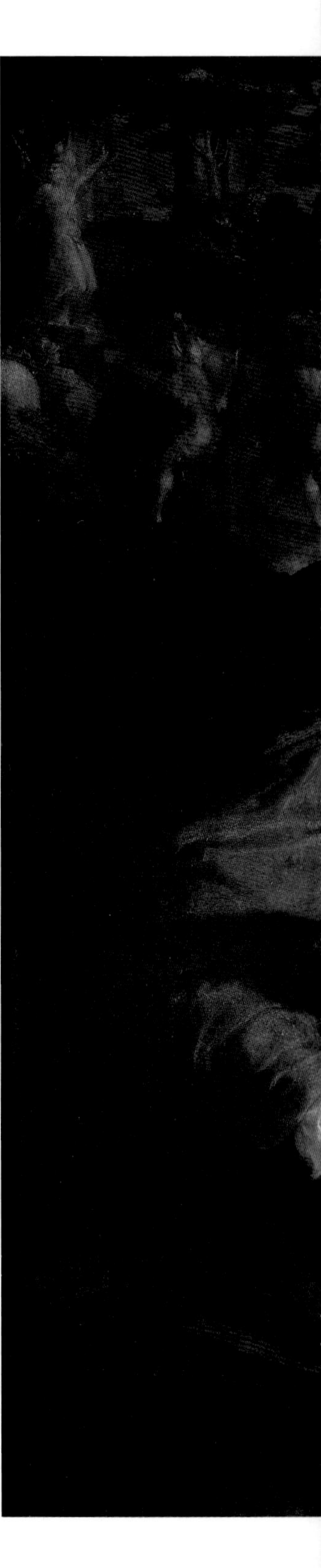

335 Paolo Caliari, known as Veronese

1528–1588

The Wedding Feast at Cana

1562–1563
Oil on canvas. 6.77 x 9.94 m
San Giorgio Maggiore, Venice
Entered the Louvre in 1798. INV. 142

Veronese crowded 130 figures into this almost 10 metres-high composition, including, as was traditional, Renaissance princes such as Charles V of Spain, Francis I of France and Suleiman the Magnificent, and, disguised as musicians in the foreground, the great Venetian masters Titian, Tintoretto, Bassano and himself, dressed in white. 'For this kind of large-format painting,' wrote Veronese, 'the painter needs, after the fashion

of the poet, the freedom to add figures supplementary to those strictly required by the story.' And the painter from Verona did indeed allow his imagination free rein in *The Wedding Feast at Cana*, in which only the disciples appear to pay attention to Christ seated in the middle. The vast architectural setting, inspired by Palladio, with lateral staircases leading up to a balustraded terrace, transforms the picture into what one imagines a theatre stage may have looked like in the 16th century. Commissioned by the Benedictine monks of San Giorgio Maggiore for the refectory of their abbey, the picture was one of the works brought back by Napolean's army in 1798. The picture's recent restoration involving the removal of the yellowed varnish and repainting, has brought out the full richness of the colours.

336 Jacopo Robusti, known as Tintoretto

1518–1594

The Coronation of the Virgin or *Paradise*

c.1580
Oil on canvas. 1.43 x 3.62 m
Entered the Louvre in 1798. INV. 570

After the Chamber of the Great Council in the Doges' Palace in Venice was gutted by fire in 1577, a competition was held for the redecoration of the end wall. Tintoretto presented this project alongside those of Palma the Younger and two other artists of his generation much in demand, Veronese and Bassano. Although Veronese and Bassano won the competition, they could not immediately execute the commission, and when Veronese died in 1588 it fell to Tintoretto and his assistants to execute the definitive composition, which is still in situ. In this sketch executed by Tintoretto himself, we see all his fiery visionary vigour, the same *furia* with which he painted the most spectacular work of his career, the cycle of paintings in the Scuola di San Rocco.

337 Paolo Caliari, known as Veronese

1528–1588

Portrait of a Lady, known as *Bella Nani*

c.1560
Oil on canvas. 1.19 x 1.03 m
Baron Basile de Schlichting Bequest, 1914
RF 2111

Veronese's undeniable talent for portraiture is manifest in the numerous figures peopling his large frescoes, but he also painted more modest-sized pictures in which he portrayed individual figures. We unfortunately know nothing of the beautiful, milky complexioned woman who modelled for him here. She may have been a courtesan or perhaps a young bride or, more probably, a patrician. It has also been argued that this is a representation of the ideal woman.

338 Federico Barocci (or Baroccio)

*c.*1535–1612

The Circumcision

1590
Oil on canvas. 3.56 x 2.51 m
Entered the Louvre in 1798. MI 315

This picture was originally painted for the main altar of the Church of the Name of Jesus in Pesaro, near Urbino, Barocci's birthplace. After training in Rome, Barocci worked for most of his career in his home town, painting mainly for the ducal family. His provincial existence enabled him to develop an original style and a highly personal interpretation of Mannerism prefiguring the Baroque. Using subtle perspective, he sets the actual circumcision scene itself quite far back, freeing the foreground for a masterfully painted still life. His colour harmonies are extremely refined and the ephemeral drapery and figures seem to be bathed in an atmosphere that is both strange and familiar.

Late 16th – 17th century

In the late 16th century and first half of the next century, Rome, the seat of the Papacy, which had recovered its prestige after the Council of Trent, became capital of the arts in Italy. The triumph of the Counter-Reformation and the Catholic Church's determination to assert its authority through ambitious artistic projects explains why painters flocked to Rome from all over Italy and exchanged views in the highly competitive atmosphere there.

Following in Michelangelo's and Raphael's footsteps came the delicately lyrical painter Guido Reni (*The Rape of Helena*, 344), a disciple of his Bolognese compatriot Annibale Carracci. The latter advocated a return to naturalism, notably through his teaching at the academy he founded in his native city. *The Virgin Appearing to Saint Luke and Saint Catherine* [341] was painted in Bologna before his departure for Rome, where he gravitated towards increasingly idealised forms.

But one of the major figures of the period was undoubtedly Caravaggio, whose revolutionary principles would have a profound influence on European painting through the movement named after him, Caravaggism. He was born in Lombardy and, after an apprenticeship in Milan, arrived in Rome around 1592, aged about 20. Violent, tormented, constantly getting into fights and preferring the company of the lower classes, he very quickly asserted his personality in his early works, in which he freely interpreted traditional schemas by introducing elements of everyday reality. His series of depictions of working class figures such as *The Fortune Teller* [340] dates from this period. His talent did not go unnoticed and soon won him numerous commissions. Whether mythological or religious in subject, his pictures reflect his will to do away with conventions. Caravaggio established no class or value hierarchy between the figures he depicted. *The Death of the Virgin* [342] is a perfect illustration of his ability to transpose reality, but also to create dramatic intensity. Badly received by the clergy but much admired, the canvas was bought by the Duke of Mantua on Rubens's advice.

Among those influenced by Caravaggio's style was the Bolognese painter Guercino, who worked for almost his entire career in his native region, devoting his life to his art and expressing sincere and ardent sentiments in works based on the imitation of nature (*The Raising of Lazarus*, 343).

339 Giuseppe Arcimboldo

1527–1593

Summer

1573

Oil on canvas. 76 x 63 cm

Acquired in 1964. RF 1964-31

The late Mannerist Milanese artist Giuseppe Arcimabaldo spent most of his career in Prague. He devised extraordinary compositions by juxtaposing objects, flowers and fruit to create human or allegorical heads. This picture is one of the *Four Seasons* series in the Louvre.

340 Michelangelo Merisi, known as Caravaggio

*c.*1571–1610

The Fortune Teller

*c.*1595–1598
Oil on canvas. 0.99 x 1.31 m
Collection of Louis XIV. INV. 55

On his arrival in Rome in around 1592, the young Caravaggio led a Bohemian life, mixing with working-class people whilst frequenting the aristocratic patrons and collectors on whom he largely depended for a livelihood. And it was the blunt everyday realities he experienced at first hand which he sought to recreate in his works, regardless of whether their subject was religious, mythological or profane. *The Fortune Teller*, whose protagonists stand out against a uniform, light background which heightens their presence, is one of a series of small easel paintings he painted during this period, in which he asserts his realist style with great power.

341 Annibale Carracci

1560–1609

The Virgin Appearing to Saint Luke and Saint Catherine

1592
Oil on canvas. 4.01 x 2.26 m
Entered the Louvre in 1797. INV. 196

This monumental *pala,* painted for the cathedral of Reggio Emilia, dates from Carracci's Bolognese period, before he moved to Rome in 1595. At that time he was still living in his hometown, often working in collaboration with his brother Agostino and his cousin Lodovico. In reaction to the excesses of Mannerism, the Carraccis advocated a return to naturalism and together founded an academy there which had a decisive influence on many painters. Having notably chosen as his masters the great Venetians and Correggio, in his view the only painters able to sublimate reality whilst respecting nature's forms of nature, Carracci imbues this picture with a lyrical grandeur which in his later works would develop into a more severe style.

342 Michelangelo Merisi, known as Caravaggio

*c.*1571–1610

The Death of the Virgin

1601–1605/06
Oil on canvas. 3.69 x 2.45 m
Collection of Louis XIV. INV. 54

Caravaggio can be considered the first 'realist' in the most modern sense of the term, because from his youth he preoccupied himself with representing the world around him and introducing the truth of everyday life into his works. This was what he set out to do in this striking picture, in which he portrays the dying Virgin Mary as an ordinary working woman with a wrinkled neck and swollen ankles. The picture, commissioned for the church of Santa Maria della Scala in Rome, was turned down by the clergy, who were shocked by his realist treatment of a sacred theme. Yet there is an intense spirituality in this harrowing scene, which Caravaggio conveys through his use of chiaroscuro, the expressive use of harshly contrasting light and shade which he pioneered.

343 Giovanni Francesco Barbieri, known as Guercino

1591–1666

The Raising of Lazarus

c. 1619
Oil on canvas. 2 x 2.33 m
Collection of Louis XVI. INV. 77

344 Guido Reni

1573–1642

The Rape of Helena

1626–1629
Oil on canvas. 2.53 x 1.65 m
Seized during the Revolution. INV. 539

Guido Reni received his initial training in his native Bologna, where the principles of a return to naturalism advocated by the Carraccis had a decisive influence on him. He left for Rome to study Raphael and antique sculpture and stayed there 12 years, developing his personal, expressive and refined style. On his return to Bologna, he pursued his brilliant career painting religious and mythological subjects of singular intensity and lyricism. He gradually lightened his palette, his colour becoming almost transparent, as in the graceful *Rape of Helena*, in which the group of figures stands out against a bright seaside sky.

345 Giambattista Tiepolo

1696–1770

The Last Supper

c.1745–1750
Oil on canvas. 8.05 x 8.95 m
Acquired in 1877. RF 176

Swansongs

Although the 18th-century Italian art scene abounds with personalities, it is difficult to group them into any homogeneous movement. Grand spiritual visions were no longer the order of the day and were superseded by a more intimate and decorative art, while the century also saw the development of portraiture, landscape painting, various types of *vedute* and genre pictures, all hitherto considered minor.

Eighteenth-century Italian painting, represented in the Louvre by over 500 works, entered the museum notably as spoils from the Revolutionary campaign in Italy, notably ten of Francesco Guardi's magnificent series of 12 paintings depicting Venetian festivities (*The Bucentaur Departs for the Lido on Ascension Day*, 348). From Louis-Philippe's reign (1830–48), a set of canvases by the Roman painter Giovanni Paolo Pannini entered the museum – the *Gallery of Views of Ancient Rome* [349], however, was a gift in 1944 – and several views of architectural ruins reflecting the prodigious interest aroused by the archaeological discoveries at Pompeii and Herculaneum.

But Venetian painting was incontestably favoured, since in the collections there were several religious and mythological works by Giambattista Tiepolo (*The Last Supper*, 345) and a more eclectic selection of biblical subjects by his son Giandomenico (*Christ and the Adulteress, Rebecca at the Well*), genre scenes (*Carnival Scene*) and decorative pieces.

The collection has been complemented since the Second World War and now includes works by Lombard, Neapolitan and Roman artists. The most recent additions were the 1970 acquisition of a picture by the Bolognese painter Giuseppe Crespi, an eclectic artist who painted numerous genre scenes (*The Flea Hunt*, 346) but who at the end of his career produced religious paintings, and the donation by the Société des Amis du Louvre in 1990 of *The Sitting* [347], a remarkable genre scene by the Neopolitan Gaspare Traversi. Settecento Roman painting is also well-represented in Louvre thanks to the Lemme Donation.

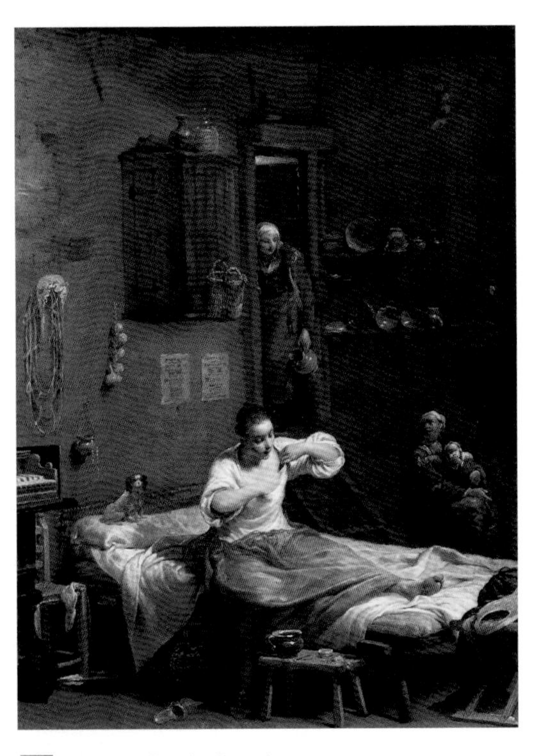

346 Giuseppe Maria Crespi

1665–1747

The Flea Hunt

*c.*1720–1725
Oil on canvas. 54 x 40 cm
Gift of the Société des Amis du Louvre, 1970
RF 1970-40

A great admirer of Dutch genre painting, which he discovered in the Medici collection, Crespi was very interested in the realistic depiction of everyday life. *The Flea Hunt* – of which he painted several versions – belonged to a series of pictures, now lost, showing the life of a singer from her debut to her late years devoted to worship. The Bolognese painter produced few pictures of this type, however, but passed on his taste for the genre scene to two of his pupils, Piazzetta and Longhi.

347 Gaspare Traversi

1722/24–1770

The Sitting

1754
Oil on canvas. 0.99 x 1.30 m
Gift of the Société des Amis du Louvre, 1990
RF 1990-1

The reserved expression of the young woman posing contrasts strikingly with those of the figures surrounding the draughtsman, who appears to be partially listening to their admiring banter. This scene from everyday life is highly representative of this Neapolitan painter's gift for observation. Gaspare Traversi honed his acutely perceptive eye for the daily life and psychology of his contemporaries, frequently painting subjects such as fights, card games and the drawing up of contracts. Yet despite their light-hearted subject matter, his extremely rigorous compositions show his perfect knowledge of the great masters.

348 Francesco Guardi

1712–1793

The Bucentaur Departs for the Lido on Ascension Day

between 1766 and 1770
Oil on canvas. 0.66 x 1.01 m
Seized during the Revolution. INV. 20009

In 1763, the city of Venice organised sumptuous festivities lasting several days to celebrate the election of Doge Alviso Mocenigo, and some years later Francesco Guardi commemorated these events in a series of 12 pictures – six of which are in the Louvre – inspired by engravings by another great Venetian painter, Antonio Canaletto. The scene here is the departure of the Doge's galley *Bucentaur* for the Lido, where each Ascension Day Venice was symbolically married to the Adriatic. Guardi recreates this picturesque scene with great sensitivity, bathing it in a festive, luminous atmosphere.

349 Giovanni Paolo Pannini

1691–1765

Gallery of Views of Ancient Rome

1758
Oil on canvas. 2.31 x 3.03 m
Princess Edmond de Polignac Bequest, 1944
RF 1944-21

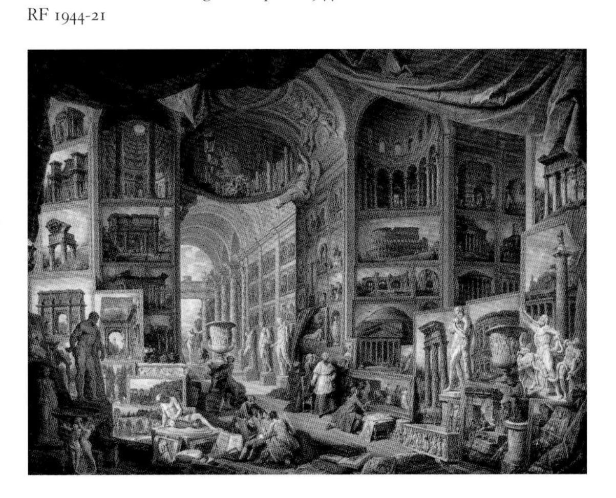

A veritable passion for archaeology swept Italy and then the rest of Europe after the discovery of the ruins of Pompeii and Herculaneum. Specialised in views of antique architecture, which he produced in great number, Pannini has brought here together most of the Roman monuments he had previously painted separately, creating a kind of catalogue of his production in the form of a picture gallery. The canvas's pendant, *Gallery of Views of Modern Rome*, repeats the same principle.

Spain

History of a rediscovery

Spanish painting was virtually absent from the royal collections until the 18th century, the only pictures under Louis XIV being a few family portraits sent from Madrid and Francisco Collantes' *Burning Bush*. Except for the acquisition of several Murillos under Louis XVI, including *The Young Beggar* [356] in 1782, there were few additions until the early 19th century. With the advent of Romanticism Spain became suddenly fashionable. Writers were captivated by its romance-steeped, contrasted atmosphere, while painters and art lovers marvelled at the dark passion of the tenebrist works of the Spanish Golden Age.

Important private collections began to be amassed, some, like Marshall Soult's, enriched under the ephemeral regime of Joseph Bonaparte, others swelled by acquisitions facilitated by the abolition of religious orders in Spain and the Carlist Wars. King Louis-Philippe, who sent Baron Taylor to look for art works for him, built up a prodigious collection of over 400 works by all the great masters. But no sooner had his famous 'Spanish Gallery' been exhibited from 1838 to 1848 at the Louvre, where its influence on painters such as Manet was decisive, than it was auctioned in London in 1853 and dispersed for ever. Only much later would one of the El Grecos, *Christ on the Cross Adored by Two Donors* [353], return to the Louvre. The dispersal of the Soult Collection did, on the other hand, enable the acquisition of two Murillos, a Herrera and three Zurbaráns, including the two *Scenes from the Life of Saint Bonaventura* [354].

Donations and purchases continued until the beginning of the 20th century, when the focus shifted to the Primitives, notably with acquisitions of works by the Catalans Bernardo Martorell [350] and Jaume Huguet [351]. The same concern for diversification led to purchases of 16th and 17th-century pictures, with the result that Louvre today offers a remarkable panorama of Spanish painting from the Gothic period to Goya.

350 Bernardo Martorell

Known from 1427 to 1452

The Legend of Saint George: The Flagellation

*c.*1435
Wood. 1.07 x 0.53 m
Gift of the Société des Amis du Louvre, 1904. RF 1572

Legend has it that Saint George, born in Cappadocia, fell victim to Diocletian's persecution of the Christians in Palestine and endured horrific torture before he was decapitated. The four scenes in the Louvre are *The Judgement of Saint George*, *The Saint Dragged Through the City*, *The Saint Decapitated* and *The Flagellation*. The central panel, *Saint George Killing the Dragon,* is in the Art Institute of Chicago. Bernardo Martorell, one of Barcelona's most successful painters, revitalised the Gothic taste of the period with his highly personal touch, imbuing his works with psychological observation and dramatic power.

351 Jaume Huguet

*c.*1415–1492

The Flagellation of Christ

*c.*1450–1455
Wood. 0.92 x 1.56 m
Chapel of Saint Mark, Barcelona Cathedral
Acquired in 1967 with the aid of the Société des Amis du Louvre. RF 1967-6

The boots on either side indicate this picture's origin: it was commissioned by the Barcelona shoemakers' guild, for the front of the altar of their chapel in the cathedral. Jaume Huguet, who trained in Martorell's studio, dominated Catalan painting in the second half of the 15th century. *The Flagellation of Christ* dates from his late period when, although remaining faithful to medieval sensibility and the dictates of the International Gothic style, his construction became ampler and his figures, set in a rigorously organised geometric space, took on more monumentality.

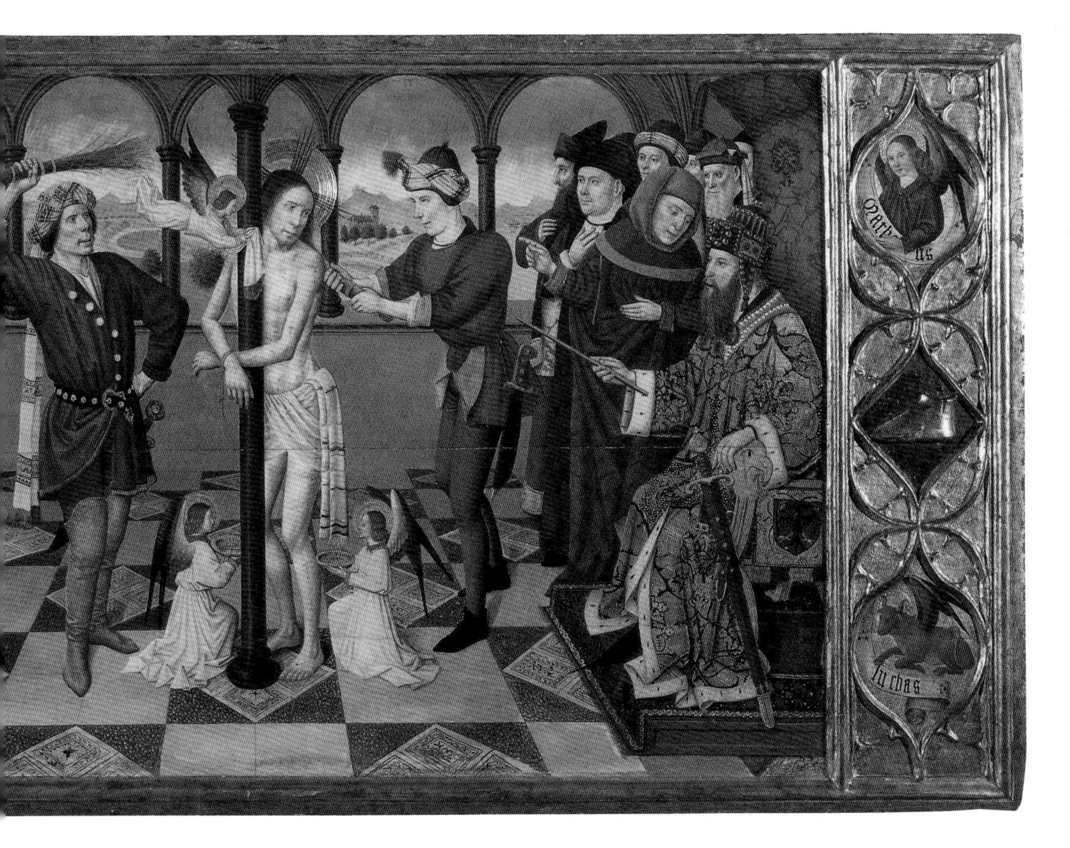

The visions of El Greco

Paradoxically, the most daring artist in late 16th-century Spain came from the Byzantine pictorial tradition, which had hardly evolved since the Middle Ages. Domenikos Theotokopoulos, later known as El Greco, began his training painting icons on his native island of Crete before leaving for Italy, where working in Titian's studio in Venice and the influence of Tintoretto radically transformed his style. After moving to Rome in 1570, he left six years later for Spain without having gained fame. During his stay in Italy, however, he had assimilated the lessons of the Renaissance and late Mannerism. In 1577, after a brief sojourn at the Escorial, El Greco arrived in Toledo to begin his first major commission, a picture for the sacristy of the cathedral. He spent the rest of his career in Spain, working under the aegis of the Church and the royal court.

The Counter-Reformation, launched by the Council of Trent, was now in full swing, and all Spanish art during this period and especially El Greco's has to be considered in this impassioned context. The vision-like *Christ on the Cross Adored by Two Donors* [353] illustrates the climate of strict piety that now prevailed, and which El Greco imbues with a genuinely sublime dimension. The sombre, tormented, stormy sky, Jesus' pallid drawn-out body on the cross and the ecstatic faces convey an atmosphere of profound mysticism. In the same manner, in conformity with the new dogma extolling active faith, divine grace no longer sufficing for salvation, he depicts *Saint Louis, King of France* [352] in armour – an allusion to the Crusades – charged with both powerful passion and infinite mercy.

El Greco both transformed and elevated the Mannerist style, imbuing it with a visionary dimension that would intensify during his late period. Although the vast majority of his works were religious subjects, he painted several magnificent landscapes and portraits (*Antonio de Covarrubias y Leiva*, Louvre).

352 Domenikos Theotokopoulos, known as El Greco

1541–1614

Saint Louis, King of France, with a Page

4th quarter of the 16th century
Oil on canvas. 1.20 x 0.96 m
Acquired in 1903. RF 1507

353 Domenikos Theotokopoulos, known as El Greco

1541–1614

Christ on the Cross Adored by Two Donors

c. 1585–90
Oil on canvas. 2.60 x 1.71 m
Church of the Hieronymite nuns of La Reina, Toledo.
Louis-Philippe's Spanish Gallery
Acquired in 1908. RF 1713

Painted during El Greco's early years in Spain, this picture once decorated an altar in the church of the Hieronymite nuns of La Reina in Toledo, but the two donors have never been identified with certainty. It is one of the earliest of the many Crucifixions he painted. The cross occupies the whole of this rigorous, cold-hued composition, powerfully imposing the fleshly presence of the Son of God on the congregation.

IHΣ NAZΩPAIΘ
OBAΣIΛEYΣ TΩN
IOYΔAIΩN

The Golden Age

Although Caravaggesque naturalism did not originate in Spain, it found an extremely original expression in the hands of Spanish painters, in works combining the concrete and the abstract, utter realism and fervent spirituality. The genius of Spain's Golden Age was embodied in the exceptional personalities of a handful of artists born at the cusp of the 16th and 17th centuries. Jusepe de Ribera, who spent most of his career working for the Spanish viceroys in Italy, gravitated from a particularly violent interpretation of Caravaggism in his early period to the lighter palette of late works such as *The Club-Footed Boy* [355], a cruelly realist yet deeply moving portrait of a young cripple, grinning as he poses like some proud hidalgo. Francisco de Zurbarán, a few years younger than Ribera, in turn produced tenebrist works of great power: the Louvre has two *Scenes from the Life of Saint Bonaventura* [354] and his exceptional *Saint Apollonia,* works highly representative of the pictorial language of his monumental compositions conveying lofty sentiments. Zurbarán's and Ribera's work, omnipresent in Sevillian collections, must have greatly influenced the young Murillo, whose early work is still marked by tenebrism, as shown by *The Angels' Kitchen*, part of his first commission, a series of pictures painted for the Franciscans of Seville. Later influenced by Van Dyck, Rubens's flamboyant dynamism and the decorative baroque imported from Flanders, Murillo lightened his palette and softened his style (*The Holy Family*, Louvre). A prolific painter, he produced a great many religious works, but also portraits and genre paintings depicting street children, *The Young Beggar* [356] being one of the most famous.

The typically Spanish tradition of social realism endured into the 19th century, later dominated by the towering personality of Goya [357, 358].

354 Francisco de Zurbarán

1598–1664

Saint Bonaventura's Lying in State

1629

Oil on canvas. 2.45 x 2.20 m

Church of Saint Bonaventure College, Seville

Acquired from the heirs of Marshall Soult, 1858.

MI 205

Saint Bonaventura died during the Council of Lyon, poisoned, it has been suggested, by those who feared his attempt at reconciliation would succeed. In the funerary scene depicted here, he is dressed in the white of triumphant purity, the luminous diagonal of his body contrasting with the muted greys of the surrounding crowd. In the same way, Zurbarán contrasts the reverence of the austerely dressed Franciscans with the attitude of Pope Gregory X and King James I of Aragon, who appear to be discussing worldly matters. And therein lies Zurbarán's genius, in his ability to fervently depict monastic spirituality without losing sight of worldly realities.

355 Jusepe de Ribera

1591–1652

The Club-Footed Boy

1642

Oil on canvas. 1.64 x 0.93 m

Dr Louis La Caze Bequest, 1869. MI 893

356 Bartolomé Esteban Murillo

1618–1682

The Young Beggar

*c.*1650
Oil on canvas. 1.34 x 1 m
Collection of Louis XVI. INV. 933

A young boy dressed in rags, his feet bare and dirty, is delousing himself in a corner, the harsh light rendering his misery even more palpable. This brutally realist yet moving 'slice of life' was the first of a series of popular scenes which Murillo continued throughout his career. His work still bears the hallmarks of the tenebrist tradition, that is, a predominance of dark tones and the use of harsh chiaroscuro for dramatic effect. This style, in which the Spaniards of the Golden Age were masters, fascinated 19th-century French painters.

357 Francisco José de Goya y Lucientes

1746–1828

The Marquesa de la Solana

Oil on canvas. 1.81 x 1.22 m
c. 1493–1495
Gift of Carlos de Beistegui, 1942.
Entered the Louvre in 1953. RF 1942-23

Aware that she was terminally ill, the Marquesa de la Solana (1757–95) commissioned Goya to paint her portrait so that her only daughter would have a picture of her. Portraying his subject standing, as he often did in his many portraits of aristocrats, he has captured the full depth of the young woman's grave expression, which is rendered even more poignant by the consummately subtle harmony of greys and blacks heightened by the pink ribbon.

358 Francisco José de Goya y Lucientes

1746–1828

Ferdinand Guillemardet

1798
Oil on canvas. 1.86 x 1.24 m
Louis Guillemardet Bequest, 1865. MI 697

A doctor and former member of the Convention, Ferdinand Guillemardet was French ambassador in Madrid from 1798 to 1800. In his old age, Goya said he considered this dazzlingly executed canvas, a veritable hymn to the French Republic, to be one of his finest works. The son of Ferdinand Guillemardet, who was a friend of Delacroix, bequeathed this work to the Louvre.

Germany

From Gothic art to Humanism

Very few museums outside Germany can boast a collection covering the entire history of painting in the Germanic countries and the Louvre is no exception, but it does possess a number of significant ensembles such as that of the School of Cologne. This prosperous city, the economic and religious capital of the Rhineland and renowned from Charlemagne's time for its priceless silverware and miniatures, became an important artistic centre in the Middle Ages. This activity culminated in the mid-15th century with Stefan Lochner, a master whose prestige endured until the end of the century in the work of disciples faithful to his brilliant colours and remarkable gift for narrative. In the rooms devoted to German painting there is a sumptuous altar picture by the Master of the Saint Bartholomew Altarpiece, *The Descent from the Cross* [360], painted in the mannerist style of very late Gothic, probably by an artist of Dutch origin, and the *Altarpiece of the Seven Joys of Mary* [359], attributed to the Master of the Holy Family.

However, the period considered to be the golden age of Germanic art came at the cusp of the 15th and 16th centuries. The German 'Renaissance', complex and so diverse as to elude definition, was above all the work of a few isolated artists, none of whom acquired any real following but who asserted themselves by their eccentric temperament. Albrecht Dürer ranks foremost among these brilliant personalities. Born into the Gothic tradition, he learned the lessons of Italian art during his two trips to Italy, combining the technical perfection and expressive force of Germanic art with the Italian assertion of individualism. In the inscription on his famous *Self-Portrait* [361], painted when he was 22, immediately before his departure for Venice, he already expresses his conviction that he had been vested with a spiritual mission: *'My Sach die gat / Als es oben Schtat'* ('My affairs follow the course assigned to them on high').

359 Master of the Holy Family

Active in Cologne 1475–1510

Altarpiece of the Seven Joys of Mary

c. 1480

Wood. 1.27 x 1.82 m

Benedictine convent of the Maccabees, Cologne. Acquired in 1912, with aid from the children of Jean Dollfus. RF 2045

On the altarpiece's centre panel, we see Mary offering two doves in sacrifice beside the priest Simon presenting the Infant Jesus to the faithful in the Temple, while the left panel shows the adoration of the Magi, and the right panel Mary and Jesus reunited after the Resurrection. From the Benedictine convent of the Maccabees in Cologne, this altarpiece originally had two wings, now in Nuremburg, *The Annunciation* and *The Nativity* on the left, and *The Ascension* and *The Assumption* on the right, which were visible only when it was open. The richness of the fabrics and intricacy of the metalwork are rendered with remarkable skill, in accordance with Gothic taste, while the vivid colours recall that the painter also produced cartoons for stained glass.

IH SVS NA
EX VDEORV

360 Master of the
Saint Bartholomew Altarpiece

Active in Cologne *c.*1480–1510

The Descent from the Cross

*c.*1501–05.
Wood. 2.27 and 1,52 x 2.10 m
Val-de-Grâce, Paris. Entered the Muséum Central des Arts in 1797. INV. 1445

One of the most striking elements of this altarpiece is the trompe-l'œil illusion it creates: Christ's limp body appears to be literally hanging out of the picture space. The work's artful composition, relief and overall theatricality are like a staging of a medieval mystery play. Seized from the Val-de-Grâce during the Revolution, the altarpiece formerly stood in the Professed House of the Jesuits in Paris, though it is not known how it found its way there.

361 Albrecht Dürer

1471–1528

Self-Portrait

1493
Oil on parchment mounted on canvas
56 x 44 cm
Acquired in 1922. RF 2382

In this self-portrait, his first, Dürer portrays himself holding a sprig of eryngium, a thistle-like plant which in Germany symbolised marital fidelity. This is why the picture is thought to have been painted for his fiancée Agnes Frey, whom he married the following year. Another hypothesis is that this prickly plant was an allusion to Christ's Passion, Dürer therefore assimilating his role as an artist to a divine mission.

362 Lucas Cranach the Elder
1472–1553
Portrait of a Young Girl (Magdalena Luther?)
c. 1540?
Oil on wood. 41 x 26 cm
Acquired in 1910. RF 1767

From Cranach to Friedrich

Unlike Dürer, Lucas Cranach showed little interest in the aesthetic innovations in Italy. Born into the Gothic tradition, he remained attached to its realism, to which he added his marked taste for precious details and background landscapes partially inspired by the works of the Danube School, which he discovered in Vienna. Official painter to the court of the Electors of Saxony for 50 years, he also participated in the great movement of humanism and the Reformation. His friendship with Martin Luther is the premise for the belief that the small Louvre portrait is of the latter's daughter (*Magdalena Luther*, 362). After producing mainly religious pictures and portraits, from around 1525 Cranach executed numerous commissions for mythological and allegorical pictures. The theme for which he became famous, the female nude standing alone in a poetic landscape (*Venus*, 363), appeared at this time.
The third great figure of the Renaissance period was Hans Holbein the Younger. The five portraits by him in the Louvre were bought by Louis XIV in 1671 from the famous Cologne-born collector established in Paris, Eberhardt Jabach: *Erasmus* [364], *William Warham*, Archbishop of Canterbury, *Nicolas Kratzer* [366], astronomer to Henry VIII, *Anne of Cleves* [365], Henry VIII's fourth wife, and *Henry Wyatt*, adviser to the English court. Several are portrayed with the attributes of their profession.
Other prestigious 16th-century German painters – Baldung Grien, Beham, Maler and Huber – are present in the Louvre. The Germanic works of the next two centuries are even more varied, ranging from 17th-century still lifes to 18th-century mythological and religious pictures, while the major 19th-century movements, Neoclassicism, the Biedermeier Period and Romanticism are also in evidence, the latter notably in two works by Caspar David Friedrich: his famous *Tree of Crows* [367] and *Seashore by Moonlight* [368], a gift of the Société des Amis du Louvre in 2000.

363 Lucas Cranach the Elder
1472–1553
Venus Standing in a Landscape
1529
Oil on wood. 38 x 25 cm
Entered the Louvre from Germany in 1806
INV. 1180

The accessories with which Cranach adorned this Venus – wide-brimmed red hat, jewelled necklace, diaphanous veil – render her nudity all the more striking. Exhibiting herself with demure unaffectedness, she stands out starkly against a dark backdrop of pines, which in turn contrasts with the luminous landscape beyond, its Gothic town reflected in water. This refined, Mannerist-inspired work dates from the artist's late period, when the Venuses and mythological works he produced in his Wittenberg studio were much in demand.

364 Hans Holbein the Younger

1497/98–1543

Erasmus

1523
Oil on wood. 42 x 32 cm
Collection of Louis XIV. INV. 1345

Commissioned to illustrate a work by the theologian Erasmus in 1516 – he was not yet 20 – Holbein struck up a lasting friendship with him and painted his portrait several times. The humanist scholar, then 56, is shown here writing his commentary on Saint Mark's gospel in *Paraphrases on the New Testament*, an exemplary portrayal of the humanist's serene scepticism amidst the religious quarrels that were tearing society apart.

365 Hans Holbein the Younger

1497/98–1543

Anne of Cleves

1539
Vellum mounted on canvas. 65 x 48 cm
Collection of Louis XIV. INV. 1348

366 Hans Holbein the Younger

1497/98–1543

Nicolas Kratzer

1528
Oil on wood. 83 x 67 cm
Collection of Louis XIV. INV. 1343

Holbein's precocious talent rapidly won him fame and entry into the humanist circles in his native Basel. Probably on Erasmus's advice, he fled the religious upheaval and civil unrest there in 1526, travelling to England, where he remained until 1528. It was there that he met his compatriot Nicolas Kratzer. The 41 year-old scientist, astronomer to Henry VIII, is shown making a polyhedral sundial.

367 Caspar David Friedrich

1774–1840

The Tree of Crows

c. 1822
Oil on canvas. 59 x 74 cm
Acquired in 1975. RF 1975-20

For Friedrich, the major painter of the Romantic movement in Germany, nature was not merely a combination of motifs but an ensemble of signs of divine revelation. The ancient barrow, the leafless oak and the crows all evoke death, the prerequisite condition for attaining eternal life, symbolised here by the distance bathed in sunlight.

368 Caspar David Friedrich

1774–1840

Seashore by Moonlight

1818
Oil on canvas. 22 x 30 cm
Gift of the Société des Amis du Louvre
RF 2000-3

Yet Friedrich conveys his spiritual preoccupations through scrupulous observation of reality. He composed his paintings from studies made from life: the white cliffs in the background, which appear several times in his works, are those of the Baltic island of Rügen, in his native region.

The golden age of Danish painting

During the last decades of the 20th century, the Louvre's Scandinavian collection became the focus of considerable attention with a series of acquisitions and the opening of new rooms. Yet the pioneer in this domain was Louis-Philippe. As early as 1847 he bought a series of views of Norway and Denmark from the Norwegian painter Peder Balke (1804–87), as a souvenir of his journey to Lapland in 1795. The 1848 revolution put an end to Louis-Philippe's reign without Balke having been commissioned any large compositions. But the exceptional ensemble of 26 sketches on card, *Norwegian and Danish Landscapes*, long unknown to the public, is now on view in the museum. Balke, who was fascinated by meteorological phenomena, vividly captured grandiose symphonies of sea and sky, some of his views verging on the fantastic (*View of the Kielhornet at Stegen*).
Yet most of the pictures in these rooms belong to the brilliant period at the beginning of the 19th century known as the 'golden age' of Danish painting. These works have a number of characteristics in common, such as close observation of nature, a taste for light, cold colours, and a predilection for intimist subjects, interiors and portraits and, above all, for that inexhaustible source of inspiration, the sea. One personality stands out among these painters, Christoffer Wilhelm Eckersberg. After training at the Academy in Copenhagen, he stayed from 1810 to 1813 in Paris, where he studied in David's studio. The strong influence of French Neoclassicism was compounded by a two-year stay in Italy in the company of his fellow countryman, the sculptor Thorvaldson. On his return to Denmark, he became a member of the Academy where as a teacher he advocated a classicism of great elegance. Apart from beautifully luminous maritime paintings (*The Port of Dragor*, Louvre), he also painted remarkable portraits (*Seated Nude*, 370). One of his pupils who went on to have a brilliant career was Christen Schjellerup Købke, represented in the Louvre by *Portrait of Adolphine Købke* [369], a landscape and *Cigar Seller at the North Door of the Citadel of Copenhagen*.

369 Christen Schjellerup Købke
1810–1848
Adolphine Købke
1832
Oil on canvas. 42 x 35 cm
Acquired in 1995. RF 1995-18

Adolphine, the painter's sister, dressed here in the checked dress that was so fashionable for young girls in Europe in the 1830s, posed for him several times. The picture was painted while Købke was still studying at the Copenhagen Academy, in Eckersberg's studio, but his personal style is already asserting itself in his fluid brushwork and choice of warm tones.

370 Christoffer Wilhelm Eckersberg
1783–1853
Seated Nude or *The Model*
1839
Oil on canvas. 45 x 33 cm
Acquired in 1987. RF 1987-27

From Eckersberg's diary we know that he began this picture on August 10th and finished it on September 6th 1839, at the Academy in Copenhagen, and that the model was Trine Nielson. The simple pose, plain decor and intimist atmosphere are Eckersberg's highly personal interpretation of Davidian Neoclassicism.

Flanders and the Netherlands

The rediscovery of the primitives

The Flemish primitives' popularity today is the fruit of a relatively recent evolution in artistic taste, since their works were not really rediscovered until the turn of the 19th century. They grew scarce on the art market, keenly sought after by museums, including the Louvre, which was anxious to complement its still incomplete collections. The painter Charles Le Brun's 1683 inventory of Louis XIV's 'cabinet of paintings' contained only one work by a 15th-century 'Flemish primitive', Gerard David's *The Marriage at Cana* [378], then attributed to Jan van Eyck, and the monarchy's lack of interest in this period of the history of painting would persist until the end of the Ancien Régime.

The sea change came during the Revolution: suddenly, the Louvre's walls were crowded with works confiscated from France's churches, monasteries and convents or requisitioned during campaigns abroad. In 1800, Alexandre Lenoir, administrator of the Muséum Central des Arts, brought back *The Madonna of Chancellor Rolin* [371] from the collegiate church at Autun. The French public discovered these ancient paintings with curiosity, and after the restitution of seized works in 1815, several Flemish paintings remained in the Louvre, including the *Annunciation* attributed to Rogier van der Weyden [373] and Joos van Cleve's *Altarpiece of the Lamentation of Christ*. This embryonic collection was added to by purchases, notably of Quentin Metsys's *The Banker and his Wife* [382] in 1806.

The collection's enrichment did not really gain momentum until the second half of the 19th century, however, and this impetus continued until the outbreak of the First World War. Acquisitions were complemented by numerous major gifts, notably of works by Van der Weyden (*Braque Family* Triptych, 372), David (*Sedano Family Triptych*), Memling (*Portrait of an Old Woman,* 376) and Geertgen tot Sint Jans (*The Resurrection of Lazarus*, 375).

371 Jan van Eyck

Died 1441

The Madonna of Chancellor Rolin

*c.*1434

Wood. 66 x 62 cm

Collegiate church of Notre-Dame, Autun

Entered the Louvre in 1800. INV. 1271

Donors appeared merely as discreet observers in 14th-century altarpieces but in the next century their presence became as imposing as the holy figures to whom they were praying. Blessed by the Infant Jesus holding an orb, symbol of the saviour's power over the world, Nicolas Rolin (1376–1462), chancellor of Philip the Good, Duke of Burgundy, is portrayed on the same scale as the Virgin Mary before whom he is kneeling. Van Eyck's strikingly realist portrayal of the man and equally meticulous rendering of this sumptuous picture's every detail are highly representative of his technique. Yet the luminous landscape with a town in the background, despite its apparent realism, is perfectly imaginary.

Flemish masters of the fifteenth century

The brilliant and refined courtly art known as International Gothic was superseded in the 1420s and 30s by a new painting rooted in a naturalist vision of reality and now mastering problems of perspective and light. The dominant figure of this renewal in the Northern countries was Jan van Eyck, to whom the invention of oil painting has often been attributed, owing to his virtuoso use of the medium. In fact, he merely perfected a technique known since the 14th century, one which enabled him to reproduce light and atmospheric effects with extraordinary fidelity, as illustrated by the sumptuous *Virgin of Chancellor Rolin* [371].
One finds this same acute sense of the real in the second generation of great masters with Rogier van der Weyden (*Braque Family Triptych*, 372), whose personality manifests itself in the clarity of his drawing and rigour of his composition. Forsaking the gentle curves customary at the beginning of the century, he created elongated figures of great elegance that would remain a prototype for several decades to come. Little is known about his life but we do know he travelled to Italy in 1450, where he particularly retained Fra Angelico's taste for symmetry. He painted the Louvre *Annunciation* [373] in Brussels, however, probably for a Piemontese banker established in Flanders or for a member of his family still in Italy.
Van Eyck's meticulous vision and van der Weyden's rigour were masterfully synthesised by Dieric Bouts, a Haarlem-born painter who produced works of great dramatic intensity. In his *Lamentation of Christ* [374], the emotions of the figures are conveyed by the mute restraint of their gestures and introspective gazes. Geertgen tot Sint Jans, also born in the Netherlands, manifested his typically Dutch sensibility through his taste for light-filled background landscapes such as the one in *The Resurrection of Lazarus* [375].

372 Rogier van der Weyden
1399/1400–1464
Braque Family Triptych

*c.*1450–1452
Wood. Central panel: 41 x 68 cm;
wings: 41 x 34 cm
Acquired in 1913. RF 2063

This triptych, an altarpiece for a private, portable altar, was commissioned by Catherine of Brabant, a wealthy widow from Tournai and Parisian in origin like her husband Jehan Braque, no doubt after his death in 1452, less than two years after they were married. Saint John the Baptist and Saint Mary Magdalen, whose face has great purity, are portrayed on either side of the central group formed by Christ the Redeemer, the Virgin Mary and Saint John the Evangelist. On the back of the triptych, the Braque family arms and a skull and cross recall the vanities of earthly existence.

373 Studio of Rogier van der Weyden
1399/1400–1464
The Annunciation

1435–1440
Wood. 86 x 93 cm
Formerly in the Galleria Sabauda, Turin
Entered the Louvre in 1799. INV. 1982

374 Dieric Bouts the Elder

*c.*1420–1475

The Lamentation of Christ

After 1468
Oil on wood. 69 x 49 cm
M. Mongé-Misbach Bequest, 1871. RF 1

Rogier van der Weyden's considerable influence on subsequent generations has led to a number of works being wrongly attributed to him, as was this picture, no doubt the central panel of a triptych whose wings have disappeared, in fact the work of Dieric Bouts the Elder. Born in Haarlem, Bouts spent most of his career in Leuven. His works show Van der Weyden's influence but he distinguished himself from the Brussels master by his more acute sense of pathos and luminous background landscapes revealing a very Dutch sensibility.

375 Geertgen tot Sint Jans

1460/65–1488/93

The Resurrection of Lazarus

*c.*1480–1484
Wood. 1.27 x 0.97 m
Acquired in 1902. RF 1285

Geertgen tot Sint Jans ('little Gerard of the Brethren of Saint John') was so-named because he lodged with the knights of that order in Haarlem. He died at 28 and therefore left us few works, hence the extreme importance of this picture, no doubt painted for a private chapel and not the habitual winged triptych format. His light, pure hues and delicate colour harmonies, the naturalist freshness of the landscapes and the delicacy of his faces are the stylistic traits which distinguish this Dutch 'primitive' from his Flemish counterparts.

376 Hans Memling

c.1435–1494

Portrait of an Old Woman

c.1470/75
Wood. 35 x 29 cm
Acquired in 1908. RF 1723

377 Hans Memling

c.1435–1494

The Virgin and Child between Saint James and Saint Dominic or *The Virgin of Jacques Floreins*

c.1488–1490
Wood. 1.30 x 1.60 m
Countess Duchâtel Bequest, 1878. RF 215

The donor, portrayed here with his family, was a Bruges spice merchant allied by marriage to Castilian merchants established at Burgos and in Flanders, hence the work's Spanish provenance. A commemorative picture, no doubt destined for a pious foundation, it has Memling's luminous palette and delicate chromatics, already much appreciated by his contemporaries.

378 Gerard David

1450/60–1523

The Marriage at Cana

c. 1501–1509
Oil on wood. 1.00 x 1.28 m
Collection of Louis XIV. INV. 1995

Gerard David has transposed the evangelical episode of Jesus's first miracle to Bruges, several of whose buildings are recognisable in the background. Some of the scene's details allude to the Easter mass celebrated by Christ and to the Eucharist. The man kneeling on the left, facing his wife kneeling on the right, is Jean de Sedano, a Castilian established in the Flemish city, for whose chapel this work was undoubtedly painted. *The Marriage at Cana* was the second picture Gerard David painted for Sedano, shortly after the *Sedano Family Triptych*, also in the Louvre.

Gerard David, who was admitted to the guild of Saint Luke in Bruges in 1484, was at the height of his artistic powers when he painted this work. His rather solemn early style has given way to a suppler treatment with solidly depicted figures set in well-defined spaces. A skilful painter of female faces, round and full of grace, late in life David painted numerous small paintings for popular worship in which the Virgin Mary appears in scenes of gentle intimacy.

379 Hieronymus Bosch

*c.*1450–1516

The Ship of Fools

After 1491
Oil on wood. 58 x 32 cm
Gift of Camille Benoit, 1918. RF 2218

The theme of humanity's vices was quite frequent in Flanders in the 15th century but Bosch was definitely the painter who depicted it with the most verve and imagination. *The Ship of Fools* was probably his first picture in this vein. Stigmatising the corruption of society and the clergy, represented here by a monk and a nun, he painted an allegory of pleasure seekers likened to a gathering of madmen crammed into a boat, drifting aimlessly as they indulge in sin and gluttony. This triptych fragment's probable pendant is *Death and the Miser* (National Gallery of Art, Washington): excess and its counterpart avarice, two of the sinful conducts which lead Christians astray.

380 Joachim Patenier

*c.*1480–1524

Saint Jerome in the Desert

*c.*1515–1520
Wood. 0.78 x 1.37 m
Gift of Sir Joseph Duveen, 1923. RF 2429

The small figure of the penitent Saint Jerome is set in one of the vast landscapes seen from an elevated vantage point that were Joachim Patenier's major speciality. Considered the precursor of the great Flemish landscape painters and greatly admired by Dürer, Patenier generally painted imaginary landscapes composed of several natural elements, sometimes adding details inherited from medieval symbolism such as the strange rocks here. The delicate harmony of greys and blues is broken only by the warm hues in the foreground and the luminous path winding away on the right.

381 Jan Gossaert, known as Mabuse

*c.*1478–1532

Carondelet Diptych

1517
Oil on wood. Both panels: 42.5 x 27 cm
Acquired in 1847. INV. 1442-1443

Archbishop Jean Carondelet, a native of Franche-Comté and advisor to Charles V of Spain, his perfectly modelled face standing out against the dark background, is shown praying before the Virgin and the Infant Jesus, who are also strikingly realistically portrayed. Painted on the backs of the two panels, in trompe-l'œil niches: a coat of arms and an exceptional vanitas still life of a skull. Gossaert's works sometimes show Dürer's influence, but also that of Italian painting, which he played a leading role in disseminating in the Netherlands in the early 16th century.

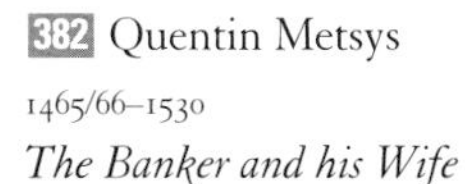

382 Quentin Metsys

1465/66–1530

The Banker and his Wife

1514
Wood. 70.5 x 67 cm
Acquired in 1806. INV. 1444

A Latin inscription from Leviticus added to the picture's frame in the 17th century indicated the scene's moral premiss: 'Just balances, just weights […] shall ye have' (Lev. 19.36). The message is emphasised by the pensive look of the woman who, having looked up from her prayer book, seems to be meditating on worldly goods as she watches her husband at work. This remarkably skilful work, considered to mark the beginning of genre painting in the Netherlands, was probably inspired by a lost painting by Jan van Eyck, a supposition confirmed by the convex mirror in the foreground, evocative of Van Eyck's famous *Arnolfini Portrait* (National Gallery, London).

383 Pieter Bruegel the Elder

*c.*1525–1569

The Beggars

1568
Wood. 18.5 x 21.5 cm
Gift of Paul Mantz, 1892. RF 730

This small picture, the only work by Bruegel in the Louvre, has been interpreted very differently: as a reflection on humanity's inherent frailty; as a social satire, with the carnival hats worn by the cripples symbolising the king, the bishop, the soldier and the peasant; and even as a critique of Philip II's policy in Flanders. Nor do we know how to interpret the figure holding out a begging bowl, or the fox's tails. Painted with remarkable realism, this picture is also skilfully staged, with the diagonals of the tangled figures giving a powerful rhythm to the composition.

384 Sir Anthony van Dyck

1599–1641

Charles I at the Hunt

c.1635
Canvas. 2.66 x 2.07 m
Collection of Louis XVI. INV. 1236

The Louvre's fine collection of Van Dycks, begun by Louis XIV, now comprises some 20 portraits, religious and mythological subjects. A smiling Charles I of England (1600–49), dressed in elegant hunting dress, is proudly posing at the forest's edge with his walking stick. Van Dyck has placed him slightly to one side, silhouetted against a bright sky, with his horse and servants blending into the magnificently executed foliage on the right. Van Dyck moved to England in 1632 and worked there for 10 years, lodged by the king, as 'principal painter in ordinary to their Majesties'. He painted several portraits of the king in various guises, as a warrior and in all his regal glory.

Antwerp, capital of the arts

Bruges was the main artistic centre in Flanders until the early 16th century and had attracted masters as prestigious as Gerard David [378] and Hans Memling [376, 377], but the city's inexorable economic decline prompted the departure of its wealthy merchant class, and therefore its artists' clientele, for Antwerp. Artists eager to train or make their fortune now congregated in the new capital of the arts. And it was in Antwerp that Pieter Bruegel the Elder developed his original, imaginative and realist style profoundly rooted in the Flemish tradition [383].

Antwerp was also an exceptional centre for the exchange and dissemination of the theories of the Italian Renaissance, and it was in this highly competitive context that Quentin Metsys pioneered genre painting (*The Banker and his Wife*, 382), Joachim Patenier set his subjects in vast and highly original landscapes (*Saint Jerome in the Desert*, 380) and Jan Gossaert put into practice the lessons he had learned in Rome (*Carondelet Diptych,* 381). Other painters borrowed Italian ornamental motifs and painted the stylistically affected pictures that engendered what became known as the Antwerp Mannerist school. One of its foremost representatives, Frans Floris (*The Sacrifice of Christ Protecting Humanity*, Louvre), known during his lifetime as 'the Flemish Raphael', trained many painters who later dispersed throughout Flanders and the Netherlands.

The artistic history of Antwerp attained its glorious pinnacle in the early 17th century, however, in the person of one outstanding personality, Rubens. This prolific and generous genius helped turn Anthony van Dyck, one of his brilliant disciples, into one of Europe's greatest portraitists (*Charles I at the Hunt*, 384).

385 Sir Anthony van Dyck

1599–1641

Venus Asking Vulcan for Arms for Aeneas

c.1627–1632
Canvas. 2.20 x 1.45 m
Collection of Louis XIV. INV. 1234

The triumph of painting

'I confess to being by natural instinct more suited to painting very large works than small curiosities,' Rubens once remarked, and the Antwerp-born artist's generous and ambitious temperament did indeed find its crowning expression in the monumental ensemble commissioned by Marie de Médicis for the Luxembourg Palace in 1622. The series of 24 pictures today hanging in the Médicis Gallery [386] is a veritable tour de force in which Rubens expressed himself with fiery freedom, mixing portraiture, historical compositions and allegorical scenes on four metre-high canvases which he painted single-handed.

Besides this spectacular ensemble, the Louvre has some thirty pictures covering all of Rubens's periods and almost every genre he worked in: altar pictures, devotional images, mythological subjects, history painting and portraiture. *Helena Fourment with a Carriage* [388], painted shortly before his death, is a moving testimony to his love for this young woman, who was only 16 when he married her at the age of 53, and whose fresh and voluptuous body he never tired of painting. His monumental *Village Fête* [387], a swirling composition in which he is at the peak of his baroque vigour, also dates from this happy period. The picture was acquired by Louis XIV in 1684.

His painterly energy found its rightful heir in Jacob Jordaens, who retained much of his master's furore (*The Last Judgement, Jesus Driving the Merchants from the Temple*, *Diana Resting*, Louvre), but who also knew how to express himself with restrained power (*The Four Evangelists*, 389). The great Rubensian inspiration also engulfed Crayer, Van Dyck, Seghers and Thulden, as several large altar paintings in the Louvre show.

386 Peter Paul Rubens

1577–1640

The Arrival of Marie de Médicis at Marseilles

1622–1625
Oil on canvas. 3.94 x 7.27 m
Collection of Louis XIV. INV. 1774

From 1622 to 1625, Rubens, commissioned by Marie de Médicis, Henry IV's widow and regent, to decorate a room in her recently built Luxembourg Palace, single-handedly painted an impressive series of 24 paintings recounting 'the queen's very illustrious life and heroic acts' from her birth to recent times. For the considerable fee of 60,000 livres, the painter set about his task of glorifying the queen with dazzling verve, mixing history painting, allegorical scenes, pagan deities and Christian references. In his depiction of the queen's arrival at Marseilles he allows his baroque genius free rein and in this respect it is rightly one of the most admired pictures in the series. Contemporary elements such as the costumes, flags and ship blend sumptuously with the generously curved Nereids at the bottom of the picture.

387 Peter Paul Rubens

1577–1640

The Village Fête

*c.*1635–1638
Oil on wood. 1.49 x 2.61 m
Collection of Louis XIV. INV. 1797

The village fête, a traditional theme in Flemish painting explored notably by Bruegel, is taken up here by Rubens very late in life. He had clearly lost none of his energy, though: women, children, dancing couples and inebriated drinkers are drawn into the swirling movement of his truculent, dynamic composition. The peace of the clear-skied landscape in the background contrasts with the tumult of the festivities, while in the shady bottom right-hand corner he has included a pig's snout poking out of a sty, a symbol of gluttony emphasing the picture's moralist intentions. This magnificent painterly tour de force was greatly admired and inspired many artists including Watteau, who copied several of its figure groups. When he bought the picture in 1684, Louis XIV could hardly have acquired a work more representative of Rubens's genius.

388 Peter Paul Rubens

1577–1640

Helena Fourment with a Carriage

c.1639
Oil on wood. 1.95 x 1.32 m
Marlborough then Rothschild collections
Donation, 1977. RF 1977-13

Rubens sometimes painted his second wife, Helena Fourment, in intimate family scenes but portrays her here in all her finery, about to go out in her carriage, in the company of their son Frans, then six or seven years old. The palatial setting and the young woman's sumptuous dress give a measure of the opulent life Rubens led in his late years. The Antwerp master is at the height of his powers here, in the subtle play of blacks heightened by the boy's red suit, the balance of volumes and the picture's warm atmosphere.

389 Jacob Jordaens

1593–1678

The Four Evangelists

c.1625–1630
Oil on canvas. 1.34 x 1.18 m
Collection of Louis XVI. INV. 1404

In the foreground, Saint John, wrapped in a white cape, and three old men are commenting on the scriptures. The Evangelists, divested of their traditional attributes, are portrayed with powerful faces whose realism is accentuated by Jordaens's treatment of light and brushwork. He achieved here one of the fullest expressions of his ample and vigorous style.

The golden age of Dutch painting

Towards the turn of the 17th century, as Mannerism was waning in northern Europe, it was undoubtedly in the Netherlands that its last fires burned brightest. The movement's main centres, Haarlem and Antwerp, were dominated by powerful personalities such as Cornelis van Haarlem, whose *Baptism of Christ* [391] peopled with elaborately posed nudes perfectly illustrates the style's refined language, and Joachim Wtewael [392], who with Bloemaert became the leader of the Utrecht School.

Meanwhile, another phenomenon, specialised painting genres, had begun to emerge in the second half of the 16th century, one which would gain pan-European ascendancy in the mid-17th century, but nowhere more markedly than in the Northern lands where Protestantism hampered the demand for church paintings (yet there were commissions in Utrecht and Haarlem). Painters were now turning to other subjects, pushing them to the utmost technical perfection in meticulously detailed still lifes, animal paintings and portraits, and painstakingly realist genre scenes.

Foremost among these 'specialists' were Ambrosius Bosschaert the Elder, considered the pioneer of the flower painting (*Bouquet of Flowers in an Arch*, 390), and Frans Hals, who devoted his entire career to individual or group portraits, generally sombre-toned and of great sobriety. One exception is *The Gypsy Girl* [393], a kind of genre picture, painted during the artist's brief Caraveggesque period.

While his fellow painters were intent on flawlessly executing coolly objective or descriptive pictures, Rembrandt asserted his exceptional personality very differently. Embodying an artistic identity that could rival with the great Italian masters and which earned him the byname 'the Titian of the Venice of the North', gifted with profound sensitivity and a remarkably inventive mind, he brought the same genius to portraiture, history painting, landscape and still life. His warm and subtle chiaroscuro imbues his religious paintings with a profound sense of mystery (*The Pilgrims at Emmaus*, 395), but with equal pictorial mastery he could convey sensuality (*Bathsheba*, 394), the dignity of an artist (*Portrait of the Artist at his Easel*, 396), and also push his gifts as a colourist to provocative, even gory extremes (*The Slaughtered Ox*, 397).

390 Ambrosius Bosschaert the Elder
1573–1621
Bouquet of Flowers in an Arch
c.1620
Oil on copper. 23 x 17 cm
Acquired with the aid of the
Société des Amis du Louvre, 1984. RF 1984-150

Flower painting, traditionally charged with symbolic meaning or used merely for decorative purposes, became an autonomous genre in its own right. Like portraiture and landscape painting, it owed its development to the demise of religious painting in the Protestant countries. Ambrosius Bosschaert, an Antwerp Protestant who emigrated to the Netherlands for religious reasons, is considered the creator of the grand floral style. But his stupefying virtuoso still lifes in which, as here, each flower is identifiable, also have a moral meaning. His arrangements of objects menaced by time, death and decay were intended as illustrations of the words from Ecclesiastes, 'Vanitas vanitatum omnia vanitas' (Vanity of vanities; all is vanity).

391 Cornelis van Haarlem
1562–1638
The Baptism of Christ
1588
Oil on canvas. 1.70 x 2.06 m
Gift of the Société des Amis du Louvre, 1983.
RF 1983-25

392 Joachim Wtewael

1566–1638

Perseus and Andromeda

1611
Canvas. 1.80 x 1.50 m
Gift of the Société des Amis du Louvre, 1982.
RF 1982-51

Perseus, mounted on Pegasus, has come to deliver Andromeda, manacled by the Nereids, to whose beauty she dared compare hers. Wtewael, the leader of the Utrecht School, gives us an elegant interpretation of this mythological episode greatly favoured by the Mannerists, mixing academic nudes, a blue-tinted landscape background and a fascinatingly precise still life of seashells and human remains. His style of this picture is quieter than that of his early works, when he was still preoccupied with the lessons had learned in France and Italy.

393 Frans Hals

1581/85–1666

The Gypsy Girl

*c.*1628–1630
Oil on wood. 58 x 52 cm
Dr Louis La Caze Bequest 1869. MI 926

This smiling young woman, traditionally described as a 'gypsy girl' even though she was almost certainly a prostitute, belonged to the famous series of 'character portraits' (*Jester with a Lute* is also in the Louvre), which Hals painted under the influence of the Utrecht Caravaggists. These genre pictures are perfect examples of Hals' brilliant touch, particularly in evidence here in the dynamic treatment of the blouse, while he uses suppler brushwork and more fluid impasto to capture the fullness of her face. This evocation of a woman of ill-repute is, however, an exception in the prolific output of this society painter, who spent his entire career in Haarlem.

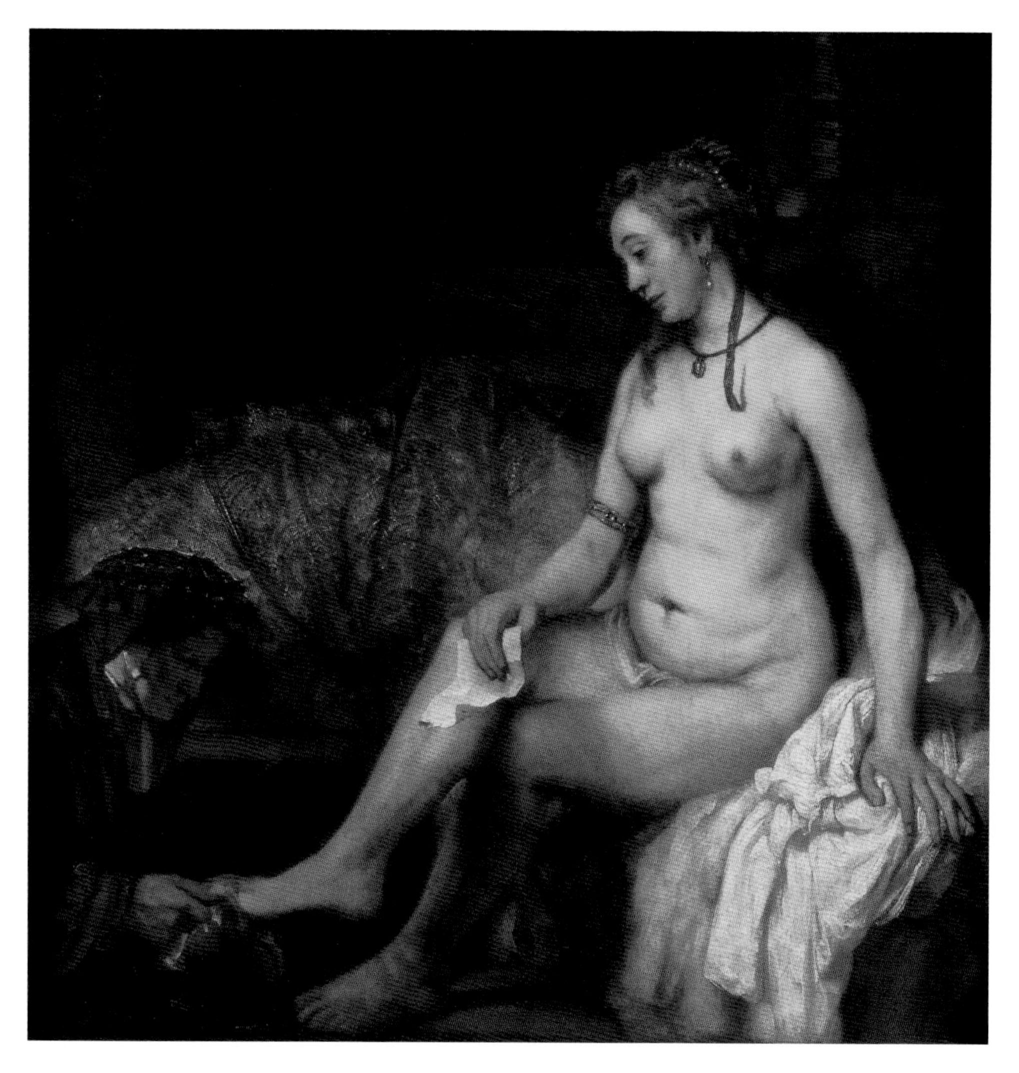

394 Rembrandt Harmenszoon van Rijn

1606–1669

Bathsheba

1654
Oil on canvas. 1.42 x 1.42 m
Dr Louis La Caze Bequest, 1869. MI 957

In the biblical episode, King David, having seen Bathsheba bathing, invites her to join him in his palace while her husband is away at war. In this brilliant deviation from the traditional iconography, Rembrandt suggests the king's presence solely by the crumpled letter in the young woman's hand. The model who posed for him was probably Hendrickje Stoffels, the painter's servant and mistress, then 22 years old. The golden light bathing her moving rather than beautiful body, the masterly treatment of the impasto and the picture's restrained composition make it one of the Dutch master's finest works.

395 Rembrandt Harmenszoon van Rijn

1606–1669

The Pilgrims at Emmaus

1648
Oil on wood. 68 x 65 cm
Collection of Louis XVI. INV. 1739

Christ's appearance after the Resurrection to two of his disciples, who recognised him when he broke bread during their meal at Emmaus, is a theme to which Rembrandt returned several times in his paintings and engravings. No doubt inspired by the composition of the great masters of the Italian Renaissance, in this version from his late period he shows Christ facing us, slightly off – centre and haloed in supernatural light: the face of a man who has returned from the dead, transfigured but still profoundly human.

396 Rembrandt Harmenszoon van Rijn

1606–1669

Portrait of the Artist at his Easel

1660
Oil on canvas. 1.11 x 0.90 m
Collection of Louis XIV. INV. 1747

Rembrandt was 56 when he painted this uncompromissing portrait of himself standing against sombre backdrop, his face already deeply etched by the trials of life. Only his white cap seems to catch the light, while his easel is merely suggested and his hand and palette are barely distinguishable in the shadows. A majestic piece of painting and the only Rembrandt acquired by Louis XIV, two years after the artist's death.

397 Rembrandt Harmenszoon van Rijn

1606–1669

The Slaughtered Ox

1655
Oil on wood. 94 x 69 cm
Acquired in 1857. MI 169

A highly unusual subject for Rembrandt – the gleaming carcass of a slaughtered ox hanging from a crossbeam in a dimly lit, empty room – and an image of rare violence transgressing every norm of propriety in the still life, but which may have been intended as a kind of vanitas still life. The casual treatment and thick, vibrant, heavily worked impasto are equally unusual.

398 Jacob van Ruisdael
*c.*1628/29–1682
The Ray of Sunlight
*c.*1660 (?)
Oil on canvas. 83 x 99 cm
Collection of Louis XVI. INV. 1820

The Dutch landscape

From the 17th century and for a long time to come, the landscape would occupy a special place in Dutch painting. Both in the idealised landscapes of the Italianate painters, with their radiant and poetic visions of nature, and the naturalist depictions of Dutch nature, Northern painters explored every evocation of the visible and perceptible world surrounding them. Water, skies, seashores and riversides were often rendered in light, subtle monochrome, as exemplified by the ethereal works of van Goyen (the Louvre has six of his paintings). Others chose more distant climes: Frans post painted fascinating visions of Brazil, while Poelenburgh and Breenbergh turned to that obligatory ideal for every artist, Roman antiquity and Italy. Aelbert Cuyp opted for rustic yet idealised views of his native land (*Landscape near Rhenen*, 399, transforming it into an opulent and peaceful northern Arcadia. Jacob van Ruisdael used real elements to create the sweeping landscape in *The Ray of Sunlight* [398], in which we find his predilection for greys and gradations of light and his restrained and refined touch.

399 Aelbert Cuyp

1620–1691

Landscape near Rhenen

c. 1650–1655
Oil on canvas. 1.70 x 2.29 m
Collection of Louis XVI. INV. 1190

It is hard not to see this extensive sun-drenched landscape as a vision of some poetic and enchanting northern Arcadia. The peaceful herd, the nonchalant shepherds, one of them playing a flute, the ethereal light bathing the scene; everything suggests this, and as he often did, Aelbert Cuyp placed our viewpoint lower than the figures to give them a kind of monumentality. Occasionally compared to Claude Lorraine because of his picture's Italianate light, Cuyp, unlike the French master, seems to have been more concerned with authenticity in his evocations of the Dutch landscape: in the haze beyond the mirror-like expanse of water we see the bell tower of the church at Rhenen.

400 Pieter de Hooch
1629–1684
A Young Woman Drinking
1658
Oil on canvas. 63 x 60 cm
Gift of Mme Grégor Piatigorsky,
née Jacqueline de Rothschild
RF 1974-29

Each figure has a precisely defined role: the soldier pouring drink for the young woman who seems to be already drunk; his companion looking on, smoking; the older woman, probably the procuress, apparently negotiating. On the wall on the right, a picture of Christ and the adulteress, the episode during which Christ said: 'He that is without sin among you, let him first cast a stone at her.' Pieter de Hooch used the theme of the flirtatious conversation, a subject he painted many times, and his extraordinarily skilful perspective to compose a masterly work bathed in a gentle golden light.

Genre painting

The cities of Leyden, Amsterdam and Delft were particularly fertile centres of genre painting in the 17th century. The early work of Gerrit Dou, who trained in Rembrandt's studio, bore his master's stamp until, working in his birthplace Leyden, he developed the extraordinarily meticulous style which won him great fame (*The Dropsical Woman*, 401). His pupil, the gifted and prolific Gabriel Metsu, left Leyden for Amsterdam where he painted masterly and very varied genre scenes (*Vegetable Market in Amsterdam*, 402). But it was in Delft, where Pieter de Hooch lived and produced the bulk of his oeuvre, that the silent interior scenes at which the Dutch became masters emerged. *A Young Woman Drinking* [400] illustrates his ability to create subtle formal and colour relationships between figures and the objects surrounding them, thereby establishing a remarkable pictorial dynamism. Johannes Vermeer, a few years Pieter de Hooch's junior and influenced by him, is today considered the major figure of the Delft School. His paintings belong to an intimist tradition which he elevated to glacial perfection in an oeuvre of absolute, poetic detachment (*The Lacemaker*, 403; *The Astronomer*, 404).

401 Gerrit Dou
1613–1675
The Dropsical Woman
1663
Oil on wood.. 86 x 67 cm
Gift of Bertrand Clauzel, 1798. INV. 1213

The medical consultation was one of the themes most frequently depicted by the Dutch genre painters. Everything about Gerrit Dou's consummately refined treatment of this scene is intended to fascinate the spectator: figures, light and objects are

402 Gabriel Metsu

1629–1667

Vegetable Market in Amsterdam

*c.*1660
Oil on canvas. 97 x 84 cm
Collection of Louis XIV. INV. 1460

depicted with the utmost precision, with the whole scene having that enamel-like smoothness for which he became extraordinarily famous during his lifetime. The picture originally had two closing wings, also in the Louvre, representing a silver ewer alluding to the woman's illness–a mental as much as a physical affliction, and water being a symbol of spiritual healing. The object stands before a trompe-l'œil niche, a motif Dou borrowed from his master Rembrandt and which became a cliché in his work.

403 Johannes Vermeer

1632–1675

The Lacemaker

*c.*1665-1670

Oil on canvas mounted on wood. 24 x 21 cm

Acquired in 1870. MI 1448

Vermeer's tight framing and use of a neutral background focuses the viewer's attention on the gestures of the lacemaker bent over her tambour, painted with great precision, whereas the foreground, in contrast, is exaggeratedly enlarged and slightly blurred, as though seen through a photographic lens. This famous picture is a perfect example of the Delft artist's conception of genre painting: concentrated, stylised and depicting merely a moment of silent, poetic intimacy. The first Vermeer to enter the Louvre, in 1870, it was joined over a century later by the equally famous *Astronomer.*

404 Johannes Vermeer

1632–1675

The Astronomer

1668

Oil on canvas. 51 x 45 cm

Donation, 1983. RF 1983-28

The celestial globe and the astrolabe next to it indicate that the man portrayed is an astronomer. The subtle light filtering through the window, the slanting shadows echoing his gesture and the delicate interplay of warm and cold tones are highly characteristic of the manner of this painter, who perfected the art of creating an atmosphere of meditative silence. Male subjects are relatively rare in his oeuvre (fewer than forty pictures) but he also painted *The Geographer* (Städelsches Kunstinstitut, Frankfurt) which, for commercial reasons, was associated with *The Astronomer* in the 18th century.

Great Britain

The art of the portrait

The repression of religious imagery in England soon after the Reformation prompted the exceptional development there of the sole genre which continued to provide artists with a livelihood, portraiture. The Louvre has a number of early works and also some fine examples from the 18th century, which is considered the golden age of portraiture. One of the genre's most brilliant exponents was Thomas Gainsborough, who was initially drawn to the Dutch-inspired landscape and who taught himself largely by making studies directly from nature. He also painted a great many portraits, especially in an outdoor setting, a genre then popular among the English upper classes. The pastoral setting for his *Conversation in a Park* [407], however, eludes conventions and has the same delightful freshness as his country scenes.

Gainsborough's contemporary Joshua Reynolds was his complete antithesis. Reynolds studied Antiquity and the great masters in Italy – particularly Raphael, Michelangelo and Titian – and on his return to England moved to London, where he remained until he died. Elected President of the Royal Academy when it was founded in 1768, he set out his artistic doctrine in lectures extolling the importance of the rules of drawing and colour and advocating that history painting should convey elevated morals. His lectures created quite a stir and his portraits were widely acclaimed. In each of them, he attempted to introduce an imaginative or sentimental dimension, or references to Van Dyck or old masters. His charming *Master Hare* [406] stands out against an autumnal landscape whose chromatic richness is a visible tribute to Titian.

The third major figure of 18th-century English portraiture was Thomas Lawrence. Trained in England, with several months spent at the Royal Academy, he pursued a career as a society portraitist. Although sometimes tempted by the 'grand style' and the history painting advocated by Reynolds, he expressed himself more faithfully in his brilliantly executed portraits (*Mr and Mrs John Julius Angerstein*, 405).

405 Thomas Lawrence
1769–1830
Mr and Mrs John Julius Angerstein
1792
Oil on canvas. 2.52 x 1.60 m
Acquired in 1896. RF 1028

John Julius Angerstein, founder of the insurance brokers Lloyds, was also a great collector. His pictures, auctioned in 1828, constituted the core collection of London's newly-founded National Gallery. Thomas Lawrence, his friend and artistic advisor, portrayed him with his wife in this elegant picture of great technical virtuosity. Some years later, he painted a group portrait of his four grandchildren (Louvre).

406 Joshua Reynolds
1723–1792
Master Hare
1788–1789
Oil on canvas. 77 x 63 cm
Bequested verbally by Baron Alphonse de Rothschild; presented to the Louvre by his heirs, 1905. RF 1580

Painted at the request of the model's aunt, who wanted a memento of the infant features of her two year-old adoptive son, this portrait illustrates the interest at the time in intimist and sensitive subjects. Painted late in Joshua Reynolds' career, it received such acclaim it was soon published as an engraving under the title *Infancy*.

407 Thomas Gainsborough

1727–1788

Conversation in a Park

*c.*1746–1747
Oil on canvas. 73 x 68 cm
Gift of Pierre Bordeaux-Groult, 1952
RF 1952-16

This early work by Thomas Gainsborough – painted before he was 20 – is a fine example of the 'conversation pieces' that were so popular in English high society in the 18th century, and which he treats here in a stylistically affected manner clearly influenced by French rococo. The leafy park and folly recalls Gainsborough's profound interest in landscape which, obliged to paint portraits for a living, he could never fully satisfy.

The invention of the modern landscape

The English landscape won acclaim in the late 18th century, thanks in particular to remarkable watercolourists such as Robert Cozens, Thomas Girtin and John Sell Cotman, whose pioneering role has often been neglected by art historians. The new vision of nature which emerged at this time was undoubtedly stimulated by the development of tourism in Europe and in wild regions of the British Isles, and by the increasing use of watercolour as a handy means of making a visual memento of admired places. It is therefore to the new 'romantic' sensibility of these artists, that we partly owe the birth of the modern landscape, despite their talent having been eclipsed by two exceptional personalities, John Constable and William Turner.

Constable, who studied at the Royal Academy but who stubbornly resisted the lessons of tradition, rapidly understood that his vocation lay elsewhere: 'I shall shortly return to East Bergholt, where I shall make some laborious studies from nature – and I shall endeavour to get a pure and unaffected representation of the scenes that may employ me.' The young Constable set about painting the landscape of his native region of Suffolk, recording on canvas its ever-changing skies, light and transient atmospheres with untiring perseverance, only ever leaving his birthplace to paint the seacoast (*Weymouth Bay*, 408) or the intimate beauty of some site stripped of all anecdote. He spent his whole life endeavouring to recreate on canvas the profound sentiments nature instilled in him, and when a town did appear in his pictures it was always in the distance, as in his famous series of views of Salisbury and its soaring cathedral spire (*View of Salisbury*, Louvre).

408 John Constable

1776–1837

Weymouth Bay

1819

Oil on canvas. 0.88 x 1.12 m

Gift of John W. Wilson, 1873. RF 39

Constable painted Weymouth Bay in Dorset in several of his works, including one dated 1816 (Victoria & Albert Museum, London), executed during his honeymoon. Some of these pictures have the same vast, overcast, menacing sky rendered in vibrant brushwork. From a young age, Constable habitually made oil sketches directly from nature, and many of his small studies vividly capture his fleeting emotions and sensations. Constable's art was first recognised in France at the 1824 Salon. His influence on French landscape painters, was considerable, in particular among the painters of the Barbizon school.

Joseph Mallard William Turner

Turner, although Constable's contemporary, was his complete opposite. Constable sought to express his emotions through familiar landscapes, Turner studied the technique of the great masters; Constable never left England, Turner the tireless voyager traveled the length and breadth of the British Isles and Europe many times, first sketching then producing finished works from memory in his studio; and whereas Constable played on the thickness of his impasto, Turner's oils attain great fluidity and his imperceptible gradations of colour rival the most subtle watercolour transparencies. At the end of his life, he achieved near-abstraction, literally dissolving forms in light and colour.

409 Joseph Mallord William Turner
1775–1851
Landscape with a River and a Bay in the Distance
c.1845
Oil on canvas. 0.93 x 1.23 m
Acquired in 1967. RF 1967-2

The majority of Turner's works – over twenty thousand – having been bequeathed to English museums in 1856, the Louvre was fortunate to have been able to acquire this magnificent canvas in 1967. It is one of a series of pictures which the artist left unfinished. Although an oil painting, the treatment of the landscape is so light it could almost be a watercolour. In its dissolved outlines we make out valleys and a river flowing into a lake or possibly the sea, motifs which Turner suggests with the lyricism so characteristic of his works.

410 Richard Parkes Bonington

1802–1828

View of the Lagoon near Venice

c. 1826
Oil on canvas. 30 x 43 cm
Acquired in 1926. RF 2558

Despite his short life – he died at 26 – Bonington is one of the masters of the English Romantic landscape. Trained as a watercolourist, his oil technique was fluid in treatment and played masterfully with transparency, notably during his stay in Venice, where he painted his finest works. His influence in artistic circles in France, where he lived much of his life, was considerable, notably thanks to his friend Delacroix, with whom he shared a studio.

Icons

411 Cretan painter
Third quarter of the 15th century?
Madonna and Child with Saint Cyril and Saint George
0.94 x 1.13 m
Acquired in 1963. RF 1972-54

The style of this imposingly large icon has been likened to that of Andreas Ritzos (1425–1492), one of the great 15th-century Cretan painters, but it cannot be attributed to him with any certainty. The depiction of the Virgin here is the *'Nikopoia'* or 'Bringer of Victory' type. She is shown full length with the Infant Jesus, with, on her right, Saint Cyril, Bishop of Jerusalem, with his attribute, the True Cross, whose discovery he recounted in his discourses, and, on her left, by Saint George in armour holding a lance and a shield.

In the 1950s, the Louvre acquired a number of Greek and Russian icons, mostly 16th and 17th-century, which were exhibited in the Department of Christian Antiquities. When this department was done away with in 1972, some of these works were shown for a while in the Byzantine room of the Department of Objets d'Art. This ensemble – complemented by the purchase in 1988 of three Greek and Cretan icons and by the presentation of works from the Campana Collection – is now on view in a small room whose meditative atmosphere reflects the sacred function with which these images were invested.

All icons depict one or two holy figures from the Bible or Christian tradition, whose very image was considered holy and whose contemplation was therefore a kind of prayer. The object's spiritual content mattered more than its actual physical reality, which explains the hieratic appearance of the subject, detached from the realities of the world, and the repetition for many centuries of a number of iconographic schemas inherited from Byzantine tradition. Thus, in the 15th and 16th centuries, images still remained faithful to this original tradition, as illustrated by *Madonna and Child with Saint Cyril and Saint George* [411], by a Cretan painter, whose gold ground is intended to suggest transfiguration by heavenly light.

Similarly, in Russia, converted to Byzantine Christianity in 988, icons obeyed the laws of these original aesthetics until the 16th century. The forms of their restrained, anti-naturalist compositions are dematerialised, and the image is devoid of space since there are no shadows to suggest volume. The *Georgian Madonna* [412] is exemplary in this respect since it derives directly from the Byzantine *Virgin Hodegetria* ('She who points the way') type, often represented in Russia with, as here, regional variations.

412 Anonymous, Central Russia
Madonna and Child,
or *Georgian Madonna*
16th century
Wood. 1.09 x 0.83 m
Acquired in 1955. RF 1972-47

Icons differ from Western representations in the active role they play in liturgical practice. Given its large size and subject, we think that this Madonna was part of an iconostasis, a wall of images separating the choir from the nave in Eastern churches. It was probably placed in the first row, next to images of Christ and the patron saint of the Church. Although its aesthetics and simplicity stem directly from Byzantine art, the elongated proportions, gentle face and thin white lines heightening the anatomy are hallmarks of early 16th-century Russian icons.

Sculptures

The Department of Sculptures is devoted to European works from the Late Middle Ages to the first half of the 19th century. It is therefore chronologically situated between the Department of Greek, Etruscan and Roman Antiquities, and the sculpture of the second half of the 19th century, which has been transferred to the Musée d'Orsay. Its collections run parallel to those of the Department of Objets d'Art, and demarcations between the two departments are not always clear: small-format works, particularly bronzes, are to be found in both sections of the museum for various reasons.

The collection of French works is the most comprehensive in the world. In 1993, after the Finance Ministry vacated the Richelieu Wing, French sculpture was moved to this part of the Louvre, whose two courtyards, the Cour Marly and the Cour Puget, have been transformed into spectacular hubs of the visitor's itinerary. Both are now devoted to open-air sculpture and were named after some of the ensembles they now contain, the sculptures from the park of the Château de Marly and the masterpieces by Pierre Puget respectively. Foreign sculptures were installed in the Denon Wing.

The Department of Sculptures is the successor to two institutions founded during the Revolution, the Musée des Monuments Français and the Musée Spécial de l'Ecole Française at Versailles. The former, created by Alexandre Lenoir (1764–1835), contained works confiscated from churches and émigrés' homes, the latter the collections of the Académie Royale, which largely consisted of the most recent 'reception pieces' of academicians. During the Revolution, 'modern' sculpture was excluded from the museum, only antique statuary being admitted. The situation changed under the Restoration, however. In 1824, five rooms in the Louvre jointly known as the 'Galerie d'Angoulême' showed works from both institutions, which had since been closed down, and works from the gardens at Versailles. This ensemble of sculptures dating from the Renaissance to Antiquity formed the initial core of a department that would experience many more trials and tribulations. It was amalgamated into the Department of Antiquities and attached to the Department of Objets d'Art. Louis Courajod, who in 1893 was appointed head of a definitively autonomous department, developed a wide-ranging curatorial policy (the appropriation of the remains of the Musée des Monuments Français, looking for new works, acquisitions). Continued by his successors and complemented by generous gifts from numerous donors, this policy has enabled the presentation today of over 1,000 French works and some 400 foreign sculptures, two thirds of which are Italian. This taste for sculpture Italian, principally from the Renaissance, prevailed for a long time to the detriment of other countries. But the imbalance has been reduced over time and the Louvre now has beautiful ensembles of sculptures from the Northern European countries.

France

413 *Daniel in the Lions' Den*

6th and late 11th century
Capital, marble. 49.5 x 53.4 x 51 cm
Church of Sainte-Geneviève, Paris
Entered the Louvre in 1881. RF 457

Romanesque France

During the centuries following the collapse of the Roman Empire, sculpture was confined to the 'minor' arts (precious metalwork, ivory reliefs). The re-establishment of an urban civilisation, the reinforcement of royal authority and the reform of the monasteries led in the 11th century to an extraordinary rich period in architecture, reflected in the reconstruction and embellishment of the great abbeys and pilgrimage sanctuaries at Cluny, Conques, Autun, Vézelay, Toulouse, and so on, and a renaissance in monumental sculpture in architecture, principally in religious buildings. On capitals, whether historiated or with abstract or floral motifs, sculptors showed great inventiveness and a delightful sense of narration. Sculpture filled cloisters but was also well in evidence on the exteriors of religious buildings. Ambitious pictorial compositions adorned doorways, the symbolic place of passage between the secular and the sacred worlds. Tympanums (Autun, Moissac, Conques) were often sculpted with apocalyptic visions of the Last Judgement. These powerful, severe, decorations symbolised the authority of the all-powerful Church and its victory in its centuries-old struggle to eradicate paganism and stamp out heresy.
Most free-standing statues, in precious materials or wood, have disappeared down the centuries. Several remarkable sculptures in wood, including the very beautiful 'Courajod' Christ [415], are on view in the rooms presenting a panorama of Romanesque art. These vividly polychromed figures were generally made to decorate altars. The worship of statues of the *Madonna and Child* [416], enthroned with the Infant Jesus on her knees, and depictions of the saints, intercessors between man and divinity, would endure throughout the Middle Ages.

414 Attributed to Monk Martin
Head of Saint Peter

Burgundy, second third of the 12th century
Stone. 21 x 14.3 x 18.5 cm
Acquired in 1923. RF 1783

This *Saint Peter* is from the great pilgrimage sanctuary at Autun, where it was part of a group depicting the resurrection of Lazarus. The regular arrangement of his curly hair is typical of the Romanesque aesthetic. The purity of line and form is akin to Provençal sculptures heavily influenced by Antiquity. But the fixity of the gaze gives the face a striking, timeless expression of fervour.

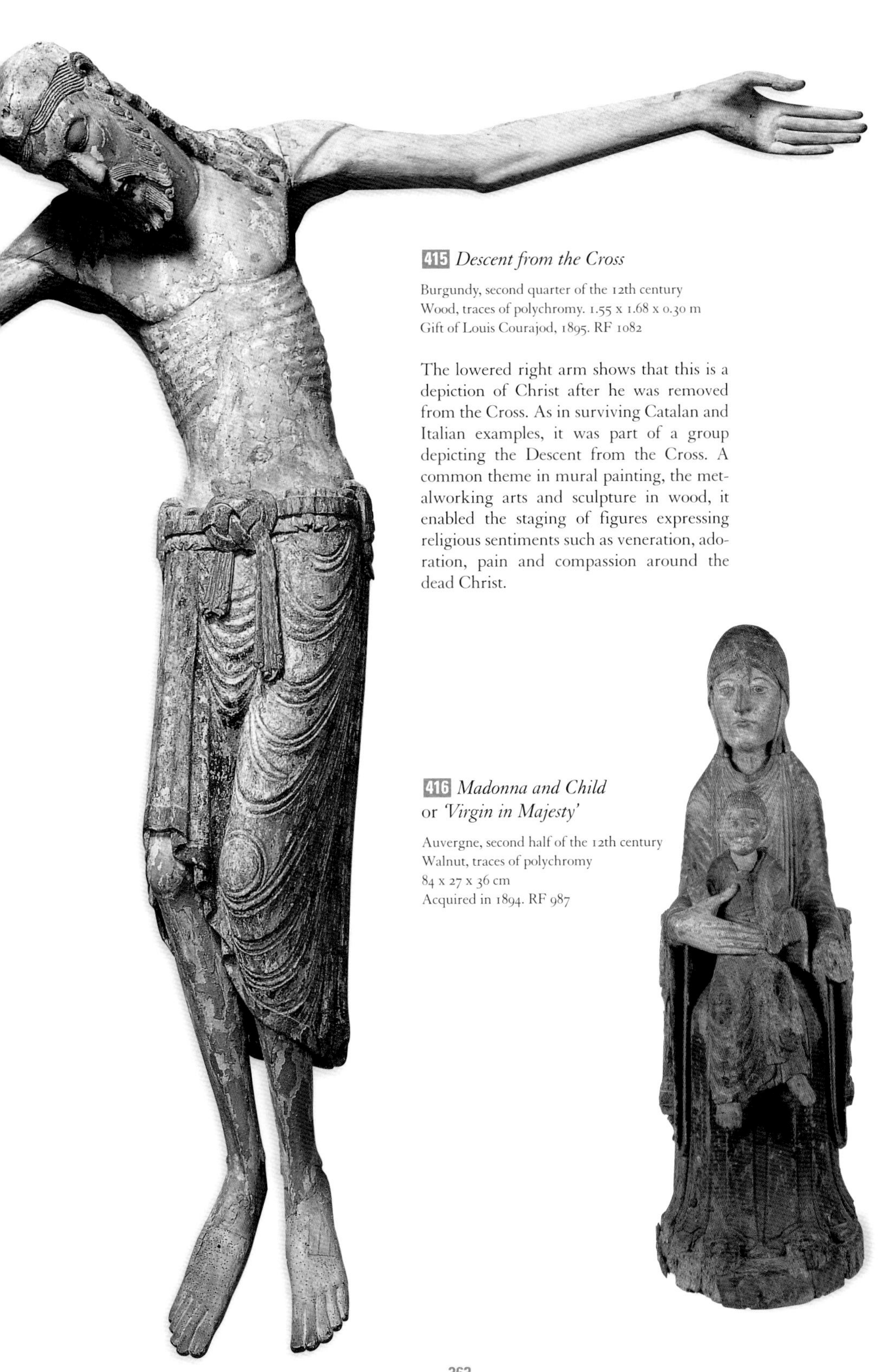

415 *Descent from the Cross*

Burgundy, second quarter of the 12th century
Wood, traces of polychromy. 1.55 x 1.68 x 0.30 m
Gift of Louis Courajod, 1895. RF 1082

The lowered right arm shows that this is a depiction of Christ after he was removed from the Cross. As in surviving Catalan and Italian examples, it was part of a group depicting the Descent from the Cross. A common theme in mural painting, the metalworking arts and sculpture in wood, it enabled the staging of figures expressing religious sentiments such as veneration, adoration, pain and compassion around the dead Christ.

416 *Madonna and Child* or *'Virgin in Majesty'*

Auvergne, second half of the 12th century
Walnut, traces of polychromy
84 x 27 x 36 cm
Acquired in 1894. RF 987

417 *King Childebert*

Île-de-France, *c.* 1239–1244
Stone with traces of polychromy. 1.91 x 0.53 x 0.55 m
Refectory of Abbey of Saint-Germain-des-Prés
Entered the Louvre in 1851. ML 93

Gothic France

The end of 12th century was marked by the evolution of the Church as an institution and the increasing power of the cities, where riches were concentrated and which stimulated innovation. The replacement of the Romanesque barrel vault by the ribbed vault and pointed arch prompted the development of a new, aerial architecture. Light now illuminated a unified space through enormous stained glass windows, first at the Abbey of Saint-Denis then in the great cathedrals of Île-de-France. Sculptural decoration obeyed the Church's doctrinal dictates. A 'scripture lesson in images', it rendered the teachings of the Bible accessible to all. But, as in architecture, it took on hitherto unknown proportions.
Sculpture espoused the edifice's vertical tension though column-statues. It spread throughout the church interior, decorating rood screens and altarpieces. The severity of Romanesque art was supplanted by a more human vision of God. Modelling became less rigid, flowing drapery followed the movement of the body and faces became more serene. In the first decades of the 13th century, sculpture attained a perfect equilibrium.
In the 14th century, the arts at court reflected the growing domination of temporal power, assimilating elements of chivalrous culture and offering its little known delights to the secular public. Religious sentiment became coloured with sentimentality. The emphasis was now on Christ's suffering and humanity and the maternal love of the Virgin Mary. In parallel, a growing sensitivity to nature pervaded both religious and secular sculpture. The first true portraits appeared. This new naturalist sensibility, which extended even to funerary sculpture and its numerous recumbent figures, developed during the next century, notably in Burgundy. However, the 'relaxation' of the style that marked the end of the Gothic period in France was above all perceptible in the workshops in the Loire Valley, with their fondness for simplicity and limpidity of form.

418 *The Angel Dictating to Saint Matthew the Evangelist*

Chartres, second quarter of the 13th century
High relief, stone. 64.5 x 50 x 15 cm
Acquired in 1905. RF 1388

This is a fragment of the rood screen that separated the choir and the nave of Chartres Cathedral, on which there was a depiction of the Last Judgement according to the Gospel of Saint Matthew. In this depiction of the angel dictating to the Saint Matthew, the evangelist looks more like a young clerk quietly working at his desk. The sculptor has depicted the scene with loving precision, infusing it with a confident familiarity and showing a new interest in concrete aspects of reality. Its monumentality is counterbalanced by the gracefully human poses and delightful references to everyday life.

419 *Altarpiece from the church of Carrières-sur-Seine: The Virgin in Majesty, The Annunciation, The Baptism of Christ*

Île-de-France, third quarter of the 12th century
High-relief, stone with traces of polychromy.
0.91 x 1.84 x 0.19 m
Acquired in 1915. RF 1612

420 *Virgin and Child*

Blanchelande, Normandy, first quarter of the 14th century
Stone. 1.75 x 0.57 x 0.34 m
Formerly in the Carlo Micheli Collection.
Acquired in 1850. ML 24

421 Attributed to Evrard d'Orléans

Known from 1292, died 1357

Angel with Cruets

Île-de-France, *c.* 1340
Wall statuette, marble. 52.7 x 14 x 8.3 cm
Gift of the Société des Amis du Louvre, 1904.
RF 1438

422 *Charles V, King of France*

Île-de France, last third of the 14th century
Stone. 1.95 x 0.71 x 0.40 m
In the Antiquities Room in the Louvre in the 17th and 18th centuries
Entered the Louvre in 1904. RF 1377

423 *Joan of Bourbon*

Île-de-France, last third of the 14th century
Stone. 1.95 x 0.50 x 0.44 m
Entered the Louvre in 1904. RF 1378

Charles V was a great patron of the arts. He built the Château de Vincennes and enlarged the Louvre. The attributes of these two famous statues were added much later. The king was originally holding the hand of justice not a model of a church, and the queen perhaps a bunch of flowers instead of a book. They are thought to come from the façade of the Louvre's east entrance. The particularly individualised and expressive features of the king make the statue a true portrait.

424 *Tomb of Philippe Pot*

Burgundy, last quarter of the 15th century
Polychromed stone. 1.80 x 2.65 m
Abbey Church of Cîteaux. Acquired in 1889. RF 795

Philippe, Lord of La Roche-Pot was seneschal to the Duke of Burgundy then Chamberlain of the King of France. His daring and original tomb borrows the theme of the procession of weeping figures that decorated the bases of the great tombs of the late Middle Ages (including those of the Dukes of Burgundy at Dijon). But here the hooded mourners bearing the stone slab with the recumbent figure are almost life-size. One of the purposes of this extremely dramatic depiction of a funerary procession was to exalt the lineage of the deceased: the mourners are also carrying the shields of the eight quarters of the seneschal's nobility.

425 *The Education of the Holy Child*

Bourbonnais, late 15th century
Stone with traces of polychromy. 85 x 59 x 46 cm
From Longvé, Allier
Acquired in 1955. RF 2763

The Virgin's distant expression gives this work a hint of gravity and emphasises its religious significance: the young mother's happiness is tinged with her awareness of her Son's destiny, announced in the Old Testament. The sculpture derives its beauty from the density of its composition and clearly defined forms, and the impression of pureness and simplicity exuded by this intimate yet sacred scene. It is an example of the refined aesthetic that prevailed at the court of the Dukes of Bourbon at Moulins, also found in the paintings of the Master of Moulins.

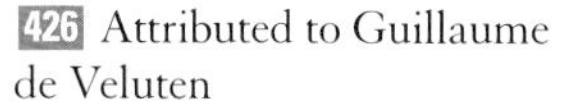

426 Attributed to Guillaume de Veluten

?–1444/1445

Recumbent figure of Anne of Burgundy, Duchess of Bedford (died 1432)

Beauvais region
White and black marble. 1.62 x 0.31 x 0.22 m
Church of the Celestines, Paris
Entered the Louvre in 1851. LP.442

427 *Saint John on Calvary*

Loire Valley, third quarter of the 15th century
Walnut. 1.40 x 0.46 x 0.39 m
Church of Loché-sur-Indrois, Touraine
Acquired in 1904. RF 1383

428 Studio of Guillaume Regnault

*c.*1460–1532

Virgin and Child

Loire Valley, *c.*1510–1520
Marble. 1.83 x 0.60 x 0.41 m
Château de Couasnon, Olivet, near Orléans
Acquired in 1875. RF 202

The Renaissance

Contacts with Italy, which intensified after the military campaigns by French kings in the peninsula, gave rise to the emergence of a new taste. Decoration in the Lombardy style, with its medallions, grotesques, foliage and volutes inspired by Antiquity, began to appear in the royal centres in the Loire Valley and also at the Château de Gaillon in Normandy. Masters of this 'first French Renaissance' such as Michel Colombe and his nephew Guillaume Regnault showed their assimilation of Italian canons (clarity of composition, monumentality, idealisation of certain features, portrait busts cut off at the shoulders, 429) yet retained a certain Gothic naivety infused with a certain realism.

The return of Francis I after his captivity in Madrid and the transfer of the court to the Paris area masked the consolidation of the French Renaissance.

The king enlisted the Italian painters Rosso and Primaticcio and their teams to oversee the refurbishment of Fontainebleau. The sculptors Dominique Florentin and more briefly Benvenuto Cellini also worked there. They imposed their typically Mannerist models (serpentine contours, elongated anatomy and twisting poses), which were assimilated and interpreted, sometimes with genius, by French artists such as Jean Goujon, who sculpted marvellous bas-reliefs with flowing drapery [432], and the then unknown sculptor of the famous *Diana* of the Château d'Anet [433]. Germain Pilon dominated the second half of the 16th century. He devoted himself largely to funerary sculpture, of which the Louvre has several fine examples: the *Monument for the Heart of Henry II*, after a project by Primaticcio, and the works for the 'Valois Rotunda', the funerary monument commissioned by Catherine de Medicis for the Basilica of Saint-Denis [436]. Germain Pilon's influence continued until the end of the century and later in the work of the artists of the 'second School of Fontainebleau', Barthélemy Prieur [434], Matthieu Jacquet and Pierre Biard.

430 Michel Colombe

*c.*1430–after 1511

Saint George and the Dragon

Marble. 1.75 x 2.75 x 0.42 with frame
Château de Gaillon
Seized during the Revolution,
entered the Louvre in 1818. MR 1645

Michel Colombe was active in Tours in the late 15th century. In 1508, he was commissioned to sculpt this altarpiece for the chapel of the Château de Gaillon, residence of Georges d'Amboise, minister to Louis XII and cardinal. Gaillon, where the cardinal introduced Lombardian decoration, became the crucible of the 'first French Renaissance'. The clumps of trees and the dragon in this relief devoted to the cardinal's patron saint are still Gothic in treatment yet the space is clear and unified. The frame, with its pilasters and grotesques, was made by Italian ornamentalists. The late style of the sculptor was perpetuated in the work of his nephew and colleague Guillaume Regnault.

429 *Louise of Savoie*

Loire Valley, early 16th century
Terracotta, 47 x 53.4 x 23 cm
Gift of the Société des Amis du Louvre, 1949
RF 2658

The portrait bust inspired by antique models, particularly the bust cut off at the shoulders, re-emerged in Italy during the Quattrocento, mainly in Tuscany, then spread into Lombardy. Whether the sculptor was an Italian working in France or a Frenchman influenced by the finest Italian examples, this portrait bust of the mother of Francis I achieves a perfect balance between realism and idealisation.

431 Germain Pilon

*c.*1528–1590

Monument for the Heart of Henry II: The Three Graces

Paris, *c.*1560–1566
Marble. 1.50 x 0.755 x 0.755 m
Church of the Celestines, Paris
Seized during the Revolution,
entered the Louvre in 1818. MR 1591

432 Jean Goujon

*c.*1510–c.1565

Nymph and Spirit

*c.*1549
Stone. 0.74 x 1.95 x 0.13 m
From the Fontaine des Innocents, Paris
Entered the Louvre in 1818. MR 1738

Recapturing the supreme elegance of Hellenic art, the architect and sculptor Jean Goujon developed a type of very shallow, extremely fluid and subtle bas-relief in which the modelling of the figures against a plain ground is enough to create an illusion of space. The *Fontaine des Innocents* was built for Henry II's entry into Paris in 1549 then re-erected as a separate monument in the 18th century. Some of the sculpted reliefs depicting nymphs are in the Louvre.

433 *Diana the Huntress*

France, mid-16th century
Marble. 2.11 x 2.58 x 1.345 m
Château d'Anet
Seized during the Revolution,
entered the Louvre in 1823
MR 1581

This *Diana* once decorated the fountain at the Château d'Anet, residence of Henry II's mistress, Diana of Poitiers. Without being a portrait, the work glorifies the memorable beauty of the king's favourite, personified as the goddess of the hunt embracing a magnificent stag embodying her royal lover. Although the figure group, with its elaborately sculpted base, is one of the masterpieces of the sophisticated art of the School of Fontainebleau, its sculptor remains unknown; it has been thought to be the work of Germain Pilon or Ponce Jacquiot. The latter sculpted *Woman Taking a Thorn from her Foot*, on view in the same room and which has the same cool sensuality.

434 Barthélemy Prieur

1536–1611

Spirits from the Tomb of Christophe de Thou

1583–1611
Bronze. Each figure: 0.46 x 1.07 x 0.35 m
Church of Saint-André-des-Arts, Paris
Seized during the Revolution,
entered the Louvre in 1824
MR 1684, MR 1685

These bronze spirits, with their taut muscles and pose inspired by the statues of Michelangelo in the Medici Chapel, along with a marble bust and two Venuses, once adorned the tomb commissioned by the historian Jacques de Thou for his father's tomb. Although a Protestant, Prieur was also commissioned to sculpt the monument for the heart of the devout Catholic Anne of Montmorency and also her recumbent figure and that of Madeleine of Savoie, wife of the Constable of France. Furthermore, Prieur seems to have played a decisive role in the development of the 'small bronze' in France.

435 Pierre Bontemps

*c.*1505–1568

Charles de Maigny

Paris, *c.*1557
Stone. 1.45 x 0.70 x 0.42 m
Church of the Celestines, Paris
Seized during the Revolution,
entered the Louvre in 1818. MR 1729

436 Germain Pilon

*c.*1528–1590

Virgin of Sorrows

*c.*1585
Polychromed terracotta. 1.59 x 1.19 x 0.815 m
Sainte-Chapelle, Paris
Seized during the Revolution,
entered the Louvre in 1890. RF 3147

This work is a study for a marble statue (now in the Church of Saint-Paul-Saint-Louis) for Henry II's funerary chapel at Saint-Denis, known as the 'Valois Rotonda', for which Pilon also sculpted *Saint François in Ecstasy*, the *Resurrection of Christ* and this mourning *Virgin*. Depicted alone, without Christ's body, the Virgin expresses acceptance of human suffering and assumes the redemptive role which the Protestants denied.

437 Pierre Francqueville (1548–1615)
Francesco Bordoni (1580–1654)
Four Captives in Chains

Paris, 1614–1618
Bronze. Each statue: 1.55 x 0.66 x 0.70 m
From the equestrian monument to Henry IV on the Pont-Neuf
Seized during the Revolution, entered the Louvre in 1817. MR 1668-1671

17TH CENTURY

During the reign of Henry IV, art became a monarchic propaganda tool. Queen Marie de Médicis had an equestrian statue of the king erected on the Pont Neuf. All that remains of this monument are the four statues of captives at the corners of the base [437]. These bronzes are fine examples of the international Mannerist style which endured in France during the first decades of the century. A new spirit manifested itself around 1640 in the work of artists such as Jacques Sarazin [438], Simon Guillain and the Anguier brothers [439]. Trained in Italy, these had both acquired the Roman Baroque sense of dynamic form and staging of a scene, yet tempered this with their observation of antique models. Their creations prefigured the birth of the classical, harmonious French art of the Grand Siècle, of which François Girardon was the exemplary exponent.
Under Louis XIV, artistic activity was controlled by the administration of the King's Buildings, in which the 'First Painter' (Lebrun, then Mignard) played a prominent role.
The creation of the Académie Royale de Peinture et de Sculpture and the French Academy in Rome, and the launching of ambitious construction projects (Louvre, Versailles, Invalides, Marly) were all part of the same political will to make artistic creation one of the instruments of royal power. A host of commissions were awarded, especially for open-air sculptures. Equestrian monuments to Louis XIV were erected in all the kingdom's major cities [443] and parks and gardens were decorated. The Cour Marly contains statues from the park of the royal residence at Marly [442]. The Cour Puget is devoted to the masterpieces of the most atypical sculptor of the period, the Marseillais Pierre Puget [440]. The completely Baroque dynamics, lyricism and passion of his works influenced the evolution of French sculpture.

438 Jacques Sarazin
1592–1660
Cenotaph for the heart of Cardinal Pierre de Bérulle

1657
Marble. 1.25 x 0.80 x 1.31 m
Acquired in 1906. RF 1430 A

439 François Anguier

1604–1669

Monument for the Heart of Henry, Duke of Longueville

c.1661
Marble. 1.48 x 0.63 x 0.52 m
Church of the Celestines, Paris.
Seized during the Revolution,
entered the Louvre in 1824
MR 1749-1752, 2669-2672, 3373-3374

This funerary monument strikes us by its imposing size, its flowing, rhythmic classicism and the sober richness of its materials. The pedestal is decorated with gilt copper reliefs depicting the duke's victories at Henry IV's side in the form of antique-style battle scenes. The corner statues depict the four Cardinal Virtues. Strength is recognisable by Hercules' attributes, the Nemean lion's skin and the club. The emblems sculpted on the base state the meaning of each Virtue. The monument is crowned by an obelisk edged with black marble and sculpted with emblems of the arts and power (war trophies). The ermine mantle originally framed a coat-of-arms.

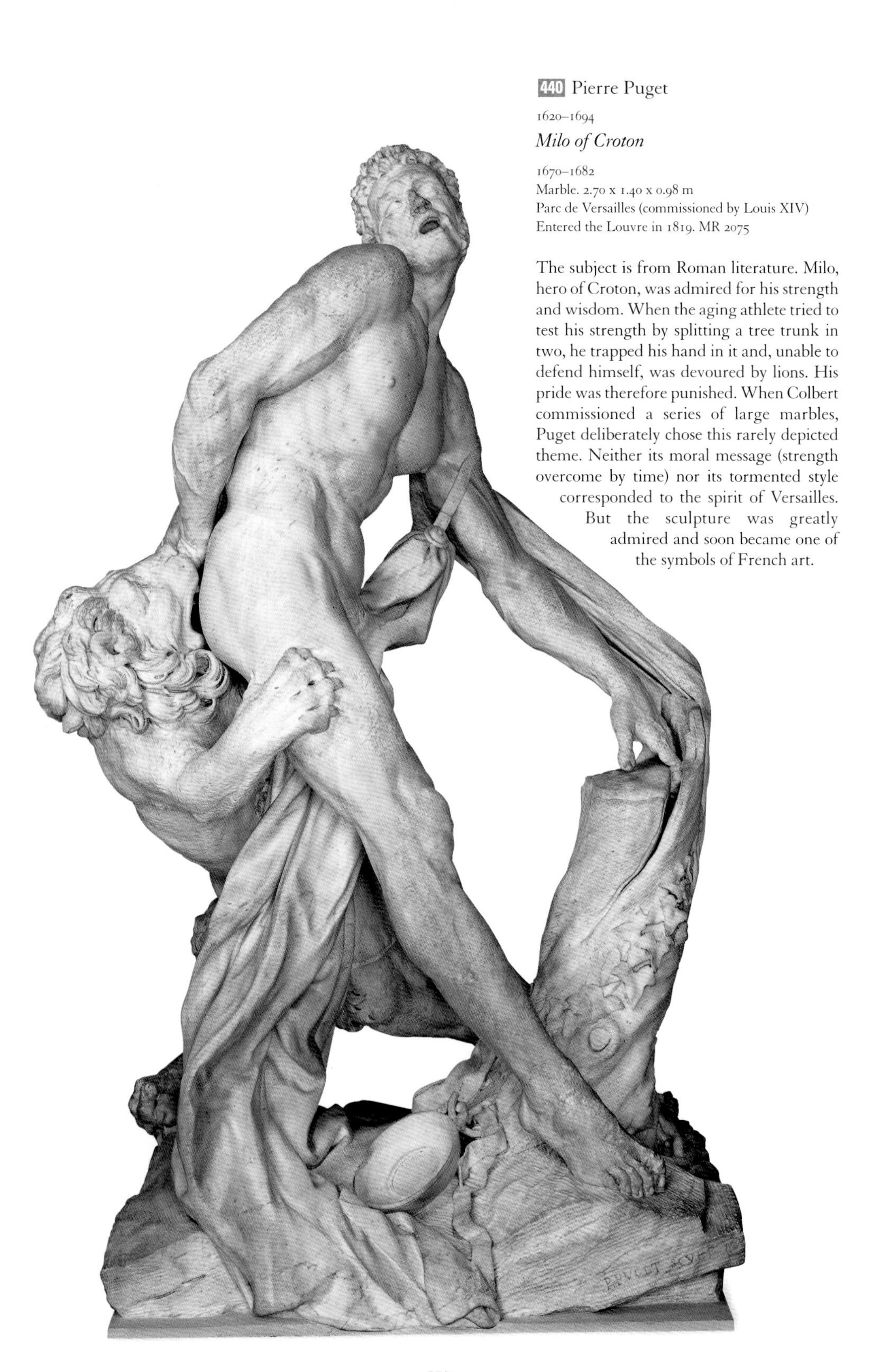

440 Pierre Puget

1620–1694

Milo of Croton

1670–1682
Marble. 2.70 x 1.40 x 0.98 m
Parc de Versailles (commissioned by Louis XIV)
Entered the Louvre in 1819. MR 2075

The subject is from Roman literature. Milo, hero of Croton, was admired for his strength and wisdom. When the aging athlete tried to test his strength by splitting a tree trunk in two, he trapped his hand in it and, unable to defend himself, was devoured by lions. His pride was therefore punished. When Colbert commissioned a series of large marbles, Puget deliberately chose this rarely depicted theme. Neither its moral message (strength overcome by time) nor its tormented style corresponded to the spirit of Versailles. But the sculpture was greatly admired and soon became one of the symbols of French art.

441 Antoine Coysevox

1640–1720

The Prince of Condé

1688
Bronze. 75 x 68 x 34 cm
Collection of the Prince of Conti
Seized during the Revolution. MR 3343

Coysevox was one of the foremost sculptors working at Louis XIV's court. In his many busts of prominent figures, statesmen, noblemen, parliamentarians, churchmen, artists and soldiers such as the Prince of Condé, he masterfully emphasised the character of his models and the importance of their office. Here Coysevox heroicises Condé with an elaborately decorated antique breastplate. But he also excelled in monumental sculpture. Largely responsible for the statues in the gardens at Marly, he produced two large groups which decorated the horse-pond, *Mercury* [442] and *Fame*. Surmounting a superb war trophy, they are typical of official depictions of the king's glory.

442 Antoine Coysevox

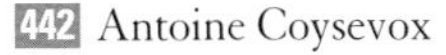

1640–1720

Mercury Riding Pegasus

Paris, 1699–1702
Marble. 3.26 x 2.91 x 1.28 m
From the horse-pond at Marly
(commissioned by Louis XIV)
Entered the Louvre in 1996. MR 1822

443 François Girardon

1628–1715

Louis XIV on Horseback

1685–1692
Bronze. 1.02 x 0.97 x 0.50 m
Crown Collection since 1784
Seized during the Revolution,
entered the Louvre in 1818. MR 3229

444 Jean Thierry

1669–1739

Leda and the Swan

'Admission piece', 1717
Marble. 81 x 40 x 44 cm
Collection of the French Academy
Entered the Louvre in 1849
MR 2100

The 18th century

Guillaume Coustou's famous *Marly Horses* [445] are a brilliant example of the Baroque style known as rococo which developed after the death of Louis XIV and culminated at the beginning of the reign of Louis XIV. The rococo aesthetic engendered a new style of interior decoration corresponding to the evolution of architecture and the needs of an aristocratic and bourgeois society seeking not pomp and splendour but the convenience and charm of more intimate interiors. All artistic disciplines became involved in the elaboration of these decors and adapted to their new demands. Monumental sculpture and heroic subjects were forsaken for 'small sculpture' and the themes of amorous mythology. The tastes of increasingly influential collectors encouraged artists to express their individuality, and in hitherto shunned materials such as clay rather than systematically demonstrating their virtuosity in marble. Portrait busts became highly fashionable [449]. In keeping with the naturalness advocated by the philosophers of the Enlightenment, sculptors endeavoured to bring out their models' individuality, character and inner feelings. This naturalism attained extremes in the work of certain sculptors such as Pigalle. Yet official art maintained strong links with tradition.

The gallery of the French Academy in the Louvre charts the evolution of sculpture throughout the century through the collection of 'admission pieces' submitted by Academy members. A new tendency began to manifest itself in the 1770s. Amorous scenes were denounced as frivolous and the virtue of 'great men' was exalted instead. Artists now aspired towards a more edifying noble art, and this Neoclassical reaction, with its references to the heroes and art of Antiquity, reflected the profound social changes that led to the Revolution.

445 Guillaume Coustou

1677–1746

Horse Restrained by a Groom,
one of the *'Marly Horses'*

1739–1745
Marble. 3.55 x 2.84 x 1.27 m
Château de Marly (commissioned by Louis XV)
Entered the Louvre in 1984. MR 1803

The 'Marly Horses' were commissioned to replace Coysevox's winged horses, which had been moved to the western gate of the Tuileries. Installed in 1746, they were moved in 1795 to the entrance of the Champs-Elysées, where they have since been replaced by copies. Wild horses held in check by grooms possibly personifying Africa and America illustrate the theme of untameable nature. Royal sculpture, at last liberated from the official iconography of the preceding reign, was now exploring the characteristic effects and movement of rococo art.

446 Edme Bouchardon

1698–1762

Cupid Making a Bow out of Hercules' Club

1739–1750
Marble. 1.73 x 0.75 x 0.75 m
Commissioned by Louis XV
Entered the Louvre before 1824
MR 1761

447 Jean-Baptiste Pigalle

1714–1785

Mercury Attaching his Winged Sandals

'Admission piece', 1744
Marble. 59 x 35 x 30 cm
Collection of the French Academy
Entered the Louvre *c.* 1848–1850. MR 1957

This work was Pigalle's first major success after he returned from Italy, and opened the doors to the Academy to him in 1744. The position of the legs, the twist of the torso and the movement of the head suggest a figure perched on a cloud about to take flight. This ingenious portrayal of concentrated dynamism was widely acclaimed when it was shown at the 1742 Salon. *Mercury* originally had a companion piece, *Venus* sitting on a rock, ordering him to go and find Psyche. The life-size marble versions which Louis XV offered to Frederick II are now in Berlin.

448 Pierre Julien

1732–1804

Dying Gladiator

'Admission piece', 1779
Marble. 60.7 x 48.5 x 42 cm
Entered the Louvre in 1866. RF 4623

449 Jean-Antoine Houdon

1741–1828

Louise Brongniart Aged Five

1777
Terracotta. 34.5 x 24.2 x 18 cm
Acquired in 1898. RF 1197

450 Jean-Jacques Caffieri

1725–1792

Canon Alexandre-Gui Pingré

1788
Terracotta. 67.5 x 51.5 x 34.6 cm
From the Observatory, Paris
Entered the Louvre in 1909. RF 1496

451 Étienne-Maurice Falconet

1716–1791

Bather

1757
Marble. 80 x 25.7 x 29 cm
Collection of Mme du Barry
Seized during the Revolution,
entered the Louvre before 1855. MR 1846

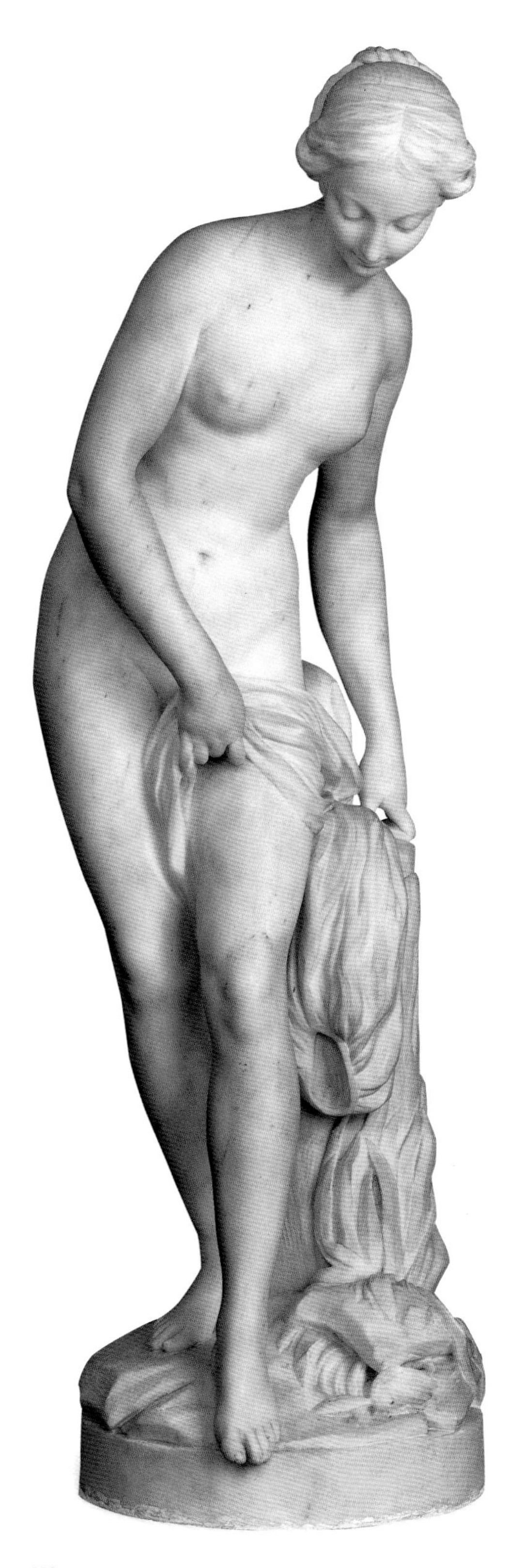

452 Jean-Antoine Houdon

1741–1828

Diana the Huntress

1790
Bronze. 2.055 x 0.795 x 0.935 m
Acquired in 1829. CC 204

453 Claude Michel, known as Clodion

1738–1814

Venus and Cupid Bathing with Leda and the Swan

c. 1782
Stone. 1.03 x 3.23 x 0.27 m
From the Hôtel de Besenval, Paris
Acquired in payment of inheritance tax in 1986
RF 4103

Clodion produced numerous sculpted decorations in collaboration with Neoclassical architects such as Brongniart. This relief was part of the decoration of the bathroom of Baron de Besenval, general of the Swiss Guard. The aquatic theme enabled the artist to depict bathers frightened by the intrusion of the cupids and the seductive swan, and is typical of the hugely popular amorous mythological scenes at which he excelled. He produced numerous highly erotic reliefs and small terracotta groups borrowing from Baroque painting, ancient Greek art and the Anacreontic poetry, which accompanied the emergence of Neoclassicism.

454 Augustin Pajou

1730–1809

Psyche Abandoned

1790
Marble. 1.77 x 0.86 x 0.86 m
Commissioned by Louis XVI
Entered the Louvre in 1829
MR Sup 62

Psyche Abandoned was commissioned in 1783 by the King's Buildings as a pendent to Bouchardon's *Cupid* [446]. Cupid and Psyche were allowed to be lovers on one condition, that Psyche never saw her partner. But she disobeyed this rule and Cupid fled, leaving her in despair – the moment Pajou chose to depict. The oil lamp, the instrument of Psyche's misfortune, is still lies at her feet. The original plaster created a scandal because of the figure's sensuality and complete nudity. When Bouchardon sculpted the marble under the Revolution, he accentuated the Neoclassical decoration of the accessories.

455 Joseph Chinard
1756–1813
Madame de Verninac
1802
Marble. 64 x 36 x 21 cm
Acquired in 1909. RF 1488

The first half of the 19th century

The canons of Neoclassical art continued to prevail in early 19th-century sculpture. Napoleon's favourite sculptor was the Italian Antonio Canova, the foremost representative, with David, of the Neoclassical School. One finds his pure, immaculate forms in numerous French works, including Chaudet's *Cupid Playing with a Butterfly* [456], in which the reference to idealised Greek art is explicit. The work is also an example of the exaltation of republican and imperial virtues using the examples of the heroes of Antiquity. This marked tendency to idealise asserted itself even in portraiture.
Artists such as David d'Angers, Pradier and Bosio, who sought their models in Antiquity, perpetuated the classical tradition under the Restoration, until Duseigneur and Barye introduced Romantic sculpture at the 1831 Salon. Romanticism forsook the antique-inspired canons and rhetoric of classical art for a new formal liberty, the primacy of the imagination, the untrammelled expression of feeling, and new themes. Next to Duseigneur's struggling *Orlando Furioso* [461], whose muscles seem about to burst, David d'Angers' *Philopoemen* [462] seems more measured in pose; yet it is still a far cry from the ideal of 'beautiful nature in repose' advocated by the theorists of Neoclassicism.
This antagonism is not always as marked. In the work of sculptors such as François Rude [459], who sculpted the famous *Departure of the Volunteers* on the Arc de Triomphe, Auguste Préault and Antoine-Louis Barye [460], one often finds 'classical' and 'Romantic' tendencies closely intermingled. Similarly, Pradier's *Satyr and Bacchante* [458] is classical in its theme, form and the antique inspiration of its fauna, and Romantic in the brutal sensuality and sensuous intensity of the nude, which is reminiscent of Rubens. The era of revolutions and scandals was over, and a certain eclecticism would characterise the sculpture of the ensuing decades.

456 Antoine-Denis Chaudet

1763–1810

Cupid Playing with a Butterfly

1802–1817
Marble. 89.5 x 64 x 44 cm
Entered the Louvre in 1847. LL 56

Chaudet was one of the leading French sculptors of the Napoleonic period. He received numerous prestigious commissions such as the colossal statue of Napoleon that stood on top of the Vendôme Column until 1814. But he was also fond of elegiac subjects, particularly those involving Cupid and Psyche, themes often depicted by Neoclassical artists. In this work greatly influenced by Antonio Canova, Cupid is offering a rose to a butterfly he is holding by the wings, an explicit reference to Psyche's butterfly wings, symbol of the soul. The reliefs around the plinth depicting love's pleasures and pains give the work its moral resonance.

457 François-Joseph Bosio

1768–1845

Henry IV as a Boy

1822–1825
Silver. 1.25 x 0.42 x 0.40 m
Commissioned by Charles X. CC 37

458 James Pradier

1790–1852

Satyr and Bacchante

1834
Marble. 1.28 x 1.12 x 0.78 m
Acquired in 1980. RF 3475

459 François Rude

1784–1855

Neapolitan Fisherboy playing with a Tortoise

1831–1833
Marble. 82 x 88 x 48 cm
1833 Salon then acquired for the Musée du Luxembourg.
Entered the Louvre before 1863. LP 63

460 Antoine-Louis Barye

1795–1875

Lion Killing a Snake

1832–1835
Bronze. 1.35 x 1.78 x 0.96 m
Formerly in the Tuileries (commissioned by Louis-Philippe). Entered the Louvre in 1911.
LP 1184

Barye's devoted much of his oeuvre to the depiction of animals. His sculptures were based on rigorous observation from life in the menagerie in the Jardin des Plantes in Paris and sometimes dissection and moulding. Although primarily concerned with realistically rendering animals' poses, muscles and coats, the artist imbued his subjects with a heroic dimension which transformed them into grandiose evocations of nature in the wild. It was the monumental plaster model for *Lion Killing a Snake* which made his name at the 1833 Salon. The lion was a discreet tribute to royalty, and the king showed his appreciation by commissioning this bronze, which was installed in the Tuileries.

461 Jean-Bernard,
known as Jehan Duseigneur

1808–1866

Orlando Furioso

Model shown at the 1831 Salon, cast in 1867
Bronze. 1.30 x 1.40 x 0.90 m
Jardin du Luxembourg. Entered the Louvre in 1900
RF 2993

462 Pierre-Jean David d'Angers

1788–1856

Philopoemen

1837
Marble. 2.46 x 0.91 x 0.98 m
Acquired in 1836. Entered the Louvre in 1858
LP 1556

Italy

463 *Descent from the Cross*

Umbria or Latium, mid-13th century
Polychromed wood. Christ: 1.83 x 1.23 x 0.43 m
Acquired in 1968. RF 2966-2969

Italy, where during the Late Middle Ages the figurative tradition perhaps remained stronger than elsewhere, and which was also more open to the Byzantine influence, produced remarkable sculptures during the Romanesque period. From a number of inscriptions and archive texts, we know the names of several sculptors active during this period. Benedetto Antelami is believed to have contributed to the introduction into Italy of forms derived from the new Gothic style that had emerged in Île-de-France. Nicola and Giovanni Pisano were the great masters of Italian Gothic, steeped in reminiscences of Antiquity. The reference to Greek and Roman models would assert itself in Tuscany in the early 15th century and lead to a rift with the International Gothic style. The aim of artistic creation was not to imitate nature but to recreate it through an intellectual process in which real forms are not reproduced directly but transcribed according to an idealised prototype. The early Renaissance was marked by exceptional figures such as Donatello [465], Ghiberti, Jacopo della Quercia [464], and later Mino da Fiesole, Agostino di Duccio [467] and Benedetto da Maiano [468]. A family of the artists, the Della Robbia, transposed the principal innovations of the Florentine sculptors of the second half of the 15th century into the new and perfectly mastered technique of enamelled terracotta [466]. The first half of the 16th century was dominated by the genius of Michelangelo, magnificently represented in the Louvre by his two *Slaves* [469]. His work rapidly became a major reference for the Mannerist movement, which spread throughout Europe. During the Counter-Reformation, when all artists became concerned with glorifying the Church, Rome became the centre of artistic life. It was in Rome that the great wind of the Baroque movement first sprang up, which Bernini [472] expressed to the fullest extent, and which would permeate Italian art until the 18th century. But it was also in Rome, that fabulous open-air museum, that the Neoclassical response came to a head, prompted by the great archaeological discoveries of the time. Yet the champion of this 'regeneration' through the art of Antiquity was a Venetian, Antonio Canova [473]. His influence was profound in Italy, France and Scandinavia, and his renown spread as far as the United States.

464 Attributed to Jacopo della Quercia
c.1371/74–1438
Virgin and Child

Bologna? c.1430–1435?
Polychromed wood. H. 1.78 m
Acquired in 1896. RF 1112

465 Donato di Nicolo Bardi, known as Donatello

1386–1466

Madonna and Child

*c.*1440–1445
Polychromed terracotta. 1.02 x 0.74 x 0.12 m
Acquired in 1880. RF 353

Donatello was one of the major figures of the Florentine Renaissance. He sculpted the first statues that were genuinely independent of architecture and also created a new kind of very flattened relief combining mastery of perspective and atmospheric effects. In this relief from the artist's late period, the expression of his figures is powerful and internalised: the Virgin Mary is lost in contemplation of the Infant Jesus who, himself deep in thought, turns his back to her.

466 Luca della Robbia the Younger and his studio

1475–1548

Christ Comforting a Pauper

Late 15th century
Enamelled terracotta. Ø 1.02 m
Acquired in 1851. ML 26

467 Agostino di Duccio

1418–1481

Madonna and Child with Angels
(known as the '*Madonna of Auvillers*')

Florence, between 1464 and 1469
Marble. 81 x 77 cm
Acquired in 1903. RF 1352

468 Benedetto da Maiano

1442–1497

Filippo Strozzi (1426–1491)

Florence, *c.* 1475
Marble. H. 51 cm
Formerly in the collection of Prince Strozzi
Acquired in 1878. RF 1169

469 Michelangelo Buonarroti

1475–1564

Slaves

Rome, 1513–1515
Unfinished, marble. H. 2.09 m
Formerly in the Châteaux d'Ecouen and de Richelieu
Seized during the Revolution,
entered the Louvre in 1794. MR 1589–1590

These two famous statues were executed for the huge tomb of Pope Julius II, a project which occupied Michelangelo for a large portion of his career and which, to his great bitterness, was never built. Unfinished, perhaps because of defects which appeared in the marble, they were given by Michelangelo to his Florentine compatriot Roberto Strozzi, who gave them in tribute to the king of France. But beyond their dazzling formal beauty, what do these *Slaves* represent? The provinces subjugated by a warrior pope, the liberal arts fallen into slavery after the death of their protector, or the soul shackled by earthly passions and imprisoned within its bodily envelope?

470 Pierino da Vinci

c.1529–1553

River God

Pisa, c.1547–1548
Marble. 1.35 x 0.48 m
Schlichting Bequest, 1915. RF 1623

471 Benvenuto Cellini

1500–1571

The Nymph of Fontainebleau

Paris, 1542–1543
High-relief, bronze. 2.05 x 4.09 m
Formerly in the Château d'Anet
Confiscated during the Revolution, entered the Louvre in 1797. MR 1706

After his arrival at the French court in 1540, the silversmith Cellini became famous for exceptional works such as the saltcellar he made for Francis I. This gigantic tympanum, the artist's first attempt at monumental statuary and originally made for the Château de Fontainebleau, was eventually mounted on the gateway of the Château d'Anet. It was intended to be supported by two satyrs and framed by two spandrels decorated with Victories. The work has all Mannerism's hallmarks – sophistication, decorative anti-naturalism and the elongated canon of the nude – and this nymph embracing a stag, whose horns protrude well out of the frame, must certainly have inspired the sculptor of *Diana,* also from the Château d'Anet [433].

472 Gian Lorenzo Bernini

1598–1680

Angel with the Crown of Thorns

Rome, *c.* 1667
Terracotta. 33 x 13 x 19 cm
Acquired in 1934. RF 2312

The inspired oeuvre of Gian Lorenzo Bernini, architect, sculptor and great organiser of pontifical pomp, constitutes the apogee of Roman Baroque. Commissioned in 1667 to decorate the Ponte Sant'Angelo in Rome, Bernini created a triumphal avenue lined by large statues of angels meditating on the instruments of Christ's Passion. This model for one of these angels already has all their dramatic energy and irresistible spiritual vigour, which Bernini conveys in the continuous, fluid movement of the drapery, arms, legs, hair and wings.

473 Antonio Canova

1757–1822

Eros and Psyche

Rome, 1793
Marble. H. 1.55 m
Formerly in the Château de Villiers-la-Garenne
Entered the Louvre before 1824. MR 1777

The story of Psyche symbolises the vicissitudes of the immortal soul of the Platonic myth. Psyche, who has fallen into a deadly sleep, is woken by the kiss of Eros, who then carries her away to Olympus. The sensual and diaphanous grace of Canova's sculpture group masterfully captures the fable's metaphysical poetry. The purity of its intertwining contours, the opening out of its forms into the surrounding space like a blooming flower, everything combines to convey the magical instant when love becomes divine ecstasy. The sculpture was acquired by Murat, who sold it to Napoleon.

474 Lorenzo Bartolini

1777–1850

Nymph with a Scorpion

Marble. H. 86 cm
Formerly in the Château d'Haroué
Gift of the Société des Amis du Louvre, 1993.
RF 4451

This beautiful nude, hailed by Baudelaire in 1845 as the 'major piece at the Sculpture Salon', illustrates the qualities for which Bartolini became famous: an idealism steeped in Antiquity in the Canova tradition, softened and invigorated by a certain naturalism in the treatment of the figures. This young woman, no doubt sculpted from life, and a nymph only in name, is merely an iconographic pretext for the artist to depict nudity in all its sensuous fullness, and without which it would have seemed too prosaic.

The Germanic countries

475 Attributed to Martin Hoffman
Known from 1507–1530/31
Virgin and Child

Basle, *c.* 1510
Limewood. 1.72 x 0.76 x 0.495 m
Formerly in the Antonite convent at Issenheim
Acquired in 1924. RF 1833

The Louvre's Germanic collections are largely composed of 15th and 16th-century works, the golden age of Germanic sculpture. The economic growth of the cities was accompanied by the considerable development of artistic life. The mass-production of altarpieces and statues catered for the needs of a huge clientele. Although works were produced in stone, wood, principally soft limewood, was the favourite material of these 'image carvers', most of whom have remained anonymous. Works, once sculpted, were polychromed to evoke, particularly in altarpieces, the splendour of the heavenly realm. Around 1400, in southern Germany and Bohemia, a local version of International Gothic flourished, known as the 'Soft Style' (*Weiche Stil*). The spread of the Bohemian 'Beautiful Madonna' model to Germany bears witness to the fervent worship of the Virgin there. Its characteristic pose is with the weight markedly on one hip, with the seemingly swaying figure enveloped in ample drapery with flowing folds.
The middle of the century saw the beginnings of the evolution towards the 'Late Gothic' style, which attained its fullest expression in the work of one major artist, Nicolaus Gerhaert von Leyden. The sinuous movements were attenuated, drapery became more angular, forms became denser and charged with a powerful naturalism, and figures were imbued with great spiritual intensity. This style was prevalent throughout the southern part of the Empire and in particular at Strasbourg. But each major centre had its masters: Basle and Nuremburg (Veit Stoss, Adam Kraft, Peter Vischer), Würzburg in Franconia (Tilmann Riemenschneider), Schwaben (Michael and Gregor Erhart, Niklaus Weckmann, Daniel Mauch). Rhenish mysticism favoured the development of private worship, and this gave rise to massive production of small-format sculptures, of variable but sometimes exceptional quality. But just as the German Renaissance was beginning to bear its first fruits, the Reformation delivered sculpture a fatal blow. Because of their materiality, statues were accused of fermenting idolatry, and incurred the wrath of iconoclasts.

476 Gregor Erhart

*c.*1460–1540

Mary Magdalen

Augsburg, *c.*1515–1520
Polychromed limewood. 1.77 x 0.44 x 0.43 m
Acquired in 1902. RF 1338

Gregor Erhart was the leading sculptor in Augsburg in the early 16th century. This famous statue, partially inspired by an engraving by Dürer, depicts Mary Magdalen in ecstasy. Legend has it that she lived in reclusion in a cave at Sainte-Baume in Provence, clad only in her hair and without food or water. Everyday she was borne up to heaven to hear the music of the angels – the statue was originally surrounded by six sculpted angels. The work's spiritual content is coupled here with a quest for physical beauty, which is enhanced by the polychromy. A new concern in German sculpture, it reflected the evolution in sensibility with regard to the Northern humanism of the late Middle Ages, at the dawn of the Renaissance.

477 Tilman Riemenschneider

*c.*1460–1531

Virgin Annunciate

Würzburg, *c.*1495
Alabaster, polychrome highlights. 53 x 40 x 19 cm
Acquired in 1904. RF 1384

This Virgin from a small altarpiece was originally accompanied by an angel kneeling on her right. Mary has stopped reading to listen to Gabriel's announcement. Her immobility and the expression of concentration on her face betray not the slightest emotion. They are the mirror of a body and soul impregnated with divine will. It is this spiritual dimension that is the hallmark of this great master of German Late Gothic. Riemenschneider's virtuoso manner manifests itself particularly in some of his large, unpolychromed limewood altarpieces. Here, the gilding and subtle colour highlights enrich without disrupting the monochrome, which exalts the nobility of the material and the sculpted form.

The Low Countries and Scandinavia

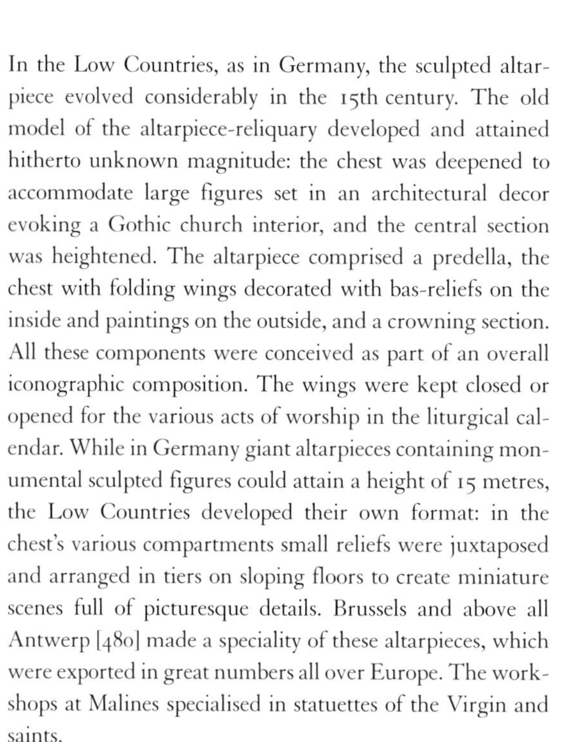

In the Low Countries, as in Germany, the sculpted altar-piece evolved considerably in the 15th century. The old model of the altarpiece-reliquary developed and attained hitherto unknown magnitude: the chest was deepened to accommodate large figures set in an architectural decor evoking a Gothic church interior, and the central section was heightened. The altarpiece comprised a predella, the chest with folding wings decorated with bas-reliefs on the inside and paintings on the outside, and a crowning section. All these components were conceived as part of an overall iconographic composition. The wings were kept closed or opened for the various acts of worship in the liturgical calendar. While in Germany giant altarpieces containing monumental sculpted figures could attain a height of 15 metres, the Low Countries developed their own format: in the chest's various compartments small reliefs were juxtaposed and arranged in tiers on sloping floors to create miniature scenes full of picturesque details. Brussels and above all Antwerp [480] made a speciality of these altarpieces, which were exported in great numbers all over Europe. The workshops at Malines specialised in statuettes of the Virgin and saints.

Northern Mannerism is represented in the Louvre by a major work by the Dutchman Adrien De Vries; the irresistible momentum and swirling lines of his *Mercury and Psyche* [479] belong to the great movment unifying the statuary of Prague, Amsterdam and the German cities.

Yet it was in the Protestant North that, much later, Neo-classical sculpture would find its promised land, in the work of the Swede Johan Tobias Sergel, known for his drawings and terracotta figure groups [478], and the Dane Bertel Thorvaldsen, Canova's only serious rival.

478 Johan Tobias Sergel

1740–1814

Centaur Embracing a Bacchante

Terracotta. 36 x 39 x 17 cm
Acquired in 1998. RF 4632

479 Adriaen de Vries

1546–1626

Mercury and Psyche

Prague, 1593
Bronze. 2.15 x 0.92 x 0.72 m
Formerly in Prague. Entered the Louvre *c.* 1877
MR 3270

481 *Calvary Virgin*

Brabant, late 15th century
Oak. 1.63 x 0.57 x 0.38 m
Probably from the rood screen of the collegiate church of Saint Gertrude, Nivelles
Acquired in 1880. RF 822

480 *Altarpiece of the Passion*

Antwerp, *c.* 1510–1510
Polychromed oak
2.03 x 2.145 x 0.265 m
From the church at Coligny (Marne). Acquired in 1922
RF 1769

Objets d'art

After the fall of the Ancien Régime, when the Louvre opened to the public as the Muséum Central des Arts, on view in the Grande Galerie there were vases, antiques and precious objects, as well as paintings and sculptures. This juxtaposition was hardly surprising since the decree of the Convention that had created the Muséum in July 1793 envisioned the bringing together of certain remarkable objects requisitioned from royal residences and religious buildings. The pieces taken from the ecclesiastical treasure from the Abbey of Saint-Denis, including the famous vases created in the 12th century by Abbot Suger as well as the coronation regalia of the kings of France, entered the Louvre collections the year the Muséum was created. They were joined by another prestigious ensemble in 1796, when the former Crown Furniture Depository ceded, among many other rare objects, the crown jewels, the bulk of the hardstone vases collected by Louis XIV, and also his bronzes – the priceless ensemble that would later constitute the core of the Louvre's collection of Renaissance bronzes.
The quality and rarity of these works naturally led to the further enrichment of the collection with exceptional pieces. There were, therefore, a number of isolated purchases: the acquisition of Charles IX's helmet and shield at public auction in 1793, and that of major private collections such as those of Edme-Antoine Durand and Pierre Révoil, during the Restoration. Both brought the Louvre a considerable

number of Greek and Roman antiquities, works from the Middle Ages and the Renaissance, ivories, tapestries, furniture, and a magnificent ensemble of enamels.

The museum's collections were greatly enriched under Napoleon III, during whose reign the Department of Objets d'art was officially created. In addition to the acquisition of entire collections, including the particularly famous Campana Collection, from 1870 further transfers of royal furniture were made, as were purchases at auctions or from collectors, and gifts or bequests received from private individuals – the prestigious Camondo and Rothschild collections, for example – and from the Société des Amis du Louvre.

Such enrichments from diverse sources have never ceased, and from the early 20th century have included pieces from all periods, from the Middle Ages to Louis-Philippe. For a long time limited to Medieval and Renaissance art, the Objets d'art collection only began to extend to later periods around 1900, with the opening of the 17th and 18th-century rooms. The 19th century is represented by numerous Empire pieces and by masterpieces created during the Restoration and the July Monarchy, and is crowned by the sumptuous ensemble of furniture in Napoleon III's apartments in the Richelieu Wing.

482 *Miracles of Christ*

Rome, early 5th century
Plaque, ivory. 19.7 x 78 cm
Acquired in 1926. OA 7876-7878

This ivory plaque depicting three of Christ's miracles was sculpted in Rome in the early 5th century. Its treatment shows that the techniques of classical Rome had not been lost by subsequent generations of ivory carvers and were still in use during the Christian Late Empire. One notices, however, that the style has evolved, particularly in the representation of the faces, which are less firmly modelled, and in the attenuated relief. These three scenes originally formed the lateral section of a large leaf of a five-part ivory diptych, another fragment of which is today in Berlin.

From the Late Roman Empire to Byzantium

Constantine the Great (306–337), a mythical figure since he was the first Roman emperor to convert to Christianity, showed great political clairvoyance in doing so, for it enabled him to restore a certain unity to the Roman Empire after a century of grave political and social turmoil. Constantine saw Christianity as a force capable of revitalising Roman civilisation without destroying its foundations. Unlike traditional religions and cultures, Christianity could ensure the acceptance of a single sovereign. The *imperator*, previously deified and worshipped, now became the first defender of Christ and his Church, and from now on would reign under his protection and govern in his name.

The iconography of the period and until the 6th and 7th centuries is a perfect reflection of this policy of the 'Christianisation' of Roman traditions. In the famous *'Barberini Ivory'* [483], for example, destined to exalt the glory of the Christian emperor, the artist uses the conventional, classical Roman representation of imperial triumphs but adds the presence of Christ. Similarly, on the diptychs, tablets traditionally sent by the emperors to consuls taking up office, it was images drawn from the evangelical texts that were sculpted from then on [482]. Thus the savoir-faire of the craftsmen of Antiquity, enlisted into the service of the new religion, would transform itself down the centuries, whilst retaining its forms and techniques.

Constantine's other decisive gesture was to found a second capital, Constantinople, in order to better administrate his empire. Out of this administrative division, at the end of the 4th century, there arose a veritable opposition between the Western Empire, Latin in culture, and the Eastern Empire, Greek in culture. The death of Theodosis I in 395 sealed this rift, and while the West was swept by the great invasions, Byzantium developed a civilisation that would endure for the next thousand years.

483 *The Emperor Triumphant*, known as the *'Barberini Ivory'*

Constantinople, first half of the 6th century
Ivory. 34.2 x 26.8 cm
Acquired in 1899. OA 9063

The conventions for representing imperial triumphs established during the classical centuries of the Roman Empire were perpetuated durably in Byzantium, to the extent that in the 6th century ivory carvers were still drawing on this iconography to exalt the Christian emperors. It is uncertain whether this figure, depicted on horseback and surmounted by Christ giving his blessing, with whom he is symbolically associated, is the emperor Anastasius (491–518) or Justinian (527–565). The skill of the artist who sculpted this diptych leaf is absolutely remarkable, both in the centrepiece, sculpted in the round, and in the lower relief depicting the defeated paying tribute. Found in Provence in the early 17th century, this ivory once belonged to Cardinal Barberini – hence its name – to whom it was offered by the scholar Claude Fabri de Peiresc. The names of Provençal Merovingian sovereigns inscribed on the back indicate that it must have already been in the region in the 7th century.

Byzantine art

The new city founded on the site of Byzantium in 330 had wide streets, a forum, public edifices, columns and several statues of the emperor. It was therefore the structure of a Roman town that Constantine adopted for his second capital, just as he relied on the administrative system and values of the Roman Empire to rule. This will to perpetuate the traditions of Antiquity, later reaffirmed during several periods of history, and which forged the particular character of the Byzantine Empire and its art, was also inherited from the civilisation of the Christian Late Empire.
The history of the Byzantine Empire began in the 5th century and ended when Constantinople was taken by the Turks in 1453: a thousand-year period, with its periods of full bloom – the reign of Justinian (527–565), for example, or that of the Macedonian dynasty (867–1056) – but also shaken by violent internal crises and armed conflicts. One dynasties followed another while the Empire transformed itself under the pressure of Islam, crusades and the proximity of the Turks. But during each period of renewal in Byzantine history – known as the 'Heraclean', 'Macedonian', 'Comnenian' and 'Palaeologan' renaissances, after the reigning dynasties – this attachment to the examples of the past was once more reaffirmed.
This constant harking back to the past profoundly affected iconography, which continued to draw its inspiration from antique sources although the themes were those of the Christian Empire (*Harbaville Tritpych*, 485). The creations of Byzantine art, particularly in precious metals and ivory, therefore have remarkable unity, irrespective of period. Yet styles can be distinguished, bearing witness to the influences of other cultures, from the East, and later from the West, with the final, Palaeologan, period of Byzantine art taking on a note of pathos.

484 *Saint Demetrios*

Constantinople, early 12th century
Medallion, gold and cloisonné enamel. 8.4 cm
Gift of Pierpont Morgan, 1911. OA 6457

This delicate enamel belongs to a series of eleven medallions – one of the other ten is in Tbilisi and the others in the Metropolitan Museum of Art, New York – which decorated the frame of a large icon of the Archangel Gabriel, formerly in the monastery at Djumati in Georgia. This object gives a measure of the degree of refinement attained under the Comnenian emperors (1081–1181), a period of exceptional artistic effervescence marked by new decorative experimentation.

485 *Harbaville Triptych: 'Deisis and Saints'*

Constantinople, mid-10th century
Ivory, traces of gilding. 24.2 x 28.5 cm
Acquired in 1891. OA 3247

The theme of this triptych is a *Deisis*, that is, a representation of Christ with the Virgin and Saint John the Baptist, to whom are associated one or sometimes several other saints, interceding with Christ enthroned on behalf of humanity. Beneath Mary and Saint John the Baptist and on the wings are figures of apostles, canonised bishops, martyrs and soldiers. The exceptional quality of this work produced in the imperial workshop known as 'Romanos', bears witness to the artistic renaissance under the Macedonians in the 10th century, but also of the persistence of references to Antiquity during this late period.

From Carolingian art to Roman art

The ambition of Charlemagne (771–814) to revive the grandeur of the Western Roman Empire led him to embark on an extensive economic and administrative reorganisation of his empire and, in parallel, to render his power sacred by leaning on the Church. In this undertaking, very comparable to that of the Byzantine emperors, Charlemagne, like them, took Antiquity as his reference. After him, his descendents would deviate little from this ideal, to the extent that Carolingian culture in the 8th and 9th centuries cannot be understood without this fundamental component: the importance of the heritage of the Late Empire. Imitating the Romans, Charlemagne and his successors surrounded themselves with a sumptuous, cultivated court, and in their palaces had workshops in which manuscripts and rare objects, themselves inspired by antiquities, were produced to their specifications. Precious metalworking achieved heights of perfection during this period (*Serpentine paten*, 487), while there was a revival of forsaken techniques such as glyptics and bronze casting (*Equestrian statuette of Charlemagne*, 488), and above all ivory carving (*Dagulf Psalter*, 486). Such was the influence of the Carolingian period that it served as a model, in the Germanic Empire, for Ottonian artists. In the 11th century, these produced particularly refined metalwork (*Maestricht binding case*, 490), while in Latin southern Europe another stylistic trend emerged towards the end of the same century: Romanesque art.
From the 11th to the 12th century, workshops producing precious objects increased in number and diversified. Each region – the Rhineland, Moselle, Spain – developed its own style. However, the universal phenomenon of this period of the Middle Ages was the triumph of enamelwork. The Louvre collection covess a wide range of techniques (*'Armilla': The Resurrection*, 493; *Reliquary of Saint Henry*, 491) and production centres, such as Conques (*Medallion decorated with a fabulous animal*, 494) and Limoges (*Alpais ciborium*, 495; *Reliquary of Saint Thomas Beckett*, 496).

486 *Leaves from the binding of the Dagulf Psalter*

Workshop of Charlemagne's palace, late 8th century
Ivory. Each leaf: 16.8 x 8.1 cm
Bremen Cathedral. MR 370-371

487 *Serpentine paten*

1st century BC or AD (stone)
and second half of 9th century (surround)
Gold, pearls, precious stones, coloured glass. Ø 17 cm
Treasury of the Abbey of Saint-Denis
Entered the Louvre in 1793. MR 415

The extremely delicate gold fish decorating this serpentine plate were undoubtedly inlaid in the early Christian era, but the gold surround dates from the Carolingian period. The combination of gold cloisonné and precious stones is a technique used until the early 11th century. King Charles the Bald donated this paten to the Abbey of Saint-Denis, where it remained until the Revolution.

488 *Equestrian statuette of Charlemagne*

9th century
Bronze with traces of gilding. H. 23.5 cm
Treasury of Metz Cathedral. OA 8260

The horseman's identity has never been ascertained but the crown and the orb in his left hand indicate that he is a sovereign, possibly Charlemagne or his grandson Charles the Bald. The figure is Carolingian in treatment but the horse, whose size does not quite match the figure, could be a reuse of a piece from the Late Roman Empire. This bronze statuette, kept in the treasury of Metz Cathedral until the Revolution, is the only Carolingian sculpture in the round to have survived intact.

489 *'Suger's Eagle'*

Antique vase; mount: France, before 1147
Porphyry, silver-gilt, niello
43.1 x 27 cm
Treasury of the Abbey of Saint-Denis
Entered the Louvre in 1793. MR 422

Abbot Suger of Saint-Denis, adviser to Louis VI and Louis VII, was keen to enrich his abbey's treasury, for which he commissioned four hardstone liturgical vases. This mount, set on an antique porphyry vase, was given the form of an eagle, no doubt by Ile-de-France silversmiths. The Louvre has two more of these prestigious pieces, the 'Eleanor' vase and a sard ewer. The fourth, a chalice, is in the National Gallery of Art, Washington.

490 *Maestricht binding case*

2nd quarter of the 11th century
Gold, cloisonné enamel, precious stones, filigree and niello on wood. 39.2 x 32 cm
Entered the Louvre in 1795. MR 349

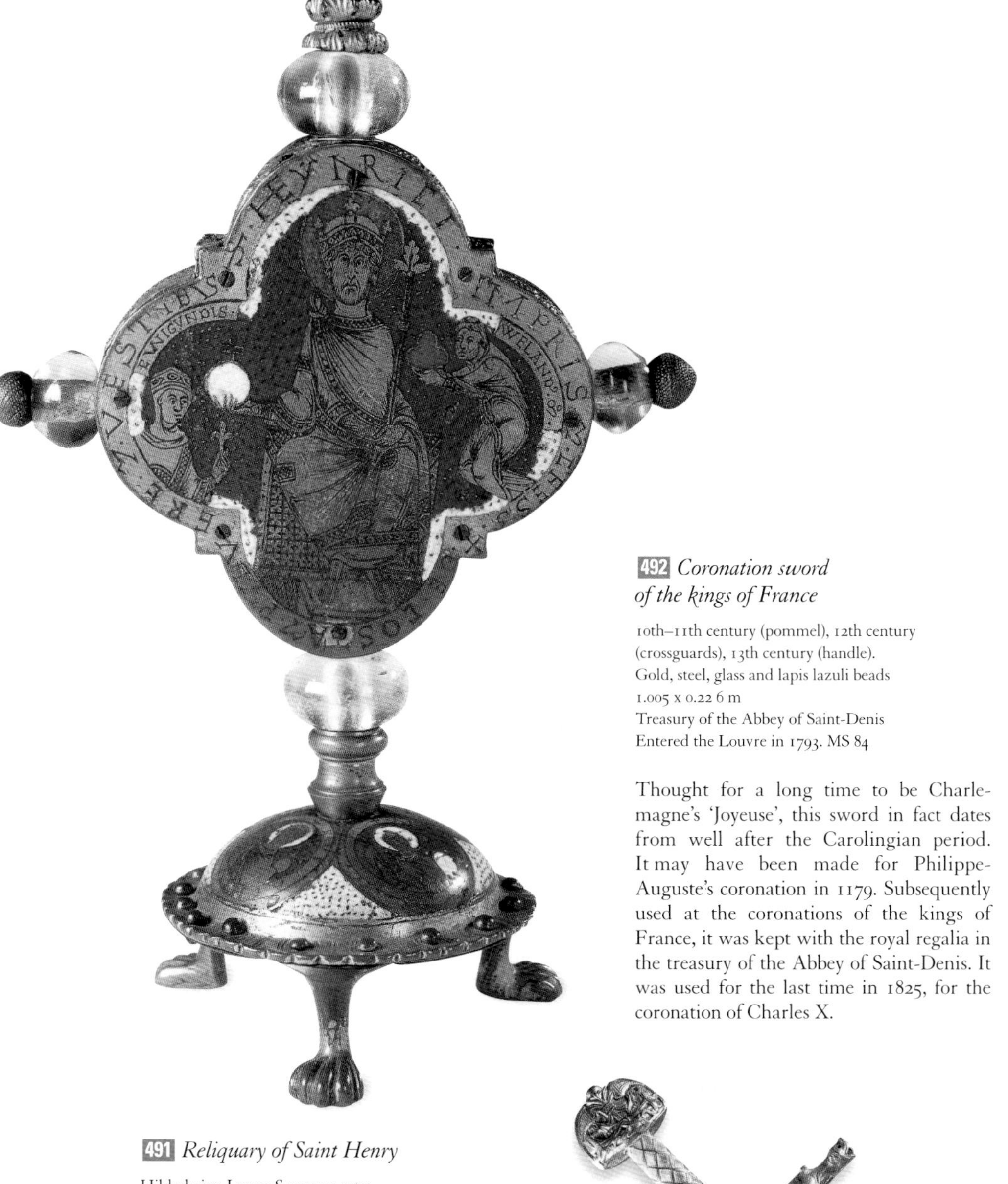

492 *Coronation sword of the kings of France*

10th–11th century (pommel), 12th century (crossguards), 13th century (handle).
Gold, steel, glass and lapis lazuli beads
1.005 x 0.22 6 m
Treasury of the Abbey of Saint-Denis
Entered the Louvre in 1793. MS 84

Thought for a long time to be Charlemagne's 'Joyeuse', this sword in fact dates from well after the Carolingian period. It may have been made for Philippe-Auguste's coronation in 1179. Subsequently used at the coronations of the kings of France, it was kept with the royal regalia in the treasury of the Abbey of Saint-Denis. It was used for the last time in 1825, for the coronation of Charles X.

491 *Reliquary of Saint Henry*

Hildesheim, Lower Saxony, *c.*1175
Gilt and engraved copper, champlevé enamel, rock crystal, silver on wood core. 23.6 x 16.1 cm
Acquired in 1851. OA 49

493 *'Armilla': The Resurrection*

Meuse, *c.* 1170
Gilt copper, champlevé enamel. 11.3 x 14.7 cm
Gift of the Société des Amis du Louvre, 1934. OA 8261

494 *Medallion decorated with a fabulous animal*

Conques?, 1107–1119
Gilt copper, champlevé enamel. Ø 8 cm
Gift of a group of friends of the Louvre, 1909.
OA 6280

This medallion and nine other similar ones now in the Metropolitan Museum, New York, and the Museo Nazionale del Bargello, Florence, once decorated a casket in the treasury of the abbey at Conques. They are the earliest surviving champlevé enamels on copper. The vivid colours, griffin and Greek fret motifs are characteristic of the Romanesque period.

495 *Alpais ciborium*

Limoges, shortly before 1200
Gilt copper, chased and engraved, champlevé enamel,
Cast added foot and finial, precious stones
H. 30 cm; Ø 16.8 cm
Formerly in the Revoil Collection
Acquired in 1828. MRR 98

The signature on the inside of the lid of this ciborium, *'Magister G. Alpais me fecit lemovicarum'*, around an engraved figure of an angel, tells us that this masterpiece was made in Limoges, where enamel production was then at its apogee. The stylisation of the figures is still Romanesque in spirit, but the openwork foliation on the base and the fine chasing of the angel on the inside of the ciborium already herald early Gothic art.

496 *Reliquary: murder and burial of Saint Thomas Becket*

Limoges, c.1180
Champlevé enamel on gilt copper
20 x 19 x 8 cm
Formerly in the collection of Martin Le Roy, Marquet de Vasselot
Donated in payment of inheritance tax, 1991.
OA 11333

497 *Virgin and Child from the Sainte-Chapelle*

Paris, third quarter of the 13th century
Ivory, traces of polychromy. H. 41 cm
Treasury of the Sainte-Chapelle, Paris
Acquired in 1861. OA 57

Gothic art

In the late 12th and early 13th century there emerged a new style in Western Europe characterised by the progressive abandonment of the conventions of Romanesque art for a more realistic representation of nature. Anatomy became more supple, drapery more flowing, or 'wet', and faces, notably that of the Virgin, ceased to be hieratic and became gentler, sometimes enlivened by a smile. This elegant movement, expressed in illumination and monumental sculpture, also bloomed in the precious metalworking arts, which underwent extraordinary expansion until the 14th century. Alongside the clientele of the Church and princes gradually developed that of the rich middle classes.
Limoges, a renowned enamel production centre, in turn adopted this style, as reflected in the *Plaque with a figure of Saint Matthew* [499], whose powerful relief and sensitive modelling are reminiscent of certain cathedral statues. Metalworking was influenced by the 'Parisian style' from the 13th century (*Triptych reliquary of the True Cross*, 498). In the same period, numerous workshops throughout Europe vied with one another in virtuosity and exchanged savoir-faire. Paris and northern France borrowed the technique of translucent enamel on silver (*Jeanne d'Evreux Virgin and Child*, 502) or gold (*Pair of mirror cases*, 504) from the Italians. In-the-round enamelling of gold developed from the second half of the 14th century – the *Sceptre of Charles V* [505] originally bore a fleur-de-lis executed using this technique – followed by painted enamel (*Jean Fouquet*, 506).
But if there is a domain in which Gothic art powerfully asserted itself, it was in ivory carving. The Louvre is particularly rich in this respect and its collection covers all its forms of expression: statuettes (*Virgin and Child from the Sainte-Chapelle*, 497); *Descent from the Cross*, 501), diptychs, triptychs, tabernacles [503] and secular pieces (*Mirror case: 'The Game of Chess'*, 500). Another art that would undergo massive development in the late 14th century was tapestry (*The Working of Wool*, 507).

The considerable development of ivory work was one of the major phenomena of Parisian artistic life in the mid-13th century. This highly refined statue of the Virgin, her back slightly arched, smiling, dressed in a skilfully draped robe, offering an apple to the Infant Jesus, is considered one of the greatest achievements of Parisian Gothic, to the extent that an entire series of ivory statuettes from the second half of the 13th century seem to have been inspired by this prestigious model. This was also the period of the development of Marian worship, which gave rise to a blossoming of Virgin and Child figurines.

498 *Triptych reliquary of the True Cross (Floreffe Polyptych)*

Ile-de-France or northern France?
After 1254
Abbey of Floreffe
Gilt copper, nielloed and gilded silver, gemstones
H. 79 cm; W. (open) 92 cm
Baron Adolphe de Rothschild Bequest, 1901
OA 5552

This reliquary, executed following a miracle in 1254 and destined to contain a piece of the True Cross, is a fine example of the elegant 'Parisian style' which emerged around 1240 and which rapidly spread throughout northern France.

499 *Arched plaque with a figure of Saint Matthew*

Limoges, *c.* 1220–1230
Gilt copper, champlevé enamel. 29 x 14 cm
Durand Collection
Acquired in 1825. MR 2650

500 *Mirror case: 'The Game of Chess'*

Paris, *c.*1300
Ivory. Ø 12 cm
Gift of A.-C. Sauvageot, 1856. OA 717

502 *The Jeanne d'Evreux Virgin and Child*

Paris, between 1324 and 1339
Silver-gilt, basse-taille translucent enamel, gold, rock crystal, precious stones and pearls. H. 69 cm
Given to the Abbey of Saint-Denis by Queen Jeanne d'Evreux in 1339
Entered the Louvre in 1793. MR 342 and 419

This silver-gilt Virgin and Child, given to the Abbey of Saint-Denis by Charles IV's widow, Jeanne d'Evreux, is holding a reliquary in the form of a fleur-de-lis which contained some of Mary's hair, milk and fragments of her clothing. The rounded face, the layered hems of her robe and the widening of figure due to the cone-shaped folds are characteristic of Parisian art in the first half of the 14th century. The translucent basse-taille enamelling on the silver base, a technique recently borrowed from Tuscan silversmiths, depicts scenes from the life of Christ.

501 *Descent from the Cross*

Paris, *c.*1260–1280
Ivory, traces of gilding and polychromy
Acquired in 1896. OA 3935 and 9443

503 *Tabernacle*
Paris, 2nd quarter of the 14th century
Ivory. 29 x 23.5 cm
Acquired in 1882. OA 2587

Tabernacles, produced in great number in the late Middle Ages, are small polyptychs composed of articulated wings folding over the central part, thereby giving them the appearance of a minute chapel peopled with one or several statuettes. Here, in the centre of the tabernacle, there is a Madonna and Child, whose round face, sinuous body and delicate cascading drapery obey the canons of monumental sculpture, whereas the scenes depicted on the wings – the Annunciation, the Visitation, the Nativity, the Adoration of the Magi and the Presentation in the Temple – are more akin to the traditional work of Parisian ivory carvers at that time.

504 *Pair of mirror cases*
Paris, before 1379
Gold, translucent basse-taille enamel. Ø 6.8 cm
Durand Collection
Acquired in 1825. MR 2608-2609

506 Jean Fouquet

c.1420–c.1477/81
Signed Self-Portrait

c.1450
Painted enamel on copper. Ø 6.8 cm
Gift of H. de Janzé, 1861. OA 56

The diptych of Notre-Dame de Melun – today in Antwerp and Berlin – from which this portrait was taken, was executed by Jean Fouquet for Étienne Chevalier, Treasurer of France and Charles VII's secretary and adviser. The missing frame comprised a number of medallions, including this one, Fouquet's signature. This self-portrait of the greatest French painter of the 15th century is the first known self-portrait in Western painting. The technique he used, enamel on copper heightened with gold, prefigures the painted enamels that would become so popular towards the close of the century.

505 *Sceptre of Charles V*
Paris, before 1380
Gold, pearls, precious stones, glass. H. 60 cm
Treasury of the Abbey of Saint-Denis
Entered the Louvre in 1793. MS 83

An inventory of the royal treasury drawn up in 1379–80 gives a detailed description of this sceptre and we know that it underwent few alterations after Charles V had it prepared for the coronation of his son, the future Charles VI. The only major difference was that the central fleur-de-lis was originally coated with opaque white enamel. The depictions of the emperor Charlemagne and scenes from his legend chased on the orb were for the House of Valois an affirmation of the legitimacy of their dynasty and clearly also an allusion to the forename of the king and his son.

507 *The Working of Wool*

Flanders?, *c.*1500
Arms of Thomas Bohier, former chamberlain of Charles VIII (died 1524) and his wife Catherine Briçonnet.
Château de Serrant (Maine-et-Loire)
Tapestry: wool and silk. 2.20 x 3.19 m
E. Larcade Bequest, 1945. OA 9408

France played a decisive role in the expansion of the art of tapestry in the 14th century before being surpassed by Flanders and the Netherlands, which became the leaders in the technique new. Works of great refinement were produced during the Late Gothic period, such as this tapestry commissioned by Thomas Bohier, former Chamberlain of Charles VIII. The pastorale-like scene shows figures against a flowered background engaged in various activities, in the midst of domestic animals.

The Italian Renaissance

The vast movement known as the Renaissance, founded on the rediscovery of the works of Antiquity, emerged in the 15th century in a prosperous and refined Italy in which culture became an instrument of a new politics of prestige for princes and the ennobled bourgeoisie. The objets d'art artists created for them reflect the aristocratic lifestyle of their clientele and the growing taste of the cultivated elite for antique art, while artists vied with one another in the invention of new techniques.
Italy's very rich production of faience in the 15th and 16th centuries is represented in the Louvre by several major examples from famous centres such as Florence (*Bowl with the arms of Florence*, 509), Urbino (*Plate from the service of Isabella d'Este*, 511), Faenza and Castel Durante. But glassmaking also progressed considerably in the same period. Its most brilliant production centre was Venice, whose principal invention, a particularly transparent and luminous glass called *cristallo*, was the envy of all Europe. Attempts at imitating it were aided by Italian emigrant glassmakers.
But the medium which underwent the greatest development was bronze. Its revival was clearly part of the return to Antiquity, whose models could still be seen in palaces and churches. Using the same materials and pictorial vocabulary, artists created small statuettes and objects destined for the houses of their patrician clients. After the Florentine masters Ghiberti and Donatello, numerous disciples furthered the tradition of sculpture in bronze, notably the Paduan Bellano (*Saint Jerome and the Lion*, 510), followed by his pupil Riccio. Among the works by the latter in the Louvre are the eight exceptional bas-reliefs from the Della Torre tomb (*Paradise*, 512). In the 16th century, bronze sculpture attained heights of elegance in the works of Giambologna, a sculptor of French origin who worked at the court of the Medicis (*Nessus and Deianeira*, 514).

508 *Cup decorated with an allegorical procession*

Venice, last quarter of the 15th century
Enamelled glass. H. 27.5 cm; Ø 14 cm
Baroness Salomon de Rothschild Bequest, 1922.
OA 7564

509 *Bowl with the arms of Florence*

Florence, *c.* 1425–1450
Glazed earthenware. H. 8 cm; Ø 64 cm
Acquired in 1897. OA 3946

Around 1400 and throughout the 15th century, Italy was the centre for the development of a type of luxury ceramics called majolica after the island of Majorca, via which transited the lustred earthenware made in the Valencia region. But whilst maintaining these imports, the Italians created their own workshops, in which they developed a style harmoniously reflecting the trends of the Quattrocento. Florence, where this bowl bearing the city's arms was made, was one of the production centres of this type of ceramic ware.

510 Bartolomeo Bellano

c. 1440–1496/97

Saint Jerome and the Lion

Padua, late 15th century
Bronze with cracked black patina. 25 x 20.5 cm
Gift of Mme Gustave Dreyfus and her children, 1919. OA 7250

The subject of this bronze is the famous episode in the life of Saint Jerome in which the hermit extracts a thorn from a lion's paw. Its sculptor, Bartolomeo Bellano, trained in Donatello's studio and was a native of Padua, a city renowned for the quality of its bronzes. This one, which appears to have been cast directly from the wax model, is a unique copy. It has been dated to the early 1490s owing to several similarities with sculptures Bellano executed at that time for the monument to Pietro Roccabonella in the church of San Francesco in Padua.

511 Nicola da Urbino

Known between 1520 and 1538

Plate from the service of Isabella d'Este

Urbino, *c.* 1525
Earthenware. H. 4 cm; Ø 27 cm
Baroness Salomon de Rothschild Bequest, 1922.
OA 7578

The arms on this plate are those of Isabella d'Este, Marquess of Mantua, patron and art lover, who commissioned Nicola da Urbino to make a service in 1525. Urbino, the town where the artist was established, was then producing remarkable faience and had made historiated scenes its speciality. This genre, called *istoriato*, enjoyed great success in Europe in the first half of the 16th century. The Biblical scene depicted on this plate, *Abimelech Spying on Isaac and Rebecca*, is a reproduction of a composition by Raphael in the Vatican.

512 Andrea Briosco, known as Riccio

1470–1532

Paradise

Padua, 1516–1521
Bas-relief, bronze with brown patina. 37 x 49 cm
Entered the Louvre in 1798. MR 1711 (OA 9099)
Part of a set of eight bas-reliefs from the funerary monument of Girolamo and Marcantonio Della Torre

513 *Gnome on a Snail*

Florence, second half of the 16th century
Bronze with cracked black patina
and brown patina. 37.5 x 19.5 cm
Acquired in 1933. OA 8252

514 Giambologna

1529–1608

Nessus and Deianeira

Florence, *c.*1575–1580
Bronze with red-brown patina. 42.1 x 30.5 cm
Crown Collection. OA 11896

This bronze of exceptional quality was formerly in the collection of Louis XIV, to whom it was given by the famous landscape gardener Le Nôtre. The signature on the centaur's headband – *Ioa Bolongie* – states that the work is by Jean Boulogne. Born in Douai, this sculptor settled in Florence where, working under the name Giambologna, he became the favourite sculptor of the Medicis. His fame throughout Europe was partially due to Medici princes' habit of offering bronzes cast in his studio as diplomatic gifts.

The Renaissance in France and Flanders

Seduced by the new art that was developing in Renaissance Italy, Europe converted to this aesthetic in the 16th century as a result of demand from its princes, the emigration of Italian artists and the circulation of objects and prints. France was at the forefront of countries won over by the lessons of the Italians, thanks largely to the will of its kings. Francis I played a decisive role by commissioning, from 1530, the decoration of his château at Fontainebleau to the multi-talented artists Rosso, Primaticcio and Nicolò dell'Abbate, whose presence in France for several decades had a profound and lasting influence on the history of art. The 'School of Fontainebleau' in turn became an international model at the end of the century.

Manifest in sculpture and painting, this Renaissance movement made an equally powerful mark on the production of precious decorative objects for palaces and residences. Sixteenth-century precious metalwork, enamel and ceramics show the adoption of new decorative elements – grotesque, Moorish and historiated scenes – first borrowed from Italy and which subsequently became European due to the dissemination of engravings. The Louvre has very little precious metalwork from this period but its collection of painted enamels on copper is exceptional. This technique, a speciality of Limoges throughout the 16th century and initially limited to the production of devotional pictures and portraits (*Portrait of the Constable de Montmorency*, 517), spread to decorative tableware and a variety of objects which had enormous success in France and abroad (*Oval plate*, 516). There were many ceramics production centres such as Nevers and Lyons, strongly influenced by Italy, Saint Porchaire, whose name has become associated with a white glazed ware with brown decoration, and the Beauvais and Saintonge regions, while Bernard Palissy, an artist elevated by posterity to the rank of a legend, solitarily created strange and poetic works (*Dish decorated with 'rustic figulines'*, 518).

515 *Ciborium from the treasury of the Order of the Holy Ghost*

Paris, *c.* 1530
Rock crystal, gilt and enamelled silver, pearls, garnets, cameos in agate and shell. H. 33 cm
Formerly in the Royal Collection (1561)
Allocated by Henry III to the treasury of the Order of the Holy Ghost. MR 547

The Order of the Holy Ghost, whose purpose was to rally the Catholic nobility around the king, was founded by Henry III in 1578. The king endowed it with a treasure comprising objects dating from the Middle Ages and the early 16th century and works in gilt silver created especially for the occasion between 1579 and 1585 (*Mace of the Order of the Holy Ghost*, 519). The ciborium, dating from the reign of Francis I, is composed of rock crystal and a rich gilt and enamelled silver mount. As an ensemble, this treasure provides a rare testament to the work of French silversmiths in the 16th century.

516 Pierre Reymond

*c.*1513–after 1584

Oval plate

Limoges, 1569
Enamel on copper. Ø 46.5 cm
Entered the Louvre in 1806
N 1280

The combat scene represented on this grisaille painted plate is after a work by the painter Jules Romain. Contemporary engravings, notably of biblical and mythological subjects, often inspired enamellers, many of whom signed their works. This plate is signed by Pierre Raymond (1513–1584). The Louvre has several of his pieces: plates, grisaille dishes and objects in polychrome enamel made for rich dignitaries.

517 Léonard Limosin

*c.*1505–*c.*1575

Portrait of the Constable of Montmorency

Limoges, 1556
Enamel on copper, gilt wood mount. 72 x 56 cm
Seized during the Revolution. Entered the Louvre in 1794. N 1254

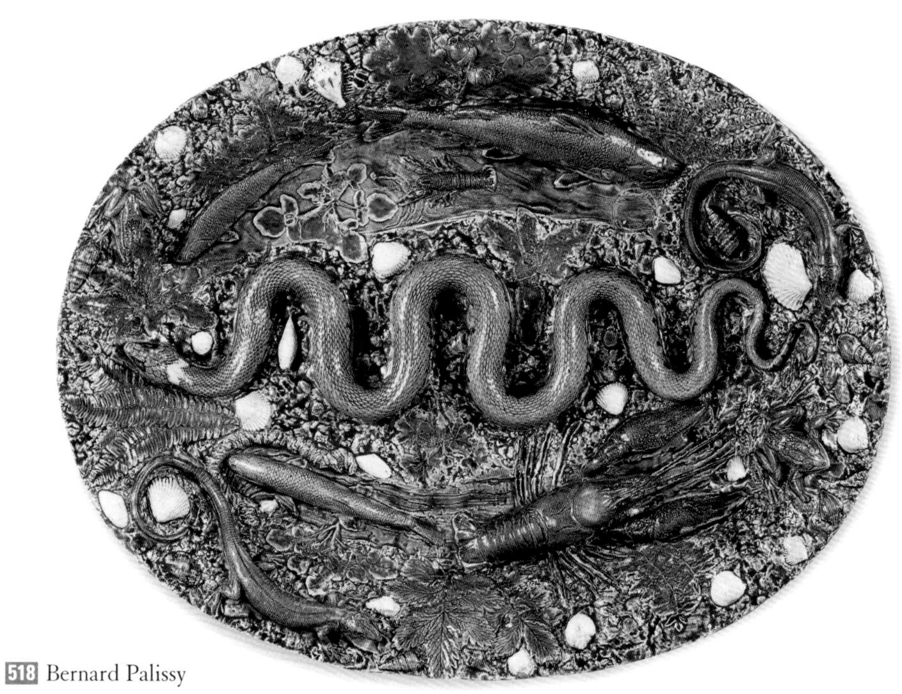

518 Bernard Palissy

1510?–1590

Dish decorated with 'rustic figulines'

France, *c.*1560
Glazed clay. 52.5 x 40.3 cm
Acquired in 1825. MR 2293

The French Renaissance was the golden age of glazed clay. Among the artists who brought great inventiveness to the medium at that time, Bernard Palissy is the most famous figure. A writer, architect and chemist, he practised his art with all the passion and curiosity of the true humanist, as shown by this remarkable piece, with its extraordinary reliefs of plants, reptiles and shellfish, apparently moulded from life.

519 *Mace of the Order of the Holy Ghost*

Paris, 1584–1585
Silver-gilt and enamel. 1.10 x 0.32 m; weight 4.24 kg
Formerly in the treasury of the Order
of the Holy Ghost
Entered the Louvre in 1830. MR 564

520 After Bernard Van Orley

*c.*1488–1541

The Month of June (Cancer)

Fourth tapestry of the *Maximilian's Hunts* series
Brussels, 1531–33
Wool, silk, gold and silver thread
4.20 x 5.82 m
Formerly in the Crown Collection. OA 7321

521 *Charles IX's shield*

Paris, *c.*1572
Embossed and gold-plated iron, enamel. 68 x 49 cm
Acquired in 1793. MR 427

This shield's accompanying helmet, also in the Louvre, was made using the same techniques: embossed and gold-plated iron heightened with opaque and translucent enamel decoration. Pierre Redon, silversmith and valet to the king, first delivered the helmet to Charles IX. The shield, made later, was bought from Redon's widow in 1572. The frame around the central bas-relief depicting Marius's victory over Jugurtha, king of Numidia, in 107 BC, is decorated with masks, trophies and fruit, motifs directly inspired by the School of Fontainebleau. Around the shield's rim, the king's K monogram alternates with medallions in cloisonné enamel.

The 17th century

At the beginning of the 17th century, Henry IV, anxious to protect the French tapestry industry from Flemish competition, decided to ban imports, thereby prompting the creation of workshops in Paris and the provinces. Foreign tapestry weavers, mainly Flemings and Germans, were invited to work in them, and the king crowned this initiative by installing a workshop in the Louvre palace. Henry IV subsequently applied the same policy to other domains of the decorative arts, and it was continued by Louis XIII, who in particular commissioned the painter Simon Vouet to design elegant tapestries (*Moses in the Bullrushes*, 523), and to an even further degree by Louis XIV. Indeed, it was due to the political will of the latter that the Gobelins Royal Manufactory of Crown Furniture was founded in 1667. All the artistic crafts were practiced there, and under the direction of Charles Le Brun, remarkable pieces were created to satisfy the sumptuous tastes of the Sun King and his court: tapestries (the *History of Scipio* tapestry series, after Jules Romain, 527), furniture and silverware, while the royal carpets were woven at the Savonnerie manufactory (*Tapestry bearing the arms of France*, 529). The noble classicism of these works gave rise to what is known as the 'Louis XIV style'.
The 17th century was also the century of the invention of a new technique, cabinetmaking, which consisted in concealing the pine or oak frame of a piece of furniture beneath a luxurious precious-wood veneer. The Louvre has a rare, ebony-veneered piece (526) from the middle of the century, but a few decades later, cabinetmaking was dominated by the refined creations of André-Charles Boulle, who incorporated brass, tortoiseshell, horn and tin, and also bronze ornaments into his marquetries. His large *Wardrobe* (528), of exceptional finesse, made at the end of Louis XIV's reign, heralds the extraordinary evolution of French furniture in the 18th century.

522 Barthélemy Prieur
1536–1611
Henry IV as Jupiter
Paris, *c.* 1608
Bronze, black lacquer and light brown patina.
H. 67 cm
Acquired in 1986. OA 11054

The portrayal of Henry IV as Jupiter is highly characteristic of the Renaissance-style references to Antiquity which endured until the early 17th century. This work's pendant, also in the Louvre, shows Marie de Médicis as Juno. Their sculptor, Barthélémy Prieur, was one of the most brilliant artists of the late 16th and early 17th century. Few works definitely attributable to him have survived, hence the importance of the sculptor's signature on this statuette.

523 After Simon Vouet

'Moses in the Bulrushes'

Third tapestry of the *Old Testament series*

Louvre workshop, Paris, *c.* 1630
Tapestry, wool and silk, 7 to 8 warp threads per cm
4.95 x 5.88 m
Transferred from the Mobilier National, 1907.
OA 6086

At Louis XIII's request, the painter Simon Vouet returned from Italy in 1627 and immediately received royal commissions, in particular for cartoons for a set of tapestries for the Louvre palace. Two of these eight biblically-inspired tapestries, including *Moses in the Bulrushes*, were woven in the Louvre workshops, which Henry IV had installed in the Grande Galerie, and which was the precursor of the Gobelins manufactory created under Louis XIV.

524 *Two-part wardrobe*

France, 1617
Walnut. H. 2.54 m
Révoil Collection. Acquired in 1828. MRR 61

French wardrobes from the Renaissance and the first half of the 17th century characteristically consist of two main parts and have four doors. Frequently, as here, the reliefs sculpted on them are derived from Flemish engravings, in this case those of Bartholomeus Spranger.

526 *Cabinet*

Paris, mid-17th century
Oak and poplar frame, ebony veneer,
blackened fruit wood. 1.85 x 1.58 x 0.56 m
Acquired in 1828. OA 6629

525 *Ewer*

1st century BC–1st century AD,
17th-century additions
Mount: enamelled gold, rubies; Pierre Delabarre,
Paris, *c.* 1630
27 x 16 x 10 cm
Entered the collection of Louis XIV
between 1681 and 1684
Sent to the Palais des Tuileries in the 19th century.
MR 445

Louis XIV manifested his interest for hardstone objects very early on by acquiring virtually all of Mazarin's collection after his death. This passion would continued unabated, as this ewer by the silversmith Pierre Delabarre, with a sard dating from the 1st century BC to the 1st century AD, so magnificently illustrates.

527 After Jules Romain
'The Arrival in Africa'

First tapestry of the *History of Scipio* series
Paris, Gobelins manufactory, 1688–1689
Tapestry, wool and silk, 8 to 9 warp threads per cm.
4.50 x 5.48 m
Transferred from the Mobilier National, 1901.
OA 5393

528 André-Charles Boulle

1642–1732

Wardrobe

Paris, *c.*1700
Ebony and amaranth veneer; polychrome wood, brass, tin, tortoiseshell and horn marquetry; gilt bronze
2.55 x 1.57 x 0.58 m
Baron Goguelat Collection
Transferred from the Mobilier National, 1870.
OA 5516

529 *Tapestry bearing the arms of France for the Grande Galerie of the Louvre*

Paris, Savonnerie manufactory, *c.*1670–1680
Wool. 5.10 x 8.95 m
Transferred from the Mobilier National, 1901.
OA 5432 bis B

During Louis XIII's reign, the royal manufactory of 'foot carpets' was set up at Chaillot in an old soap works, after which it was named. The Savonnerie manufactory underwent remarkable development under Louis XIV, who notably commissioned 93 pieces for the floor of the 500 metre-long Grande Galerie of the Louvre. Woven after compositions by Charles Le Brun, they illustrate royal glories and virtues. Never installed, they were used to decorate other royal residences and as diplomatic gifts.

The Louis XV style

The ordered opulence of Louis XIV's century was superseded several decades later by an art that was all lightness and curves, perfectly echoing the elegance and refinement of society under the Regency and in the early years of Louis XV's reign. Interiors, now more intimate and decorated with fine wood panelling and light-toned pictures, required objects and furniture which were also more adapted to this light atmosphere. Interior decoration, inspired by the art of the landscape gardeners, now indulged in fantasy and flowery decoration or turned to mythology. Ornamentalists such as Meissonier, Pineau and the Slodtz brothers triumphed, as did painters such as Boucher (*Eros and Psyche*, 540) and sculptors such as Cressent (*Wall clock: 'Love Conquering Time'*, 534). This new aesthetic reached its apotheosis in the mid-18th century in the rococo style.
Decorative objects were now being produced in abundance and the remarkable inventiveness of artists was stimulated notably by patronage, in which Madame de Pompadour, the king's mistress, was highly instrumental (*Pot-pourri 'vessel' belonging to Madame de Pompadour*, 538). New models were created, furniture diversified, cabinetmakers were now using lacquer and porcelain, silversmiths were inventing ever more refined combinations of materials and exporting their masterpieces all over Europe, particularly tables, snuffboxes [531], and caskets. In the middle of the century, high-fired faience, produced at Rouen and Moustiers, supplanted the low-fired earthenware perfected in Strasbourg and Marseilles, while porcelain triumphed thanks to the royal manufactory at Vincennes (*Naiad,* known as *'The Spring'*, 536), which was later moved to Sèvres.
The third quarter of the 18th century, however, saw the first stirrings of a strong counter-movement to the rococo style. A more classical aesthetic emerged, inspired both by Antiquity and the 'Louis XIV' spirit, which became known as the the 'Greek style'. Forms became rectilinear and more architectural, as shown by the furniture Leleu made for the Prince de Condé (*Commode*, 539).

530 *The Regent*

Diamond, 140.64 metric carats
Crown Diamond Collection. MV 1017

531 Daniel Govaers or Gouers

1717–before 1754

Snuffbox

Paris, 1725–1726
Enamelled gold, gold-inlayed tortoiseshell, miniatures, diamonds. 3 x 8.5 x 6.5 cm
Anonymous gift, 1978. OA 10670

532 Augustin Duflos, after Claude Rondé
Crown of Louis XV

Paris, 1722
Silver-gilt. H. 24; Ø 22 cm
Given to the treasury of the Abbey of Saint-Denis in 1729. MS 61

Louis XV's crown, the only surviving crown of a king of France, was part of the treasure the king donated to the Abbey of Saint-Denis after his coronation – having first replaced its original precious stones with copies. One of these gems was the *Regent* (530), a magnificent diamond found in India and acquired by Thomas Pitt, who had it cut in England, and from whom the Regent bought it in 1717 for the French Crown. It was subsequently used for the coronation of Charles X and on one of the Empress Eugénie's diadems.

533 Henri-Nicolas Cousinet
Died *c.*1768
Set made for Queen Maria Leczinska: chocolate pot, lamp and stand

Paris, 1729–1730
Silver-gilt, ebony. Chocolate pot: H. 19.4; stand: H. 12; lamp: H. 4.5 cm
Gift of the Société des Amis du Louvre with the aid of M. Stavros S. Niarchos, 1955.
OA 9598

Louis XV's wife, Maria Leczinska, was probably given this chocolate pot and stand inscribed with her arms on the birth of their first son, after bearing three daughters. The theme of the dolphin would corroborate this. The decorative motifs – flowers, reeds shells, cartouches – and also its dissymmetry are typical of the rococo style then beginning to manifest itself in official art. The talented silversmith who chased these motifs, Henri-Nicolas Cousinet, was subsequently appointed sculptor to the Prince de Condé.

535 François-Thomas Germain

1726–1791

Dish cover from a silver service belonging to Joseph I of Portugal

Paris, 1758
Cast and chased silver. 47.5 x 57.3 x 53.6 cm
Acquired in 1983. OA 10923

534 Charles Cressent

1685–1768

Wall clock: 'Love Conquering Time'

Paris, *c.*1740
Gilt bronze, brass and tortoiseshell marquetry
1.40 x 0.50 m. Crown Collection
Transferred from the Mobilier National, 1953.
OA 9586

The asymmetric composition of this wall clock perfectly illustrates the rococo style that bloomed in the mid-18th century. It is the work of the cabinetmaker Charles Cressent, who trained as a sculptor and created particularly elaborate furniture which he embellished with bronzes sculpted by himself. Love, dominating the composition, is overcoming Death, symbolised at the bottom of the clock by a figure holding a scythe.

536 *Naiad,* known as *'The Spring'*

Vincennes Royal Porcelain Manufactory, 1756
Soft-paste porcelain, gilt bronze. H. 26 cm
Mme Adolphe Thiers Bequest, 1880. TH 693

537 Jacques Dubois

*c.*1693–1763

Desk

Paris, mid-18th century
Oak, pine and fruit-wood frame, Chinese lacquer, black varnish, gilt bronze, leather.
0.81 x 1.87 x 1.02 m
Château du Raincy. Seized during the Revolution
Transferred from the Ministry of Justice, 1907. OA 6083

The originality of this piece of furniture bearing the stamp of Jacques Dubois, a cabinet-maker from the Faubourg Saint-Antoine district of Paris, consists in its use of lacquer panels taken from objects imported from the Far East, an idea which inspired the great Parisian *marchand merciers* (dealers in decorative arts) from the 1730s onwards. Before the Revolution, this desk was in the Château de Raincy, a property of the Duke of Orléans.

538 *Pot-pourri 'vessel' belonging to Madame de Pompadour*

Sèvres Royal Porcelain Manufactory, 1760
Soft-paste porcelain. 37 x 35 cm
Acquired in 1984. OA 10965

As was the fashion at the time, there is a chinoiserie scene on the side of this pink Sèvres porcelain pot-pourri vase, whose form is reminiscent of the sumptuous *nefs* (boat-shaped centrepieces) which decorated royal tables. This 'vessel' was bought by Madame de Pompadour in 1760, and was on the mantelpiece of her bedroom in her Parisian mansion, the present-day Elysée Palace, when she died four years later.

539 Jean-François Leleu

1729–1807

Commode belonging to the Prince of Condé

Paris, 1772
Oak, amaranth veneer, marquetry in various woods, gilt bronze, red breccia marble.
0.88 x 1.17 x 0.56 m
Acquired in 1953. OA 9589

The Palais Bourbon, purchased in 1764 by Louis-Joseph de Bourbon, Prince de Condé (1736–1818), underwent extensive refurbishment and the cabinetmaker Jean-François Leleu was commissioned to make numerous pieces of furniture for the newly-decorated palace. This piece's remarkable marquetry recalls that he had worked in the workshop of a great master of this technique, Jean-François Oeben, himself a former apprentice of a son of André-Charles Boulle. This commode's antique-inspired architectural structure and decoration are characteristic of the 'Greek' style which emerged in the 1760s.

540 After François Boucher

Eros and Psyche

Paris, Gobelins manufactory, *c.*1770
Tapestry, wool and silk, 10 to 11 warp thraeds per cm
4.25 x 3.80 m
Crown Collection, 1825
Transferred from the Mobilier National, 1901.
OA 5118

For fifteen years, the painter François Boucher was artistic director of the Gobelins royal manufactory, for which he produced a considerable number of cartoons, including the central drawing of four tapestries celebrating the 'Loves of the Gods'. The decorative elements surrounding them were designed by Maurice Jacques.

541 Georges Jacob

1739–1814

Chair for the 'Turkish Room' of the Count d'Artois, Palais du Temple, Paris

Paris, 1777
Gilt walnut. 94 x 70 x 76 cm
Baroness Gourgaud Bequest, 1965. OA 9987

For his Paris residence, the Palais du Temple, the Count of Artois, Louis XVI's brother and king himself after the Revolution, commissioned the architect Etienne-Louis Boullée to create a 'Turkish Room' in keeping with the fashion of the moment. The furniture was made by the cabinetmaker Georges Jacob, whose elegant and fanciful pieces prefigure the Empire style.

The Louis XVI style

The discovery of Pompeii and Herculaneum in the mid-18th century played a decisive role in determining the aesthetic tastes of the cultivated European elites and gave rise a few decades later to the vast movement that became known as Neoclassicism. Its beginnings manifested themselves as early as the 1760s in the decorative arts, with the appearance of an ornamental vocabulary directly inspired by Antiquity – fluting, straight lines, symmetrical garlands, bucranes and claws – and new forms of great sobriety. This new aesthetic attained heights of refinement in one art in particular: cabinetmaking.

The extraordinary boom in French luxury furniture production in the late 18th century was partially due to the importance of royal commissions and the personal role played in this by Marie-Antoinette. Artists vied with one another in the production of masterpieces for the queen and her court, sometimes enlivening their classically inspired works with pseudo-oriental or naively exotic motifs. The priceless *Writing table belonging to Queen Marie-Antoinette* (542) by Adam Weisweiler is a fine example of the elegance and technical mastery of furniture in the Louis XVI style, but other great names also excelled in this: Martin Carlin, in his virtuoso use of lacquer (*Commode belonging to Madame Victoire*, Louvre), Jean-Henri Riesener, Jean-Baptiste Séné and Georges Jacob, several of whose pieces are in the Louvre (*Chair for the 'Turkish Room' of the Count d'Artois*, 541).

The same quest for perfection drove other great artist to create sumptuous pieces of silverware (Robert-Joseph Auguste, *Service belonging to George III of England*, 543), bronzes and elegant porcelain, of which the Sèvres manufactory produced pieces of rare quality throughout the second half of the 18th century.

542 Adam Weisweiler

1744–1820

Writing table belonging to Queen Marie-Antoinette

Paris, 1784
Oak, ebony veneering, lacquer, mother-of-pearl, steel, gilt bronze. 82 x 47 x 44 cm
Collection of the French Crown
Transferred from the Mobilier National, 1901.
OA 5509

The role played by Marie-Antoinette in royal commissions proved crucial for the blooming of the decorative arts in the late 18th century. The cabinetmaker Adam Weisweiller produced this table, extremely daring in its use of steel and bronze for the sides and legs. The design of the cross-strut is characteristic of his style, as is the decoration of the drawers, veneered on the inside with a diamond mosaic. On the eve of the Revolution, this table was in the queen's inner study in the Château de Saint-Cloud.

543 Robert-Joseph Auguste

1723–1805

Service belonging to George III of England

Paris, 1776–1785
Cast and chased silver
Donation in payment of inheritance tax, 1976.
OA 10602-10624

544 François-Honoré-Georges Jacob-Desmalter

1770–1841

Empress Joséphine's jewel cabinet

Paris, 1809
Oak, tropical yew and amaranth veneering, Mother-of-pearl, gilt bronze. 2.75 x 2 x 0.60 m
On loan from the Musée National du Château de Fontainebleau, 1964. OA 10246

Despite the upheavals of the Revolution, the taste for antique aesthetics became more marked under the Empire in the workshops of master craftsmen who had served the Ancient Régime. Jacob-Desmalter, son of Georges Jacob, furthered the family tradition by creating furniture of great purity of form, such as this monumental jewel box decorated with a gilt bronze Birth of Venus in the middle. Made for Empress Joséphine, it stood in her bedroom in the Tuileries Palace.

The pomp of the Empire

Interrupted by the Revolution, the production of objets d'art made a spectacular recovery under Napoleon I, during whose reign it benefited from economic prosperity, but also from the encouragement of the emperor and his wish to create a court around him worthy of the pomp of the Ancien Régime. Workshops and artists who had previously worked for the kings now executed commissions for furniture, silverware and sundry precious objects for the imperial residences. The works they produced are remarkably aesthetically homogeneous, so much so that they gave rise to what is now known as the 'Empire style'.
The characteristics of this style are most manifest in furniture: simple, sometimes imposing forms, a taste for symmetry, the decorative vocabulary of Antiquity (*Madame Récamier's bed*, 546). The great master cabinetmaker of the time was Jacob-Desmalter, who supplied the imperial household with remarkable pieces (*Empress Joséphine's jewel cabinet*, 544) inlaid with mother-of-pearl and rare tropical woods, and decorated with bronzes by Pierre-Philippe Thomire, also one of the Emperor's suppliers.
The tableware crafts also greatly benefited from imperial commissions. Napoleon I had numerous silver and porcelain services made, and his personal silversmith, Martin-Guillaume Biennais, created sumptuous ensembles at his behest, such as the famous silver-gilt *Tea service* (545), fourteen of whose pieces are in the Louvre along with several other works by the artist. Porcelain production, particularly refined under the Empire, was largely concentrated at the Sèvres manufactory, which supplied the court with luxury tableware and also decorative pieces, notably monumental vases.

545 Martin-Guillaume Biennais

1764–1843

Tea service belonging to Napoleon I

Paris, 1809–1810
Silver-gilt. Tea urn: 80 x 45; teapot: 18 x 32; tea caddy: 14.5 x 15.5; milk jug: H. 27 cm.
Gift of the Société des Amis du Louvre, 1952. OA 9537

546 Jacob Frères, after Louis Berthault
Madame Récamier's bed

Paris, *c.* 1798
Mahogany, gilt and patinated bronze
1 x 1.33 x 1 m
Gift of the Société des Amis du Louvre, 1991.
OA 11344

The celebrated turn-of-the-century socialite Juliette Récamier was the young wife of a successful banker, who bought the former Necker mansion in Rue du Mont-Blanc. The architect Louis Berthault was entrusted with its refurbishment, and its greatly admired decoration, already prefiguring the empire style in 1798, marked a turning point in the history of the decorative arts. Mme Récamier's room, known from engravings, was furnished by the Jacob brothers and has been partially reconstructed in the Louvre.

Both the forms and decoration (by the architect Percier) of this tea service illustrate the enduring taste for the aesthetics of Antiquity under the Empire. The 'Etruscan'-style teapot, the tea caddy with a reproduction of a famous fresco from the Augustan period and the decorative elements – palmettes, water-leaf, winged figures – are straight out of the Greco-Roman repertoire. The style is highly representative of the prolific production of Biennais, silversmith to the Emperor.

547 Frédéric and Evrard Bapst
The Duchess of Angoulême's diadem

1819–1820
Gold, silver-gilt, 40 emeralds, 1031 diamonds
Formerly in the Crown Diamond Collection
Sold in 1887. Acquired in 2002. OA 11982

This diadem was made by the silversmiths Frédéric and Evrard Bapst for the Duchess of Angoulême, at the request of Louis XVIII. The complete parure consisted of bracelets, a necklace, earrings, a comb and this diadem, recently acquired by the Louvre. It was also worn by Empress Eugénie, wife of Napoleon III.

The Restoration – The July Monarchy

Napoleon's final defeat in 1815 enabled Louis XVIII to ascend the French throne for a reign of less than a decade. The court which formed around him was lacklustre and the king himself was content to live in the Emperor's rooms in the Tuileries Palace without making any changes to them. His brother Charles X, on the other hand, despite his even shorter reign, seems to have shown a certain interest in the decorative arts, as reflected in his porcelain collections and the spectacular giltwood bed in the Neoclassical style he commissioned Pierre-Gaston Brion (Louvre). Yet, despite the low level of royal patronage, the production of precious objets went on unabated under the Restoration, generally prolonging previous styles, with the exception of a few highly original works (*Dressing table*, 549).
Louis-Philippe, 'King of the French' after the July 1830 uprising, reigned over a society in which the values of the Ancien Régime rapidly faded. The change in mores was accompanied by a need for renewal among artists, who would now seek inspiration in the heydays of the Middle Ages and the Renaissance. The decorative arts participated enthusiastically in this rediscovery, borrowing themes, pictorial elements and sometimes forgotten techniques. The rise of the middle classes and the democratisation of taste opened up broad new areas of opportunity for craftsmen and industrialists. The most diverse trends emerged, illustrated by curious 'neo-styles', while in parallel there developed a taste for exoticism (*Chinese openwork breakfast service belonging to Queen Marie-Amélie*, 548). The eclecticism of this period is largely due to personalities such as Chenavard and the Grohé brothers, who created Renaissance-style furniture, the sculptors Liénard and Feuchère, and Froment-Meurice, an inventive silversmith who also drew inspiration from mythological ages to create objects of admirable finesse (*Grape harvest chalice*, 550).

548 *Chinese openwork breakfast service belonging to Queen Marie-Amélie*

Sèvres Royal Porcelain Manufactory, 1840
Hard-paste porcelain. H. 29.5; Ø 50 cm
Gift of M. and Mme Jean-Marie Rossi, 1987.
OA 11098-11111

The characteristic eclecticism of the second half of the 19th century first manifested itself under Louis-Philippe. Artists were now turning to very different sources for their inspiration: the Middle Ages, the Renaissance, the 18th century and the Far East. This breakfast service is a rather fanciful Western interpretation of Chinese models, from which have been borrowed the technique of adding an openwork layer to the outside of a piece. The first set was presented at the Exhibition of Products of the Royal Manufactories in 1835. Marie-Antoinette was so taken with it she ordered several sets from the Sèvres manufactory.

549 Marie-Jeanne-Rosalie Désarnaud-Charpentier and Nicolas-Henri Jacob

Dressing table

Paris, *c.*1819
Cristal, gilt glass, gilt bronze, H. 1,71 m
Gift of Claude Ott with the participation of Maurice Segoura, 1989
OA 11229-11230

This extraordinary dressing table in diamond point, fluted and gadrooned crystal on an iron frame was designed by Nicolas-Henri Jacob. It was commissioned by Mme Désarnaud-Charpentier, who ran a famous shop *A l'Escalier de crystal*. The table, supported by dolphin-headed rhytons, has a mirror fixed to candelabra with the figures of Flora and Zephyr. The table and chair were bought by the Duchess of Berry for her château at Rosny. They show the extraordinary progress made in crystal cutting under the Restoration, notably by the Saint-Louis, Baccarat and Le Creusot manufactories.

550 François-Désiré Froment-Meurice

1802–1855

Grape harvest chalice

Paris, *c.*1844
Agate, silver, enamelled and gilt silver, pearls
35 x 27 x 15 cm
Acquired in 1984. OA 11011

One of the major economic phenomena of the 19th century was the increase in international, so-called 'universal' expositions and of national exhibitions of industrial products. Although commercial ventures, they were opportunities for artists and craftsmen to create and present exceptional pieces, whose quality was sometimes rewarded by medals. During the 1844 exposition, particularly brilliant in the silverware field, Froment-Meurice received a gold medal for his *Grape harvest chalice*, a masterpiece of elegance and inventiveness inspired by late Gothic motifs.

The Napoleon III rooms

The uniting of the Louvre and Tuileries palaces, first envisaged in the 17th century, was not finally completed until the Second Empire (1856–1871). Napoleon III entrusted the building work successively to the architects Louis Visconti and Hector Lefuel. It was the latter who built the new wing along the rue de Rivoli, in which the emperor wanted to install the reception rooms of the Minister of State, whose residence was in the Tuileries Palace. After the violent events of the Paris Commune and the fall of the Second Empire, the new wing was allocated to the Finance Ministry. Subsequently ceded to the Louvre Museum, it was refurbished as an exhibition space in the 1990s.

The interior decoration, carried out under the close supervision of the minister Achille Fould and completed in 1861, illustrates the Second Empire taste for styles inspired by France's artistic past. The choice here was the Louis XIV style, in an exceptionally luxurious manner in certain rooms, notably in the Grand Salon, with its sumptuous panelling, gilding, sculptures, painted ceilings, decorative objects, chandeliers and carpets. Brilliant artists and craftsmen worked on these remarkable decors: Louis-Alphonse Tranchant (sculptures), Christofle and Barbedienne (bronzes and objects in precious metal) and Charles-Raphaël Maréchal (frescoes).

The rooms fortunately still have their original furniture, in perfect harmony with the decoration since they are also in the Louis XIV and Louis XV styles. The contents of each room are remarkably homogeneous: walnut furniture in the Large Antichamber, in darkwood in the Dining Room and in giltwood in the other rooms. The Small Dining Room, with its furniture inspired by Boulle's marquetries, painted decoration and gilding, is an exemplary illustration of the 'historicist' style of the period.

551 *The Grand Salon*

1856–1861
After Hector Lefuel
Sculptures: Louis-Alphonse Tranchant
Painted decor: Laurent-Jan Lausanne

This drawing room, the largest and most sumptuous of the reception rooms, could be converted into a theatre seating over 250 people, with the adjoining drawing room serving as stage. Above the abundant sculpted decoration, the paintings in the ceiling arches, by Marechal fils, depict the successive stages of the construction of the Louvre and the Tuileries under Francis I, Catherine de Médicis, Henry IV and Louis XIV. The apotheosis of this building project appears on the ceiling itself, with an allegorical representation of the uniting of the two palaces by Napoleon III and Eugénie, while the banderoles depict the emperor's great military, economic and social deeds.

Graphic Arts

The Department of Graphic Arts, although exceptionally rich and comprising some 130,000 pieces, is the least known to visitors to the Louvre. This paradoxical situation can be explained by the very nature of the works themselves – drawings, pastels, miniatures, engravings, books, manuscripts – whose fragility prevents them from being permanently on show. They can, however, be seen during regularly organised temporary exhibitions. A host of publications, the computerisation of the collections and the viewing rooms have also enabled a fuller knowledge of these works.

As is the case of the Department of Paintings, the former Royal Collection constitutes the Department of Graphic Arts' historic core, and more specifically, the Cabinet des Dessins, founded in 1671 by Louis XIV. A patron and protector of the arts, he also created an engravings collection, originally consisting of the 'King's Cabinet of Engraved Plates' and the 'Collection of the Royal Academy of Painting and Sculpture', and which after the Revolution became the National Engravings Collection.

The vagaries of history, acquisitions, donations and the very evolution of art naturally modified the structure of these institutions. Today, the Department of Graphic Arts comprises several collections. The first is the Cabinet des Dessins proper, which is particularly rich in French drawings from the 15th to the 19th century, but which also has very fine examples of the Italian, German and Dutch Schools (Leonardo de Vinci, Raphael, Michelangelo, Dürer, Holbein, Rembrandt). In 1977, responsibility for the drawings of the second half of the 19th century (artists born after 1820, with the exception of Courbet, Daumier and Millet) was transferred to the Musée d'Orsay; however, the Louvre department continues to ensure their classification and conservation, in collaboration with the Musée d'Orsay.

The department's second collection, the Engravings, presently has over 13,000 copper plates dating from the 16th century to the present day, prints of which are marketed by the Réunion des Musées Nationaux.

Finally, the Edmond de Rothschild Collection was donated to the Louvre in 1935 and installed close to the Cabinet des Dessins in accordance with the wishes of Baron Edmond de Rothschild. The strong points of the collection this generous donor amassed are incunabula, German engravings, the work of Rembrandt and 18th-century French engravings. It comprises over 40,000 prints and engravings, some 3,000 drawings and 500 illustrated books.

The Cabinet des dessins

When Louis XIV acquired the collection of over 5,500 drawings amassed by the German banker Eberhard Jabach in 1671, he created the core of what would become the Louvre's Cabinet des Dessins. A few years later, this was complemented by the appropriation of the drawings in the studio of Charles Le Brun, First Painter to the King, after his death in 1690 (*Three Men's Heads in Relation to a Tawny Owl*, 553), then by those of Pierre Mignard in 1695 and Antoine Coypel in 1722. In the 18th century, one of the major acquisitions was made at the auction of the famous collection of Pierre-Jean Mariette in 1775. When the Cabinet des Dessins became 'property of the Nation' after the Revolution, it contained some 11,000 pieces, a number very soon doubled by seizures of collections belonging to the émigrés, in particular those of the Counts of Orsay and Saint-Morys. The Revolutionary period also coincided with a considerable enrichment of the Italian School, with the collection of the Dukes of Modena, brought back from Italy, and volumes from the studio of Carlo Maratta, found in the Netherlands. Almost 1,200 drawings entered the Louvre in 1806 when Dominique-Vivant Denon acquired albums compiled by the Florentine art collector Filippo Baldinucci. The Cabinet de Dessins experienced another extraordinary period in the second half of the 19th century thanks to its curator Frédéric Reiset. Apart from major acquisitions such as the Codex Vallardi (Pisanello, *Bearded Tit*, 554) in 1856, he attracted donations such as those of Sauvageot (Jean Fouquet, *Saint Margaret*, 552), His de la Salle and the sculptor Gatteaux. There were also exceptional donations in the 20th century, including those of the painter Léon Bonnat, Etienne Moreau-Nélaton, who bequeathed several thousand works (Delacroix, *A Courtyard in Tangiers*, 557), Claude-Roger Marx and many others. These gifts enriched the collection with remarkable ensembles by 19th-century artists and rare miniatures (Doistau and David-Weill Donations), while in parallel an active acquisition policy was being pursued (Chardin, *Self-Portrait at the Easel*, 556). Today, in addition to its acquisitions, the Cabinet des Dessins continues to benefit from the generosity of collectors (Louis-Antoine and Véronique Prat) and the support of the Société des Amis du Louvre.

552 Jean Fouquet

*c.*1420–1477/1481

Saint Margaret Tending the Sheep

Miniature on parchment
*c.*1452–1460
9.1 x 11.7 cm
Sauvageot Donation, 1856. MI 1093

According to Jacques de Voragine's *Golden Legend*, Margaret, born at Antioch, converted to Christianity when she was still only a young shepherdess. Having resisted the advances of the Roman governor Olybrius, she was thrown into prison and devoured by a dragon. But thanks to the small cross she had kept, she pierced the monster's belly and escaped miraculously unharmed. Saint Margaret, very popular during the Middle Ages, was particularly venerated by pregnant women hoping to ward off birth pain. Marguerite is in fact portrayed pregnant herself in this delicate miniature with skilfully modulated tints, in which Olybrius appears in the background. This priceless page was part of Jean Fouquet's famous *Hours of Etienne Chevalier*, dispersed in the 18th century, of which the Cabinet des Dessins has another miniature, *The Charity of Saint Martin*.

553 Charles Le Brun

1619–1690

Three Men's Heads in Relation to a Tawny Owl

*c.*1698
Graphite, pen and black ink, grey wash, gouache, squared with graphite
23 x 32 cm
INV. 28113

The expression of human passions, considered a fundamental element of artistic language, was a constant preoccupation of painters in the 17th century. In 1668, Charles Le Brun gave two lectures on facial expressions at the Académie Royale de Peinture et de Sculpture, and a third three years later on the physiognomy of man and its relationship to that of animals. Although his texts have disappeared, his drawings and his studio in the Louvre became the property of Louis XIV after his death and are therefore today in the Cabinet des Dessins. In 1806, some of the works were engraved for the Engravings Collection of the 'Musée Napoléon' at the request of its director, Dominique-Vivant Denon.

554 Antonio Puccio, known as Pisanello

*c.*1395–1455

Male Bearded Tit Depicted in Flight and Perching

Velum, watercolour, white heightening, pen and brown ink
11.7 x 15.5 cm
Formerly in the Vallardi Collection.
Acquired in 1856
INV. 2476

The painter Pisanello, highly sought after at Italian courts from Milan to Naples, was a tireless draughtsman. Throughout his career he produced numerous compositional studies and studies from nature (nudes, portraits, animals, costumes) but also independent works in which he gave free rein to his extraordinary virtuosity. The Department of Graphic Arts has an exceptional number of drawings amassed by the collector Giuseppe Vallardi, from whom they were acquired in 1856.

555 Antonio Allegri, known as Correggio

1489?–1534

Allegory of the Vices

*c.*1528–1530
Tempera on canvas
1.42 x 0.85 m
Collection of Louis XIV. INV. 5927

This work's matching piece, *Allegory of the Virtues*, is also in the Louvre. Both were executed for Isabella d'Este's *studiolo* in the ducal palace at Mantua. The subject has given rise to many interpretations. It has been seen as a mythological scene depicting Apollo and Marsyas, and as a representation of Silenus, spirit of Vice and Drunkenness, tormented by Maenads and Erinyes. Correggio was at the height of his powers when he painted these two enigmatic allegories. In order to match the technique of his two compositions to those of the pictures already in place (Mantegna, Costa, Perugino), he used tempera, but there is nothing archaic about his style, as his mastery of anatomy, the mobility of the poses and his use of light colours so eloquently demonstrates.

556 Jean-Siméon Chardin

1699–1779

Self-Portrait at the Easel

1779?
Pastel on blue paper mounted on canvas
40.7 x 32.5 cm
Acquired in 1967. RF 31748

Chardin did three pastel self-portraits during the last ten years of his life, and this one seems to have been the last. He shows himself with his head wrapped in white linen held in place by a ribbon, dressed in a grey jacket and scarf, and slightly drawn and unsmiling. And unlike his previous self-portraits, he has included the instruments of his trade, his hand, a piece of red pastel and the edge of the easel, leaving his face in shadow. Could this have been the image of himself he wanted to leave to posterity, that of an artist at work?

557 Eugène Delacroix

1798–1863

A Courtyard in Tangiers

1832
20.7 x 29.4 cm
Watercolour and graphite
Moreau-Nélaton Donation, 1907
RF 3375

When the Count of Mornay was charged by Louis-Philippe with a diplomatic mission to Morocco, Eugène Delacroix went with him. The Orient, until then an imaginary world for the painter, had already inspired two of his masterpieces, *The Massacre at Chios* [287] and *The Death of Sardanapalus* [290]. 'I am at present like a man who is dreaming and who sees things he fears will escape him,' the painter wrote to a friend on his arrival in Tangiers in January 1832. And precisely in order not to forget them, he filled his sketchbooks with written and drawn notes on costumes, landscapes and architecture. The seven albums of sketches he brought back from Morocco – three of which are in the Louvre – would be a constant mine of inspiration for him until the end of his career. Several years later, Delacroix used this sun-drenched view of the interior of a house in Tangiers as the basis for his famous painting *Jewish Marriage in Morocco* (Louvre).

Engravings

The Louvre's Engravings Collection was founded in 1797, during the Revolution, with the aim of supporting this art and exploiting the collections of engravings amassed under the Ancien Régime, which largely consisted of the Cabinet of Engraved Plates of the King and the Collection of the Royal Academy of Painting and Sculpture. It was on Louis XIV's initiative and with the same aim of supporting the art of engraving that these collections had originally been created. In 1660, the Sun King created the workshop of the 'King's ordinary engravers' at the Gobelins manufactory, whose initial task was to create reproducible images of the royal treasures and thereby exalt the glory of the monarch. Leading artists, including Mellan, Rousselet, Audran, Silvestre, Leckkerc and Bosse, were enlisted to produce engravings of the royal residences and the paintings and sculptures they contained (Claude Mellan, *Agrippina,* 558), to which was added the representation of plants and animals and all things 'rare and singular', and the great events of the reign. Over 1,300 plates were engraved for the *Cabinet du Roy* and compiled in volumes or later sold separately. The other major collection consisted of the 'admission pieces' of engravers admitted to the Academy from 1672, each candidate being required to reproduce a picture by one of the Academy's members. The commercial exploitation of this collection enabled its enrichment through purchases and commissions.

This policy of enrichment and commercial exploitation, pursued by the National Engravings Collection, continued throughout the 19th and 20th centuries. Today, the collections are still being complemented with acquisitions of ancient and modern engravings and, since 1990, by commissions that have involved the Louvre's Engraving's Department in contemporary creation (Pierre Alechinsky, *The Wandering Brush*, 559).

558 Claude Mellan

1598–1688

Agrippina, also known as *Mnemosyne*

1677

Burin.

40.8 x 29 cm

INV. 1314

This engraving, commissioned by Louis XIV, was published in the first volume of *Pictures in the King's Cabinet. Antique Statues and Busts in the Royal Houses*, published by the Royal Printing Works in 1677. Its model was a sculpture that today stands on the terrace of the Palace of Compiègne. Mellan was no beginner: in 1630, during a stay in Italy where he studied under Francesco Villamena and Simon Vouet, he had worked on the *Galleria Giustiniana*, an album of engravings reproducing Marquis Giustiniani's collection of statues, the first illustrated catalogue of its kind. Although still young, the artist was already known for his exceptional virtuosity with the burin. He considered a single line was enough and rejected hatching, creating shadow using parallel lines and obtaining tonal variations by modulating their thickness. His famous *Holy Face*, an early work, is a prodigious illustration of this technique, the engraving being composed of a single, continuous spiral, beginning at the centre of the image, on the end of Christ's nose.

559 Pierre Alechinsky

Brussels, 1927

The Wandering Brush

1998
Etching and aquatint on copper. 55 x 68 cm
On BFK Rives velum 63 x 92 cm
INV. 11134

In the tradition of the French conservatory, the Engravings Collection commissioned a number of contemporary artists who already had an engraving to their name to produce an original work. Pierre Alechinsky was perhaps evoking here his trip to Japan in 1955. But the historiated frame echoes and superbly articulates the circles, folds and volutes which seem to escape from his brush and spread their arabesques around the edges of the motif.

560 Hans Baldung Grien

1484/1485–1545

The Witches

1510
Monochrome print, two blocks (grey and black)
37.8 x 25.8 cm
Edmond de Rothschild Collection,
bequeathed in 1935
INV. 784 LR

This monochrome print was produced using two separately engraved wooden blocks. Baldung Grien used this technique, particularly popular with German and Dutch artists in the 16th century, to strikingly depict a nocturnal witches' sabbath. Witches, women and death are the themes which this pupil of Dürer greatly explored between 1509 and 1512 while he was living in Strasbourg, where he became a burgher and then a master in 1510. Despite his young age, the artist is already revealing his powerful temperament and remarkable sense of composition. The composition here is almost geometric, based on a pyramidal group and diagonals that appear to radiate from the central cauldron.

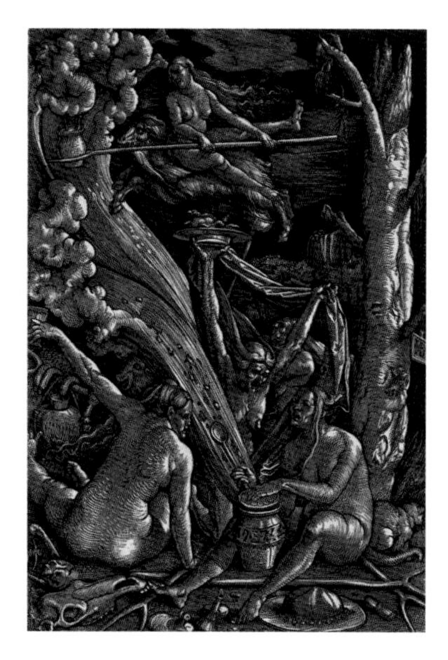

The Edmond de Rothschild Collection

Baron Edmond de Rothschild (1845–1934), son of James de Rothschild, founder of the famous family's French line, first showed his generosity to the Louvre by offering the museum the results of the excavations carried out by the archaeologist Rayet at Miletos and Didyma (*Male Torso*, 145), then again in 1895 with another spectacular donation, the famous 'treasure' found at Boscoreale near Naples [187]. Yet his name has become synonymous with an entirely different domain, that of drawings and prints. He spent his life amassing a collection unique both in its quality and quantity. According to his wishes, this collection of over 40,000 engravings, around 3,000 drawings and some 500 illustrated books, including several incunabula, was bequeathed to the Louvre after his death by his children.
Edmond de Rothschild was himself an extremely scholarly man, advised by the leading specialists in engraving such as Danlos and his friend Doctor Roth. He was particularly interested in German art, acquiring the entire engraved work of Dürer without neglecting 15th-century masters lesser known at the time such as Martin Schongauer, Hans Baldung Grien [560] and Israel van Meckenem. Other strong points of his collection are 18th-century French engraving and, above all, the drawings and etchings of Rembrandt, for whom he had the profoundest admiration.
The Rothschild Bequest's entry into the Louvre in 1937 provided the museum with an exceptional collection of the Dutch master's work: over 200 etchings but also the rarest ensemble of Rembrandt etching proofs in any museum. These include famous landscapes such as *The Three Trees* (1643), portraits and self-portraits, genre scenes and religious subjects such as *Christ Healing the Sick*, known as *The Hundred Florin Piece* (1642-49) [561], and the famous *Three Crosses* (1653).

561 Rembrandt Harmensz. van Rijn

1606–1669

Christ Healing the Sick,
or *The Hundred Florin Piece*

c. 1642–1649
Drypoint and burin; first state
27.8 x 38.8 cm
Edmond de Rothschild Collection,
bequeathed in 1935
INV. 2382 LR

A master of chiaroscuro in his painting, Rembrandt captured effects of light and shade with the same subtlety in his engravings, frequently using several different techniques in a single work. This is the case here in this religious scene, engraved with both drypoint and burin, the former for its light touch, the latter for its incomparable velvety effect, notably in the darkest areas. It was given its traditional title, *The Hundred Florin Piece,* because of the high price that his works commanded even in the 17th century, and not for its subject matter. The engraving mixes several scenes from the Gospel according to Saint Matthew concerning Christ's healing of the sick: the episode of the rich young man torn between his worldly preoccupations and his conscience, and on the left, the councils of the Pharisees. There are also allusions to other biblical passages. This iconographic richness can be explained by the ten-year meditation which seems to have preceded this engraving, which is of exceptionally broad scope for Rembrandt.

Arts of Africa, Asia, Oceania and the Americas

'The Louvre should take in certain exotic masterpieces whose appearance is no less moving than that of the fine specimens of Western art,' Guillaume Apollinaire declared in the 13 October 1909 edition of *Le Journal du Soir*. But it would take almost a century for his wish to be fulfilled. On 13 April 2000, some 120 works from Africa, Asia, Oceania and the Americas were installed in the Pavillon des Sessions, idealised by Jean-Michel Wilmotte's elegant and spare museography. The brain-child of Jacques Kerchache (a leading specialist in non-Western cultures) and endorsed by the President of the Republic, Jacques Chirac (a fervent admirer of these 'distant' arts), this rehabilitation was something of a consecration. The project's detractors had indeed been legion. Indeed, not so long ago these arts were still considered 'primitive', 'tribal', or simply 'negro'. The crusade for the recognition of these peoples and the masterpieces they created is completely symbolised by these light-flooded riverside rooms. Majestic on their metal bases, the sculptures selected by Jacques Kerchache's infallible eye deliver their aesthetic message in a straightforward, relaxed manner.

There is no hierarchy between the works, and even less attempt to seduce. Wilmotte's presentation heightens the transparency around the masks and sculptures, rejects all dramatisation (as in those exhibitions that plunge visitors into half-darkness to make them tremble in front of fetishes and 'gris-gris') and excludes any kind of exotic reconstruction (no field photographs on the walls, no casts). The exhibition itinerary is logical, both historically and geographically, beginning with Africa, going on through Asia then, via Easter Island, to South America and finally the Arctic. Although composed of the finest pieces in France's public collections (Musée de l'Homme, Musée National des Arts d'Afrique et d'Océanie and regional museums such as those at Boulogne-sur-Mer and Rochefort), this anthology certainly does not claim to be exhaustive. In both its aesthetic and scientific intentions, it brilliantly heralds the opening of the Musée du Quai Branly in 2006. And, in the words of Jacques Kerchache, 'What remains of these cultures except the traces their artists left?'

562 *Ife civilisation: head*

12th–14th century
Nigeria
Terracotta
H. 15.5 cm
Formerly in the Barbier-Mueller Collection
Musée National des Arts d'Afrique et d'Océanie
INV. A. 96.1.4.

According to the German ethnologist Leo Frobenius, who explored the site in 1910, the extreme realism of the terracottas and bronzes of ancient Ife (southwest of present-day Nigeria) was the mark of a colony of Mediterranean origin that had founded a line in the interior of the Yoruba kingdom. As if the sheer perfection of these sovereign heads could have been due to anything but the African genius... We now know that this city-state, governed from the 11th to the 14th century by a king or *oni*, produced a court art of rare sophistication, as attested by this slightly smaller than life-size head, no doubt a portrayal of a servant, with wavy hair, outlined lips and cheeks striated with scarifications or ritual paintings.

563 *Sapi people: side-blown horn*

15th–16th century
Sierra Leone
Ivory
L. 79 cm
Formerly in the Bibliothèque Nationale,
Cabinet des Médailles, Paris
On loan from the Museum National d'Histoire
Naturelle-Musée de l'Homme since 1933
INV. D. 33.6.4

In François Rabelais' time, many a 'cabinet of curiosities' was crammed with 'exotic' objects such as savages' garments, animal skins, ivory tusks, idols and so on. The appeal of these collections of ill-assorted oddities soon gave rise to a thriving market in Africa itself and European courts rapidly became inundated with hybrid pieces – saltcellars, sculpted horns, spoons, forks and sundry bowls, ordered directly from African ivory sculptors – which, as well as being 'commissioned works', were the first testaments to a meeting of two worlds. Covered with crocodiles and snakes, this magnificent 'object-sculpture' was most probably created for an African sovereign before its arrival at the court of a European king, possibly Louis XIV himself.

564 *Dogon plateau: mother and child*

14th century
'Master of the Red Mother and Child'
Mali
Wood, pigments
H. 75 cm
Acquired by Maurice Nicaud in 1954
Formerly in the Maurice Nicaud and
Hubert Goldet Collections
Musée du Quai Branly (donated 1999)
INV. 70.1999.9.3

One of the themes dearest to African sculptors is the mother and child, which they depict in a near-obsessive and sacred manner. This hieratic sculpture coated with a beautiful red patina was discovered in the northwest of the Dogon plateau, in the remote Tintam region. Despite its lithe, rounded forms, it exudes a definite impression of severity, even stiffness. We feel no tenderness between this mother and child, not the slightest love in the Western sense of the word. Yet this allegory of fecundity and fertility, an incarnation of the clan's lineage, is nonetheless the work of a very great artist.

565 *Luba people: headrest*

19th century
'Master of the Cascading Hairstyles'
(Kinkondja workshop)
Democratic Republic of Congo
Wood
H. 18.5 cm
Formerly in the Baron Henri Lambert and Hubert Goldet Collections
Musée du Quai Branly (donated 1999)
INV. 70.1999.9.1.

The everyday objects – headrests, seats, spoons, jewellery, musical instruments – fashioned by the expert hands of African sculptors reveal a rarely equalled sense of beauty. Akin to ceremonial signs, they also act as mediators between the worlds of the living and of spirits, accompanying and emphasising life's every stage: birth, puberty, marriage, childbirth, death. The rigorous geometry and sophisticated hairstyles of this headrest's two caryatids make it a genuine masterpiece.

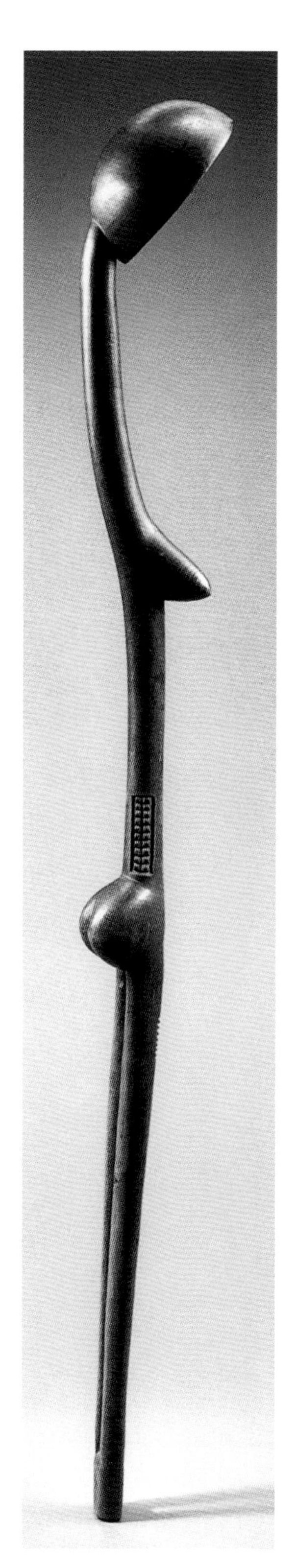

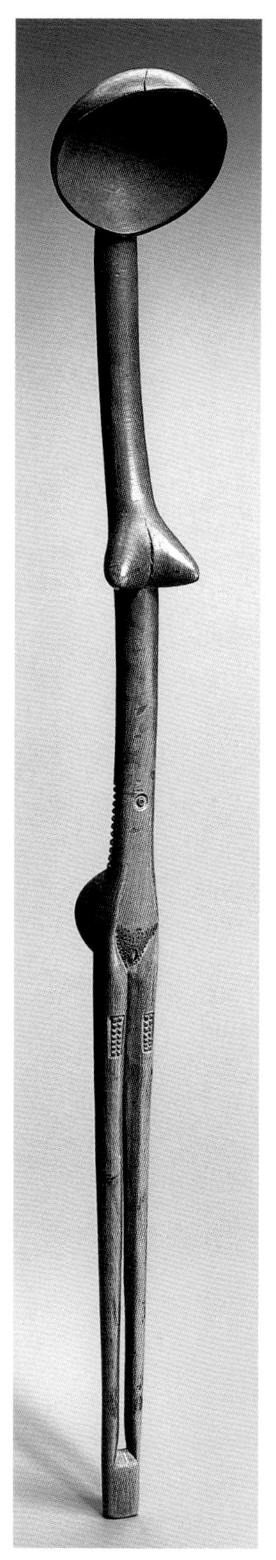

566 *Zulu spoon*

19th–early 20th century
Kwazulu-Natal, South Africa
Wood
H. 57 cm
Edouard Saint-Paul Bequest, 1977
On loan from the Museum National d'Histoire naturelle-musée de l'Homme
INV. M.H. 977.52.14

It was not until several decades after it entered the Musée de l'Homme, registered as a work of Oceanic origin, that this refined sculpture was recognised as being African. The object's workmanship is definitely Zulu, but there is still doubt as to its actual use. Is this sublimely perfect 'woman-spoon' indeed a spoon, a highly personal possession in the African world, or could it be one of the sticks brandished by warriors during their virile dances?

567 *Toba Batak sculpture*

Mid-15th century
North Sumatra, Indonesia
Wood, soot patina
H. 1.28 m
Formerly in the Count Baudouin de Grunne Collection
Musée du Quai Branly
INV. 70.1998.9.1

The Batak people, who inhabit most of Sumatra's mountainous northern province, comprises six ethnic groups speaking Austronesian dialects. Even after they were Christianised, the Batak continued to obey the *adat* code, a veritable 'law of the sky' regulating life's intense moments. Several magical practices have also endured, ranging from the simple philtre to wizardry, and from the making of amulets to the creation of sculptures with prophylactic properties. With its hands joined in offering and bent knees, this enigmatic statue seems to be beseeching a divinity to ward off a danger. The absence of a cavity for a magic substance tends to prove that a 'medicine' was probably placed alongside it to increase its redoubtable potency.

568 *Nias Island, Indonesia: ancestor statue*

19th century
Indonesia
Wood, crusty red patina
H. 55.7 cm
Formerly in the collections of André Breton, Helena Rubinstein and Alain Schoffel
Gift of Alain Schoffel, 1999
Musée du Quai Branly
INV. 70.1999.3.1

Unlike the highly Indianised kingdoms of Bali and Java, the traditional cultures of Southeast Asia (also called Insulindia) developed a tribal art of prodigious inventiveness. Permanent features of these warrior societies were the practice of head hunting, the use of communal longhouses or 'chief's houses' and above all ancestor and spirit worship. Famous for several reasons (it once belonged to André Breton and was photographed by Man Ray), this sculpture from the north of Nias Island is probably a depiction of an *adu siraha salawa*, a village chief, recognisable by his high, fern-decorated hairstyle, cabled necklace and long pendant hanging from the left ear.

Oceania

569 *Malo Island: tall male figure*

Early 19th century
Village de Sakavas, Vanuatu
Wood (Instia bijuga)
H. 3 m
Sent back to France by the Korrigane Expedition in early 1935
On loan from the Museum National d'Histoire Naturelle-Musée de l'Homme
(Desgranges Donation)
INV. M.H. 38.42.8

How could one possibly truss up the art of these myriad islands, these microcosms scattered all over the Pacific, in definitions? Unlike the African artist, the Oceanian artist is willfully rebellious, unpredictable and disconcerting. He eludes all rules, all models, transcends all artistic practices and constantly invents new ones, and above all opens wide, beautiful doors onto the world of dreams, the irrational and ecstasy. Covered with an extraordinary blue patina (a coloured coating obtained by mixing lime, burnt coral and dolly blue), this hieratic sculpture with scarified sides captivates us by its mysterious formal presence. Hence its nickname in one of the languages of Malo Island: 'He who stands before you and looks at you.'

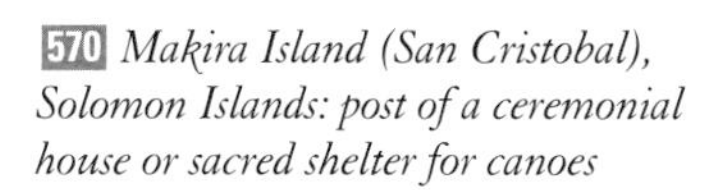

570 *Makira Island (San Cristobal), Solomon Islands: post of a ceremonial house or sacred shelter for canoes*

17th century
Former village of Nagura
Wood
H 2.11 m
Collected by Pierre Langlois *c.* 1960
Formerly in the Musée Barbier-Mueller Collection
Gift of Monique and Jean-Paul Barbier-Mueller, 1999
Musée du Quai Branly
INV. 70.1999.5.3

The inhabitants of the Solomon Islands customarily erected vast ceremonial houses intended as shelters for canoes and also for chests containing the bones of their most important ancestors. This vigorously sculpted post, from one of these sumptuous residences, forcefully depicts the copulation of two figures of unclear identity and function. We have no way of telling whether this a particularly venerated couple of village ancestors or, on the contrary, a contemporary couple with considerable aura within the community.

571 *New Ireland, Papua New Guinea: Uli figure*

18th–early 19th century
North central New Ireland
Hardwood, red ochre, charcoal, limestone, rootlets, resin, turban shell (*Turbo petholatus*) opercula
H. 1.50 m
Collected in New Ireland by Franz Boluminski; bought in 1908 by the Museum für Völkerkunde, Leipzig; formerly in the A. Schoffel Collection
Musée du Quai Branly
INV. 70.1999.2.1

There is something triumphantly virile about this *uli* figure, with its bearded head, face contorted in a rictus, stocky female torso and short legs. The vivid polychromy emphasises the brutal vigour of its hermaphrodite anatomy. Used during ceremonies honouring the dead, this effigy is one of the most striking formal creations of Oceanic art.

572 *Hawaii: figure of a god*

18th century
Wickerwork, thin liana, cord, feathers, mother-of-pearl, dog's teeth, wood
H. 67 cm
Collected before 1796; transferred from the Museum d'Histoire Naturelle to the Musée des Antiques in 1797
Gift of the Bibliothèque Nationale to the Musée d'Ethnographie du Trocadéro, 1878
On permanent loan from the Museum National d'Histoire Naturelle-Musée de l'Homme
INV. M.H. 78.30.15

Oceanic art pulls out all the stops: mannerist and stylistically affected, or morbid and disconcerting... It resorts to every means at its disposal, or rather every material: everything from palm leaves to human hair, every kind of seed, fruit, coloured soil, and of course the skins of certain mammals and shimmering birds' feathers, seashells, tusks, sculls and sundry teeth, even the immaterial and fragile spider's web. And this frightening Hawaiian war god, at once grotesque and macabre, is no exception.

From the Americas to the Arctic

573 *Chupicuaro sculpture*

600–100 BC
Mexico
Glazed terracotta
H. 31 cm
Formerly in the Guy Joussemet Collection
Musée du Quai Branly
INV. 70.1998.3.1

What, at first sight, do the mosaics of cultures and peoples grouped together by ethnologists under the convenient appellation of the Americas, have in common? On the one hand, sedentary states with the same calendar, writing, sacrifices, offerings and polytheism: the Mayas and Aztecs of Middle or Central America, the Tainos of the Caribbean islands and the Incas of Peru; on the other hand, the nomadic, 'empireless' and 'historyless' peoples spread out over vast territories: the Indians of the forests and plains, the Haidas of the northwest coast, the Inuit of the Gulf of Alaska. Yet one practice common to all these cultures has manifested itself down the ages, that of an art entirely devoted to the sacred. This female figure with generous forms from Chupicuaro in western Mexico, placed in graves to celebrate the perpetual cycle of seasons, is a dazzling example.

574 *Mask from Teotihuacán*

Classical period, AD 200–600
Mexico
Stone
H. 20 cm
Formerly in the collections of Diego Rivera and André Breton
Musée du Quai Branly
INV. 70.1999.12.1

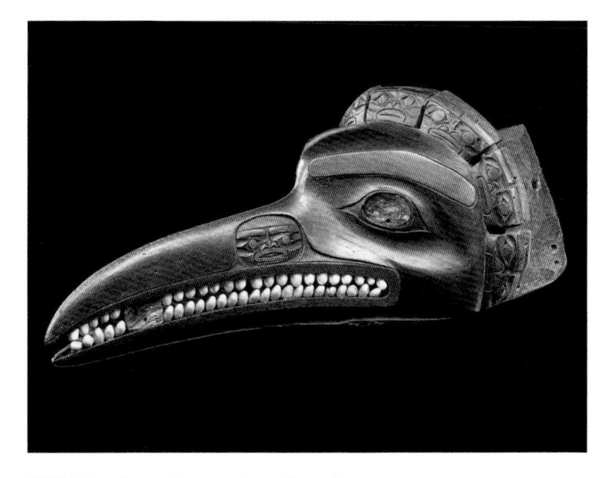

575 *Nisga'a sculpture: frontal mask*

19th century
British Columbia, Canada
Wood, graphite, paint, abalone fragments, shellfish opercula
H. 16 cm; W. 38 cm
Collected by George T. Emmons in the Lower Nass region; formerly in the Museum of the American Indian, Heye Foundation, New York; acquired by exchange by Julius Carlebach in July 1944; bought by Claude Lévi-Strauss the same year; formerly in the collection of Claude Lévi-Strauss
Donated anonymously through the intermediary of Mme Georgette Soustelle, 1951
On loan from the Museum National d'Histoire Naturelle-Musée de l'Homme
INV. M.H. 51.35.3

From the 1880s to the late 1920s, the American navy lieutenant George Thornton Emmons collected a considerable number of pieces from the northwest coast for the American Museum of Natural History and the Smithsonian Institution in Washington, and subsequently for the Museum of the American Indian. Part of this extraordinary harvest was this mask from British Columbia, whose expressiveness is equalled only by its technical virtuosity. With its dragonfly eyes inlaid with mother-of-pearl, two rows of seashell operculum teeth, and engraved decoration of human heads, one can imagine it suddenly appearing during a shamanic ceremony.

576 *Yup'ik (Inuit) sculpture: fish mask*

Early 20th century
Goodnews Bay district, south coast of Kuskokwim Bay, Alaska
Polychrome wood, feathers
H. 48 cm
Collected by Adams Hollis Twitchell in the early 1920s
Museum of the American Indian, Heye Foundation, New York
Formerly in the collection of André Breton
Musée du Quai Branly
INV. 70.1999.1.2

It was thanks to their exile in New York during the Second World War that the Surrealists discovered with wonder the collections of Museum of the American Indian, created some thirty years earlier, in 1916. When the museum, in financial difficulty, was obliged to sell some of its major pieces, André Breton's friends did not have to be persuaded to buy some of the most beautiful masks from the Arctic and the northwest coast known today. Half-man half-fish, this mask could but seduce us by its 'convulsive beauty' and mute ambivalence.

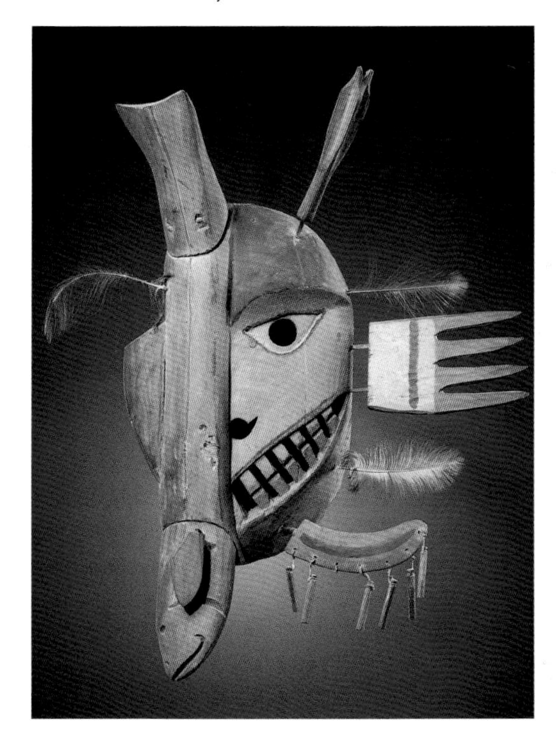

Index

Photographic credits

Numbers refer to figure numbers.

Paris, Hugues Charreyron: 49, 57, 125.
Paris, Louvre Museum: 197 (base); Louvre / Ali-Meyer: 48; Louvre / Revault: 31; Louvre/Claire Tabbagh: 204.
Paris, Quai Branly Museum / photo Hughes Dubois: 562-576
Paris, Réunion des musées nationaux: 7, 25, 37, 47, 54, 56, 66, 146, 147, 167, 192, 197 (candle ring), 200, 237, 240, 241, 242, 320, 330, 345, 347, 370, 377, 407, 490, 509, 513, 514, 516, 517, 529, 530, 531, 550, 552, 553. Transfer MET NY: 38. Daniel Arnaudet: 220, 224, 259, 260, 262, 265, 280, 284, 300, 350, 361, 380, 392, 482, 483, 489, 491, 494, 495, 496, 498, 499, 500, 503, 508, 510, 512, 515, 518, 520, 523, 524, 526, 534, 536, 537, 538, 539, 540, 541, 542, 544, 546, 548. D. Arnaudet / J. Schormans: 19. Martine Beck-Coppola: 419, 429, 437, 466, 486, 501, 502, 525, 527, 532, 533, 551. Michèle Bellot: 557, 559. J.-G. Berizzi: 107, 211, 213, 229, 246, 253, 283, 309, 311, 312, 313, 322, 324, 337, 340, 368, 385, 389, 399, 477, 504, 545, 547, 554, 556. P. Bernard: 21, 236. Gérard Blot: 28, 30, 117, 214, 218, 228, 232, 251, 267, 269, 272, 275, 277, 278, 298, 299, 317, 343, 353, 355, 360, 373, 374, 375, 393, 397, 400, 402, 447, 449, 561. G. Blot / Coursaget: 405. G. Blot / C. Jean: 245, 249, 378, 414, 431, 433, 461, 463, 480 and page 6, 8. G. Blot / J. Schormans: 234. Les Frères Chuzeville: 8, 17, 20, 26, 27, 29, 34, 45, 46, 50, 55, 60, 65, 67, 69, 71, 72, 73, 74, 76, 77, 80, 81, 84, 90, 92, 94, 95, 97, 102, 105, 106, 112, 115, 119, 123, 124, 144, 149, 156, 173, 174, 176, 177, 178, 179, 183, 184, 189, 205, 206, 208, 413, 493, 511, 519, 521, 535. Jérôme Galland: 2. B. Hatala: 64, 78, 113, 348. C. Jean: 217, 338, 391, 416, 421, 426, 435, 441, 444, 448, 450, 451, 455, 456, 458, 459, 467, 468, 471, 481, 560. C. Jean / Popovitch: 543. C. Jean / J. Schormans: 6, 187, 188, 190, 191, 457. Lebée: 63. Le Mage: 227, 287, 289, 328, 349. Hervé Lewandowski: 3, 4, 5, 9, 11, 12, 14, 23, 24, 35, 36, 39, 40, 41, 52, 53, 58, 59, 61, 62, 75, 82, 87, 89, 91, 93, 98, 99, 100, 109, 110, 111, 114, 116, 118, 120, 126, 127, 128, 129, 130, 131, 132, 133, 134, 137, 138, 139, 141, 142, 143, 145, 148, 150, 152, 153, 154, 155, 157, 159, 161, 162, 163, 165, 168, 169, 170, 172, 182, 186, 193, 194, 196, 198, 199, 201, 202, 203, 207, 209, 212, 252, 255, 257, 258, 264, 271, 281, 285, 290, 292, 294, 295, 305, 315, 318, 321, 351, 352, 364, 365, 366, 367, 369, 386, 387, 388, 394, 395, 396, 398, 401, 408, 409, 417, 427, 428, 430, 432, 452, 470, 478, 555. R. G. Ojeda: 83, 96, 101, 103, 104, 180, 216, 231, 238, 239, 270, 273, 276, 279, 291, 293, 297, 310, 329, 331, 332, 336, 341, 342, 357, 358, 363, 372, 404, 420, 425, 434, 436, 453, 454, 462, 464, 469, 474. R. G. Ojeda / Hubert: 439, 472, 479. R. G. Ojeda / Néri: 325, 326, 333, 334. R. G. Ojeda / Le Mage: 221, 475. Thierry Ollivier: 438. Franck Raux: 10, 18, 22, 51, 86, 88, 195, 226, 243, 244, 346, 390, 411, 412. Jean Schormans: 304, 344, 354, 359, 381, 410, 507.

Coordinating editor
LAURENCE POSSELLE
Réunion des musées nationaux

Graphic design and layout
FRÉDÉRIC CÉLESTIN

Copy-editing (English)
ALEXANDRA KEENS

Corrections and Index (French)
MARTINE HUOT

Picture research
CATHERINE BOSSIS, PHILIPPE COUTON,
STAN GUICHARD, PIERRICK JAN, ANNIE MADEC,
SOPHIE VASSOGNE

Production
HUGUES CHARREYRON

The texts were typeset in Granjon and Univers

Photoengraving: I.G.S., L'Isle d'Espagnac, France

Printed in July 2015
by Deckers-Snoeck, Gent, Belgium

First Registration of copyright April 2005
Registration of copyright: July 2015

I.S.B.N.(RMN) : 2-7118-4592-3
I.S.B.N.(Louvre) : 2-35031-013-3

GK 19 4592